Politics and Pan-Africanism

Politics and Pan-Africanism

Diplomacy, Regional Economies and Peace-Building in Contemporary Africa

Dawn Nagar

I.B. TAURIS
LONDON • NEW YORK • OXFORD • NEW DELHI • SYDNEY

T&T CLARK
Bloomsbury Publishing Plc
50 Bedford Square, London, WC1B 3DP, UK
1385 Broadway, New York, NY 10018, USA

BLOOMSBURY, T&T CLARK and the T&T Clark logo
are trademarks of Bloomsbury Publishing Plc

First published in Great Britain in 2020
Paperback edition first published 2021

Copyright © Dawn Nagar 2020

Dawn Nagar has asserted her right under the Copyright,
Designs and Patents Act, 1988, to be identified as Author of this work.

For legal purposes the Acknowledgements on p. xiv constitute
an extension of this copyright page.

Cover design by Charlotte James
Pattern © Elysart / iStock
Map by Free Vector Maps

All rights reserved. No part of this publication may be reproduced or transmitted in any form or by any means, electronic or mechanical, including photocopying, recording, or any information storage or retrieval system, without prior permission in writing from the publishers.

Bloomsbury Publishing Plc does not have any control over, or responsibility for, any third-party websites referred to or in this book. All internet addresses given in this book were correct at the time of going to press. The author and publisher regret any inconvenience caused if addresses have changed or sites have ceased to exist, but can accept no responsibility for any such changes.

A catalogue record for this book is available from the British Library.

A catalog record for this book is available from the Library of Congress.

ISBN: HB: 978-1-7883-1743-6
PB: 978-0-7556-3683-9
ePDF: 978-1-7867-3645-1
eBook: 978-1-7867-2639-1

Typeset by Newgen KnowledgeWorks Pvt. Ltd., Chennai, India

To find out more about our authors and books visit
www.bloomsbury.com and sign up for our newsletters.

This book is dedicated to my mother, Elaine Florence Jampies Nagar, for her tremendous efforts towards my education, and to my Father, Davidson Bhana Nagar, who taught me about politics in his own simplistic way.

Contents

List of Figures	xi
List of Tables	xiii
Acknowledgements	xiv
List of Key Abbreviations and Acronyms	xv

1   Introduction: Pan-African integration 1

2   The evolution of Pan-Africanism: Regional integration theories and
    approaches 11
    Assumptions of new theories and definitions 11
    Situating Pan-Africanism within the divergence and convergence
        debates of regional integration 14
    The second wave of Pan-Africanism towards modernity 20
    The third wave of Pan-Africanism from modernity to dependency ... 22
    Neoclassical economics: Divergence and convergence 24
    Market-driven trade liberalisation and economic growth 27
        Pan-Africanism: Free trade agreements and intraregional
            trade: Divergence and convergence 30
        Macroeconomic policies: Divergence and convergence 33
        Multiple memberships: Divergence and convergence 36
    Neoclassical realism approach: Security 38

3   Pan-Africanism's birth, burial – reincarnate: A historical trajectory
    of divergence and convergence 43
    The birth and death of a Pan-African idea 43
    Pan-Africanism reincarnate 45
    The convergence of regions 46
        The Frontline States and the making of an alliance 46
    Political and economic courtship – policy of détente 49
        The Frontline States and external actors 51
    The formation of SADCC: A European agenda 53
        SADC's institutional architecture 57
        Funding SADCC and SADC 62

	The formation of the PTA and the incorporation of EAC member states	67
	COMESA's institutional architecture: Economic regional convergence	72
	Rationalisation period of 1993 and 1994 of SADCC and PTA: A failed convergence	74
4	**The era of convergence: COMESA, EAC and SADC**	**91**
	The period 1998–2008: Convergence of a Tripartite Agreement	92
	States, markets and developmental integration: 1998–2008, divergence or convergence	96
	COMESA, EAC and SADC's diplomatic efforts of the main summits and meetings: The period 1998–2008	103
	Diplomatic efforts: A move towards establishing the COMESA, EAC and SADC Tripartite free trade area	106
	Progress of the Tripartite MOU towards convergence	109
	The Tripartite merger and progress of the free trade area roadmap	109
	Efforts towards the establishment of a Tripartite free trade area	111
	Regional transport master plan	114
	Concluding remarks	117
5	**Convergence and consolidation of multiple memberships: An attempted convergence**	**119**
	Management of multiple memberships	121
	Variable geometry and the Tripartite bloc	124
	Rules of origin and external trade agreements: AGOA and EPAs	127
	Regional arrangements in multiple memberships: Hindrance or promotion?	131
	Management of multiple memberships by member states: The case of South Africa in SACU	138
	Concluding remarks	142
6	**Pan-African economic integration**	**147**
	Intraregional trade: An agricultural comparative advantage	149
	Information and technology systems control: Achieving value addition	158
	Comparative advantage and economic growth for Africa's geostrategic economic convergence with the Caribbean and Pacific	162
	Blue economy: The Africa, Caribbean and Pacific Bloc	163
7	**Pan-African security convergence: The evolution of collective security**	**167**
	Africa's attempts of achieving collective security	168
	Regional security complex framework: Evolving domestic actors and factors	171

	Towards Pan-African security convergence	177
	Concluding remarks	182
8	Analysis and normative proposals: Pan-African convergence theories	185
	Rules of origin	186
	Total factor productivity	186
	Protecting Tripartite member states' industries is much more than just variable geometry, free trade and the principle of acquis	187
	Multiple memberships	190
	Infrastructure gaps	191
	Security convergence	191
9	Conclusion	193

Notes	197
Bibliography	245
Index	269

Figures

3.1	SADCC's agricultural exports to the rest of the world, 1985–9	56
3.2	SADC's restructuring and organogram	62
3.3	SADCC's agricultural exports to South Africa, 1989	77
4.1	2008 bilateral contracts in SAPP	97
4.2	Growth in micro-regions: Mozambique and South Africa	99
4.3	Major sugar producers in COMESA, EAC and SADC	103
4.4	Direct employment in the sugar industry (COMESA, EAC and SADC member states)	103
4.5	Overview of air markets of COMESA, EAC and SADC member states (2011)	107
4.6	Total economic impact stimulated by airspace market liberalisation in COMESA-EAC-SADC member states (2013)	108
5.1	Major partners of COMESA and South Africa with the AGOA market in 2013	129
5.2	Five top export commodities from AGOA to COMESA in 2013	130
5.3	Major export goods from COMESA to AGOA in 2013	130
5.4	SACU trade as a percentage of GDP, 2005–13	135
5.5	Total trade of SACU member states, 2005–13	135
5.6	Trade growth of SACU member states, 2005–12	136
5.7	Trade growth convergence of Botswana and South Africa, 2005–12	136
5.8	Trade growth convergence of Lesotho and South Africa, 2005–12	137
5.9	Trade growth convergence of Namibia and South Africa, 2005–12	137
5.10	Trade growth convergence of Eswatini and South Africa, 2005–12	138
5.11	Total GDP of BLNE member states, 2005–13	140
5.12	South Africa's total trade with BRICS states, 2010–14	141
6.1	South Africa's total import trade with main partners, January–December 2016	150
6.2	South Africa's total export trade with main partners, January–December 2016	151
6.3	South Africa's generic leather processing chain	156

6.4	EU–Caribbean countries: Total trade in goods, 2014–16	161
6.5	EU–Pacific trade flows in main commodities, 2016	162
7.1	Smuggling from the Eastern DRC to Uganda, Rwanda and Burundi	175
7.2	COMESA profile	180

Tables

3.1	PTA: Countries – main economic indicators, 1987	69
3.2	Composition of manufacturing value added (MVA), 1987	75
3.3	South Africa's regional trade, 1984	78
3.4	South Africa's leading export markets in Africa, 1990	78
3.5	South Africa's trade to the rest of the world, 1990	79
4.1	SAPP's planned regional generation projects commissioned and funded up until 2017	98
5.1	Membership in RECs and FTAs in the Tripartite bloc	122
7.1	State interventions in conflict areas from 2008 to 2015	178

Acknowledgements

I would like to express my sincere gratitude to Tomasz Hoskins, chief editor at I.B. Tauris, and his publication team, particularly Mr Nayiri Kendir and Mrs Kalyani Kanekal, for their tremendous support in completing this book. My sincere appreciation goes to Professor Gilbert M. Khadiagala, former head of international relations at the University of the Witwatersrand, for his incredible knowledge and tremendous support afforded to me during my doctoral studies of which this book is a product of. I am also equally grateful for the support of my four daughters, Simóne, Danielle, Marcel and Nina, as without them I would not have completed this publication. I also express my sincere gratitude to the Faculty of Humanities, University of Johannesburg, as my affiliation status during the completion and production of this book, for allowing me the opportunity to contribute to African knowledge. All thanks goes to the Almighty God.

Key Abbreviations and Acronyms

4IR	Fourth Industrial Revolution
ACFTA	African Continental Free Trade Agreement (also referred to as the Continental Free Trade Area (CFTA)
ACIRC	African Capacity for Immediate Response to Crises
ACP	African, Caribbean and Pacific group of states
ACRF	African Crisis Response Force
ACRT	African Regional Centre for Technology Design and Manufacturing
ADF-NALU	Allied Democratic Forces – National Army for the Liberation of Uganda
AEC	African Economic Community
AfDB	African Development Bank
AGOA	African Growth and Opportunity Act
AHI	Afrikaanse Handelsinstituut
AMU	Arab Maghreb Union
ANC	African National Congress
APPER	Africa's Priority Programme for Economic Recovery
APRM	African Peer Review Mechanism
APSA	African Peace and Security Architecture
ARCEDEM	African Regional Centre for Engineering Design and Manufacturing
ARF	African Renaissance and International Cooperation Fund
ARTIN	African Regional Transport Infrastructure Network
ASEAN	Association of Southeast Asian Nations
ASF	African Standby Force
ASYCUDA	Automated System for Customs Data
AU	African Union
β	beta-convergence
BLNE	Botswana, Lesotho, Namibia and Eswatini bloc
BRICS	Brazil-Russia-India-China-South Africa
CAP	Common Agriculture Policy
CCR	Centre for Conflict Resolution
CEAO	West African Economic Community (*Communauté économique de l' Afrique de l' ouest*)
CEMAC	Central African Economic and Monetary Community
CEN–SAD	Community of Sahel-Saharan States
CEOs	chief executive officers
CEWARN	Conflict Early Warning and Response Mechanism
CFTA	Continental Free Trade Area
CIA	Central Intelligence Agency (US)

CIDA	Canadian International Development Assistance
CMA	Common Monetary Area
COMESA	Common Market for Eastern and Southern Africa
COSATU	Congress of South African Trade Unions
CPA	Comprehensive Peace Accord
DAC	Development Assistance Committee
DAFF	Department of Agriculture (South Africa)
DAM	day-ahead market
DBSA	Development Bank of Southern Africa
DFID	Department for International Development
DIRCO	Department of International Relations and Cooperation
DPKO	UN Department of Peacekeeping Operations
DRC	Democratic Republic of the Congo
DTI	Department of Trade and Industry
EAC	East African Community
EACB	East African Central Bank
EAMU	East African Monetary Union
EAPP	East African Power Pool
EASBRIG	Eastern African Standby Brigade
EASFCOM	East African Standby Force Coordination Mechanism
ECB	European Central Bank
ECCAS	Economic Community for Central African States
ECGLC (CEPGL,	Economic Community of the Great Lakes Countries (*Communauté économique des pays des Grands Lacs*)
ECLA	Economic Commission for Latin America
ECLAC	Economic Commission for Latin America and the Caribbean
ECOSOC	United Nations Economic and Social Council
ECOWAS	Economic Community of West African States
ECSC	Economic Coal and Steel Community
EEC	European Economic Commission
EFTA	European Free Trade Association
ELSA	Exotic Leather Sub-National Cluster
EMU	European Monetary Union
EPAs	Economic Partnership Agreements
ESAMI	Eastern and Southern African Management Institute
EU	European Union
EU-SA TDCA	Europe-South Africa Trade Development and Cooperation agreement
FARDC	Armed Forces of the Democratic Republic of the Congo (*Forces Armées de la République Démocratique du Congo*)
FDI	foreign direct investment
FDLR	Democratic Forces for the Liberation of Rwanda (*Forces démocratiques de libération du Rwanda*)
FIB	Force Intervention Brigade
FLS	Frontline States

FRELIMO	Mozambique Liberation Front
FTA	Free Trade Area
G-20	Group of Twenty
GATT	General Agreement on Tariffs and Trade
GDP	gross domestic product
GERD	Grand Ethiopian Renaissance Dam
GIGA	German Institute of Global and Area Studies: Institute of African Studies
GNP	gross national product
HAT	High Transitional Authority (*Haute Autorité de la Transition*)
HCTs	High Commission Territories
HDI	Human Development Index
HSRC	Human Sciences Research Council
ICGLR	International Conference on the Great Lakes Region
ICJ	International Court of Justice
ICM	Integrated Committee of Ministers
IDT	Independent Development Trust
IGAD	Intergovernmental Authority for Development
IGADD	Intergovernmental Authority for Drought and Development
IMF	International Monetary Fund
IMO	International Maritime Organization
IRP	Integrated Resource Plan
ISDSC	Inter-State Defence and Security Committee
ISIC	International Standard Industrial Classification
ISPDC	Inter-State Politics and Diplomacy Committee
JCA	Joint Competition Authority
JOC	Maputo Corridor Joint Operating Centre
JPC	Joint Planning Committee
LAPSSET	Lamu Port for Southern Sudan–Ethiopia Transport corridor
LDCs	least developed countries
LDF	Lesotho Defence Force
LLPI	Leather and Leather Products Institute (COMESA)
LPA	Lagos Plan of Action
LRA	Lord's Resistance Army/Movement
M23	March 23 rebel group movement
MANU	Mozambican African National Union
MC	ministerial committee
MCLI	Maputo Corridor and Logistics Initiative
MDC	Maputo Development Corridor
MDGs	Millennium Development Goals
MERCOSUR	Mercado Común del Sur
MERG	Macro-Economic Research Group
MFN	most-favoured nation
MNCs	multinational corporations

MONUSCO	United Nations Organisation Stabilisation Mission in the Democratic Republic of the Congo (*Mission de l'Organisation des Nations Unies pour la Stabilisation en République Démocratique du Congo*)
MOU	memorandum of understanding
MPLA	Popular Movement for the Liberation of Angola
MULPOCs	multi-national programming and operational centres
MVA	manufacturing value added
MW	megawatts
NCACC	National Conventional Arms Control Committee (South Africa)
NCBLI	National Bargaining Council for the Leather Industry
NDP	National Development Plan
NEPAD	New Partnership for Africa's Development
NGP	New Growth Path (South Africa)
NIEO	New International Economic Order
NIPF	National Industrial Policy Framework
NP	National Party
NRA	National Resistance Army (Rwanda)
NRA/T	New Regionalism Approach/Theory
NSDS	National Skills Development Strategy
NTBs	non-trade barriers
NULAW	National Union for Leather and Allied Workers
σ	sigma-convergence
OAU	Organization of African Unity
OCAs	optimum currency areas
OECD	Organisation for Economic Co-operation and Development
OPDS	Organ on Politics, Defence and Security
OPDSC	Organ on Politics, Defence and Security Cooperation
OPEC	Organization of Petroleum Exporting Countries
PAFMECA	Pan-African Movement for East and Central Africa
PAP	Pan-African Parliament
PCRD	Post-Conflict Reconstruction and Development Programme
PIDA	Programme for Infrastructure Development in Africa
PTA	Preferential Trade Area for Eastern and Southern Africa
R2P	Responsibility to Protect
REC	regional economic community
REIPPP	Renewable Energy Independent Power Producer Programme
RENAMO	Mozambican National Resistance (*Resistência Nacional Moçambicana*)
REPSS	Regional Payment and Settlement System
RIA	regional integration agreement
RISCO	Rhodesian Iron and Steel Corporation
RISDP	Regional Indicative Strategic Development Plan
ROOs	rules of origin
RPTC	Regional Peacekeeping Training Centre

RSC	regional security complex
SACCAR	Southern African Centre for Cooperation in Agricultural Research
SACTWU	Clothing and Textile Workers Union
SACU	Southern African Customs Union
SADC	Southern African Development Community
SADCC	Southern African Development Coordination Conference
SAFTO	South African Foreign Trade Organisation
SAIIA	South African Institute for International Affairs
SANDF	South African National Defence Force
SAP	structural adjustment programme
SAPP	Southern African Power Pool
SATCC	Standing Committee of Officials
SDGs	sustainable development goals
SDI	Spatial Development Initiative
SETA	Skills Education Training Authority
SHALC	South African Skin, Hide and Leather Council (SHALC)
SIPO	Strategic Indicative Plan of the Organ
SITC	Standard International Trade Classification
SMMEs	small, micro, and medium enterprises
SNCs	SADC National Committees
SPA	SADC Programme of Action
SPLA	Sudan People's Liberation Army
SPLM-IO	Sudan People's Liberation Movement in Opposition
SSR	security sector reform
SWAPO	South West Africa People's Organization
SWIFT	Society for Worldwide Interbank Financial Telecommunication
TBTs	technical barriers to trade
TCSO	Tripartite Committee of Senior Officials
TDCA	Trade, Development and Cooperation Agreement
TFP	total factor productivity
TFTA	Tripartite Free Trade Agreement
TOR	terms of reference
TPSF	Trade Policy and Strategy Framework
Tripartite FTA	Tripartite Free Trade Area
TTCID	Tripartite Technical Committee on Industrial Development
TTCM	Tripartite Trade and Customs Committee
TTF	Tripartite Task Force
TTNF	Tripartite Trade Negotiating Forum
TTWGs	Tripartite Technical Working Groups
UAPTA	unit of account of the Preferential Trade Area
UDENAMO	National Democratic Union of Mozambique
UEMOA	Western African Economic and Monetary Union
UFIR	Upper Flight Information Region
UNAMI	National African Union of Independent Mozambique
UNCTAD	United Nations Conference on Trade and Development

UNDP	United Nations Development Programme
UNECA	United Nations Economic Commission for Africa
UNEP	United Nations Environment Programme
UNIDAT	United Nations Multinational Interdisciplinary Development Advisory Teams
UNITA	National Union for the Total Independence of Angola (*União Nacional para a Independência Total de Angola*)
UN-PAAERD	United Nations Programme for Action for African Economic Recovery and Development
USTDA	US Trade and Development Agency
WTO	World Trade Organisation
YD	Yamoussoukro Declaration
ZANU	Zimbabwe African National Union
ZAPU	Zimbabwe African People's Union
ZMM-GT	Zambia–Malawi–Mozambique Growth Triangle

1

Introduction: Pan-African integration

The first and primary aim of the book is to reach a better understanding of Africa's efforts at promoting Pan-Africanism, its relevance to the continent, and to achieving socio-economic growth, political stability and continental security. This book makes two main arguments focused on divergence and convergence of regional economic integration and regional security by incorporating two new theories – Pan-African economic integration; and Pan-African security convergence – that have been first coined and developed for, and are applied in, this book. These theories are updated and premised on theories deployed in a doctoral thesis as well as several research outputs and critical analyses conducted on Africa's political economy, international relations, and security issues in the period 2000–19. The second purpose of this book is to provide a historical critical analyses of the regional experiments in Africa and thus, the book expands on the divergence and convergence debates, as imperative analyses in understanding the coming together of the key African regions as stepping stones in Africa's integration process, namely, the Common Market for Eastern and Southern Africa (COMESA), the East African Community (EAC), and the Southern African Development Community (SADC) and their initial signing of the Tripartite Free Trade Agreement (TFTA) in 2008. These three regional communities have also signed the African Free Trade Agreement in March 2018 and the extent of this convergence towards Pan-African economic integration is thus assessed.

An assessment of Africa's historical regionalism, further allows a critical debate on the extent of the evolutions of divergences and convergences – providing different periods of time in which a momentum towards both divergence and convergence is demonstrated within these regional groupings. The third purpose is to assess the convergence of the African security mechanisms and to analyse the actors and factors of such roles in understanding the divergence and convergence debates within the continent's security apparatuses used to achieve continental security.

Numerous books have been written over the decades on Africa's attempts at regional integration, with various concepts developed, but no theory to date has been developed or produced by African scholars, for Africa that is premised on a Pan-African regional integration trajectory. This book thus, proffers two new theories: Pan-African economic integration theory, which is premised on the relationship between divergence and convergence of regional economic integration policies and initial implementation towards a continental convergence, that is premised on COMESA, the EAC and SADC in their attempts to achieve economic convergence through conducting trade, while also putting in place regional security mechanisms, in paving the way for trade. A decade later, after the signing of the FTA in 2008, in March 2018, the African Continental Free Trade Agreement (ACFTA)'s (also referred to in this book as the Continental Free Trade Area (CFTA)) legal instruments were formally signed by twenty-one out of fifty-five African countries – with Gambia signalling its ratification to the ACFTA in April 2019 – which brought the total tally to twenty-two out of fifty-five African states for the trade agreement to take effect on 30 May 2019.[1] Africa is thus envisaging exponential annual continental trade growth of 53 per cent, with its African FTA as the largest in the world in terms of the number of countries, and a market of 1.2 billion people.[2] However, the reality is that during the October 2008 COMESA-EAC-SADC trade partnership comprised of about twenty-six countries, total intracontinental trade remained at a paltry 16 per cent in 2019, with the majority of trade being conducted with mega international partners such as the United States, China and Europe, working against the modalities of boosting trade of the ACFTA. Hence, it will be underdevelopment and poverty that will be experienced, and not economic growth.

The theory of Pan-African economic integration, therefore, advocates that global economic inequality warrants that Africa's governments and regional communities adopt stronger partnerships and specifically have trade relations with those economies that are on a more equal socio-economic footing, such as countries from the Caribbean and Pacific and that are developmental orientated, namely, the Africa, Caribbean and Pacific (ACP) group of states.[3]

With economic stability feeding off security – and within a neorealist framework, the second theory coined in this book is the Pan-African security convergence, which assesses the progress, problems and prospects of achieving the objectives of a continental – African Standby Force (ASF), which has been conceived as Africa's rapid deployment force composed of troop contributions of regional standby brigades – from South, West, Eastern, Central and North Africa.[4] The divergence and convergence of the ASF are assessed under a political economy lens in order to gauge the realist debates within this theory.

Both theories outlined above serve as principal indicators in the book for understanding Africa's political economy and interpreting continental socio-economic and security convergences and divergences respectively.[5]

Chapter 2 provides an overview of the literature reviewed, in offering critical analysis that reflects degrees of divergence and convergence of regional integration efforts within major regional economic communities (RECs) that lead to the CFTA, namely COMESA, EAC and SADC, and their workings towards achieving Pan-Africanism, which were challenged by historical internal and external actors and factors that have filtered into existing regional practices. Such challenges have constituted uneven economic growth of the member states at the national, regional and continental levels. Stronger economies like those of South Africa attached to a Southern African Customs Union (SACU) and SADC, Angola in SADC, Egypt in COMESA and Kenya in EAC, are all linked to regional and international bilateral trade arrangements and customs unions (such as the EAC) that dominate the trade markets, leaving very little room for the smaller economies to manoeuvre. Such impact on the smaller economies destroys infant industries or threatened by becoming insolvent and leading to divergence and not Pan-African integration. Therefore, the concepts of divergence and convergence raised in the theories reviewed in Chapter 2 offer important analytical lenses for understanding and explaining the issues of a continent battling to achieving Pan-African economic integration and Pan-African security convergence.

The theory of Pan-African economic integration as developed further lays claim that, because open markets and trade are largely premised on neoclassical economics – as also outlined by the General Agreement on Tariffs and Trade (GATT) (now called the World Trade Organization (WTO)) principles – open markets cannot be simply wished away since they are part of the real world. This theory, therefore underscores that owing to individual regional integration policies such as COMESA, EAC and SADC, and their integration policies at regional level (of both institutions and member states) of free trade agreements, and customs unions which are largely premised on neoclassical economics linked to open markets and free trade, and due to the unequal nature of intraregional trade, regional trade policies will cause divergence in Africa's attempts of achieving Pan-African economic integration. This divergence is inevitable, even though a CFTA is in place, with continental security and instability having been perpetual throughout the continent with several intra- and interstate conflicts transpiring since the 1970s.

The national interests of states have set the pace for the continental peace and security agenda, particularly those of the ASF, and not the African Union (AU) – as the architect of the African Peace and Security Architecture (APSA). Such interests have derailed policy implementation and are misled by the state's parochial domestic conditions, resulting in a nationalist approach to dealing with external affairs. Africa's continental peacekeeping has also become squarely linked to the economic interests of the state, with security issues coming to be viewed by governments through the lens of realism and trumped by concerns of political economy over regional and human security. Furthermore, neorealists define a hegemonic state as a powerful, strong economy that sets the rules of the game, having a greater advantage over its partner states, and one which exerts power. The theory of 'neorealist security convergence'[6] goes further in proposing that a hegemon has the ability to converge the security apparatuses of other member states within a region or regional bloc, based on its own conception of interests. In other words, a regional hegemonic power – a state with immense political clout and authority within a regional bloc, but bound by the need to address its own domestic socio-economic concerns – will set the rules of the game for its own benefit. Moreover, such a state will have the political will to militarily intervene in support of other states in its region to achieve regional security, and, only do so when this is linked to its own national interests. This also means that national level challenges, particularly in the case of regionally powerful states, will tend to filter into the continental-level aim of achieving convergence of regional security mechanisms.[7] Hence Chapter 6 applies the theory Pan-African security convergence, which assesses the ability of the ASF to converge given the protection warranted by powerful states in minimising conflicts and in securing an expanded CFTA.

Chapter 3 expands the divergence and convergence debates, as imperative analyses and also providing an understanding of the coming together and the historical experiments of the regions of COMESA, EAC and SADC. The assessment of the historical period critically focuses on the evolutions of divergences and convergences – providing different periods of time in which a momentum in both divergence and convergence is demonstrated within these regional groupings – and include a discussion of the Preferential Trade Area (PTA) for Eastern and Southern Africa and its formation, which subsequently evolved into COMESA. Also provided is a commentary on the historical period and an assessment of the Frontline States (FLS) that evolved into the security Organ of SADC. In order to facilitate an understanding and gauge the extent to which their existence filtered into the new COMESA, EAC and SADC, the discussion expands on how these institutions evolved during their rationalisation process. The book considers PTA's initial ten states – Burundi, Ethiopia, Kenya, Madagascar, Malawi, Mauritius, Rwanda, Somalia, Tanzania and Zambia (in the 1990s Comoros (who also joined SADC in 2017), Djibouti, Lesotho, Mozambique, Swaziland (now known as Eswatini) and Uganda joined, followed by Angola, Namibia and Zimbabwe), and the Southern African Development Coordination Conference's (SADCC) nine states – Angola, Botswana, Lesotho, Malawi, Mozambique, Eswatini, Tanzania, Zambia and Zimbabwe (and later Namibia, which joined SADCC in 1990), were forced to consider a difficult decision during the 1990s: whether to incorporate a post-apartheid South Africa into COMESA or SADC or whether to merge into one institution.

These processes are discussed during the period of rationalisation. The book therefore, focuses on regional and subregional cooperation in industrial policy and programming of the PTA that became the cornerstone for rapid industrial development in Africa. It was seen as an important mechanism in addressing issues of colonialism and racial discrimination in Northern and Southern Rhodesia and confronting the apartheid regime in South Africa.[8] The book assesses the impact that non-trade barriers had on the potential of economic convergence and trade creation for PTA member states, which allows for a greater understanding and analyses in assessing the convergence and divergence debates in Africa's current regionalism trajectory.

In the case of Southern African states, SADCC conducted trade since 1980, without a trade protocol or treaty, but the PTA was formed in 1981 and its Treaty was signed in June 1982. In assessing the period between 1980 and 1992, it is thus critical to examine how PTA member states have benefited from their treaty and the implications that this has had for Southern African states. Such assessments, similarly, allows the book to gauge the potential for convergence of the current CFTA. Similarly, not all member states are signatory to the legal instruments in the current CFTA, which was also the case during the historical regional evolution with most African countries subjected to an apartheid regionalism during the 1970s, and in particularly during the 1980s regional destabilisation practices of Pretoria. The historical challenges that both the PTA and SADCC member states faced in becoming economically and regionally stable is therefore assessed. Thus, the establishment of SADC in 1992 and COMESA in 1993 are critical cases in the understanding the historical period of the divergence and convergence debates.

The major relations with the donor community and the policy of détente provide further critical thought and understanding in the convergence of the regions and their divergence from Africa's achieving of regional integration during that time in relation to external roles played by historical external actors. EAC and its relations with the PTA are further expanded in the historical analysis as the EAC attempted a regional integration strategy for its region, which failed dismally.[9]

Chapter 4 incorporates and expands the understanding of economic integration in discussing the evolution of African integration with the key building blocks – COMESA and SADC's period after the rationalisation process (1991–7) (EAC was not involved in the rationalisation process, although some of its member states also belonged to COMESA and others were in SADC) – and this discussion, thus, focuses on the period between 1998 and 2008. The book uses the literature on regional integration and convergence to help illuminate this period in explaining how Africa's regionalisation attempts have further evolved with the adoption of an action plan by the AU in 2012 to boost intra-African trade through the main pillar of integration – the COMESA-EAC-SADC's 2008 Tripartite Free Trade Area (TFTA). This discussion provides an understanding of the three RECs: COMESA, EAC and SADC and the evolution of their convergence, that joined forces on 22 October 2008 to create a tripartite alliance towards Africa's regional integration efforts, by integrating trade and economic development towards creating a CFTA with a promised date of 2017 (a missed deadline), which was established in March 2018 and ratified a year later in March 2019 by twenty-two out of fifty-five African member states. The COMESA-EAC-SADC Tripartite FTA was not incorporated into the CFTA – but evolved separately. Also, though a Continental Customs Union by 2019 is envisaged, member states of the EAC belongs to their own EAC Customs Union, and similarly, is the SACU in place with South Africa, Botswana, Lesotho, Eswatini (formerly known as Swaziland) and Namibia. An African Common Market by 2023, and a Continental Economic and Monetary Union and Pan-African Parliament by 2028 is also envisaged.[10]

The analysis in Chapter 4 also include the levels of convergence of the regional policies based on the Tripartite 2008 memorandum of understanding (MOU) as the stepping stone towards achieving an ACFTA: (i) trade protocols and legal instruments; (ii) regional FTAs relating to intra- and interregional trade policies and total trade; (iii) obstacles to trade (trade barriers and non-trade barriers (NTBs) such as border posts, industrialisation, value-added chains, and rules of origin (ROOs)); (iv) customs unions; (v) legal binding commitments; (vi) macroeconomic frameworks towards establishing a monetary union; (vii) progress in infrastructure development such as transport corridors (rail, road, air and ports), regional electricity generation (trade, demand and supply), and information and technology; and (viii) sociopolitical issues touching on education and migration policies.

Chapter 5 considers multiple memberships of member states within the Tripartite FTA. Arguments indicate that owing to trade liberalisation and tariff adjustments, conditions concerning economic pressures leave member states either joining other regional groupings or remaining in the bloc, but not adhering to the RECs' policies or else, delaying trade agreements by not signing agreements that could facilitate trade because they are unable to do so, largely due to the fragility of their markets.

A larger market though, can create a larger space for competitive pricing of goods within an economic grouping. This further creates a larger geographical scale and more purchasing power, thus creating economies of scale. Each REC also has its own trade processes of liberalisation according to its protocols; hence reforms towards a single CFTA have been signed on paper, but the reality is that trade diversion stalls growth, owing to various regional trade policies including customs unions and the regional integration process is concomitantly delayed – for example, not all legal instruments for the operationalisation of the CFTA were ratified by all members.[11] The non-commitment of some member states will create an open market for external actors such as the European Union (EU) and therefore distort trade further. Therefore, the book further addresses how the African states are approaching this issue, which allows states to enter agreements and liberalise trade at their own pace – the variable geometry approach that COMESA, EAC and SADC have embraced.

But, the variable geometry approach becomes unwieldy when the slower members sign on as members in either blocs or other adjacent regional groupings.[12] The book provides a further understanding by explaining the degree of Africa's convergence and divergence set off against major blocs such as COMESA, EAC and SADC working in unison and regionally managing relations with external trade partners like the African Growth and Opportunity Act (AGOA) with the United States and the Economic Partnership Agreements (EPAs) with the EU, as well as multilateral trade arrangements with the emerging powers in the Brazil-Russia-India-China-South Africa (BRICS) bloc. The various evolving bilateral and multilateral agreements of member states similarly provide an in-depth analysis to ascertain their relevance in the regional integration process of how they deal with these phenomena are further lines of enquiry pursued in the book. A deep analysis of assessing Africa's place in the world is also carried out, seeing Africa as the periphery of the periphery of the world.

Further assessed are SACU and the Common Monetary Area (CMA), which were established to create a customs union and monetary area for SACU. This discussion is set off within a critique provided of the century-old SACU that has been at the forefront of trade processes in Africa, comprising of a powerful economy – South Africa – also viewed as a benign hegemon (since the book consider South Africa's developmental regional integration role with smaller countries like Mozambique during the late 1990s to spur Maputo's economic growth) and malign hegemon with 80 per cent of South Africa's economic wealth in the hands of white monopolies, their dominance in the region and unequal partnerships in socio-economic inequalities and injustices of land and capital deprivation remain in the hands of apartheid architects in their pursuit of integration.[13] The analysis thus assesses the impact that the SACU bloc has on Africa's regional integration attempts given South Africa's numerous bilateral and multilateral trade agreements – which also consider how these agreements impact Africa's achieving of Pan-Africanism. The debates therefore, in this book are centred on a critical review of what the key mechanisms are that converge economies.

Chapter 5 applies the neoclassical economic integration theory[14] that demonstrates how smaller economies alongside a hegemonic partner in a regional bloc can converge. The theory further stipulates that a strong economic partner bound to smaller economies in a regional bloc can grow the economies of the smaller economies over a long-run convergence period like South Africa attached to SACU. The flipside of the neoclassical economic integration theory, which also considers long-run convergence debates, underscores that liberal tariffs could diverge smaller economies within a regional grouping in the absence of strong value-driven industrialisation policies while taking into account sparingly conducted international trade. Member countries including – Botswana, Lesotho, Namibia and Eswatini (BLNE) – are trading with member states that are attached to the SACU bloc with South Africa. This argument carefully applies and considers the earlier work done in Europe of 'long-run convergence and regional trade schemes' by regional integrationists and trade economists like Walter Mattli,[15] as well as that of Anthony Venables,[16] Steve Dowrick and Duc-Tho Nguyen's total factor productivity (TFP) as a catch-up variable for downstream industries and smaller economies,[17] (since these are the original theorists and scholars of this work). Moreover, African voices and perspectives of intellectual academic debates of Africa's Pan-African discourse are provided by several African scholars, which is incorporated into the book and include Ali Mazrui, Ibrahim Gambari, Lynn Mytelka, Justin Malewezi, Walter Orchoro and Phillip O Nying'uro, among several others.

Chapter 6 applies the theory of Pan-African economic integration and claims that the implementation of effective policies of the CFTA with members also belonging to existing regional blocs, carefully and sparingly considers the impact of external international agreements that favours regional trade, and also considers stronger Africa trade partnerships that can benefit trade growth such as agro-industrialisation driven commodities and the blue economy. Pan-African economic integration theory also underscores that regional policies should consider value-driven industrialised-manufacturing that includes endogenous factors of growth, such as technology, research and inputs of smaller industries and smaller economies into the outputs of stronger economies and industries and in strengthening Africa's efforts within the Fourth Industrial Revolution (4IR). Production of regional trade should link clear agreed to ROOs with a view to spurring real economic growth; and incentivising poorer economies of its member states could create the necessary economic conditions for achieving Pan-African economic integration.

Such considerations have the potential of strengthening small industries as well as small economies and ultimately converge the continent. Pan-African economic integration theory also lays claim that the consideration of trade relations, however, should balance or lessen international trade partners such as those with Europe, the United States and China but strengthen trade relations with developmental states such as those within the ACP and to which Africa belongs when the continent signed the 2000 to 2020 ACP–EU Cotonou Agreement with Europe,[18] which had already begun in 1975.[19] This approach has therefore, huge potential to converging Africa's regional trade policies, increasing regional trade, and lessening trade diversion, while fostering growth for the poorer economies and infantile industries of member states within a bloc. This discussion is applied and critically demonstrated in Chapter 6. The discussion similarly takes into account, Jan Tinbergen's Gravity theory of trade.[20]

The book takes into account the pernicious effects that the direction of trade can have on infant economies that are associated with liberal tariff adjustments, such as commodity prices and price volatility, which play a major contributing role in diversion. Similarly, the discussion also take into account recessions and economic downturns, when markets could swing either way, from low to massive surpluses, with prices falling either way.[21] Thus, Africa's states may also gain incentives to join and form a region to attract direct foreign investment in favour of their own markets, or join security mechanisms which could divert it from other members.

Chapter 7 critically assesses and applies the second important theory that considers the security of the region and its fragile regional security mechanisms linked to economics as well as providing the requisite literature for understanding security convergence and cooperation. Member countries are now faced with various challenges in COMESA, EAC and SADC to commit to the CFTA bloc without workable infrastructure, and major national interests that impact on remaining economically viable and regionally secured turn fragile states into rogue states. Because, effective regional economic integration does not only comprise intraregional trade, but of numerous other factors as well, inter alia, transaction costs; infrastructure systems such as transport, information and communications; commitment at national government level to regional policy and hence to implementation of agreed tariffs; trade creating and trade diverting effects; multiple regional arrangements by states; and regional security mechanisms, the end game is that economics trumps politics. The lack of a workable infrastructure has thus placed a damper on Africa's integration. Member states have indicated that it may be more economically viable to do business with Europe, among other powerful global actors, rather than conducting trade interregionally or intracontinentally, owing to the poor African infrastructure condition. For example, COMESA, EAC and SADC comprise ten landlocked states: Botswana, Burundi, Ethiopia, Lesotho, Malawi, Rwanda, Eswatini, Uganda, Zambia and Zimbabwe. Only 30 per cent of the roads on the entire continent are paved. Mechanisms such as infrastructure (rail, roads, ports, air, water and electricity) are important in assessing Africa's integration attempts. Chapters 4 and 5 link these factors and discusses a regional security complex framework (RSC) theory, which provide assistance in understanding security complexities, but this theory falls short in adequately explaining the findings of the research in this book.

In support of the overall literature review under security in Chapter 7, critical elements include that of realism and security and its role in convergence of regional security practices and the geopolitical interests of a hegemonic state converging regional security within a regional grouping. With economics that trumps politics, evidenced in the establishment of the ACFTA that include major economies of Egypt, Kenya and South Africa, this allows for greater security and stability to be prevalent in the continent with a view to achieving effective economic benefits through trade. Therefore, the theory of Pan-African security convergence is critical in strengthening the overall analysis and theoretical arguments and academic debates germane to achieving continental security. Chapter 7, thus, provides the main tenants of the continental security, namely the APSA framework. The discussion delves into and expands Barry Buzan and Ole Wæver's[22] observations that are a starting point for such an analysis and should be based on a clear definition of a regional security system. The analysis is also guided by Amitav Acharya's observations on regional security within regionalism that sees security complexes as a national threat and discusses determinants of security interdependence.[23] The chapter expands on the main conflict areas and states in the African regions and discusses the convergence of Africa's member states in managing these conflicts in the continent.

Six overarching questions guide discussions in this book: (i) How did COMESA, EAC and SADC evolve from their predecessor institutions, the PTA and SADCC respectively, and who were the actors and what were the main factors that informed their relationship? (ii) What explains the evolution of convergence of the three major regional communities, COMESA, EAC and SADC, in signing a 2008 Tripartite agreement? Can this convergence create Pan-African economic integration? (iii) How much trade have these three regional institutions (COMESA, EAC and SADC) promoted? What do the literature and theories on divergence and convergence tell us about their trade liberalisation processes? (iv) What is the impact of multiple memberships on Pan-Africanism? Thus, how are these three regional institutions (COMESA, EAC and SADC), as both institutions and member states, managing multiple memberships? (v) Can Africa achieve convergence of continental security? And, (vi) How are Africa's main regional institutions (COMESA, EAC and SADC) as well as African states managing the issue of regional security?

These six overarching questions help the analysis to interrogate the RECs of COMESA, EAC and SADC, with member states that are straddling national positions and regional obligations. The relationship is a divided one, with values such as power and wealth filtering into the regional economic fraternity.[24] Because the concepts of states, markets and power cut across and form the core building blocks of several theoretical strands, the book utilises two mutually supporting approaches to link these concepts to guide the study: the neoclassical economics approach and the neorealist approach which will serve as principal indicators for conceptualising the literature review and interpreting the research findings as well as the conclusions presented in the book.

Chapter 8 provides a substantial conclusion highlighting the importance of the research for the field of international relations. Gaps are identified and explanations provided. Also highlighted within the concluding Chapter 9 are possible policy recommendations to be considered, for trade, governance and security officials and policymakers within the CFTA, COMESA, EAC, SADC and SACU Secretariats and their governments. It is envisaged that the South African government, Africa's continental bodies (the AU), other important African bodies (such as the New Partnership for Africa's Development (NEPAD)), the African Development Bank (AfDB), the Development Bank of Southern Africa (DBSA), the United Nations Economic Commission for Africa (UNECA), the EU, the United States, and donor community as well as civil society actors, and human rights institutions and organisations will find the recommendations provided in this book useful to their work. In an attempt to understand knowledge production in Africa, two new regional integration theories are coined in this book: Pan-African economic integration and Pan-African security convergence – two first-of-their-kind theories in the continent with a focus on Pan-African convergence and divergence. The findings of the book will therefore be relevant to Africa's think tanks and policy institutes, and for universities and libraries in Africa where emerging academics and students could assess, address and expand on gaps in this book and provide further critique on these theories. These could possibly further strengthen future studies in this area and on topics pertinent to Africa's development for sustained, solid socio-economic growth, security, and continental stability within the divergence and convergence debates of Pan-Africanism, and to which we now turn.

2

The evolution of Pan-Africanism: Regional integration theories and approaches

This chapter provides a platform and base for discussing the primary focus of this book – the evolution of Pan-Africanism and assessing the major factors and actors in Africa's Pan-African Integration of divergence and convergence – in critiquing Africa's main regional economic communities (RECs), the Common Market for Eastern and Southern Africa (COMESA), the East African Community (EAC) and the Southern African Development Community (SADC) that signed a Tripartite Free Trade Agreement (TFTA) in 2008, setting the stage for continental integration, through the creation of the African Continental Free Trade Area (ACFTA), that was established with twenty-two of Africa's fifty-five member states in March 2018.

Informed by the diverse body of literature, debates and issues established in regional integration and divergence and convergence literature, the chapter articulates two analytical frameworks to navigate this terrain: the neoclassical economics approach and the neoclassical realist approach, which provide an understanding of the literature review and interpreting the findings as well as the conclusions presented in the book.

Thus, this chapter provides an understanding of the politics and economics surrounding the two concepts, which lays the foundation for the examination of the different meanings, goals and specific approaches employed in achieving Pan-Africanism through a regional integration lens in contemporary divergence and convergence discourse. The literature review on regional integration also provides a broad scope within which multiple memberships and regional security are discussed.

Assumptions of new theories and definitions

First, the theory of neoclassical economic regional integration,[1] as the first main argument, demonstrates how economic convergence could occur, and applies the case of South Africa and the Southern African Customs Union (SACU) under a regional economic integration lens (elaborated in Chapter 5). Regional trade schemes assume that owing to free trade being promoted and conducted and within the logic of trade creation and diversion, empirically it is envisaged that regional economic groupings, when opening their markets, should yield positive results in increased levels of trade.

The assumption is that South Africa, as a malign hegemonic state, manages the multiple memberships of the SACU bloc by incentivising poorer economies through the trade revenue generated in the bloc and critique is provided within the four approaches discussed in Chapter 5 demonstrating this regional convergence.

Second, COMESA, EAC and SADC have, on the one hand, converged (joined forces and have come together) to trade and to promote attempts towards continental integration; but on the other hand, they are also faced with open markets and free trade as neoclassical economics outline. Thus, the flipside of the assumption of neoclassical economic integration that is largely premised on open markets and free trade concerned with economic growth – an approach used by the CFTA – is that divergence will occur, moving away from the ideals of achieving Pan-African integration.

A further assumption underscores that globalisation of open markets and trade as defined in neoclassical economics contradicts Africa's regional integration approaches of a market-led strategy (neoclassical economic approach) of free trade and relaxing tariffs, amid the acceptance of multilateral international agreements of its member states within regional blocs and thus, are further contradictory to the principles of variable geometry of protecting member states against discriminatory free trade. The analyses of multiple memberships of Africa's states within various regional groupings is thus critically assessed, in understanding the prospects for African integration. Third, the theory Pan-African economic integration, therefore, claims that conducting stronger trade relations among Africa's countries with similar developmental economies like those of the Caribbean and Pacific countries can create the necessary conditions to achieving Pan-African economic integration and ultimately economic growth and analyses are applied and illustrated in Chapter 6.

Having said that, the preferences of Africa's governments have erroneously leaned more towards relations with exploitative and powerful international actors including Beijing, Brussels and Washington – viewed largely by Africa as the saviours to achieving economic growth for the African continent. These trade relations will erode any ideals of creating a Pan-Africa and achieving the African Union's (AU) Agenda 2063 framework of continental integration. Moreover, Africa's much stronger economies, such as South Africa for instance, have since the 2000 Cotonou EU and African, Caribbean and Pacific (ACP) group of states trade agreements began distancing itself from the Caribbean and the Pacific countries. This divergence was successfully orchestrated by Europe when it succeeded in evoking a developed economic status on South Africa, while rejecting its least developed country (LDC) status.[2] Similarly, Africa's stronger economies such as Kenya and Egypt are important actors in conducting viable trade relations for Africa's achieving of Pan-African economic integration and moving its economies from remaining the under-periphery of the world to the semi-periphery.

But, Africa's governments' foreign policy trends with external powers are further supported in justifications and arguments made by Africa's leaders that lay the blame on poor infrastructure as the main barrier for effective intercontinental trade. The book therefore explains these debates concerning North-South and South-South Africa trade in relation to infrastructure in Chapter 4 and provides expanded critiques of ACP, African Growth and Opportunity Act (AGOA), Economic Partnership

Agreements (EPAs) and Brazil-Russia-India-China-South Africa (BRICS) trade relations with Africa in Chapters 5 and 6.

Fourth, this book addresses Africa's security issues and factors in the analysis focused on Barry Buzan and Ole Wæver's regional security complex, as well as Amitav Acharya's observations on regional security within regionalism, which provides a further lens for examining how Africa's states are dealing with the issue of regional security within a regional security complex framework. However, the theory on Regional Security Complex (RSC) will not be able to adequately explain the convergence of Africa's states in managing regional security and achieving Pan-African security convergence which this book is interested in. The theory of neorealist security convergence[3] underscores that owing to the presence of a hegemonic power within a regional bloc that has both a strong economy as well as military strength[4] with geopolitical interests will intervene in regional security issues that are linked to its own national interests of both security and economic concerns. The key variable of the malign hegemon that has the ability to converge the security apparatuses of other member states within a regional bloc, is expanded from the concept of 'neorealist' that defines a malign hegemonic state as a powerful state with a strong economy that has the power and authority of setting the rules of the game, the hegemon acts out of self-gain, and has a greater advantage over its partner states, and is able to exert such power.

Such an observation directly points to numerous examples that are directly linked to countries like South Africa, Uganda, and Rwanda – and their domestic problems owing to their socio-economic, political or security conditions that they face by using the region's security agenda. Hence, such states have the ability to converge national brigades such as the Neutral Intervention Brigade or the African Capacity for Immediate Response to Crises (ACIRC), for that matter, or intervene unilaterally. Such states are also contributing troops elsewhere and intervening in hybrid missions (e.g. South Africa's three thousand troops in the Democratic Republic of Congo (DRC)), achieved regional convergence but divergence of the continental brigade and its operationalisation agenda, through the creation of those interventions.[5] The assistance from external actors is also prevalent, like France, the United States and China in the G-5 Sahel initiative with the operationalisation of the Cross-Border Joint Force in Bamako sponsored by France;[6] and in the case of the United States, Washington houses two thousand of its troops as a vital link to the war on terror in the Horn of Africa ever since the 11 September 2001 attacks that occurred in New York.[7]

Having said that, if Africa's states that are resource-rich, economically poor, with intense levels of corruption and fragile security are allowing powerful states to intervene militarily, indeed only a degree of regional security convergence would be achieved through such interventions and convergence of regional security apparatuses. However, in the absence of Africa's governments creating the necessary conditions to address socio-economic inequalities and injustices and with their failure to uphold human rights laws, peace and security is unlikely to be achieved. Moreover, with the key continental framework of the establishment of the CFTA in March 2018, economics trumps politics, thus, the degree of commitment to continental security could be greater in achieving Pan-African security convergence, which is a key factor in gaining further understanding of who the real actors and factors are that are prohibiting or promoting the operationalisation of Africa's achieving of Pan-African security convergence discussed in Chapter 7.

Further debates in the book concerning discussions on regional security are also reinforced by providing a historical security lens to explain the evolution of Africa's security convergence and divergences and include Gilbert Khadiagala's theory on alliance, which provides a good basis for the historical security evolution that includes the Frontline States (FLS) in setting the stage for understanding the security convergence debates discussed in Chapter 3.

Situating Pan-Africanism within the divergence and convergence debates of regional integration

A debate of the historical dimensions of Pan-Africanism and what this meant for Africa also briefly centres the discussion on Europe's earlier success at economic integration of incremental lobbying, as well as getting the buy-in of its member states at each stage of the process and which has much relevance in understanding Africa's unification.[8] Although, on 23 June 2016, the European Union (EU) had to bid farewell to one of its powerful members – Britain – when it reached the pinnacle of its dissatisfaction with EU policies and decided in their country referendum to abandon the EU. Such global events in international relations should now become a drawing card for Africa's countries to unite and strengthen its Pan-African vision. But regional integration processes in Africa and elsewhere have been considerably slow, with most regions confronting the same needs, forces, obstacles and constraints in various forms as Britain has orchestrated its exiting from the EU.[9] Regional economic integration has been viewed by many states as a mechanism for sovereign states to come together and to conduct economic integration in trade and is able to link government's national policies to a supranational entity.[10] Regional economic integration that is linked to market factors and open trade can thus more easily dictate the outcome of regional integration schemes that are linked to regional institutions.[11]

For Africa, the traditional intellectual debates of integration schemes have been influenced by experiences of integration by Western countries.[12] This discussion further outlines the regional economic integration theories starting from the 1950s. These views were expressed in various approaches and schools of thought: federalism, functionalism, and neofunctionalism. Regional economic integration is also different from pure economics, since it can dictate the outcomes of integration linked to open trade. Africa however, has been too overzealous in its efforts to conduct trade with Europe. Although African countries were in a trade bloc – as part of the seventy-nine-member ACP bloc – it failed to use to the ACP bloc to benefit intra-trade relations within the bloc.[13]

Initially, between the 1950s and 1960s, regional integration processes were particularly concerned with how supranationalism could modify state behaviour in community building, while viewing sovereignty as an important component in the promotion of economies of scale. Karl Deutsch stressed the importance of this, by noting that Europe had to consider and focus on the real reasons for joining a supranational organisation and forego sovereignty.[14] Deutsch also described supranationalism as a vehicle whereby the behaviour of the state could be modified through building a community of values and attitudes that could promote cooperation.[15] Supranationalism therefore implied that an international institution was able to exercise authority over its members (states), which involved elements of authoritative power in the political and legal areas, and which limited the autonomy of sovereign states. The EU is the only example of a supranational entity which serves as the primary decision-making organ through the Council of the European Union.

Region builders of the federalist school (1950s) viewed politics and state governments as the cornerstones of regional integration processes. The federalists held the view that politics trumped economics, and integration had to be pursued through the creation of a centralised, supranational entity. For the federalists, maintaining a national identity and promoting economic growth could best be achieved by creating a central government, joint institutions and a common constitution. Ernest Haas was the first proponent to write on the logic of integration, and his efforts pioneered analysis on the European Community as a supranational entity that led to the development of the framework for his theory of 'neo-functionalism'.[16] Leon Lindberg shared similar frameworks to those of Haas.[17] Spillover from institutions was seen to further the neo-functional discourse. This entailed that, through enhanced increased transborder exchanges and cooperation in technical areas (as was the case of the Economic Coal and Steel Community (ECSC)), the integration processes could lead to an increased transnational interdependence, which in turn would create functional spillover into other areas and ultimately, the integration process could become more sustainable.[18]

But federalist thinkers in Europe were challenged in the 1960s by functionalism and neo-functionalism approaches. David Mitrany, who was also known as the father of functionalism, in his concept articulated as, 'peace by pieces', argued that a functional alternative to international integration was essential. For Mitrany, international cooperation had to be premised on the view that non-political issues of the state, such as 'socio-economic, technical and issues of a humanitarian nature, could be separated' and dealt with independently.[19] A functional approach was therefore seen by Mitrany as a pragmatic one, which instead of placing emphasis on the state, should be created, and constitute units of sectoral activities in the economic fields, for market regulation, communications, and management of natural resources. Furthermore, sectoral units had to be given a sense of autonomy and power for such units to solve the problems of the state. These efficiencies would spill over into the political fields and, in so doing, ultimately avoid war and violent conflicts.[20]

As noted earlier, Africa's regional blocs have largely been created from a difficult past. The EU that emerged from the Second World War provides a pertinent analogy. In the case of Africa, its regional integration processes have faced underdevelopment and poor integration processes that either failed or have been ineffective. The majority of Africa's economies and states are peripheral economies with five large core economies: Nigeria, Kenya, Egypt, Angola and South Africa. Africa's regions still lack regional integration policies viable for economic growth, such as government support for businesses of small, micro and medium enterprises (SMMEs) that can grow industrialisation alongside value-added production through intraregional trade and manufacturing. Such factors are important in fostering endogenous growth through the transference of technology and skills to boost development, research and education supported by strong government policies. Such factors should therefore be considered and engender support through state-led policies that are implemented at both national and regional levels.

External bilateral and multilateral relations have, however, flourished more amid regional trade agreements on the African continent. There is very little traded on the continent, with only 16 per cent of intraregional trade in 2018. African countries still face similar issues as those prevalent at independence, with largely mono-crop economies that spend a large part of their resources on the production of export commodities. For instance, the 1980s was viewed as 'Africa's Lost Decade', since economic integration was ineffective because there was debt build up and no economic growth. Region builders in Africa further evolved from the AU's predecessor's plan, the Organization of African Unity (OAU) that defined regional integration as a vehicle for states to build regional institutions and to advance economic growth, as defined in its charter.[21] Further spearheading Africa's regional integration cause, United Nations Economic Commission for Africa (UNECA) was seen as the master builder of Africa's integration, and assisted in the creation of the EAC established in 1967, involving Kenya, Uganda and Tanzania.[22]

The grandiose integration plans pursued regionalism solutions – a plan and concept on paper that collapsed within the reality of Africa's own political economy of strong sovereign states holding onto power.[23] But what is the place for regional integration in Africa, which had already begun during the early 1900s? Pascal Lamy notes that regional integration is not a new process and that the African continent had seen the creation of the first of such processes of integration in 1910, with the creation of SACU, while 1919 saw the birth of the EAC.[24] Regional integration processes only really took root in the rest of the world about forty to fifty years later.

Such integration processes, for example in Europe, formed the ECSC, created in 1951. Other regional mechanisms were also formed such as the Association of Southeast Asian Nations (ASEAN) created in 1967; and in South America, the Mercado Común del Sur (MERCOSUR) created in 1991. In retrospect, although Africa was the first integrator and builder of RECs, it is currently lagging behind in intra- and interregional trade and still facing major infrastructure impediments. In Europe, for example, the level of interregional trade was 60 per cent, while ASEAN's interregional trade levels were between 30 and 40 per cent. MERCOSUR is a further example, with an interregional trade level of 40 per cent in 2016.

On the other hand, the developmentalist approach of UNECA stressed the need to develop cooperation integration that centred on well-strategized projects and that could promote integrated markets and co-investments. Through the efforts of UNECA's commitment, regional economic cooperation and integration evolved and initially only the Economic Community of West African States (ECOWAS) and the Preferential Trade Area (PTA) for eastern and Southern Africa were established with the EAC already being in existence.[25] The EAC was Africa's most successful regional cooperation and sophisticated regional grouping until it failed.[26] Kenya had a strongly developed industrial base and was seen as the major beneficiary of the community's economic development, but the economic and political ideologies of Idi Amin, the former Ugandan president, contributed greatly to the demise of the community in 1977.[27]

In furthering the regional integration cause in Africa, the key goals of the PTA were advanced by UNECA to promote trade liberalisation and state cooperation in specialised development industries such as production of food crops and livestock, development of science and technology, exploitation and utilisation of natural resources, human resources development and creation of transport and telecommunications networks.[28]

But it was also a difficult period for eastern and Southern African states that faced regional wars targeting economic integration and destroying their infrastructure – valuable to the growth of the economy. But while South Africa had an influence on Southern African Development Coordination Conference's (SADCC's) non-growth on the one hand (by destroying its infrastructure), on the other hand, the Federation of Rhodesia and Nyasaland, created through British imperialist objectives and interests, was a step ahead of the rest of the SADCC states. Those countries linked to the Federation – Northern Rhodesia (Zambia), Nyasaland (Malawi) and Southern Rhodesia (Zimbabwe) – had access to railways. Through the railway system, these three countries had access to South Africa through Bechuanaland (Botswana) and further access to the ports of Beira and Lourenco Marques (Maputo) in Portuguese East Africa (Mozambique).

Aside from rail access, the countries linked to the Federation had telecommunications as well as electricity generated from the Zambezi River and accessed through Northern Rhodesia, Nyasaland and Southern Rhodesia; this energy was generated from the Kariba power station. Throughout South Africa's apartheid years, the South African government had developed most of its neighbours' economies in some way or another, other than those of Angola and Tanzania.[29] Africa's slow economic growth among the regional communities has largely been attributed to the inappropriate integration models used, as well as to major global events.

Lynn Mytelka,[30] Ibrahim Gambari,[31] Gerald Meier[32] and Lamy[33] all argued that global events that compounded the regional integration cause for Africa were largely due to the 1973 oil crisis, which triggered a threefold increase in the price of oil demanded by the Organization of Petroleum Exporting Countries (OPEC).[34] The soaring oil price increase of 400 per cent in 1980 led to an increase in production and transport costs overall and placed a further burden on Africa's economies.[35] External involvement also had implications for autonomous development and against regional political and economic cooperation agendas.

While restructuring institutions, the region's concern was focused on whether SADCC would have attained a level of economic development and integration that could withstand a powerful economy like that of South Africa. The major factor was the historical legacy of apartheid South Africa in terms of its aggressive military role in the region. SADCC member states viewed their organisation as a political institution designed to reduce dependence on the economy of South Africa in terms of trade, transport, communications and infrastructure, either individually or jointly as a regional bloc. It is necessary to understand these debates in the theory and literature review, in order to have salient discussions in the book on how COMESA, EAC and SADC and belong to individual regional schemes intend addressing the issue of regionalisation and convergence of their own protocols and treaties to remedy the economic growth for their member states and moving closer towards Africa's goal of achieving a Pan-African integration.

As noted by Gambari, it was not possible for Third World countries to separate economics from politics, nor would the spillover of economic to political cooperation be a natural process.[36] Many African countries, having gained independence in the late 1950s and early 1960s, became protective of their independent states after the end of the colonial period. African states were therefore guarding their sovereignty. According to Gambari, the LDCs in Africa viewed the role of the sovereign state as paramount in attempting integration, since these states were more intent on pursuing wealth and enhancing economic growth and less concerned with the issue of avoidance of war and conflict that concerned the functionalist scholars like Mitrany.[37] Regional integration in the 1970s expanded more on economic cooperation, intergovernmentalism, developmental regionalism, political cooperation, economic cooperation, old and new regionalism and regionalisation and other integration processes that evolved across the world. Scholars of regional integration like Joseph Nye,[38] Robert Keohane[39] and Andrew Moravcsik[40] all viewed successful integration as interdependent. Their view was that for integration to materialise, member states in a regional group should have the ability to adapt and respond to cooperative agreements through negotiation between governments, which in their view was a viable strategy which could lead to successful outcomes of integration.

These scholars further noted that such negotiation processes should consider two important variables: 'bargaining' and 'negotiating' among powerful members within the group. Also, it was through such a move that Europe's economic policy converged. The literature provides various views on regionalism. These views articulated regionalism seen as processes that have evolved from being state led, to constituting important dimensions of global restructuring processes. Similar concepts are expanded on by scholars like Margaret Lee, who writes on regionalism. She indicates that regionalism is 'the adoption of a regional project by a formal regional economic organisation designed to enhance the political, economic, social, cultural, and security integration and/or cooperation of member states'.[41] Samuel K. B. Asante's discussion on Africa's regional integration within economic integration views integration as: 'A process where two or more countries in a particular area voluntarily join together to pursue common policies and objectives in matters of general economic development or in a particular economic field of common interest to the mutual advantage of all the participating states.'[42]

Old and new regionalism concepts were succinctly argued by Alex Warleigh-Lack as overly exaggerated political and economic projects. Warleigh-Lack explained that this was not sufficient, by drawing on Haas's neo-functionalist theory in describing regional integration projects as being dependent on certain factors for success, such as increasing transaction levels between states that could benefit all member states, with wealthier participating states providing side-payments when necessary. Warleigh-Lack drew on a range of regional integration debates, including the constructivist approaches of Björn Hettne and rationalist perspectives of James Mittleman. Warleigh-Lack identified the importance of four independent variables in exploring regionalism within the political economy framework and these he defined as the rationale or genesis, functionality, socialisation and the impact of the regionalisation process. Warleigh-Lack therefore noted that a successful regional project should concentrate on homogeneity of wealth and size of the participating members within a regional grouping.

However, a clear focus should be on institution building when creating a common market.[43] For example, SADCC, and the PTA, were very closely linked regions, owing to both their geography and colonial heritage. During the 1980s, however, when the PTA and SADCC were formed, they had different regional perspectives to contend with. SADCC was saddled with apartheid regional practices, and in the 1980s, Zimbabwe had the second largest economy in Southern Africa after South Africa but it remained impoverished. The PTA, however, was faced with complying with the Lagos Plan of Action (LPA). The true realities of struggling economies set in, as the apartheid government in South Africa began its wars against the liberation movements in Angola, Mozambique, Zimbabwe, Namibia and within South Africa. A further issue was the SACU agreement that generated trade revenue for the weak economies of Lesotho, Eswatini and Botswana and that was linked to a monetary area.

John Akokpari defines regional cooperation as cooperation between states, which translate to regional integration and which is also a starting point for regional integration to advance. Regionalism, in his view, is a broadened concept that is beyond economic and market integration. Regionalisation, on the other hand, is seen as a broader process to include elements of both regionalism and interactions of formal and informal structures in a region. Later these processes could result in regionalisation.[44] Marianne Marchand, Morten Bøås and Timothy Shaw similarly describe region-ness or regionality as the various dimensions and exchanges of cultural affinities, political regimes, economic policies and security arrangements.[45] Tanzania for example, was instrumental in assisting with the liberation movements of Southern Africa. Tanzania, Angola and Mozambique became active participatory states in the involvement of the FLS and their liberation movements and struggle against white superiority and racism. Angola joined the Alliance members of Southern African states after independence in 1975. During the 1960s, Mozambique found a safe haven in Dar es Salaam for its Mozambique Liberation Front (FRELIMO). The historical dimension of EAC also stems from the 1969 Lusaka Manifesto, and Tanzania was a key player in forming the FLS.

Regional integration became the entry point for Africa to create the necessary conditions to achieve Pan-Africanism. Akokpari provides a more definitive analysis of theories on regional integration in defining 'regional integration' and 'regional cooperation', as well as 'regionalism' and 'regionalisation' and his view is that theories have become conflated because these terms involve policies and harmonisation of such policies among states, as well as activities aimed at 'accelerating regional development'.[46] He also describes regional integration as a process that 'takes various forms including market integration [common markets] and development integration'.[47]

The link between the Botswana, Lesotho, Namibia and Eswatini (BLNE) and their attachment to South Africa was SACU established in 1910, which remained a significant economic link during the 1980s and beyond. South Africa's attachment to Zambia for example, was linked to the mining industry.[48] Zambia received most of its mining equipment from South Africa and was also equipped by the South African government with mining skills and technology. South Africa has built up extensive investments in neighbouring countries that were aligned with the BLNE states. But in considering Warleigh-Lack's views noted earlier, an assessment of the historical legacy should thus be undertaken in relation to the economic, social, political and infrastructural development of the region. These socio-economic and political factors as well as security issues cannot be ignored and they define the pace and intentions of regional integration. Such factors include skills and education; labour migration; infrastructure such as transport and communications; trade and finance and other critical components important for achieving regional development.

The second wave of Pan-Africanism towards modernity

South Africa as a hegemonic power has been a prominent player in regional integration efforts. Post 1994, South Africa assumed a market-driven developmental regional integration approach and a micro-regional approach. However, many states in the region accused South Africa's multinational corporations (MNCs) of regional investments that benefited South Africa more.[49] South Africa's regional strategy involved using Spatial Development Initiatives (SDIs) as a springboard to assist South Africa's neighbours, while also attempting to improve South Africa's own socio-economic and poverty-stricken society with its huge shortages of skills and poor education, poverty and lack of the most basic of services such as running potable water, housing and sanitation. For example, the Maputo Development Corridor (MDC) that evolved from SADC's SDIs was developed by South Africa with billions of dollars provided by the South African government.[50] These issues are critical in order to grasp why Africa is struggling to grow its economies as Gregg Mills posits in his account of the reasons for Africa's poverty and why the continent has lagged behind amid an abundance of natural resources.[51]

According to Ian Taylor, new regionalism is seen as having three different levels – macro, sub and micro – within regional projects that interact with and react to other elements of the global economy. Taylor also viewed these three levels as important in understanding how macro-regions generate tensions and contradictions, for example within the SDIs of SADC that are linked to private partnerships and MNCs. These debates also evolved from the growing climate of globalisation in defining a new regional strategy for groupings like SADC and that focused on 'developmental integration'.[52] Taylor, Hettne, András Inotai, Osvaldo Sunkel and Mittleman all expanded on the 'New Regionalism Approach/Theory (NRA/T)' that includes regionalism, regionalisation and transnational cross-border flows, which are seen as interdependencies within a global perspective and at multiple levels.[53] John Ravenhill is also of the view that if political cooperation is effectively facilitated and institutionalised, African agency would be enhanced, could serve as a collective voice and become meaningful at international forums (such as the WTO, or Group of 20 (G-20) summits).

Therefore, one of the main reasons for creating RECs in Africa was to promote sustainable regional economic policies to address the imbalance of weaker economies against stronger ones within regional economic clusters. Africa's states were clustered into regional groupings based merely on geographical proximity. As noted earlier, the Federation of Rhodesia and Nyasaland was established in August 1953,[54] and alliances such as these had to spearhead infrastructure; however, the region's infrastructure, depleted by apartheid South Africa in its wars against regional states, did not bode well for socio-economic development. Neither did the migration movements from neighbouring states to South Africa advance regional integration during the 1970s–80s, with labour continuously ebbing from the Southern African states. This left neighbouring countries in a dire predicament in their attempts to rectify the damage and contend with a deteriorating infrastructure. It was therefore imperative for the OAU to consider the production of economic growth for Africa's development.

The three RECs comprising eastern and Southern Africa were identified as starting pillars for Africa's integration. These three RECs constitute twenty-six of Africa's fifty-five countries, and have a combined population of 530 million people and a total gross domestic product (GDP) of $1.3 trillion, with a total GDP per capita averaging $1,180. Furthermore, they encompass over half of the AU's membership and more than half of the African continent's 1 billion people. They are COMESA, EAC and SADC. The AU's Constitutive Act of 2000 and the Abuja Treaty of 1991 both viewed all three as the building blocks for achieving an African Economic Community (AEC).

Furthermore, the RECs also manage regional security mechanisms which place a further strain on these communities. Hence, for African agency to benefit the African continent, Ravenhill suggests that political cooperation should be encouraged, instead of being imposed by the AU. Regional institutions should therefore serve as vehicles that strengthen the state; simultaneously sovereign capacity should be considered that could enhance regional cooperation and promote greater economic cooperation and, ultimately, regionalism.[55]

In addition to the 'New Regionalism Approach/Theory'[56] of Fredrik Söderbaum and Björn Hettne, other forms of integration emerged in Africa, such as micro- and macro-regionalism. Micro-regions had seemingly become the backbone in public–private partnerships, and were more transborder in nature, existing at both national and local levels and unlike macro-regions (world regions), as noted by Söderbaum and Taylor.[57] Macro-regions are defined as 'larger territorial units or sub-systems between the national and the global levels'.[58] Söderbaum and Taylor draw this analysis from Mozambique and South Africa's development corridor, where macro-regions are defined as larger territories or subsystems between national and global levels.[59] Similarly, Nikki Slocum-Bradley discusses similar regional schemes such as the Zambia–Malawi–Mozambique Growth Triangle (ZMM-GT, which covers the Zambezi Valley in Mozambique and certain micro-regions of Malawi and Zambia that border Mozambique) and defines them 'as subjective phenomena that are continuously re-created through discourses by various actors and for various purposes … the existence of regions is preceded by the existence of region builders'.[60]

However, an opposing view is provided by Olubanke King-Akerele and Kojo Asiedu of micro-regions to that of Söderbaum and Taylor and Slocum-Bradley that is also based on the ZMM-GT. King-Akerele and Asiedu observed that micro-regions could be an innovative step to grow economies and a mechanism to withstand global competition.[61] Further afield, ASEAN, for example, experienced the emergence of such subregional growth, comprising three-tier growth triangles. ASEAN's growth triangles were believed to have contributed to economic growth because of the success of ASEAN's economic growth trajectory. Ravenhill also provides a specific example and defined 'the Johor–Singapore–Riau Growth Triangle within ASEAN, which took advantage of Singapore's skilled labour and developed infrastructure, Johor's land and semiskilled labour and Riau's land and low-cost labour'.[62] Quebec's large industrialised region is another example of an economy's forming successful micro-regions, which were both independent and technologically advanced. Therefore, new regionalism can be defined as a process that develops in a multipolar context where the drivers do not have to be superpowers but can be more spontaneous; it includes states of semi-core and peripheral economies.[63]

The AU's agenda on regional integration is also aimed at creating more efficient ways of building regional communities – hence the prominence afforded to fast-tracking regional integration through growth triangles with greater focus placed on the private sector. This is central in growth mechanisms that also include public–private sector partnerships as important strategies to achieve economic growth and that can contribute towards regional integration. South Africa's micro-regional developmental integration approach in building infrastructure, such as the MDC and the energy grid – the Southern African Power Pool (SAPP) – established in 1995, did so in gaining economic integration and convergence largely affected by South African government's domestic condition, which in turn created its regional response.

The third wave of Pan-Africanism from modernity to dependency

Africa's regional integration attempts cannot be discussed without assessing open markets of open trade and liberal agreements to assess economic growth. In taking these views into account, Bela Balassa posits that, 'economic cooperation among member states to include actions aimed at lessening discrimination such as concluding international agreements on trade policies; and, economic integration and comprises measures and actions taken that suggests suppressing some forms of discrimination through removal of trade barriers.'[64]

Currently it appears that Africa's efforts of liberalising its markets, and, 'lessening discrimination such as concluding international agreements on trade policies' by finalising trade policies and deals with the international community, such as the EPAs[65] with the EU and other agreements such as the Europe-South Africa Trade Development and Cooperation agreement (EU-SA TDCA) of 1999, have impacted negatively on the region and may have further negative impact on diverging trade integration schemes.

John Friedmann explains this impact of trade divergence within the unequal nature of growth in world systems theory, and contends that wealth from the 'core' or 'semi-core' will not automatically filter down to peripheral economies. The periphery is always dependent on the core for its market, technology and production (spillover). World systems theory posits that as the market economy of the core grows, it continually expands, ultimately creating a larger periphery (or a semi-periphery), which gradually transforms, taking on similar attributes to the core, which may include advanced levels of technology, production and an efficient market. However, the core can also be seen to be dependent on the periphery through market exploitation, creating a periphery of the periphery (with poor, vulnerable and resource-depleted economies).[66] The reality is that the region builders (government leaders) have not sufficiently merged policies of trade and policies of migration (labour). These policies remain at AU ambassadorial level.

The decade-old Tripartite bloc's (COMESA-EAC-SADC) stages of development and trade since 2008 lacked endowment factors concerning input and output, which has not been overly advantageous for regional integration. Knowledge spillover has been lagging behind as well. This, the book views as important, and will expand on in addressing these conflicting views. As Justin Malewezi suggests, technological advancement and knowledge spillover are important to any region-building efforts; this the book considers in discussing the trajectory of the economic integration processes of COMESA, EAC and SADC's Tripartite agreement and their efforts to converge policy, implementation, and practice leading up to the CFTA.[67]

Instead, Africa's regional integration processes have adopted a market-led strategy of free trade – a neoclassical economic approach of open markets that works against the principles of variable geometry, which the COMESA–EAC–SADC have adopted as a mechanism and framework designed to protect smaller economies and infant industries when it converged in 2008. Several smaller economies have therefore become dependent on other forms and ways of economic growth to protect their infant industries. Such mechanisms entail signing external trade agreements and creating several multiple memberships in trade.

While market integration and regional trade are important factors to consider in African integration attempts, state capital of hegemonic states has become increasingly important in influencing the pace of economic and regional growth and setting the pace for integration efforts. Robert Putnam's 'two-level game' model, adequately explains 'how the relationship between diplomacy and domestic politics can be integrated', and 'domestic politics and international relations [are seen as interlinked and entangled]'.[68] Stephan, Power, Hervey and Fonseca clearly define Africa's regional integration condition as being 'constrained by globalisation, with realities of inadequate investment flows, adverse trading regimes, and the legacy of colonialism'.[69] According to Putnam's two-level game theory,

> Each national political leader appears at both game boards. Across the international table sit his foreign counterparts, and at his elbows sit diplomats and other international advisors. Around the domestic table behind him sit party and parliamentary figures, spokespersons for domestic agencies, representatives of key interest groups, and the leader's own political advisors. The unusual complexity of this two-level game is that moves that are rational for a player at one board (such as raising energy prices, conceding territory, or limiting auto imports) may be

impolitic for the same player at the other board. Nevertheless, there are powerful incentives for consistency between the two games.[70]

In expanding on Putnam's two-level game theory, South Africa's investment through its market-driven approach, recognises the importance of increasing intraregional trade while balancing external trade within the SACU bloc. Ian Bremmer further explains that the role of the hegemonic state in an integration process can either slow down economic growth by over regulating markets, or use the market as a means to bolster self-fulfilled trade for a state's own gains and for domestic and political positions.[71] Moreover, regional integration has been affected by state capitalism, which has become prominent in state interrelations, and has placed a damper on regions by stifling trade liberalisation and distorting markets.

According to Bremmer, 'government sectors that own the world's largest oil companies, and those controlling three-quarters of the world's energy reserves, have huge influence on the direction of trade and have further influenced the pace of regional integration'.[72] Various other processes have also hampered regional integration efforts in Africa. Globally, regional integration had been overshadowed by competing rounds of over 200 bilateral agreements, a mechanism to circumvent the Uruguay Rounds of General Agreement on Tariffs and Trade (GATT) (now called the WTO) to raise tariffs. Bremmer also suggests that 'protectionism begets protectionism, and subsidies beget subsidies'.[73] From the neoclassical realist perspective, the literature on regional integration identifies that 'tit-for-tat' tactics and various power games exercised by states can erode cooperation and disadvantage peripheral economies; this creates regional economic divergence instead of convergence. For example, the Doha Round of international trade talks that failed in 2008, was affected by the US and the EU's agricultural tariffs, leaving China and India dissatisfied with the Doha Round process and wanting to protect both their farmers and infant industries.[74]

Regional integration discussed above highlighted the attempts made by Africa to join forces and integrate the region through RECs through promoting open markets and free trade areas but as discussed above divergence and convergence of regional integration attempts in Africa can occur. Because economic growth linked to open markets and free trade (pursued by COMESA, EAC and SADC's Tripartite Agreement of 2008) is largely based on neoclassical economics, the discussion now turns to understanding this debate and the literature review is thus premised on the divergence and convergence literature of neoclassical economics and to which we now turn.

Neoclassical economics: Divergence and convergence

Like the concept of regional integration, divergence and convergence is a multidimensional concept to analyse and to assess through a single prism, which is economic growth policy. This discussion thus expands on economic growth models demonstrating that divergence and or convergence in regional groups and countries can be achieved which favour free trade through eliminating discriminatory policies as well as fostering industrialisation, technology and knowledge-driven production factors in endogenous growth models.

Early studies (during the 1960s) on divergence and convergence focused primarily on the United States, as well as states and groups in Europe. Traditional industries in these countries were strongly driven by rules of competition, combined with intensified levels of knowledge production in technology and research design.[75]

The prediction of the theory is that 'poorer economies will show faster growth than richer economies, which will therefore converge over time towards common levels of per capita income'.[76]

As suggested by Meier,

> According to the second generation of development economists, correct policies were to move from inward-looking strategies toward liberalization of foreign trade regime and export promotion; to submit to stabilization programmes; to privatize state-owned enterprises; and to follow the dictates of the market price system. Through its guidance toward the correct policies, neo-classical economics were believed to be the safeguard against policy-induced distortions and nonmarket failures.[77]

Classical economic growth model indicates 'that a reduction of barriers to trade associated with economic integration will lead to increased growth for poor countries'[78] and will show faster growth for poor versus rich countries, with economies converging 'over time towards a common level of per capita income associated with strong, absolute, and unconditional convergence'.[79] But there was also a divergence in this understanding of economic growth, with Western and Eastern economic performances showing different development outputs. Within the classical economic approach there was poor economic performance in the West, but growth in Eastern economies was observed in technology and space shuttle (Sputnik) launches, as well as in the rapidly growing economies in the Soviet Union.[80]

The concepts of divergence and convergence have been evolving since the work of Robert Solow in 1956, and have as their origins classical economics linked to economic growth theory.[81] These two concepts stem from the 1929 Great Depression, and the 1940s–50s aftermath of underdevelopment after the Second World War. Paul Samuelson's (1948) writing on classical economics was conducted through abstract modelling and began setting a new path and a different model for classical economists.[82] However, theories also differed among economists. The Solow theory predicted that economic integration would lead to an increase in efficiency, and hence an increase in income per capita with growth accelerating to a new equilibrium. But it does not provide explanations for how technology spillover could affect economic growth. At that time, Solow's model was seen as an idealised case, not sufficiently taking into account the real world. This reality portrayed various frictions and deviations from the ideal conditions caused by monopolistic and oligopolistic imperfections of the market, external economies, price and wage rigidities, and lack of information and technological advances.[83]

The huge underdevelopment of LDCs was an added factor to the debate of classical economics. The classical economic model was attempting to find the ways and means to address the LDCs' underdevelopment and poor conditions. For example, Theodore W. Schultz, in 1964, noted that the LDCs were poor economic performers, largely owing to government failures. Therefore, fixing markets through government intervention would not rectify the economies of the poor states.[84] Governments of LDCs were to conform to principles of market openness, fiscal discipline, and non-interventionism in order to gain from economic development, and hence growth rates and national wealth of LDCs would over time equal those of developed countries. Theories varied and scholars differed in their understanding of and solutions to why some states remained impoverished, and tried to deploy strategies that would assist LDCs to grow their economies, and similarly grow out of poverty. Solutions were also sought by classical economists in trying to understand the protracted decline of the US production industries and failing world markets. In Robert Gilpin's view, the controversy that ensued was between the development economists and development theorists. For the development school, LDCs were different from the industrialised group, functioned in a different economic setting, and were victims of 'late-late' development.[85]

Development theorists also believed that the strategy for development should be trade protectionism and import substitution, as well as building industrial structures behind high tariff walls. These ideas were proposed by leading economists, like Raúl Prebisch, who was heading Economic Commission for Latin America (ECLA) and United Nations Conference on Trade and Development (UNCTAD). Prebisch's ideas also became central to the import-substitution strategies of Latin America.[86] For the classical economic historians, productivity and related variables were inconclusive; they operated in silos without linkages afforded to long-term economic growth, which omitted historiography from the debate. These ideas found expression in the views of Alexander Gerschenkron,[87] arguing against the neoclassical economists' view that US productivity growth rates had been low relative to those of Germany, Japan and many other countries. Other spurts of integration with Solow's economic growth model contributed to the public finance work undertaken by David Cass, which addressed his question of determining factors on optimal savings.[88]

While the Keynesian model contributed to the neoclassical economic approach, various global events were equally responsible in shaping the mind-set of thinkers.[89] Such events were when the 1973 OPEC saw huge financial surpluses later recycled as international bank loans to LDCs, which resulted in a wave of global financial shocks and debt crises.[90] The neoclassical economic model evolved largely from the success of East Asia in 1997, which ushered in variables of endogenized growth theory and accumulation of factors. This success was attributed to rapid accumulation of capital and labour, and the basic factors of production in supporting the neoclassical growth model.[91] Attempts made to understand how economic growth could be accurately measured in the divergence and convergence fraternity of debates, with claims that labour productivity and per capita income levels in the industrialised market economies that have tended to converge since the Second World War (the period from 1945 to the 1980s), with convergence implying a tendency for the poorer countries in the group to grow more rapidly than the richer ones – also led to doubts in terms of the empirical evidence.

It was not clear to all scholars whether the Solow model suggests that when broadening the analysis of endogenous growth theory to a wider spectrum within a regional grouping, convergence necessarily leads to growth, as it was assumed that it is due to absence of income convergence among countries. Robert Lucas[92] and Paul Romer[93] suggested that convergence would only occur in an endogenous technological change model that considers 'an equilibrium model of endogenous technological change in which long-run growth is driven primarily by the accumulation of knowledge by forward-looking, profit maximizing agents'.[94]

The divergence and convergence theories further expanded into the business, labour, finance, and history economic paradigms. Edward Prescott used the Solow technology parameter to develop the neoclassical stochastic growth model in their study. The study assessed business cycle fluctuations to estimate aggregate consequences of public finance and terms of trade shocks. Expanding on the Solow model predictions, 'the neoclassical stochastic growth model unravels the argument that: "Once the model has a multistage production process, the neoclassical growth theory predicts the high volatility of inventory investment and also the fact that inventory stocks lag the business cycle."'[95] Similarly, business economist, Gary Hansen, expanded his model based on the Solow model and 'introduced non-convexities into the mapping between hours allocated to market activities and units of labo[u]r service produced, a feature of the economy well documented by micro observations'.[96] The neoclassical economic growth model expanded into the financial markets and complemented the Stanford Grossman and Robert Shiller study of stock market volatility.[97]

Market-driven trade liberalisation and economic growth

Building on the theories and empirical evidence of endogenous growth factors that lead to convergence, Lucas also argued that the endogenous growth model lacked the variables of diversity across countries, labour mobility, and the enormous pressures for immigration seen in the real world.[98] As suggested by Lucas, it was necessary to consider such variables, based on the fluidity of movement of people in the world. The analysis observed that the endogenous growth model was missing key variables such as human capital and government policies, and the incorporation of these variables would provide a different result.

The literature on divergence and convergence was also focused on conventional integration theories which tend to concentrate on economic factors and promote more efficient use of resources, eliminating discriminatory practices such as import substitution, and free movement of goods and services in a customs union. These older debates are discussed by Gambari, Mytelka and also Walter Ochoro.[99] As Gambari posits, not all these processes have been conducive to Africa's integration attempts. They constitute regional integration driven by developed countries, causing divergence in trade that has not been profitable for trade creation. Particularly in the areas of eliminating import substitution, Africa's governments have neglected to implement such policies, which are relevant for supporting LDCs in markets of free trade. Such views outline that regional economic integration is a concept that involves state actors coming together in their economic activities to trade, and, in the case of COMESA, EAC and SADC, to create free trade. African governments have been attempting to address the obstacles of regional integration. These obstacles include barriers to trade: 'a) to reduce supply-side constraints, improve competitiveness and promote industrialisation and diversification; b) to take practical steps to reduce trade barriers and facilitate trade; and, c) to deepen regional integration.'[100] Neoclassical economics is based on conventional neoclassical growth theory, as it is assumed that economic integration will occur when there is a reduction of barriers to trade and will lead to increased efficiency and income per capita convergence.

In measuring economic growth in trade liberalisation, Robert Barro and Xavier Sala-i-Martin provide an understanding of economic growth convergence by outlining two levels of convergence models as a basis for their theory. These are defined as beta-convergence (β) or, absolute convergence (also defined as the catch-up process), and sigma-convergence (σ) (when the dispersion among a group of countries tends to decrease over time).[101] Barro and Sala-i-Martin assessed the European economic and monetary policies measured against the removal of trade barriers, harmonisation of regulations, and liberalisation of capital and labour movements. The main empirical study was applied to patterns of convergence across seventy-three regions of Western Europe, as well as growth across the United States. The findings suggest that countries like the United States as well as European markets experienced club convergence in increased economic integration processes of trade liberalisation when factors of mobility were considered, and this led to opportunities for economies of scale and specialisation. Barro and Sala-i-Martin also observed that reducing transport and transaction costs could lead to greater 'spatial agglomeration' as well as specialisation. These findings also suggest that easing and reducing costs of settling payments with a single currency led to convergence of factor prices across the United States and European markets, but in addition also led to convergence in economic structures as well as per capita incomes.[102]

But as Rob Davies has indicated, in Africa, which is lagging behind in economic growth and is saddled with many weak economies, the benefits of functional spillover have not been as significant as in the instances of the EU and the United States, given the infrastructure incapacities that Africa has yet to deal with.[103] In shaping growth model studies, research measuring growth performance in trade liberalisation by Steve Dowrick and Duc-Tho Nguyen[104] focused on comparative economic growth performances of the Organisation for Economic Co-operation and Development (OECD) countries using trade liberalisation as a criterion. Their results indicated that labour productivity as a convergence variable was inadequate to measure economic performance. The model proposed total factor productivity (TFP) as the 'catch-up' and as a variable: 'TFP catch-up implies a tendency for income levels to converge, but such a tendency may be masked or exaggerated if factor intensity growth varies systematically with income growth.'[105] Furthermore, Dowrick and Nguyen observed that if poorer countries were to invest substantially more in employment and output than richer countries did, the convergence in labour productivity would be more rapid than in total factor productivity, since faster capital accumulation assisted the least developing countries to catch-up with the industrialised countries in their model testing.

Various approaches conducted in divergence and convergence growth economic models have provided different results. For instance, Oded Galor's theory on divergence and convergence was a response to the controversy in the debates of the neoclassical economic growth theory models in frameworks by Paul Romer; Barro and Sala-i-Martin; and Gregory Mankiw, David Romer and David Weil. Galor's findings indicated that the absolute convergence hypothesis suggests that

> per capita incomes of countries converge to one another in the long run independently of initial conditions as inconclusive; since an economy's long-run equilibrium depends on its structural characteristics (example technologies, preferences, population growth, government policy, factor market structure, among others.) Absolute convergence [therefore] requires convergence in structural characteristics across countries.[106]

Galor's work on divergence and convergence further argued that the 'traditional neoclassical growth paradigm in club convergence hypothesis as well as in the conditional convergence hypothesis is empirically linked and therefore should include key variables such as human capital, income distribution, and fertility in conventional growth modelling, along with capital market imperfections, externalities, and non-convexities'. Galor also posits the following: (i) The absolute convergence hypothesis – per capita incomes of countries converge to one another in the long run independently of their initial conditions (Paul Romer; Robert Lucas; and Barro). (ii) The conditional convergence hypothesis – per capita incomes of countries that are identical in their structural characteristics (e.g. preferences, technologies, rates of population growth, government policies, and among others) converge to one another in the long run independently of their initial conditions (Barro; Gregory Mankiw, David Romer and David Weil; and Barro and Sala-i-Martin). (iii) The club convergence hypothesis (Steven Durlauf and Paul Johnson; and Danny Quah) (polarisation, persistent poverty and clustering) – per capita incomes of countries that are identical in their structural characteristics converge to one another in the long run provided that their initial conditions are similar as well.[107]

Divergence among groups was also discussed by Matthew Slaughter, who provided an expanded understanding of the difference-in-differences methodology (comparative methodology approach) to assess income dispersion, and which compares convergence patterns among countries before and after liberalisation of open trade in those countries, as well as with the convergence pattern among a control (selected group) group of countries before and after trade liberalisation. Slaughter's methodology tested trade liberalisation effects on income convergence over four liberalisation groups: the European Economic Commission (EEC); the European Free Trade Association (EFTA); trade liberalisation between the EEC and EFTA; and the Kennedy Round of the GATT. The main empirical result was that trade liberalisation did not foster significant convergence among liberalisers in any of the four controlled groups.[108]

The divergence and convergence literature outlined various historical models and studies and provided empirical evidence that largely centred on the neoclassical growth model, which focused on growth paths. However, a more holistic approach is required to assess convergence of free trade agreements and intra-, inter- and extra-regional trade which we now discuss.

Pan-Africanism: Free trade agreements and intraregional trade: Divergence and convergence

The main custodian of Pan-Africanism of African Unity, with a view to fostering intercontinental trade, was Ghana's first president, Nkrumah, who advocated for a federalist, supra-national approach to propelling trade through gaining African unity. The conceptualisation of Pan-Africanism by the continent's leaders, was an important traction and move beyond the origins of the Pan-Africanism movement against racial and cultural discrimination, and Europe's economic dominance – a movement which originated with Africans in the Diasporas including Trinidad lawyer, Henry Sylvester-Williams and African American scholar, William E. B. Dubois. But the Pan-African cause of strengthening its economies and building political unity was stalled by the increasing challenges of decolonising Africa, ending apartheid was eroded with the consistent interferences of international powers like the United States, France and Britain. The rethinking of tackling liberalism and capitalism later translating into the LPA adopted in the 1980s also did not add up to much.

The 1973 oil crisis and subsequent global events precipitated other equations and findings to the neoclassical economics debate. These events were mainly centred on the success achieved by Asian countries in the period 1997–8, which was after the collapse of major markets in 1973 with OPEC's increase of oil prices. During the same period, Europe's economic growth was not as successful in managing the financial global crisis as it was for Asian countries, as Richard Griffith[109] contends. Asian countries' growth levels were due to their dynamic economic performance and achievements, largely drawn from specialisation and market competitiveness, whereas European businesses needed to improve their international competitiveness. Japan, for example, was undercutting Europe's products in consumer heavy-duty products, and also in car manufacturing. In addition to the economic crisis, Europe was also faced with the Bretton Woods system that collapsed in 1973, leaving the EEC unable to support its member states.[110] Further studies conducted in Europe during the 1990s by Dan Ben-David were based on the trade arrangement of EU member states. These deliberated how to improve their economies and whether there had been any success achieved in economic and social conditions in free trade areas among the member states of the group. The findings noted that convergence led to growth for poorer economies and highlighted that trade agreements in free trade areas and customs unions could have a significant effect on growth in this region. Therefore, the hypothesis supported the finding that trade liberalisation in a group of states could lead to economic growth in income per capita convergence.[111]

Since the GATT processes of 1990, literature on exports and growth started rapidly evolving in the convergence debates. Francisco Rodriquez and Dani Rodrik made this clear distinction on the evolving nature of the trade growth divergence and convergence debate that was centred on openness and growth. Rodriquez and Rodrik noted that 'between 1980 and 1991, studies were conducted that were more concentrated on per capita income growth modelling in openness and growth, which focused on exports and growth in trade. However, since the GATT negotiation processes, studies conducted from mid-1991 onwards focused more on trade policy and economic growth.'[112] On its part, Africa was looking to South Africa's strong economy to advance industrialisation infrastructure, in the hope the negotiated settlement between the African National Congress (ANC) stalwart, Nelson Mandela, and the National Party (NP) leader, F. W. de Klerk that ended apartheid and ushered in a democratic dispensation in South Africa, engendered the notion of good neighbourliness in the country's foreign policy, which would subsequently relate to Tshwane (Pretoria) becoming an important player in Africa. However, South Africa's ideas for the integration of the continent was opposite to those of Nkrumah's United States for Africa and Libya's former leader, Muammar Qaddafi who favoured a federalist, supra-national approach to African unity.

South Africa as Africa's strongest economy, however, is not a custodian of the Pan-African vision. Instead, South Africa believes in a Union of African states to promoting a functionalist approach to African integration based on building norms, values, institutions and partnerships as its former president, Thabo Mbeki, had orchestrated in the implementation of the African Peer Review Mechanism (APRM), the New Partnership for Africa's Development (NEPAD) and the Pan-African Parliament (PAP). But Mbeki's grandiose ideas and implementation schemes were neglected by the Zuma administration when Jacob Zuma took the helm of South Africa's presidency. Even though a 2009 document of South Africa's Department of International Relations and Cooperation (DIRCO), 'conceptual framework on identification of anchor states in five geographical regions recognised by the AU', South Africa's engagements advanced with more external engagements. South Africa's engagements and trade relations with the BRICS bloc, for example in 2009–10, increased the SACU revenue pool relating to considerable trade revenue being generated for the BLNE group with a huge financial incentive scheme, leading to convergence of the SACU bloc. But while more revenue generation equates a strengthening of SACU's intra-trade relations and thus convergence of this bloc, the flipside of this convergence is divergence, and this divergence of Africa's economies and economic growth is strained. The straining of intercontinental trade further equates to trade divergence owing to South Africa's foreign policy approach of stronger multilateral trade relations with powerful global actors which directly impacts negatively on Africa's liberal trade schemes. Moreover, Africa's countries have also further created trade diversion in the continent owing to their own extensive external trade being conducted with Europe and the United States and with powerful countries like Kenya (an EAC member) and Egypt (a COMESA member) further eroding Africa's achieving of Pan-African economic integration. South Africa has also neglected trade relations with critical international partners such as those of the Caribbean and Pacific countries in the ACP bloc as was aforementioned. The EU's deliberate segregation – a move by the EU in defining South Africa as a developed state with different trade tariffs than the remaining seventy-eight African, Caribbean and Pacific countries – was a deliberate attempt on Europe's part in keeping South Africa unattached to the ACP bloc – which undoubtedly affected the psyche of South Africa's foreign policy, thus hastening Tshwane into a bilateral trade partnership created with Europe in 1999 (the EU-SA Trade, Development Cooperation Agreement (TDCA)) diverging trade and creating a poorer Africa.

Further debates made by leading economists, Paul Krugman[113] further advanced research on divergence and convergence in free trade agreements. He provided an expanded view of Asia's economic performance, termed the 'Asian Miracle', and the ability of Asian economies to weather the economic crisis of 1997–98. In studying Asia's growth patterns, Krugman indicated that extrapolating growth favours a progressive policy and not a laissez-faire approach, where states leave it all up to the markets. But instead, to experience economic growth in trade liberalisation, states needed to implement economic policy that incorporated sophisticated industrial policies and selective protectionism. He further contended,

> On one side are increases in "inputs": growth in employment, in the education level of workers, and in the stock of physical capital (machines, buildings, roads, and so on). On the other side are increases in the output per unit of input; such increases may result from better management or better economic policy, but in the long run are primarily due to increases in knowledge.[114]

Krugman's growth accounting tautology also outlined that a developed index is important to combine all measurable inputs that are able to measure the rate of growth of national income relative to that index. Krugman's hypothesis, defined in endogenous growth, which assumes that convergence in economic integration can contribute to and yield higher growth rates, and allow states to converge regional economic systems relatively easily, is in contrast to Gambari's view.

Both Gambari and Mytelka observed that for the economies of LDCs, larger markets might not be able to enhance greater flows of foreign capital and endogenous factors of spillover in skilled labour, and suggested that there should be processes in place to support import substitution, with trade in Africa being conducted in foreign currency, leading to trade diversion. Krugman's literature on regional convergence[115] is of particular relevance to the book. As Martin also suggested, 'the dependence of regional economies on export clusters held together by local Marshallian[116] type external economies, reaps benefits from specialised labour of technological spillover, and leads to increasing economic returns that can benefit the regional states, by placing them at a competitive advantage'.[117] For Krugman, growth accounting needs to calculate explicit measures of both 'increases in the output per unit of input'. Increases in knowledge can be positive for growth convergence. However, growth measurements must be considered in the process of economic growth. The view is that 'per capita income can only occur if there is a rise in output per unit of input'.[118]

Krugman does not take into consideration the aspects of rules of origin (ROOs) that concern inputs of production in his accounting index. However, Frank Flatters[119] underscore that ROOs could lead to divergence of trade policies in regional schemes, should policies not conform or be streamlined and addressed at both national and regional levels. Of equal relevance is endogenous growth factors in support of industrialisation and value addition and meaningful for achieving African integration.

A more expanded critique of regional convergence is provided by Ochoro.[120] He holds the view that 'convergence is more likely to occur when technology and production are adequately incorporated into a regional grouping and where governments play more of a central role. Policies should therefore reflect such strategies that develop appropriate technologies, promote research and development address essential tax credits, develop new ways for infrastructure, and formulate strategic trade policies.'[121] Moreover, when all these factors are considered, infant industries could then be protected and have the tenacity to foster further innovation across a range of other related industries, which could also converge regional integration policies.[122] Besides considering technology, and research and development to spearhead production and economic growth convergence, various other factors are also at play. For example, technical barriers to trade (TBTs) are viewed as the yardstick for the harmonisation of technical regulations and standards of conformity, as well as assessment of products traded in goods and services. Similarly, Carolyn Jenkins and Lynne Thomas highlighted that governments should coordinate effective policies that can mitigate the effects of labour associated with services, but taking into account skills and research costs within national economies: to gain from remittances and income flows is an important mechanism in converging economic growth. Therefore, governments should also ensure that opportunities for labour are concentrated in industries that could mitigate the effects of trade diversion and allow for growth.[123]

Macroeconomic policies: Divergence and convergence

The literature review further explores the divergence and convergence debate of macroeconomic policies within regions. A study conducted by UNECA, which tests macroeconomic policies using econometric testing of income per capita, GDP, and economic fiscal growth factors within regional economic groups, noted that 'African governments should consider harmonising and coordinating macroeconomic policies at national levels as a first step first in considering a monetary union'.[124] Similarly, David Dollar, notes that 'within a macroeconomic regional framework, weak trade policy must be addressed and prioritised early on in an integration process. This will help in financial integration at the regional level and facilitate the institutionalisation and implementation process thereof, which constitutes more than just focusing on trade liberalisation.'[125] Ogochukwu Nzewi stressed that 'weak national economies are also characterised by poor organisational learning, lack of resources (human, technical, and financial) and weak, politically marginalised secretariats,'[126] and such factors should be equally taken into account when considering regional monetary schemes.[127] According to UNECA, the extent to which national macroeconomic policies reflect government's monetary, fiscal, trade and exchange policies, often discriminates against regional trade and is seen as the main impediment to viable integration.[128]

More progressive regional blocs such as Europe, Bernard Fingleton, Harry Garretsen and Martin contended that the European Monetary Union (EMU) was not able to support EMU member states' economies during the 2008–9 global economic crisis and caused divergence among members.[129] They also observed that during the first major economic shock in 2008, the EMU's meltdown raised several questions of whether monetary integration for regions, which had a shared institutional monetary policy, would lead to divergence or convergence in conditions of economic crisis. Europe is still trying various mechanisms to address its falling economy in the eurozone. While geography played a major role in the economic and monetary integration plans for Europe, peripheral eurozone members were also tied to a monetary policy and to the European Central Bank (ECB) that was largely dominated by the large economies of Germany, France and Italy (eurozone member states). Hence, Fingleton, Garretsen and Martin argued that the peripheral eurozone members lacked the adjustment mechanisms needed to avoid a severe negative economic shock in the 2008–9 economic crises and were worse off than those states of non-eurozone members.[130]

Ever since the economic crises, the European Commission has battled to keep some of its economies afloat. For example, in January 2015, the ECB launched a government bond-buying programme of 1 trillion euros, known as the quantitative easing programme, as a rescue plan to revive the economic growth and to ward off deflation for Europe.[131] According to an article by Reuters, this meant that the ECB would purchase bonds to deal with sovereign debt from March 2015 to the end of September 2016, and release bonds into the EU market to the value of 60 billion euros ($68 billion) a month in the form of cheap loans to banks.[132] Fingleton, Garretsen and Martin observed that a monetary union could lead to regional divergence and greater disparity, and make regions more vulnerable. They also observed that optimum currency areas (OCAs) were not part of the initial planners and were not incorporated into the EMU's framework when it was created. 'The OCA theory highlights that symmetry, flexibility, and integration are key variables to consider when forming a monetary union.'[133] They also noted that 'within the eurozone, core states that were closely connected to economic powerhouses like Germany, suffered less in terms of employment loss, which was in contrast to those states of the peripheral regions (Ireland, Spain, the Baltic states, and Greece)'. 'These peripheral states had also fared worse during the financial recessions of 2008 and 2009 and experienced greater divergence.'[134] The difficult EU policies of the eurozone have impacted on several of the semi-peripheral economies. Evidently, Catalonia's push for independence from EU member Spain and Italy's upcoming elections in 2018 will also demonstrate which way the pendulum will sway for Rome with tensions raising the alarm of Italy's possible exit from the EU to shortly follow Britain's move of 2016 when the UK too severed its umbilical cord from Brussels and decided on going it alone.[135]

Various scholars suggest that African economies are not ready for macroeconomic convergence.[136] This is mainly due to the caveat that states regional blocs must have sound financial policies that are resilient and able to support the bloc during global financial crises, and the ability to handle market crises and shocks. Such factors require strong macroeconomic principles as suggested by Jenkins and Thomas.[137] In the instance of eastern and Southern Africa, the closest to a monetary union has been the trilateral monetary agreement among the governments of Lesotho, Eswatini and South Africa, which established the Common Monetary Area (CMA) on 1 April 1986, and links member states of SACU (excluding Botswana in the case of the CMA).

In reviewing the benefits of a monetary unification model for Africa, the continent has a ways to go in forming a monetary policy managed by a regional central bank and fiscal policies managed with national governments, as in the case of the EU. Keith Jefferis, in studying the SADC region, observed that not all macroeconomic convergence processes are designed to support the processes of monetary unions.[138] There are both economic and political costs associated with monetary union formations. Such costs are high for some states, since ceding levels of autonomy in the fields of monetary and exchange rate policy could have various implications at the national level.[139] At the economic stage, implications may be associated with reducing and minimising economic policy instruments, which could have been previously available to bear the burden of adjustment to economic shocks for national economies. But as the OCA literature highlighted, a monetary union must have the flexibility over fiscal policy to compensate for the loss of policy instruments such as monetary and exchange rate policies.[140] Jenkins and Thomas also observed that efforts to grow economies in Africa through regions have generated slow growth due to the huge differences in economies, geography, technology advances and poverty levels. Therefore, efforts of trade liberalisation must become the driving force to effect growth. Converging currency could lead to divergence in economic growth, but Africa's states are not ready to manage macroeconomic convergence, which would require implementing sound macroeconomic principles. Such principles must be informed by macroeconomic policy, fiscal adjustment, foreign investment, and socio-economic policies that are able to support infrastructure and education, export promotion, and compensatory mechanisms. Similarly, Africa's financial instruments are weak and not able to promote the basic sound macroeconomic policies of financial jurisprudence with a view to circumventing corrupt financial practices. The take away is that Africa is losing billions due to capital flight, estimated at $50 billion annually.[141]

Moreover, policies should be aligned with and coordinated between domestic economic policies and reform strategies in trade reforms.[142] Jenkins and Thomas further suggested that more emphasis should be placed on economic and trade policy reforms at national level. At the regional level, a medium-term coordinated approach should be underpinned by the direct effects of cross-border transactions.[143] Richard Gibb observed that 'regional integration has been a contested issue in Africa, but there is no doubt that the level of intraregional trade provides a useful indicator of economic integration and regional convergence'.[144] 'RECs boost regional trade through tariff reductions and limit non-tariff barriers.'[145] The neoclassical growth model also stresses the importance for governments to focus more on physical investment to expand national outputs. Investment in equipment and research is critical to advance technology; equally important is investment in infrastructure (roads, ports and railways).[146] Africa's states are also confronted with member states belonging to more than one regional grouping.

Multiple memberships: Divergence and convergence

Pan-African integration is challenged by member states belonging to more than one regional economic community. Multiple memberships have consequently been seen as both a hurdle and also as a positive step towards integrating regional schemes.[147] James Gathii highlights that multiple memberships are created by states when governments use the market as a means to benefit domestic economies.[148] This Gathii attributes to the proliferation of multilateral trade agreements which lead to divergence in regional integration efforts.[149] Rodriquez and Rodrik also noted that trade growth and growth rates will diverge to the extent that trade policies are reinforced and trade volumes increased; therefore other forms of integration will be pursued by states in an attempt to remedy skew trade in order to protect infant industries.[150]

Robert Gilpin[151] provides an expanded view framed in the neoclassical realist approach, whereby states use the market as a means to achieving wealth and in exercising power. The state can use the market (or the market is used) as a means to gaining wealth; the state and the market are therefore seen as inseparable, and both are important entities for economic interaction and influencing the direction of the market due to distribution of power and wealth in a global economy. Gilpin further indicates that regional integration can exploit the effects of functional spillover, and integration of regional markets can create economies of scale. Gilpin is of the view that to exploit opportunities for comparative advantage, state policies must inform outputs of production and distribution of production. Such policies then ought to take into account the extent of the state's political interests (in terms of its partners/agreements and economic interests), which can ultimately affect the overall regional economy. On the other hand, Jens Haarløv[152] argues that developmental integration could rectify the 'anomalies or discrepancies' of open regionalism, in considering three aspects: (a) changing the objectives of the integration process, (b) changing the timing and level of interstate binding commitments and (c) changing the distribution of costs and benefits of cooperation. Anthony Venables posits that 'states belonging to a free trade agreement and that have a higher income member relative to the other members within that FTA and also relative to the world average than the lower income members, are likely to converge with the high income partner and benefit from such an FTA'.[153]

Ravenhill discusses the 'domino theory' of proliferation of membership. Preferential trade agreements have proliferated among states within a bloc or regional grouping once exporting interests of disadvantaged groups in a region are contested by imports that flood the markets of mainly peripheral economies. Similarly, Ravenhill notes that the proliferation of trade agreements between East Asian governments was in part a response to the government policies which set business groups at a disadvantage.[154] Ravenhill also contends that while an increased interdependence among East Asian economies had been largely responsible for the growth seen in intergovernmental collaboration, these benefits were not evenly spread within their economies in Asia.[155] Views expressed by scholars have been mixed; while some view multiple memberships as positive, others adopt a more pessimistic stance. According to Arvind Panagariya, a proliferation of regional agreements has occurred, since states are trying to circumvent or replace the non-discriminatory most-favoured nation (MFN) tariff associated with the WTO regulations for trade by 'crisscrossing FTAs'.[156]

Phillip O Nying'uro holds the view that the capitalist global order has been more diverging than converging.[157] Such studies on divergence and convergence in trade liberalisation was mainly centred on by Western scholars in the United States and Europe. Furthermore, these studies mainly focused on measuring 'factor outputs against intermediate inputs' and on economic divergent or convergent economic growth and per capita income convergence. The literature review also discussed trade liberalisation and open market performance by measuring population, as well as income per capita and endogenous growth factors such as technology, skills, and production spillover that could lead to growth.

A report of the UNCTAD[158] outlined several studies on various continents, including Africa. The report highlighted that globalisation and technological change can affect income distribution. The report's findings also revealed that since policies influence the nature and speed of economic integration, they will also influence and affect the process of structural change and the related creation of employment and wage opportunities in high-productivity activities.[159] Therefore UNCTAD highlighted that economic structures should not be implemented in silos and should neither be independent of trade and financial integration, nor its management and implementation, but should be seen as a joint process.

The G20 Summit, which met in Brisbane on 15 November 2014, highlighted in their meeting that Africa's economies were over-reliant on natural resources; Africa's services sector was similarly weak. At the G20 Summit meeting that was held in Hangzhou, China, in July 2016, German Chancellor, Angela Merkel, noted that Germany has ten times more direct investment in the EU than in the whole of Africa.[160] This startling revelation is a clear message to Africa's governments to conduct more internal Africa trade and place less emphasis on powerful global actors. Germany's position changed towards Africa in 2017, when Hamburg conducted the G20's Compact Initiative with Africa at a G20 Africa-Conference on 12–13 June 2017 in Berlin. Germany's federal minister of finance Wolfgang Schäuble noted, 'We see the Compact with Africa as a long-term demand driven process. The African countries will determine what they want to do to improve conditions for private investment, with whom they want to cooperate, and in what form.'[161] Africa's policymakers should therefore consider enhancing the productive capacity in its manufacturing sectors, and create partnerships that benefit skills and technology for continent, which are believed to be the key to Africa's convergence of regional policies.

But the reality is the missing piece in trade convergence and the sluggish growth is owing to the slow pace of industrialisation, and it is unlikely that Africa could replicate the convergence dynamics evident in Europe and Asia.[162] Similar views were expressed by William Baumol in respect of how to increase convergence through productivity levels without a concerted effort at enacting trade policies.[163] Such an approach needed to take into account the macroeconomic principles that are able to support the concepts to which endogenous growth theorists like Gene Grossman and Elhanan Helpman allude.[164]

Concepts that pertain to knowledge spillover and specialisation in Robert Baldwin's discussion on openness and growth, highlight that endogenous factors that lead to increasing returns do not adequately inform how trade policy can affect growth rates.[165] In expanding the literature on endogenous factors leading to growth, Baldwin discussed policy and implementation levels and suggested that policies affecting the 'openness' of trade and investment or its 'inward orientation' or 'outward orientation' should incorporate components of 'outward-looking development policies that take into account endogenous growth factors as well as addressing government's inward-looking and outward-looking policies, which involve more than just trade and trade policies.'[166] Baldwin further noted that

> consideration of such factors would then lead to growth convergence for poorer economies. Policies should therefore also include the willingness of governments to accept foreign direct investment (FDI) so that market-oriented exchange rates are maintained; budget deficits and corruption are tightly monitored; and monopolistic behaviour by firms and industries is controlled so that trade and growth are not restricted to individual states within a group.[167]

But as Keohane and Nye observed, the process of economics theory does not have a theory of international regime change.[168] Neoclassical economic analysis was developed not as a faithful description of reality, but as a simplified explanation for suggesting policies to increase economic efficiency and welfare. Economists have therefore focused on economic theory, without considering issues that centred on power, which is further outlined below in the neoclassical realism approach.

Neoclassical realism approach: Security

The neoclassical realist approach applied in this book helps to understand and assists in examining the interactions of member states, since the neoclassical realist approach incorporates both domestic and systemic factors. It similarly helps to explain the convergence of COMESA, EAC and SADC in managing regional security. The neoclassical realism approach is a modification of the realist approach, which has evolved since the 1970s.[169]

> Realism as a theoretical approach analy[s]es all international relations as the relations of states engaged in the pursuit of power. Realism cannot accommodate any non-state actors within its analysis. Neorealism evolved since the 1970s and recogni[s]es that economic resources in addition to military capabilities are a basis for exercising influence. The most significant change in neorealism was in abandoning the concept of a single international system in favour of there being many issue-specific systems, each characterised by their own power structure. [For example] Saudi Arabia may be the most powerful state in the politics of oil, while Brazil is the most powerful in the politics of rainforests.[170]

Classical realism had built its concepts of international relations on the literature of the Melian dialogue and Thucydides' account of the Peloponnesian War between Athens and Sparta. Thucydides noted that the resolve of Athens was to remain in power and act in the self-interest of the state. The Melian dialogue provides an understanding of how powerful states create and join institutions in self-interest, based on their domestic concerns.

Political realists' view of the nation state is that of a malign hegemon (regional superpower) that has as its principal gain self-interest; hence realists' analyses of self-interest are associated with dominance and mercantilist strategy. The political realists view the hegemonic state as a powerful, strong economy that sets the rules of the game in economic relations, and always has a greater advantage over its partner states. But the downside is imperial overreach through greed for power and wealth, with the state seeking more international influence than it can maintain, leading to the decline of the hegemon's dominance.[171]

Gideon Rose provides a critical approach to understanding the concept of neoclassical realism. Neorealism consists of two theories of foreign policy: offensive and defensive realism. Defensive realism theory provides switches between systemic and domestic factors as causal variables of foreign policy.[172] In this regard, it is argued that while systemic factors explain some foreign policy decisions, domestic factors are the drivers of the state's external decisions.[173] Offensive realism, on the other hand, argues that systemic factors are the main determinants of foreign policy decisions. Offensive realism also argues that the anarchic nature of the international system, combined with the state's relative capabilities, drives and shapes foreign policy decisions. Such policies are historically linked to African states associated with state formation and sovereignty. Realism is situated in mercantilist policies that are not primarily economic, but policies subjected to force economic policies into the service of power. Mercantilist policies are closely linked to state struggle and survival to help achieve unity through the centralisation and concentration of power.

The main link to the mercantilist political economy is external trade through foreign exchange and economic development. Hence state power is able to increase levels of economic development through the supply of foreign exchange by increasing the volume and types of trade and policies. Thomas Callaghy observed that the mercantilist political economy is situated in development projects that 'foster the well-being of the ruling group, designed primarily to expand the control capabilities of the state, increase exports, regulate imports and promote economic autarky'.[174] Therefore, what offensive realism postulates, is that domestic factors do not carry much weight in influencing foreign policy, since offensive realism is often offset by international pressures. For example, member states of COMESA, EAC and SADC regional blocs are largely aspirational developing states; they, therefore, may at times have to consider their domestic situation in relation to how they engage in liberal trade agreements regionally and globally, which may or may not be based on their domestic situation. Similarly, this will affect how they engage with regional and external actors. These issues become more complicated for states when faced with complicated security concerns.

In building on the Melian dialogue, neoclassical realists argue that relative material power establishes the basic parameters of a country's foreign policy as noted by Thucydides: 'The strong do what they can and the weak suffer what they must.'[175] As Rose points out, there is no immediate or perfect transmission belt linking material capabilities to foreign policy behaviour. 'Foreign policy behaviour and foreign policy choices are made by political leaders and elites, and so it is their perceptions of relative power that matter, not simply relative quantities of physical resources or forces in being.'[176] Attempts made by EAC, SADC and COMESA in building a security community were hampered by several obstacles. Agostinho Zacarias[177] outlines these obstacles in his literature on defining a security community like Southern Africa, and draws on various constraining factors that impeded earlier attempts at building a security community. These impediments Zacarias defines as 'regional instability, political fragmentation, economic imbalances, and fears which weakened the security system, particularly in relation to SADCC'.[178] The book finds the literature by Zacarias relevant in comprehending the security evolution of the divergence of SADCC and PTA during their rationalisation processes. The literature also provides greater insight in respect of how security relations unfolded among COMESA, EAC and SADC.

What drives states in conflict regions, and why do states play one region off against another, or one state against another? In the realist debate, the region has been seen as the instrument to gain power and wealth. As asserted by Edward Mansfield, in unstable regions, the effects of political–military factors affect bilateral trade and regional integration. In examining how state conflicts and security conditions can affect trade relations, alliances can help to minimise the damages of state conflict to the benefit of the regional integration process through trade and spillover into wealth generation.[179]

In William Zartman's view, regional security is seen as a perennial problem that is still embroiled in past roles of former colonies in Africa's postcolonial government security apparatus and structures. Zartman notes that Africa's security development is therefore still hampered by and indicative of past internal systems that have infiltrated the existing (new government system) internal workings of the state. External relations of the formative years (such as colonial links) have continued into the new state, with linkages in the history of the new state, which makes understanding regional security quite complex.[180]

Therefore, Zartman defines regional security as a complex phenomenon that has various dimensions involving not only neatly defined 'military and security dimensions', but which also involves economic, military, political, and social and international actors and factors. Zartman suggests that stable states with legitimate regimes have often faced territorial insecurity within the first few decades of independence, such as border conflicts. In the 1990s, for instance, regional security evolved into secessions, and regions disengaged from weak and oppressive state systems.[181] Moreover, regional security became interwoven, given the lack of security mechanisms within the new state, with states having to 'borrow power' from outside, providing an opportunity for external powers to become embroiled in African conflicts.[182] This borrowed power allowed external powers and former colonial regimes access to newly independent states, contributing to the complexity of Africa's security architecture.

Similarly, Rok Ajulu makes a key observation that regional conflicts in Africa have been generated by ruling elites, therefore any emerging security architecture ought to address the issue of political power and political will. A question that is necessary, then, and ought to be considered, is to analyse whether there is sufficient political will from the main players to address regional conflicts, and if not, then what kind of institutional arrangement will assist or force conflicting parties to reconsider their adversarial stance.[183]

Defining regional security through the integration lens has elicited a multidimensional approach that also centres on the Responsibility to Protect (R2P) framework that encompasses potential actors under three pillars: prevent, react and rebuild. Africa's RECs, like the Intergovernmental Authority on Development (IGAD), are participating in an emerging African R2P-oriented security culture, but not all its members appeal to the R2P doctrine like Sudan does. John Siebert notes that 'the striking characteristics of the R2P security model shift emphasis from state sovereignty to state responsibility for the wellbeing of citizens, with an obligation placed on the international community to intervene in specific humanitarian interventions like genocide, where a country is unwilling to protect its citizens'.[184] RECs are seen to be making concerted efforts, like SADC and ECOWAS, to include R2P in their frameworks for securing regions.[185] Hany Besada, Ariane Goetz and Karolina Werner, however, view the concept of R2P as a security intervention that has undermined the state's sovereignty and strengthened the role of the international community. R2P, in their view, is largely a top-down approach and not an inclusive one where all parties are significant in the conflict. The framework seems to lean more towards peace enforcement ideals, and does not take into account the wars and violence in regional conflicts associated with economic and resource disputes which involve both internal and external actors and militia groups particularly in the East Africa and Sudan regions.[186]

Peter Vale's analysis of security and sovereignty premises that the core understanding of the security discourse cannot be built on representations of sovereignty alone. Vale expands his views on the 1980s security conditions in Southern Africa and posits that regional security in the case of Southern Africa has been too easily dismissed as a 'security community'. According to Vale, security and sovereignty are both unstable concepts, since both are socially constructed. Vale notes that security should not be too loosely associated with community building in regional frameworks to resolve regional conflicts. Such a view would be problematic and would offer a false perspective of the reality of the past when dealing with present and future security dynamics. Security studies should therefore be conceptualised in terms of a realist security framework that can accurately reflect the regional nomenclature framework. Vale notes, 'The epistemology offered by realist security studies genuflects toward the statist taxonomy that gave Southern Africa its current form.' This 'powerful ensemble of science, the bureaucratic state, individualism and continuous advancement'[187] offers no place for people, only for power.[188] With reference to Deutsch,[189] Naison Ngoma outlines a security community as a belief in common institutions and practices to resolve social problems through peaceful change.

Barry Buzan and Ole Wæver view regional security as a situation when both sides in a conflict are dependent on the same power, and it is consequently possible for such a power to pressurise the conflicting parties to move towards peace processes.[190] Therefore, Buzan and Wæver suggest a clearer description of a regional security system to be 'the possibility of systematically linking the study of internal conditions, relations among units in the region, relations between regions, and the interplay of regional dynamics with globally acting powers'.[191] These factors further determine the structural logic of the region, as regional security operating at four levels of a security constellation simultaneously: the international world, domestic, regional and global factors.

States in regions are to some extent linked to security interdependence and may join regions for security reasons. For the FLS, security objectives were largely driven by 'the structure, distribution of power, and the state of relations among nations in the international system'.[192] In assessing the literature by Khadiagala,[193] a key observation is made central to the role of the FLS – as small states, their behaviour evolved within an asymmetrical and a hierarchical system of power relations. These behaviours are defined in the theory of alliances and describe how 'subordinate states in these systems augment their power capabilities to confront the interests of dominant actors'. The book will further explore the literature on 'alliances', which provides an understanding of the historical relations of COMESA, EAC and SADC member states and the various intricacies and dynamics in state behaviour of PTA and the FLS, as highlighted by Khadiagala.

3

Pan-Africanism's birth, burial – reincarnate: A historical trajectory of divergence and convergence

The first wave of Pan-Africanism represented a bid to promote the political, socio-economic and cultural liberation attempts of Africa, which had a short life, as Africa's governments diverged from the Pan-Africanism views of solidarity in creating an African Unity owing to the enduring tensions between advocates for an immediate continental political union. The second wave of Pan-Africanism witnessed the emergence of divergent interpretations of Pan-Africanism and alternative strategies to achieve it, as evidenced in the reincarnation of, and divergence from, Pan-Africanism in carving up regional communities. This second wave was thus, an opportunity and an invitation for powerful actors to remain involved in the politics and economics, particularly, in trade relations with Africa.

This chapter, therefore, provides a historiography of Africa's attempts at integration, as well as a brief historical account of the short-lived birth and death of Pan-Africanism, preceded by a historical discussion on Africa's attempts at reincarnating Pan-Africanism but in a different form – which demonstrates the divergence from continental integration. Pan-Africanism returns, in a different form presented in the five miniature continents of Africa, but with the same international countries closely by its side – the architects of divergence of the 1883 Berlin Conference. The analysis outlines the 1960s, which takes on the process of a gradualist approach adopted of converging Africa and resurrecting Pan-Africanism and bringing it back to life reincarnated into regions, and subsequent wish lists generated by Africa's leaders of a Continental Free Trade Area (CFTA) outlined in the Abuja 1991 Treaty. The chapter further outline the formations of the three blocs: the East African Community (EAC, largely part of the Preferential Trade Area (PTA)) and Common Market for Eastern and Southern Africa (COMESA) leading up to the attempted rationalisation process with Southern African Development Community (SADC) and the divergence of the EAC.

The birth and death of a Pan-African idea

During the end of the colonial regimes in Africa the initial logic was for Africa to follow Pan-Africanism, which defined a political integration as the foundation for economic integration, but it was only an idea. This idea stemmed from political leaders like Ghana's Kwame Nkrumah, Mali's Modibo Kéïta, Senegal's Cheikh Anta Diop and Guinea's Sékou Touré, who promoted the formation of a single African government aligned with common institutions.[1] This period 1935–57,[2] therefore, marked the colonial phase of a much earlier attempt of regional integration for Africa. In 1945, the Fifth Pan-African Congress, held in Manchester, England, called for concrete recommendations towards combating the exploitation of Africa's resources. Further calls were made at the 1955 Bandung Afro-Asian Conference and the subsequent declaration, which also attempted to address the political and economic liberation of both Africa and Asia. These earlier ideas stemmed from a deep political and cultural notion of a unified Africa, and African unity – meaning a complete political union of Africa.[3] Between 1957 and 1960, nineteen African states achieved independence[4] from colonial rule, with Ghana signalling the first integration efforts after having attained independence in 1957 under the leadership of Kwame Nkrumah.

Africa's anti-colonial struggles received the backing of fellow veterans from the 1955 Bandung Conference, as well as from an earlier conference staged in Brussels in 1927. The League against Imperialism and Colonialism included Asian and African leaders like Senegal's Lamine Senghor, India's Jawaharlal Nehru and Vietnam's Ho Chi Minh.[5] Five Pan-African Congresses took place between 1919 and 1945.[6] Africa's regional economic integration was largely based on Europe's arrangements in integrating markets and institutions that started in the 1950s, also spilled over into their integration models.[7] Thus, Europe's views informed Africa's early attempts at Pan-Africanism in the creation of a political union. Africa was enthused by Europe's rapid economic growth. Arguments were also put forward by Africa's leaders for the possibilities of regionalism among least developed countries (LDCs) by other integration economists like Raúl Prebisch while he was head of the Economic Commission for Latin America (ECLA), which became the Economic Commission for Latin America and the Caribbean (ECLAC) during the 1960s. Prebisch reinforced Pan-African views among Africa's governments.[8]

The practical successes of Europe therefore dominated theories of integration, and also influenced region builders' to attempt economic integration in Africa, and to apply it in their own regions.[9] Africa believed that it could adopt a similar regional integration model and cure the ills of post-colonialism plaguing its weak economies. In Africa, regional integration meant strengthening the fragile economies of newly independent states, while Europe, since its integration processes had started after Second World War,[10] was left wanting to avoid war at all costs. Africa's regional integrationists appeared to have had no urgency, and took on a gradualist approach adopted through subregional organisations, but socio-economic conditions and a paucity of technology and minimal industrialisation militated against the desired functional spillover and linkages originally envisaged as outlined by Robert Henderson, Richard Gibb and Samuel K. B. Asante.[11] Pan-Africanism never really took root because no real commitment was established among Africans to conduct trade and converge their economies. Other than the EAC, which attempted region-building in 1917 and established the Kenya-Uganda Customs Union,[12] and Southern African Customs Union (SACU) in 1910[13] – which was an agreement between the Union of South Africa and the British High Commission Territories (HCTs) (Basutoland (Lesotho), Bechuanaland (Botswana) and Eswatini (Swaziland), with Namibia (South West Africa) a de facto member, which became a de jure member when it gained independence in 1990) – there were no formal economic integration schemes.

Pan-Africanism reincarnate

In 1960, the nineteen independent African states recommended the creation of Africa's Council for Economic Cooperation, a Development Bank, a Commercial Bank, an African Common Market, a Payments Union, and an African Bank for Economic Development. The United Nations Economic Commission for Africa (UNECA), established on 29 April 1958, facilitated, monitored, developed and strengthened Africa's economic development agenda.[14] As a first step to reconstructing and boosting economies weakened during the Second World War, the ECA was established by the United Nations Economic and Social Council (ECOSOC), under its resolution 671A (XXV), as one of five regional economic commissions alongside the Economic Commission for Europe; the Economic Commission for Asia and the Far East (currently Asia and the Pacific); the Economic Commission for Latin America (currently Latin America and the Caribbean); and the Economic Commission for Africa and the economic commission for Asia (currently the Economic and Social Commission for Western Asia).[15]

Although the ECA was primarily concerned in boosting Africa's economies and in developing the continent, the ECA was cumbersome to operate and struggled to execute its tasks optimally. In addition, the ECA found it difficult to build the good relations with African states which were necessary for gaining their full cooperation and understanding its raison d'être. The leaders of Africa's newly independent states were also impatient, wanting to see quick fixes to their frail economies, and were reluctant to cooperate with the leaders of other independent states. The ECA was also confronted by its own internal dynamics; with colonial powers like Britain and France sitting on the Commission, much of the ECA's attention was afforded to the non-independent African states, as well as on addressing issues of colonialism and racial discrimination in Rhodesia (Zimbabwe) and the apartheid regime of South Africa.[16] The initial years of the ECA were marked by trepidation, and it lacked authority. The prevailing African view was that the Commission's executive secretary (Adebayo Adedeji), being from an Anglophone background, would promote Anglophone interests over those of his Francophone neighbours, who also depended heavily on France and other countries in Europe for aid.[17]

Africa had also put several initiatives in place in its attempts to unite the continent through UNECA. In 1967, a permanent consultative committee was set up in North Africa between Libya, Morocco and Tunisia. Ghana's Kwame Nkrumah noted the importance of seeking a political union for the continent, though he was a solitary figure among the leaders of Africa's newly independent states. All the rest of Africa's independent states sought functional regionalism through regional organisations that were to become economically and politically independent through freer trade and interlinking customs unions in order to build strong economies. During the Cold War, some African leaders leaned more towards pro-East camps and ideologies (the Casablanca group), while others were more pro-West (the Monrovia group), which led to many meetings and debates to resolve their differences before the signing of the Charter of African Unity on 25 May 1963, as well as the establishment of the Organisation of African Unity (OAU).[18] As a first step on Africa's regionalism agenda, in 1967 the EAC was established, involving Kenya, Uganda and Tanzania. But this initiative collapsed in July 1977 and was only restored on 1 December 1999 at Arusha, in Tanzania, after eight years of negotiation.[19]

Other regional initiatives included the Central African common market, made up of the five states of the Central Africa subregion: the Central African Republic, Congo, Chad, Gabon and Cameroon (UDEAC), created in 1964; the Economic Community of West African States (ECOWAS), which was established in 1975; the West African Economic Community (CEAO), in 1973; the Council for the Entente and the Mano River Union, also in 1973; the Economic Community of the Great Lakes Countries, or CEPGL (*Communauté économique des pays des Grands Lacs*), created in 1976, included Burundi, Rwanda and Zaire (the Democratic Republic of the Congo (DRC)).[20]

It was against the background of Pan-Africanism that the East and Central African states formed the Pan-African Movement for East and Central Africa (PAFMECA) in Tanganyika in 1958. The PAFMECA grouping, which later included the Horn of Africa states, Somalia and Ethiopia, fought white supremacy in South Africa and Southern Rhodesia by supporting the liberation movements of South Africa, as well as those of South West Africa, Northern and Southern Rhodesia, and Mozambique.[21] In 1962 the Mozambique Liberation Front (FRELIMO) replaced the rival nationalist groups – the National African Union of Independent Mozambique (UNAMI), the National Democratic Union of Mozambique (UDENAMO), and the Mozambican African National Union (MANU).[22]

The convergence of regions

The Frontline States and the making of an alliance

The main regions formed in Africa's attempts to achieving the convergence of its countries after their divergence from Pan-Africanism included: EAC, SADC and COMESA. The Frontline States (FLS) was created in 1975, and the Southern African Development Coordinating Conference (SADCC) was formed in 1980; both were precursors of SADC. The PTA, created in 1981, was a precursor of COMESA, formed in 1993.

The goals of the founding leaders of the FLS – Tanzania's Julius Nyerere, Zambia's Kenneth Kaunda and Botswana's Seretse Khama – were to create political cohesion and a stronger security regime to support the region's national liberation movements, gain political freedom from colonial rule, and overthrow white minority rule.[23] Zambia (formerly known as Northern Rhodesia), and Malawi (formerly known as Nyasaland) were colonised in the late nineteenth century by the British South Africa Company;

they both gained their independence in 1964.[24] In response to South Africa's apartheid government and in support of liberation movements, the FLS were created in 1975, comprising the governments of Angola, Botswana, Mozambique, Tanzania and Zambia. These were formed in support of the national liberation movements, South Africa's African National Congress (ANC), Namibia's South West Africa People's Organization (SWAPO), the Popular Movement for the Liberation of Angola (MPLA), the FRELIMO, the Zimbabwe African National Union (ZANU), and the Zimbabwe African People's Union (ZAPU) (the latter two attempted to unite, but failed).[25] The Southern African states that were directly affected by apartheid South Africa's destabilisation policies, and those states that gained independence and vociferously fought for the liberation movements included Angola, Botswana, Lesotho, Malawi, Mozambique, Tanzania, Eswatini, Zambia and Zimbabwe.

In forming the FLS, the major socio-economic constraints that confronted Southern Africa were weak states and fragmented domestic political situations. A security society, to some scholars like Zacarias, is seen as 'the first stage in building a security community'.[26] Headley Bull identified a security society as a group of states 'where states are in regular contact with one another, and where ... there is interaction between them [that is] sufficient to make the behaviour of each a necessary element in the calculations of the other',[27] and a society of states 'where a group of states, conscious of certain common interests and common values, form a society in the sense that they conceive themselves to be bound by a common set of rules in their relations with one another'.[28]

The FLS was carefully designed and primarily directed towards coordinating political, economic, diplomatic and security objectives. The objectives of the FLS were defined by the hierarchical systems of power relationships among the group of states. But the alliance could only be as strong as its members. The FLS was formed when members of its group were already involved in economic ties with the state (South Africa) that they fought against. As suggested by Gilbert Khadiagala: 'In addition to geographical contiguity and economic interdependence, political interaction in the subsystem led to increased organizational expression of common and also conflicting interests.'[29] Khadiagala contends that the member states of the Southern African system were conscious of their own relations, and their relations and behaviours within the subsystem, which was critical for its demise or success.

When the FLS was formed, Angola and Mozambique were still under Portuguese colonial control. The independence of Angola and Mozambique brought about violent regional conflict and war that provoked a regional nervousness for the South African government as it feared that Marxist power could be unleashed to dominate the entire region, jeopardising the apartheid ideology.[30] Radical members of Angola's MPLA supported Zaire's secessionist forces by invading Zaire twice – in 1977 and again in 1978 – which effectively destroyed relations between the leaders of the two countries. Zaire's Mobutu Sese Seko responded with support from his Western allies, the United States, France and Belgium together with his African counterpart, Morocco.[31] The United States provided $5 million in funding towards upgrading the Beira port and railway line in Mozambique, while also openly supporting the National Union for the Total Independence of Angola (UNITA) to overthrow the government of Angola.

The earlier moves in the formation of the FLS during the1970s were 'non-confrontation' and 'non-aggression', which evolved out of interactions with the former South African President Vorster, and former Zambian President Kaunda, the former whom Kaunda called the 'voice of reason for which Africa and the rest of the world have been waiting'.[32] Portugal's precipitous departure from Mozambique, which was brought about by the April 1974 Portuguese coup, created a security vacuum that left both Rhodesia and apartheid South Africa vulnerable and exposed to regional and international politics. Kaunda capitalised on Rhodesia's impasse with Mozambique. Rhodesia's problems were twofold: a security vacuum and the importance of the transport trade routes. Rhodesia shared a 700-mile eastern border with Mozambique, which provided access for 80 per cent of land-locked Rhodesia's trade exports through the transport network of Mozambique's port facilities of Beira and Lourenço Marques. On the South African side, Vorster was left unshielded and exposed by the removal of the buffer zone between the belligerent armed forces of Mozambique's nationalist movement, FRELIMO, which had collaborated closely with ZANU and operated from Mozambique's Tete province, and which also showed solidarity with the black Rhodesian majority by militarily rebelling against Ian Smith's white regime in Rhodesia. From the Namibian side, Nujoma led SWAPO in the years of struggle for Namibia's independence. From 1975, SWAPO worked closely with the MPLA,[33] as well as with FRELIMO, and later in the same year moved its headquarters from Lusaka, Zambia, to Luanda, Angola.[34] On the Rhodesian side, the Rhodesians had previously relied heavily on the Portuguese military support in fighting FRELIMO, and in trying to fill the military vacuum, called on the support of Vorster.[35] Through a calculated move, and having weighed the costs of war with Mozambique, Vorster refrained from conceding to Rhodesia's request, and instead Vorster pushed for a non-aggression pact of non-intervention and non-interference with offers of economic incentives for the regional states of Southern Africa.

Zambia furthered its regional support strategy to include Botswana, Mozambique and Tanzania in the region's diplomatic quest, as Zambia's first line of defence was engagement with racist minorities and in so doing supported the liberation movements to achieve the region's goal. Aside from Lesotho, and Eswatini's close economic affiliation with South Africa, which was linked to the SACU 1969 agreement,[36] the FLS sought to wean Lesotho and Eswatini from deeper economic relations with South Africa. Pretoria's strong opposition did not deter the FLS, and Lesotho nevertheless diversified its political and economic relations by establishing diplomatic relations with Cuba in 1979 and with the Soviet Union in 1980.[37]

During the early years of the formation of the FLS, the roles between alliance members and the apartheid government of South Africa became one of dual dependence. South Africa was dependent on the Southern African region for trade export. For example, in 1973, SACU was listed as one of the twenty-two top exporters for forty-one commodities in the Standard International Trade Classification (SITC) categories 5–8 for Eastern and Southern African markets. These trade commodities were exports such as paper and board, glass and metal-working machinery, diamonds, basic inorganic chemicals, unworked metals and the least advanced iron and steel products, which found access to major international markets.[38] Similarly, Zambia was listed as one of the twenty largest importers, since Zambia received 39 per cent of South Africa's exports in 1973.[39] SACU member states saw South Africa as the means of extracting benefits from cooperation through the SACU agreement on trade.

Political and economic courtship – policy of détente

The awkward co-dependence and balancing roles of the governments of the FLS with the apartheid government of South Africa resulted in the convergence of the weak Southern African states. The alliance was a regional subsystem with distinctive units that assumed a pivotal role in international relations. The primary emphasis of a regional subsystem, according to Khadiagala, was one that embraces geographic regions and was characterised by patterns of relations of levels of cohesions, types of communications and a configuration of power structures that were divided by boundaries and constrained by behaviour. In building on the concept of the subsystem, the preponderance of race and class conflict subsumed the formation of the regional cluster of states and economic linkages that bound the subsystem together, and which had no outer limits. Mel Gurtov similarly suggested that Southern Africa's governments did not speak with one voice, nor did they act in unison, which allowed South Africa, and the West, easy entry into the region. Gurtov suggested that 'for realists, power is the essential ingredient of politics … the instinctive goal of persons … A paradigm of the philosophy, strategy, and objectives that define the national security state, that complex of institutions, special interests, and powerful bureaucracies that govern all societies.'[40]

The interaction between South Africa and some of the FLS leaders like Kaunda and Banda was meaningful for the Southern African states, and a farce for the South African government as Robert Mugabe recognised when he said, 'The coincidence of interests between Zambia and South Africa of avoiding confrontation in Southern Africa set the stage for new attempts as a peaceful resolution through meaningful accommodation.'[41] These attempts became popularly known as regional détente. Khadiagala noted that 'Southern Africa's political lexicon was a logical corollary to Pretoria's reassessment of her relationship with Rhodesia for the explicit purpose of establishing a different kind of relationship with neighbouring states'.[42] According to Khadiagala, secret negotiations between Zambian and South African officials emerged in mid-1974 as a détente scenario. A Zambian official noted the engagements as an undertaking to use the détente exercise to buy Vorster's confidence in resolving the Rhodesian conflict.[43] This position – détente – later became the basis for the OAU's Dar es Salaam Declaration on Southern Africa.

Détente also came under fire when South Africa used it to make diplomatic inroads throughout Africa, and the OAU member states became disgruntled by this move, criticising Kaunda for spearheading the policy. Furthermore, Kaunda did not envisage the problems that détente could engender, like the conflict division that erupted when a militant wing of ZANU, led by Mugabe (prior to his becoming Zimbabwe's president), rejected Muzorewa's leadership and resumed guerrilla infiltration in north-eastern Rhodesia. Mugabe too criticised the FLS for having used détente, which he viewed as 'political chicanery', which stampeded the Zimbabweans in a false unity.⁴⁴ The détente engagements made varied political and economic inroads. Kaunda and former president, Houphouët-Boigny, of the Ivory Coast were at the forefront to assist Jonas Savimbi, the UNITA leader in Angola's fight against the MPLA in Luanda.⁴⁵ While Zambia made strong calls for a government of national unity in Angola, President Kaunda was also siding with the UNITA radicals. For Zambia, what mattered most was to secure export routes and trade from South Africa, given the major obstacles that the Zambian government had faced with its economy during 1975. For instance, Lusaka's balance of payments deficit was kwacha 180 million and its foreign exchange reserves dropped from £370 million to £12.4 million. Zambia therefore turned to South Africa for assistance and negotiated was an export credit agreement of one-quarter of Zambia's import oil bill.⁴⁶

Many other complexities also arose through the regional détente policy of making inroads through concessionary practices. Vorster provided loans to Malawi of R14 million for building a new capital in the centre of the country, at Lilongwe (the capital city was not completed until much later, largely by international donors). Vorster also gave Malawi R11 million for a railway line to connect Mozambique with the port of Nacala to facilitate the transport of Malawian migrant workers to South Africa. These numbers increased from 50,000 in 1966, to 100,000 in 1971.⁴⁷ Malawi's behaviour also appeared contradictory, with a despondent civil service on its doorstep and government technocrats backing Southern Africa's liberation leaders, while its president was backing South Africa. As Douglas Anglin⁴⁸ pointed out, the FLS presidents' motives were to extend the hand of friendship to their less resolute comrades in the hope that they thereby be weaned from their errant ways. Other controversial roles were seen in the issues dealt with by the international community. The International Monetary Fund (IMF) and World Bank forced Malawi to work with South Africans and the heads of Malawi Railways and Press Holdings were both South Africans. Malawi went as far as allowing the Mozambican National Resistance (Resistência Nacional Moçambicana, RENAMO) to use the country as a rear base to launch invasions, even though the same militant group had destroyed Malawi's second rail link to the sea, Nacala.⁴⁹

As noted by Khadiagala, the FLS welcomed Malawi into their circle and suggested that Malawi cultivate cordial relations with its neighbour Mozambique for its trade outlets (ports). The suggestion was 'rather than treating him as an outcast, we showed our goodwill … Like the prodigal son, we [FLS leaders] told him: [Banda] "Come back home."'⁵⁰ Various contradictions similarly prevailed in the region, as was seen in Mozambique's 1976 support of US sanctions against the Ian Smith regime and closure of its borders, while also allowing Soviet assistance and a military presence in the country to thwart South Africa's regional destabilisation. Between 1976 and 1979, Mozambique paid a heavy price for backing South African and Zimbabwean liberation movements, when it experienced attacks from Ian Smith's Rhodesian regime and from RENAMO.⁵¹ Paradoxically, the United States, while enforcing sanctions against Southern Rhodesia, supported proxy wars backing the South African-led UNITA army in Angola.⁵² The US–South Africa relationship was further concretised when Fidel Castro (former Cuban leader) sent thousands of its troops to assist Angola.⁵³ As described by William

Lindeke, economic interests in Africa were deep entrenched in mining and petroleum and 'coexisted with security ones, sometimes in complex ways such as in Angola'.[54] Mobutu Sese Seko, through fuelling rebels in Angola, too had reaped huge profits through UNITA in diamond-smuggling trade deals with the United States that were conducted via the Kamina airbase in Southern Zaire and amounted to $5 billion per year.[55] This powerful backing allowed UNITA to control the diamond fields of Angola and mine $3.7 billion worth of diamonds during the 1990s.[56]

The FLS alliance had a number of awkward relations among its members and with South Africa. Victor Olorunsola and Dan Muhwezi noted that varying degrees of state power and mercantilist policies were used as 'pretence' for bottom-up integration. These subterfuges entailed a degree of government corruption of unaccounted government funds. In the case of Tanzania, unaccounted funds stood at 327,000 shillings in 1967–8; this amount increased to 43 million shillings from 1977–8. These figures further advanced to a total of 437 million shillings in 1980–1.[57] African governments were also faced with economic realities of underdevelopment, of race and class formations, and ethnic divisions that spilled over into the political economy of the state. These complexities gave rise to new pressures, with governments trying to maintain political officialdom combined with high living standards in Africa's post-independence era.[58] Therefore, the African state was absorbed in maintaining political power, and also maintaining exorbitant lifestyles at the expense of its people. Ruth First noted in 1970, 'The resources of the new states were being devoured by a tiny group whose demands distorted the budgets and economies of the states they governed.'[59] Owing to the regional environment, and in forming an alliance, at times its members could be challenged by resources, as Khadiagala noted in his work on FLS history, that an alliance 'might have to pay the price of a drain on domestic resources and some significant loss of national autonomy'. It was inevitable therefore, that alliance members would pursue certain foreign-policy goals that could assist them, as small vulnerable states, when the costs became too high for their domestic situations.[60] Zacarias also noted that the divergent political interests were a mere expression of survival, rather than an expression of cooperation among states with similar values. Khadiagala also highlighted that when the costs and benefits became too large for the alliance members, states pursued other interests.[61]

The Frontline States and external actors

The weaknesses of the state and the exploitative roles of external actors on the resources of fragile states, diverged economic integration, however, strengthened the security convergence of Southern Africa's states. Extra-regional actors contributed to the weakness of the region's economies. The FLS constituted a group of states eager to create adequate mechanisms for addressing violent conflict without the initial intervention of great powers, but their weakness forced them to draw on external powers to fulfil and realise their goals.[62] There was also the self-interest of external actors, and which too was involved for their own needs and not so much for wanting to assist regional states. Instead of assisting the region after the end of the Rhodesia/Nyasaland Federation in 1963,[63] the World Bank approved an investment of £80 million to develop Rhodesia's railways for Britain to have access to the region's resources, given British interests elsewhere in Southern Africa. With the World Bank's refusal to complete the Tazara railway, Chinese funds of $450 million helped fund its completion.[64] British investments and capital were enormous in Rhodesia, like the Rhodesian Iron and Steel Corporation (RISCO), with proceeds of £24 million. Other British firms in Rhodesia were Salisbury Portland Cement; Marley; Tate and Lyle; Brooke Bond; Unilever; Cadbury-Schweppes; and Lonhro and British Petroleum (BP) Industries. The United States had a chrome mining plant, Union Carbide and Foote Minerals, estimated at £20 million. Other countries with interests in Rhodesia were France, Germany, Switzerland, Austria and Japan.[65] Namibia was also a contested state because of its wealth in diamonds, and was managed by the South African government when its Union was formed in 1910.[66] The United States' relations with Southern Africa did not only concern security issues; America had over 1 per cent of foreign investments and bank loans in South Africa and a $7.6 billion share ownership.[67] Currently (2014), approximately 60 per cent of Namibia's diamond exports go to Japanese and US markets.[68]

South Africa's Anglo-American Corporation was the key mining conglomerate extracting diamonds in Namibia's mines. In order to gain international purchasing power, Anglo-American Corporation made large offshore investments through its Minorco company, based in the United States, with mining interests in South Africa.[69] In terms of oil exports, before Angola's independence in 1975, the country produced 135,000 barrels of oil daily. By 1985, Angola's oil production had increased to 278,000 barrels per day, with oil trade that amounted to $2.5 million. Angola's major oil-trading partners and private businesses were the United States' Chevron, Texaco and Mobil; Belgium's Petrofina; Italy's Agip; France's Total and Elf Aquitaine; Spain's Hispanoil; the UK's British Petroleum; Germany's Diminex; and Brazil's Petrobras.[70] With such huge investments it appeared that the US government and its private businesses had a lot to lose in Angola's conflict, since the United States had a $600 million investment in Angola in its Chevron oil company between 1975 and 1985.[71]

The South African government was a contributing force towards the neighbouring states' foreign exchange budgets in mine wages.[72] As early as 1942, South Africa had 215,000 mineworkers from the region working in its own mines: in 1971 – 86,000, in 1970 – 100,000 Mozambican miners worked in South Africa, while Malawi had over 100,000 migrant miners in South Africa. These numbers decreased when President Banda required more labour for his own country's tobacco plantations in Malawi. Mozambique also reduced its number of miners to 60,000 after its independence. However, South Africa also crippled Southern Africa's manufacturing mining sector by taking labour away from the region's own mines, and therefore less gold and fewer diamonds were produced in those Southern African states. Even though Angola, Botswana and Namibia, as well as Zaire, were gold, diamond and other mineral and precious metal producers (as is still the case), South Africa for the period of 1984 exported to these states amounts totalling R11,684 million in gold; R2,387 million in diamonds and precious metals; and R5,515 million in other minerals and mineral products. In 1984, other exports from South Africa to the region included fruit, grain and vegetables (R480 million); other agricultural products (R833 million); and chemicals (R672 million).[73]

On its part, Southern African states benefited from labour migration and this trend continued, since it provided worker remittances to an amount of $350 million due to labour migration, which comprised 40 per cent of the non-South African mining force.[74] While South Africa was befriending Banda, it also crippled Malawi's economy. South Africa came to Malawi's rescue by giving the Malawian government kwacha 5 million worth of fertiliser. Yet, South Africa destroyed a 600-kilometre Beira railway line that resulted in additional transport costs for the government of Malawi of kwacha 16 million on imports. Malawi was then faced with stockpiling of 130,000 metric tonnes of sugar and shortages of fuel and fertiliser.[75]

As Robert Keohane and Joseph Nye observed, in complex interdependence the role of a military can exert substantial power and authority through other means:

> If there are no constraints on one's choice of instruments ... the state with superior military force will prevail. If the security dilemma for all states were extremely acute, military force, supported by economic and other resources, would clearly be the dominant source of power. Survival is the primary goal of all states, and in the worst situations, force is ultimately necessary to guarantee survival. Thus military force is always a central component of national power.[76]

Keohane and Nye also observed that besides using the state military to gain power, other multiple issues in their foreign policy agenda would be used to force control over weaker states, such as energy, resources, environment, population and territorial rivalry. Adebayo Adedeji believed that the trade routes of Southern Africa would not be ideal for economic development for SADCC states and they would be subjected to a problematic South Africa. At the time of setting up the PTA, the Southerners were not interested. He patiently sought to get the states of Southern Africa to join the PTA and tried to secure funding through the European Commission with which he had had several meetings while he was setting up the PTA. He had worked on a plan for ten years as well as a framework for eastern and Southern Africa's states.[77]

The formation of SADCC: A European agenda

Unlike the FLS, the formation of SADCC was driven by external involvement leading to the region converging with was its determination of coordinating trade and infrastructure linkages for its member states. But, the apartheid destabilisation activities of South Africa during the 1980s challenged Southern Africa's states' attempts of economic convergence. As aptly described by Zacarias, when he observed that SADCC was a strategy to create economic relations in the region that were not driven by market forces; it was a deliberate choice of incorporating the majority of the Southern African states into its organisation to reduce dependence on South Africa. The political values of its member states were heterogeneous, and Zacarias outlined, 'Liberal democracies of Botswana coexisted with Malawian dictatorship, and the monarchies of Lesotho and Eswatini, Marxist regimes of Angola and Mozambique, and single-party states with mixed economies such as Tanzania and Zimbabwe, all coexisted alongside one another.'[78] This coexistence of heterogeneity of different political values was a sensitive point that could jeopardise the SADCC configuration, and these dynamics also demonstrated the inability of the Southern African states to develop a supranational functional institution.[79] Kaire Mbuende, a former executive secretary of SADC, outlined the phases of regional integration that had characterised the process of Southern Africa.[80] These phases of integration entailed a phase of political solidarity when the FLS joined in the liberation struggle against colonialism. It was this sense of a common cause that led the first members to meet initially in Lusaka and form SADCC. The Organisation allowed for a strong tradition of solidarity among members, enabling a cohesive organisation. The second phase of regional integration was coordinating and consolidating programmes in transport and communications. Critical sectors for regional development were introduced, including agriculture, energy and human resources, and which constituted programmes for regional development coordinated by SADCC.

The independence of Africa's states represented the beginning of Southern Africa's opportunity to boost the performance of its economies. The Democratic Republic of the Congo (DRC) and Madagascar were the first to gain independence, in 1960.[81] The momentum towards independence subsequently increased, with Tanganyika gaining independence in 1961 and Zanzibar in 1963, which then together formed Tanzania in 1964; Malawi and Zambia both gained independence in 1964, followed by Botswana and Lesotho in 1966. As a successor to the FLS, in April 1980, the leaders of Angola, Botswana, Lesotho, Malawi, Mozambique, Eswatini, Tanzania, Zambia and Zimbabwe met in Lusaka, Zambia, to adopt the 'Southern Africa: Toward Economic Liberation' declaration and formed SADCC in 1980.[82] In July 1981, the SADCC structure was ratified at a summit of heads-of-state meeting. SADCC adopted the SADCC memorandum of understanding (MOU)[83] that provided members states with an institutional framework. The headquarters were established in Gaborone, where they are still located.

The SADCC Summit of Heads of State and Government oversaw policymaking and met on an annual basis.[84] The SADCC Council consisted of ministers tasked to oversee the economic affairs of the region. Sectoral Commissions comprising the Southern African Centre for Cooperation in Agricultural Research (SACCAR), the Standing Committee of Officials (SATCC), and the Secretariat were the other structures completing SADCC.[85] In 1987, SADCC states had a total gross domestic product (GDP) of nearly $20 billion, 68.7 million compared to South Africa's GDP of $54.4 billion and a population size of 32.3 million.[86]

While SADCC was formed to promote cohesion among its members and wanted to assist its economies in becoming less economically dependent on South Africa, various views and opinions existed concerning its creation. Anglin, for example, noted that the European Economic Commission (EEC) and certain of its officials served as the midwife to SADCC, discreetly promoting the birth of SADCC.[87] External actors and international donors also provided 90 per cent of SADCC's budget; however sometimes these funders played ambiguous roles. For example, between 1980 and 1986, the US government indicated that it did not see the Southern African region developing without apartheid South Africa's participation, owing to its strong economy.[88] For example, funding from the United States during the 1980s for SADCC's regional transport and communications sector, which was overseen by Mozambique, was limited. Being averse to Marxism, the United States refused funding as Mozambique was a Marxist-led country at that time.[89]

As noted by Mbuende, in 1980 an economic dimension was added to political cooperation through a different entity, which allowed for broader membership within SADCC.[90] SADCC's member states had always envisaged a democratic South Africa as eventually being part of its organisation. Both the ANC and the Pan-Africanist Congress had observer status at SADCC's annual summits and annual consultative conferences. Although SADCC was formed to build confidence among its member states, SADCC member states were unable to provide one another with sufficient goods and services. Members were also not at the stage of converging trade policies. Trade encompassed transport; agricultural goods such as animals and animal products; animal and vegetable fats; vegetable products; foodstuffs and beverages; mineral products; chemical products; plastics and rubber; hides, skins and leather; wood; pulp and paper; textiles; footwear; stone; jewellery; base metals; machinery and appliances; vehicles; and optical equipment, among other items necessary to support independence.[91]

Key to SADCC's regional integration efforts was the adoption of its action programme, which was seen as an important vehicle to promote and obtain regional cooperation. SADCC member states were tasked to oversee sectoral and sub-sectoral activities, at both national and regional levels.[92] The SADC Programme of Action (SPA) was viewed as a means to achieving the participation and involvement of all SADCC members. In mid-1993, the SPA had 464 projects requiring funding of $8.8 billion, with only 22 per cent of those projects being truly regional (also as is later discussed in this chapter under the rationalisation period). By the late 1990s there were nineteen sectors and the SPA had 380 projects. Although the main goal was to retain regional projects with adequate funding, only 49 per cent of funds were secured. Similarly, members failed to provide the required resources for the adequate functioning of the SADCC Secretariat.

The lack of sufficient funds, coupled with insufficient staffing of the Secretariat, made it difficult for SADCC, and later also for SADC, to fulfil its regional role adequately. SADCC soon realised that financing was difficult to manage, and even more difficult to coordinate through its Secretariat. Only twenty sector coordinating units were truly regional, and the rest lacked a regional focus. This led to the adoption of a new strategy beginning in 1985,[93] focusing on coordination through a more robust emphasis on sectoral regional activities. Sectoral activities were very important to SADCC's efforts in fostering security for the region through political and economic stability. The sectoral activities were coordinated nationally through member states' national ministries.[94]

The decentralised approach adopted by the SADCC action programme became problematic for the region, negatively affecting the integration process. These problems faced by SADCC member states varied. For example, donors preferred to fund the sectoral activities and projects that they deemed most important, while failing to fund sectoral activities that SADCC member states deemed equally important for the region. Levels of competence also varied among SADCC member states, with some states being more effective than others in executing sectoral responsibilities. Lobbying for sectoral funding also occurred in advance, with member states seeking donor support unilaterally and not adhering to SADC procedures. Therefore, SADCC's annual consultative conference, held with its international partners, was described by Garth le Pere and Elling Tjønneland as a dress rehearsal for discussions on donor support.[95] While SADCC was faced with regional instability, it was conducting more trade with the rest of the world and divergence in intra-regional trade was hampered at these early stages of SADCC owing to the damaged infrastructure of roads and railway lines. Figure 3.1 highlights SADCC's trade with global markets, as seen in the exports

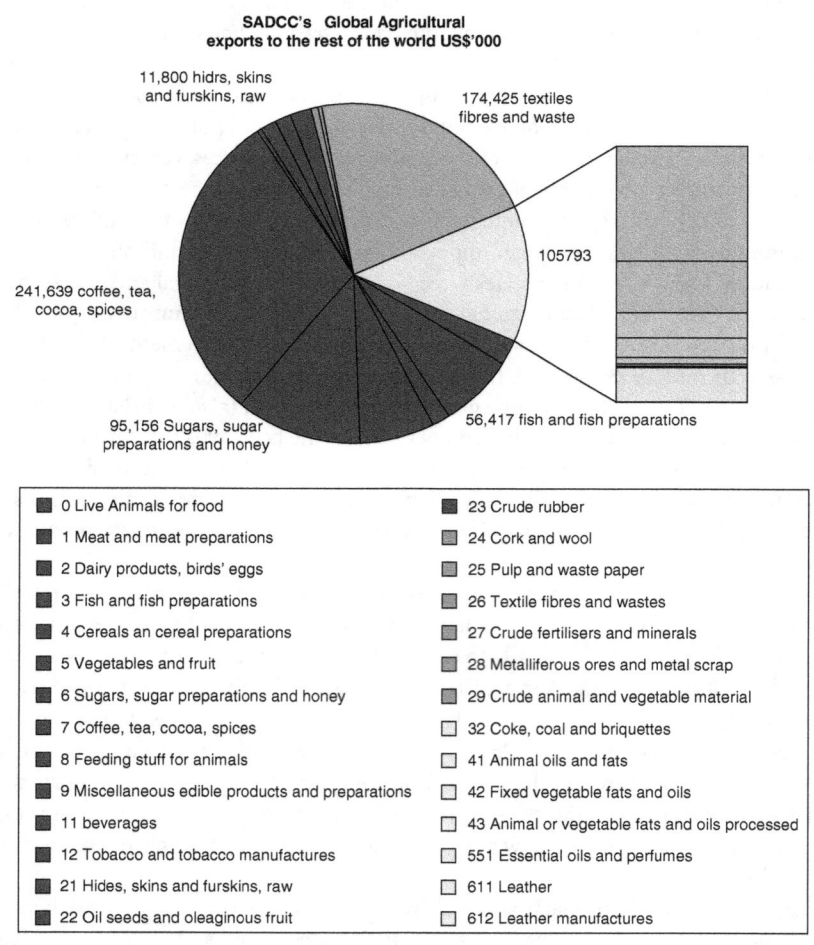

Figure 3.1 SADCC's agricultural exports to the rest of the world, 1985–9.

Source: Data provided by the African Development Bank (AfDB) on SADCC's regional growth indicators for trade, GNP, GDP versus regional trade and overall economic growth based on, AfDB, Economic Integration in Southern Africa, vol. 2 (Oxford: Oxprint,1993), pp. 80–4 and 90.

of agricultural trade from SADCC to the rest of the world for the period from 1985 to 1989.

While, this trade with external markets demonstrates the ability for SADCC to produce agricultural exports, and trade externally, it also shows the inability for regional integration and for trade convergence between member states during this period in its history. These are all primary products as per the SITC 7; export amounts from SADCC to the rest of the world for the period 1985-9 totalled as follows: coffee and tea – $241,639 million; sugar – $95,156 million; fish and fish preparations – $56,417 million; textiles – $174,425 million; skins and fur skins raw – $11,800 million; and smaller agricultural commodities for the same period – $105,793 million. Besides the sectoral coordinating structures, SADCC also faced internal organisational problems and in its security and secretariat structures as is discussed next.

SADC's institutional architecture

The institutional journey of SADCC, which became SADC, and the restructuring of its Secretariat in region-building attempts were largely orchestrated by Europe.[96] SADCC's evolving security architecture embarked on a difficult journey. Defence and security issues were initially a sub-structure under the FLS. The Inter-State Defence and Security Committee (ISDSC), the security leg of the FLS formed in 1976, was operating with no formal charter or institutional framework. Zimbabwe held the chair of the FLS and played an integral role in the ISDSC. SADCC's key hegemonic player between 1975 and 1990 was Zimbabwe, and was viewed as the economic and military giant. With South Africa joining the Southern African fraternity in 1994, SADC had new battles to fight that did not encompass a political agenda of racism and colonialism, but was instead a battle over a clash of personalities,[97] evident in Zimbabwe's Robert Mugabe and South Africa's Nelson Mandela's relations. Robert Mugabe was the longest serving head of state in Southern Africa, as well as chairperson of the FLS, with Zimbabwe therefore having significant regional status. The issues between these two presidents varied. Mugabe remained wary of South Africa's new political transformation; Mandela, on his part, had misgivings about human rights and democracy issues in Zimbabwe.

Robert Mugabe and Nelson Mandela's disagreements and discontent further divided the region and issues pertinent to regional security became problematic. Issues arose where SADC member states were left having to choose between South Africa's (Mandela) advocating for an Organ on Politics, Defence, and Security (OPDS) integrated regional security approach, incorporated into SADC and reporting to the summit. Mugabe, on the other hand, strongly opposed South Africa's idea and felt that the Organ should be autonomous and have its own summit, while security should not be integrated into the SADC structures. Overall, member states felt that security needed to be part of the SADC agenda.[98]

Member states were generally unhappy with the role that the Secretariat played, particularly with the inadequate staffing structure. By 1996, the Secretariat had ten professional and twenty administrative staff. SADC's security architecture was further challenged by Zimbabwe when it sent troops to the DRC with Angola and Namibia and signed its own Mutual Defence Pact with all three states.[99] To pull the region's member states together and attempt to converge SADC's security policies, in June 1996, at a SADC Summit meeting in Gaborone, Botswana, the OPDS of SADC was established.[100] Since the establishment of SADC's OPDS in 1996, the Organ's mandate has been to oversee conflict prevention, establish a regional peacekeeping force, coordinate foreign and security policy of member states, strengthen democracy and human rights, and establish a mutual defence pact. The establishment of the OPDS showed a tentative commitment by member states to consolidate SADC's regional security policies. Even with the establishment of the Organ, it too had no clarity how it would relate to the wider SADC structures and how it would report to the executive secretary or under SADC.[101] In August 1999 (three years later, and after the SADC 1996 Summit), at a heads-of-state meeting in Maputo, Mozambique, SADC's foreign and defence ministers met to develop the subregion's collective security system.[102] In an attempt to further consolidate cooperation and trust among SADC member states, two bodies were established: the Inter-State Politics and Diplomacy Committee (ISPDC) of subregional foreign ministers, and an ISDSC from the FLS, comprising ministers of foreign affairs, defence, public security and state security.

SADC experienced many difficulties in the operationalisation of the OPDS mandate.[103] When the objectives of SADC were stipulated in its founding treaty of 1992, these objectives defined the economic and political values of the institution and include the promotion of defence and security. Issues arose with the manner in which the executive secretary executed his duties and the infighting within the Secretariat led to the public dismissal at an SADC Summit of its independent-minded executive secretary, Namibia's Kaire Mbuende, in 1999. A substantive executive secretary, Mauritius's Prega Ramsamy, was appointed only in 2001 (and served in this capacity until 2005).[104]

Further concerns were raised concerning the vague work programme and lack of focus that could not be reconciled with SADC's overall objectives.[105] In 2000, at an Annual SADC Consultative Conference held in Ezulwini, Eswatini, the meeting highlighted that the defence and security committee, in comparison with the foreign affairs committee, appeared to be more effective.[106] In 2001, SADC's organisational structure still appeared inadequate in terms of resources and staffing. In addition, the political tensions and divisions that emerged between Zimbabwe and South Africa threatened the Organisation's security work. As a regional economic community, SADC was able to legally address security functions.[107]

Hence, in August 2001 at a summit of heads of state in Blantyre, Malawi, the OPDS was restructured into the Organ on Politics, Defence and Security Cooperation (OPDSC) providing SADC members with an institutional framework to coordinate policies and activities in the areas of politics, defence and security.[108] The 2001 summit also recommended improvements and changes to SADC's institutional framework for it to execute its original 1992 mandate and SADC staff increased to 384, comprising 194 professional and 190 support staff.[109] The OPDSC comprises the chairperson and the office of the chairperson, the troika, the ministerial committee (MC), the ISPDC and ISDSC. Together the MC, ISDSC and the ISPDC are the SADC Organ's MC.[110] The

Organ was also brought under the authority of the SADC Summit and chairmanship and became rotational from being solely chaired by one country, Zimbabwe.[111]

A further SADC extraordinary meeting in January 2002 in Blantyre mandated the Organ on Politics and Defence Cooperation to provide guidelines for its Protocol on Politics, Defence and Security Cooperation. Hence, the Strategic Indicative Plan of the Organ (SIPO) was created by SADC focusing on four main areas: the political, defence, state security and public security sectors.[112] Also approved were the Terms of Reference (TOR) for the development of SIPO, and a task force comprising the Troika of members was established, with a one-year rotating chair to coordinate SADC's security policy.[113] SIPO provided a five-year strategic and activity guideline for implementing the OPDS Protocol. It covered a range of objectives and activities. SIPO also developed additional policy documents such as the Mutual Defence Pact signed at the August 2003 SADC Summit. SIPO still had to operationalise and develop an implementation apparatus and business plan to engage with its politics, defence and security remits effectively. In August 2003, the Mutual Defence Pact was signed, committing member states to develop both individual and collective defence capabilities and to cooperate on defence training, research and intelligence issues.[114]

SIPO[115] had a broad understanding of security through its governance and democratisation objectives as well as its defence and security issues, but with divergent opinions and approaches. Hence, some member states in the region placed more emphasis on state security issues, while others placed more emphasis on human security.[116] SADC's security convergence of its member states' various protocols took five years since the establishment of the security Organ in 1996 – the Organ received guidelines only in 2004 through SIPO.

SADC's security convergence gained support with the availability of donor funding, 'which always got SADC member states to respond' (as a SADC Secretariat official indicated).[117] By the end of 2004, the Secretariat managed to appoint the heads of its four directorates and staffing for each directorate to the extent of ten officials per cluster. Previously, the most basic administrative resources such as adequate access to email and communications had been hampered at the Secretariat. A relationship gap between the Secretariat and member states remains a challenge, since the mandate of the Secretariat is mainly administrative, with no political decision-making powers. An additional secondment was made from South Africa to the Organ's Chair in 2005. Persistent problems still existed with the relations between the Organ and the Secretariat. This remains a major challenge, with both the Organ and the Secretariat sharing the same support staff, but having entirely different governing structures.[118]

SADC social and economic areas are supported by the Integrated Committee of Ministers (ICM), the Council of Ministers, the Troika (past, current and incoming Chairs of SADC) and the Summit. The ICM lacked the ability to provide direction on programmes and activities for the various sectors and similarly lacked the ability to provide strong policies and a coherent flow of information between government departments at the national level.[119] According to Elling Tjønneland, Jan Isaksen and Garth le Pere, the Council of Ministers spent much of their time and capacity on administrative detail and seemed to lack overall leadership.[120] The Troika system had also failed to provide strong political leadership between the meetings of the ICM and the Council of Ministers.

To narrow this gap between rhetoric and implementation, SADC established a Committee of Ambassadors in February 2005 in Gaborone, Botswana. The Organ has its own Troika.[121] The Organ operates at the level of heads of state, consisting of three heads of state with its own Troika, and it reports to the SADC Summit. How this works in practice, is through the ministerial committee, which in turn reports to the Troika and makes the key decisions. The ministerial committee consists of ministers of defence, police and intelligence from SADC's fifteen member states (SADC has sixteen member states since 2017 with Comoros joining). The Organ's operational work is carried out through the two committees of senior officials, the ISPDC and ISDSC. The main responsibility of the Organ is security cooperation for member states, based on principles of common and collective security and mutual defence, and it provides a framework for operationalising the SADC Brigade. The protocol for the OPDSC empowers the Organ to deal with both interstate and intra-state conflict such as civil wars, military coups or gross human rights violations. The SADC OPDSC was put firmly under the control of SADC and a small Secretariat of the Organ was established at the SADC Secretariat in Gaborone.[122]

The SADC Troika system – sometimes referred to as the Double Troika – has an incumbent chairperson, an incoming chairperson who also serves as the deputy chairperson for one year, and an immediate or previous chairperson who can take quick decisions on behalf of SADC that are not taken at SADC's regular policy meetings. The Summit of Heads of State and Government Summit meet annually, while the Council of Ministers meets biannually. These meetings occur in February to approve SADC annual budgets, and also in August to prepare the Summit agenda. Provision is also made for extraordinary Summit and Council meetings if and when the need arises. The Troika is also applicable at the level of the Standing Committee of Senior Officials comprising the permanent or principal secretaries accounting for government offices and ministries. These rules of engagement also apply to the Troika of the OPDSC. The chairperson of the Organ does not hold the chair of the Summit simultaneously.

SADC's National Committees (SNCs) were established according to its Treaty of 1992, to coordinate programmes and policies for its government, civil society organisations, and the private sector. The SNCs are mandated to ensure that SADC programmes are implemented at a national level. The reporting line for state-directed SNCs is to the SADC Secretariat. This posed a problem for the Secretariat, since the SNCs are state directed at national level and therefore accountability to the Secretariat became a challenge. The Secretariat's lack of power and authority could not hold SNCs accountable at national level. Furthermore, the SNCs do not exist in all SADC member states (this is still the case)[123], and those that do exist are largely dysfunctional, lack technical capacity and have ineffective coordinating mechanisms and inadequate resources.[124]

SADC officials noted that as soon as funding was imminent from the European Union (EU), it would be linked to restructuring of the Secretariat.[125] At a SADC Summit in Maseru, Lesotho, in August 2006, two important decisions were made: first, to establish a task force on regional economic integration; and second, to strengthen the role of the Secretariat, and to review the role of the ICM.

At a further consultative meeting in April 2008, in Port Louis, Mauritius, SADC's role was re-examined to address the organisation's capacity and performance issues against the commitments made at its 1992 Windhoek Declaration. Furthermore, the Council of Ministers instructed the Secretariat to participate in an evaluation of all its staffing positions with an attempt to realign the Secretariat's organisational structure with SADC's priorities. Evaluations were conducted by KPMG, and also by the Ernst and Young auditing firm, which undertook an institutional assessment of the Secretariat, which focused on operational policies and procedures. Germany financed a similar evaluation through GTZ and InWent (Germany's capacity-building international organisation), focusing on SADC's capacity needs.[126]

The evaluation findings observed that the need to address capacity constraints of the organisation was critical. The findings of the evaluators also noted that SADC's Secretariat remained weak, lacked human and financial management capacity, and was not able to facilitate strategy development and policy harmonisation within the region.[127] The February 2008 meeting of the SADC Council of Ministers proposed a number of changes to the internal structures of the Secretariat (see Figure 3.2). The main purpose of the meeting was to clarify the lines of authority and to improve the coordinating activities of the Secretariat's senior management. Hence, the vacant post of chief director was to be eliminated and replaced by positions of two deputy executive secretaries.[128] The deputy executive secretary for regional integration was made responsible for regional integration within the technical directorates: trade and industry; finance and investment; food, agriculture and natural resources; infrastructure and services; health; labour and skills development; and policy, planning and resource mobilisation. In addition, the deputy executive secretary for regional integration also provides direction to the Secretariat by recommending regional policies, and by providing strategic impetus and coordination with other RECs. The role of the second deputy executive secretary for finance and administration oversees two directorates and is responsible for the human resources and administration, and budget and finance clusters.

The August 2008 Mauritius conference also proposed a Capacity Development Framework for SIPO. The assumption was that the Secretariat should embrace the priorities of the framework encompassing both the Regional Indicative Strategic Development Plan (RISDP) of 2003, and the 2004 SIPO. The priorities should therefore also include functions such as (i) a think tank to guide members on the implementation of SADC's common agenda; (ii) a principal regional coordinator of policies, strategies and programmes for regional integration; (iii) a provider of support services to the technical directorates and convenor of annual consultative conferences for SADC's decision-making structures; and (iv) a professional programme manager to facilitate, implement and systematically prioritise programmes within a business plan and budget. Furthermore, the SADC Capacity Development Framework included ten intervention areas to strengthen the SADC Secretariat's capacities and for a bridging facility through which donor funding could be channelled. The Bridging Fund Facility was to address the needs of the Secretariat, other SADC treaty-established institutions such as the SADC Tribunal (but this institution was cancelled in 2011), SADC subsidiary institutions such as the Regional Peacekeeping Training Centre (RPTC) and the Development Finance Resource Centre.[129]

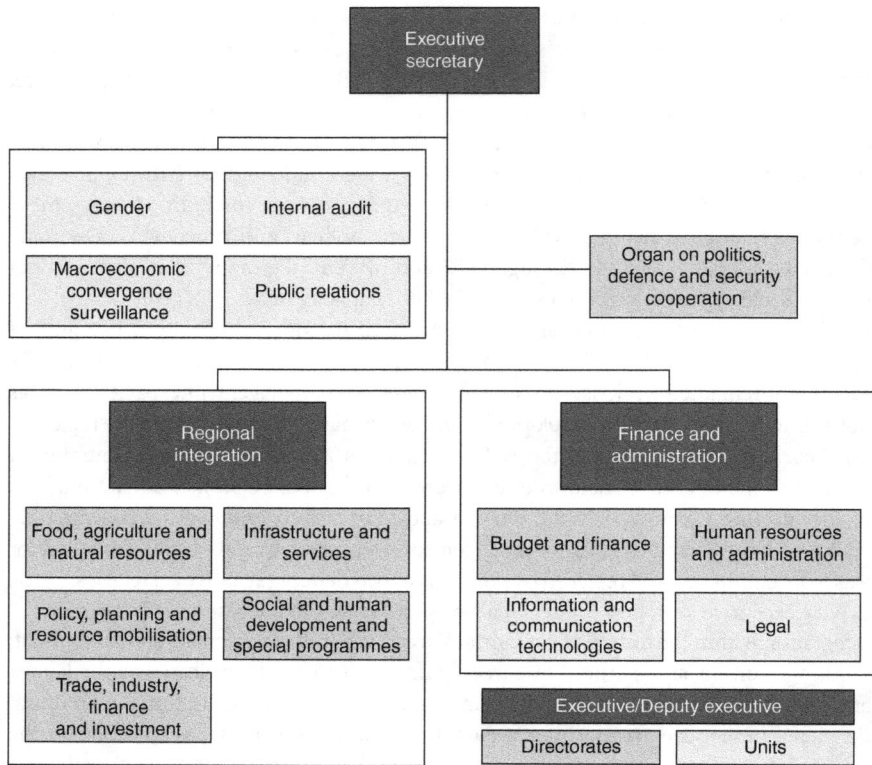

Figure 3.2 SADC's restructuring and organogram.

Source: SADC Secretariat, http://www.sadc.int/english/sadc-institutions/sadc-Secretariat/.

SIPO was revised into SIPO II in 2012 – a detailed programme of activities against key political, defence, public security sector (policing) and state security objectives. The current structure of the SADC Secretariat had been revamped to a staff capacity of 400 personnel.

A special Project Preparation Facility Fund was established and funded by Development Bank of Southern Africa (DBSA). The purpose of the Project Preparation Facility Fund was to assist SADC member states, in an intermediary capacity, to develop projects, up to the point that they were at a 'bankable stage'.[130] The EU commissioned an institutional assessment of SADC that strongly recommended that SADC bring its financial management up to international standards.

Funding SADCC and SADC

In allowing the convergence of SADC, heavy involvement transpired with donors providing funding for the functioning of the Secretariat (which still is the case currently), inadvertently allowing a firm European footing in Southern Africa's trade.

SADCC members relied heavily on the support of external actors for funding; this was seen as a continuation of the FLS to reduce economic dependence on South Africa. Transport and infrastructure were vital to the survival of the SADCC economies. In 1984, which was four years after the donor conference, SADCC had generated 250 projects, an estimated $5 000 million, but had obtained only 20.8 per cent of the required funds.[131] SADCC had its origins in the diplomatic initiatives of African and Western states, and envisaged a huge programme of reconstruction in Southern Africa after the years of war, with a sort of Marshall Plan for the region.[132] As suggested by Øostergaard,[133] Anglin,[134] and Leys and Tostensen,[135] donors remained involved in SADCC and also in SADC. Europe, in particular, is forcing a regional integration role in existence onto SADC – which weakens intra-regional trade and Brussels has gained easy access into its economies.

The funding for SADCC was a two-pronged approach: SADCC's dependence on foreign aid and the Nordic countries' political and economic interests in Southern Africa. Previous instances had been during the post-Cold War era, when Southern African states received US aid of $53.7 million between 1975 and 1979; and $154.4 million between 1980 and 1984.[136] Global events like the fall of the Berlin Wall in 1989 resulted in a further increase in aid by the United States, which played a supportive role to promote countries evolving into democratic regimes, like Malawi ($58.4 million) and Zambia ($41.7 million), and assisting with the resolution of civil wars in Angola ($29.4 million) and Mozambique ($102 million).[137]

SADCC formed the SATCC, which was to integrate all transport systems with the four regional ports of Dar es Salaam in Tanzania, Lobito in Angola, Beira in Maputo and Nacala in Mozambique, for which the donor community pledged $650 million.[138] In 1988, estimated costs for 188 important projects were $4.6 billion; 42 per cent ($1.9 billion) was fully secured, with $241 million under negotiation. Such challenges increased for SADCC when national policies conflicted with regional policies, as in its regional food security projects proposed by Zimbabwe. In 1986, SADCC had to abandon its agrarian programme when it shifted focus from transport to production of goods and services in the industrial, mining and trade sectors under the 1987 SADCC theme, Investment in Production, which also conflicted with regional as opposed to national policies.[139]

As noted by Øostergaard, Friedland, Anglin and Meyns, Organisation for Economic Co-operation and Development (OECD) governments of Britain, France, Canada, West Germany and Japan funded only 21.2 per cent of SADCC's total sectoral distribution and contributed to the transportation and the communications sectors.[140] SADCC required funds to establish plants to produce cement, paper and packaging, natural and synthetic textiles, and salt, as well as farming requisites such as tractors, chemical fertilisers and pesticides/insecticides for enhancing food production, which would have led to stronger economies and seen an increase in its per capita income.[141] At the 1985 SADCC Summit held in Arusha, the report on the SADCC Programme of Action was tabled, covering the period of July 1984–July 1985, which provided the results for five years of cooperation for economic liberation in Southern Africa. Of the nearly $2.3 billion required, over 50 per cent was secured by donors.[142] The Council of Ministers on the Nordic/SADCC initiative provided a report that detailed expanding and deepening relations between the two regions in the areas of development assistance, trade, industry, investment, finance and culture. The Joint Declaration on Expanded Economic and Cultural Cooperation between the Nordic countries and the SADCC member states was signed in January 1986,[143] as well as the memorandum of understanding (MOU) for the Programming of Regional Cooperation Funds under the Third Lomé Convention for the African, Caribbean and Pacific (ACP) group of states of Southern Africa that provided for the joint programming of regional resources, including food security, transport and communications. These two agreements were important for SADCC member states, and the funding and joint venture programmes assisted the Southern African states to withstand the attacks by the South African apartheid government on their trade transport routes.

The total Nordic (Denmark, Sweden, Finland and Norway) funding support received in 1985 for SADCC projects was $369 million. While funding was provided, there was also trade conducted. For example, trade from Nordic countries to SADCC for 1986 totalled $4,328 million, and total exports from SADCC to Nordic countries totalled $4,267. The trade amounts between Nordic and SADCC countries during the 1980s did not reflect a major difference.[144] Trade with SADCC was only to ensure that Nordic countries' motives for funding SADCC served as a form of cushioning for Nordic markets in instances of vulnerability, owing to the Nordic countries' relatively high ratios of foreign trade to their gross national product (GNP).

On the part of SADCC, the items traded from SADCC to Nordic countries had potential for specialisation within the region to boost trade prospects. Exports from SADCC to Nordic countries were: Angola (coffee); Botswana (live animals); Lesotho (mohair, textiles); Malawi and Zimbabwe (tobacco); Zambia and Tanzania (coffee and tea); and Mozambique and Eswatini (sugar). Also suggested at the SADCC Summit of heads-of-state meeting held on 22 August 1986 in Luanda, Angola, was for member states to consider the intra-SADCC trade programme that incorporated a system to direct trade and bilateral trade agreements, multi-purchase annual agreements, and counter purchase preferential import licensing.[145] The SADCC Summit in 1986 also addressed the exchange trade preferences among member states that needed to take into account their existing obligations and a supplementary financial mechanism for intra-SADCC trade to ease the constraints arising from foreign exchange difficulties. Therefore, the Summit meeting of August 1986 considered the establishment of a regional export credit facility and a national export refinancing revolving fund to promote trade.[146] SADCC's Nordic agreement in 1986 expanded to include both economic and cultural cooperation, which was as a result of the stalemate in the UN programme for a New International Economic Order (NIEO).

Denmark's trade to SADCC in 1986 amounted to 506 million Danish krone and consisted of machines, metal goods, transport equipment and chemicals. SADCC's exports to Nordic countries met none of the real funding objectives of SADCC, which were to enhance trade conducted within the region and to obtain meaningful integration.[147] Such real objectives did not result in a reduction of economic dependence, mainly on South Africa; mobilisation of resources that reflected promotion and implementation of national, interstate and regional policies; and a lack of effort to secure international cooperation within the framework of its strategy for economic liberation. Nordic funding commitments also moved to bilateral funding later on in 1987 and 1988. For example, Nordic countries' commitment to the Beira system amounted to $37.4 million; and $575 million for the transportation development plan for Angola's Lobito corridor as well as the critical food shortages programme. The Nordic countries' move in providing the funds allowed SADCC to accept and make quick decisions in embracing a developmental integration approach, which called for a regional industrial strategy.[148]

Ian Bremmer argues that growing economies through an integration strategy had been equally daunting for regions when governments used state assets to regulate the markets, and used the markets to bolster domestic and political positions.[149] Regional integration becomes affected by state capitalism and interstate relations, places a damper on regions, and stifles trade liberalisation, in particular that of weak markets. Tanzania's private sector development accompanied massive privatisation, as was the case in most other African economies alongside deregulated import-export regimes.[150] African markets in SADCC were very weak, and the opening of its markets led to a massive export sector with a weak local manufacturing sector that invariably provided a link for external trade. Furthermore, these economies experienced dumping from capitalist countries, and a meagre surplus was made available for implementing development programmes.[151] Crawford Young notes that a declining state loses its credibility when 'its ability to transform allocated public resources into intended policy aims'[152] fails.

Not all Nordic funding was directed purely to commitments in SADCC's sectoral programmes. Tanzania received the lion's share of total Nordic donor funds for its national projects, which were listed and categorised as SADCC projects. A case in point was the Mufinidi Project that received $187 million in 1987. SADCC's industrial projects received only $66 million, which was the balance of the total SADCC industrial projects' amount of $253 million of Nordic funds.[153] SADCC needed to improve its industrialisation base,[154] which required not only funding and resources, but also the willingness of member states to industrialise. However, as observed by Elaine Friedland, since the worldwide supply of most raw materials exceeded demand, it was not possible for SADCC member states to export on a sufficient scale and to simultaneously fund industrialisation projects. SADCC's member states, Angola, Malawi, Mozambique, Tanzania, Zambia and Zimbabwe had trade with the EEC in 1987 that amounted to $4,267 million, while exports from the EEC to SADCC totalled $4,328 million.[155]

At the Lusaka SADCC Summit in 1984, the Canadian International Development Assistance (CIDA) noted that they were evaluating progress before funding SADCC to determine whether it would go the same way as the EAC had done, which had failed owing to a heavy centralised bureaucracy. The funding received from donors for SADCC sectoral projects was an apt opportunity for the region to develop its technology and skills, with spillovers that could have enhanced economic growth as well as improved trade opportunities. For example, Malawi was considered an important source in technology transfer in the fishing industry.[156] During 1989 and 1990, SADCC faced huge food shortages in the Southern African region. At the 1990 and 1991 SADCC Summits, particular concern was expressed by governments at the extreme low levels of regional food shortages, with food deficits of an estimated 2.8 million tonnes for cereal and grain.[157] Therefore, the use of donor funds to develop comprehensive regional approaches for agricultural production and food security programmes could have advanced the expansion of production given the complementary, comparative advantage in Southern African states. SADCC states declined a US offer to fund an $18 million-dollar regional sorghum and millet research project, which had the potential for the coordination of field tests and applied research. However, the agreement did not sit well with SADCC leaders, since the United States had a proviso attached that excluded project components from Angola, Mozambique and Tanzania.[158]

The United States also showed little interest in initially funding SADCC and contributed only $50 million to SADCC programmes between 1980 and 1985; only much later, during the late 1980s, did the United States provide funding as mentioned earlier.[159] Besides the objections of SADCC in relation to the United States and its $18 million offer, such agreements could have been beneficial to regional economic growth in the long run, as highlighted by economists like Robert Baldwin.[160]

Neoclassical economic models have succeeded amid the growth of massive privatisation schemes and alongside import-export regimes that resulted in perpetual underdevelopment of Africa's economies. The model de-emphasises the role of the state in economic development. The importance for SADCC members to boost intra-SADCC trade promotion programmes in 1986, was to assist with low levels of production in the region.[161] But, as noted by Khadiagala, Southern Africa's regionalism had also been largely tied to external intervention from the West that was mainly linked to interventions via Bretton Woods Institutions – the World Bank and the IMF.[162]

Controversial aid from donors also funded South Africa during the apartheid regime as well as post 1994. South Africa received aid from the United States of $112 million for the period 1995–6 that made it the largest American aid recipient in Southern Africa.[163] Also, between 1989 and 1994, South Africa received $75.3 million in annual funding from the United States to work with the ANC regime towards a multiracial democratic society.[164]

At a two-day conference held in Windhoek in September 1993, the focus was on development issues and the future role of aid in the Southern African region. Government actors promoted the conference with a view to economic reforms through donor commitments and aid and trade packages. In attendance at the this meeting were the OECD and the Development Assistance Committee (DAC) chairman, Alexander R. Love, and Swedish ambassador to Namibia, Sten Rylander, among twenty leading experts from the Southern African region. These included Z. Ngavirue, director general of the National Planning Commission; Attorney General Hartmut Ruppel, minister of agriculture, rural development and water affairs; and Kaire Mbuende, former SADC executive secretary. Also included were representatives from SADC and PTA. SADC officials were trying to lobby for financial assistance for SADC's sectoral action programme. Love noted: 'It will be important that the donor community reconfirms its long-term commitment to provide aid to Africa, both timely and commensurate with the needs of the countries moving towards political reform and economic liberalisation.'[165]

Funding allocations were therefore determined and done by the donors. For example, if the funding for governance and security were not provided, the Secretariat would cancel its regional security and governance programmes, and project implementation would be delayed and hampered at national and regional levels. Similarly, funding of Millennium Development Goal (MDG) projects at the regional level was delayed because of the embargo on funds.[166] Furthermore, if the donors, upon evaluation, were not satisfied with the outcomes of the programmes funded and rolled out at the Secretariat level, funding would be stalled, and the integration programmes would not be rolled out.[167]

The formation of the PTA and the incorporation of EAC member states

The formation of the PTA, which became COMESA in 1993, shows a very different convergence to that of SADC, which was faced with regional wars. On its part, the PTA was a direct beneficiary of the pursuit of several strategies with the assistance of UNECA and through the creation of its regional economic communities within its five subregions: West, Central, North, East and South Africa. Regional integration efforts also stemmed from historical development ideologies, largely prioritising 'good governance' principles and structures, as well as stable economies. One of the main reasons for creating the RECs in Africa was to promote such structures with sustainable economic schemes to address the imbalance of weaker economies against stronger ones within regional clusters. As Anglin noted, UNECA was designed to 'force the pace of cooperation among African states in trade, transport, and industry through the mechanism of sub-regional coordinating bodies'.[168] In 1965, at a Lusaka meeting, eastern African states met to harmonise industrial development and establish an economic community for East and Central Africa with a Secretariat based in Lusaka. However, within two years it dissolved. The next attempt to create the EAC was in 1967, comprising Kenya, Tanzania and Uganda, but that collapsed in 1977.[169]

The next attempts at regionalism were the joining of the eastern and Southern African states. The cooperation framework was designed by the Economic Commission for Africa, which sought to promote regional economic cooperation that could eventually evolve into common markets through the establishment of multi-national programming and operational centres (MULPOCs) in Africa's five subregions. The funding for MULPOCs was extensive and consumed an annual budget of $7,045,393 over four years in financing projects in statistics, industry, national accounts, transport and communications, and integration of women in development.[170] MULPOCs were set up by the ECA as a response to the failed United Nations Multinational Interdisciplinary Development Advisory Teams (UNIDATs) created by a 1969 UN General Assembly Resolution 2563 to provide services at the subregional level to improve the operational and economic capacity and performance of Africa's subregions. MULPOCs own role was ambiguous and unclear and failed dismally. Programming and development in Africa were to be the cornerstones for rapid industrial development. This led to the establishment of three institutions for manpower, industry and technology being implemented: the African Regional Centre for Technology Design and Manufacturing (ACRT) in Dakar, Senegal; the African Regional Centre for Engineering Design and Manufacturing (ARCEDEM), Ibadan, Nigeria; and, the African Institute for Higher Technical Training and Research, Nairobi, Kenya.

The PTA member states had relatively stable economies, aside from the impact of regional conflicts, such as the intra-state conflicts in Ethiopia and Somalia's Ogaden War, fought between 1977 and 1978; the intra-state conflict in Rwanda from 1993 to 1994, which led to the genocide in which eight hundred thousand people were killed through 'ethnic cleansing'; the border dispute between Eritrea and Ethiopia from 1998 to 2000; and the military coup in Sudan in 1985, which brought General Omar Hassan Ahmad al-Bashir to power.[171] But these conflicts did not affect the PTA's vision of forming an economic community and a free trade area (FTA), and ignoring the plight of Africa's people and the death of millions of people – it was 'business as usual'. As shown in Table 3.1, PTA member Kenya had the highest per capita GNP of $7,500 with its average growth at 3.8 per cent of GDP between 1980 and 1987, and its population in 1987 was 22,097,000 million – almost half that of Ethiopia's, which had a population of 44,788,000 million people in 1987. Ethiopia had the second-highest GNP of $5,537 and its annual growth rate for the period 1980–7 was 3.8 per cent of GDP.

PTA members and observers also pledged towards MULPOCs: Botswana pledged $12,000 towards the ECA MULPOC, as well as Tanzania, while also informing the ECA during that time, that the country would be settling the arrears of $298,000 in 1985 and in addition would contribute an additional Tanzanian shillings of 1,800,000 to the fund in 1985–6. Angolan and Zimbabwean representatives also promised contributions to the MULPOC fund after consultation with their governments during that period.[173] However, some slight success was achieved through the MULPOC programme, namely, the establishment of the Intergovernmental Authority for Drought and Development (IGADD) and the Eastern and Southern African Management Institute (ESAMI). It also evolved into four years (1977–81) of negotiations among leaders of eastern and Southern Africa that culminated in the establishment of the PTA in 1981, one year after the formation of SADCC in 1980.

In 1980, Africa's balance of current account deficit was $3.9 billion and in 1988 $20.3 billion; health and education in total expenditure fell from 25.2 per cent in 1986 to 21.3 per cent in 1988; external debt was $48.3 billion in 1978 and $230 billion in 1988; and trade deteriorated at an annual rate of 10 per cent.[174] The narrowness of the markets to develop industries of economies of scale and to create more interregional trade was not possible. With the adoption of the UN General Assembly's Declaration on the Critical Economic Situation in Africa in Resolution A39/29 of 1984, brought about the adoption of Adedeji's Africa's Priority Programme for Economic Recovery 1986–90 (APPER) and a special session was held in May/June 1986 essentially implementing APPER and set the scene for further discussions on the United Nations Programme for Action for African Economic Recovery and Development (UN-PAAERD). Adedeji furthermore published a 56-page report based on a study of *South African Destabilization: The Economic Cost of Frontline Resistance to Apartheid*, which was unveiled in Zambia in October 1989.[175]

Table 3.1 PTA: Countries – main economic indicators, 1987

Country	Population (000) Mid-1987	GNP (million US$) 1987	Average[172] annual growth rate of GDP (%) 1980-7	GNP per capita 1987
Burundi	4,978	1,205	6.6	250
Comoros	424	160	–	380
Djibouti	–	–	–	–
Ethiopia	44,788	5,537	3.8	130
Kenya	22,097	7,500	4.3	340
Lesotho	1,629	270	12.9	370
Malawi	7,629	1,233	–	160
Mauritius	1,042	1,524	10.9	1,490
Rwanda	6,454	2,008	2.5	310
Somalia	5,712	1,656	–0.5	290
Eswatini	713	496	–	700
Tanzania	23,884	5,202	–3.5	220
Uganda	15,655	3,550	–0.9	260
Zambia	7,196	1,696	0.8	250
Zimbabwe	9,001	5,265	1.8	590

Source: German Institute of Global and Area Studies: Institute of African Studies (GIGA). 'The Preferential Trade Area (PTA) for Eastern and Southern Africa: Achievements, Problems and Prospects', *Spectrum*, vol. 24, no. 2 (1989): 157-71.

Focusing on regional and subregional cooperation in industrial policy and programming, the PTA became the cornerstone for rapid industrial development in Africa. With relatively stable economies, ten member states (Ethiopia, Kenya, Lesotho, Malawi, Mauritius, Somalia, Eswatini, Uganda, Zambia and Zimbabwe) of the twenty potential members of the PTA signed up on 21 December 1981. (Zimbabwe ratified the COMESA treaty in 1998 when the PTA became COMESA; Mauritius left the Treaty and joined again much later.)[176] The PTA was also formed on the basis of increasing intra-regional trade for the states of Southern and eastern Africa. Opportunities to join PTA were important for some SADCC member states since SADCC did not have a trade protocol and the ideologies of SADCC were different from those of the PTA. Eligibility for PTA membership was defined by UNECA's geographical scope outlined for eastern and Southern African states, with Comoros, Djibouti, Mauritius, Lesotho, Eswatini and Zimbabwe receiving temporary exemption from the full application of certain provisions to the Treaty. Zambia and Malawi joined the PTA when it was established in June 1981.[177] Tanzania was an active participant in the establishment of the PTA but, in the end, did not join the PTA and instead asked for an abstention. According to Anglin, Tanzania was averse to sharing trade relations with Kenya, owing to the breakdown of their relations during the collapse of EAC and the trade difficulties it had had with Kenya.[178]

During the preparation years of 1981-4, the PTA experienced various obstacles. SACU members were still linked to South Africa through the SACU 1969 agreement (as still is the case), and the Botswana, Lesotho and Swaziland (BLS) states were hesitant to sign the PTA, while Botswana refused to sign the Treaty. Comoros was reluctant to be part of the PTA because of its trade relations with France. The Marxist-Leninist countries, Angola, Madagascar, Mozambique and Seychelles also refrained from signing the PTA treaty.[179] Mozambique did not join PTA because of the civil strife, adverse climatic conditions and continuing destabilisation by the Mozambique National Resistance (MNR) and South Africa. The major critique of the PTA, as noted by Bax Nomvete,[180] was that the PTA was seen as a misnomer and not synchronised with one of its major objectives – that of promoting cooperation and development through trade liberalisation. The PTA's regional integration approach was similar to the neoclassical economic approach of trade liberalisation through growth, which was associated with regionalism of open markets and North-South trade liberalisation.

The PTA took a functional approach which entailed a step-by-step mechanism designed sectorally and inter-sectorally. As Nomvete also noted, the PTA, 'combined the careful balancing of the project-by-project approach within each sector, with inter-project and inter-sectoral programmes of trade promotion mechanisms that [were] aimed at gradual integration of all sectors in all countries'. Furthermore, as he suggested in 1983, 'it is not trade promotion or trade liberalisation measures that will increase the volume of intra-PTA trade, but self-reliant, and self-sustaining development through agricultural [and] industrial production, and transport and communications'.[181]

Intended to be one of Africa's main regional institutions, the PTA had seven main objectives:

1. Simplifying trade liberalisation and customs procedures and regulations; collection and dissemination of trade data.
2. Providing local currencies for intra-PTA business transactions; a clearing and payments system to formulate and implement measures to harmonise monetary policies and programmes.
3. Having complementary transport and communications policies and systems for cross-border movement of goods, capital, labour and services.
4. Improving on enterprise efficiency and product quality through specialised research development and training facilities designed to complement the PTA's productive sectors.
5. Increasing standards of living within PTA member states in order to promote intra-PTA trade and growth.
6. Establishing a common market by the year 2000.
7. Contributing to the progress and development of other African states.

At the end of 1992, the PTA had established seventeen legal instruments pending ratification by its member states. Angola, Comoros, Djibouti, Mozambique, Somalia and Sudan ratified some instruments. The other member states ratified none. The PTA clearinghouse was established alongside the PTA to create a set of accounts in the Unit of Account of the Preferential Trade Area (UAPTA) (equal to one standard depository receipt), mainly used as travellers cheques enabling credit and debit balances between members' central banks and in turn reflecting imports and exports financed by their national commercial banks. Debit limits were set at 25 per cent of the average value of a country's total trade. Other finance arrangements included a traveller cheque facility, from 1992 to 1996; limited currency convertibility and an informal exchange-rate union;[182] and fully fixed exchange rates, between 2000 and 2024. National fiscal and monetary policy was to be coordinated by a PTA monetary institution. By 1996 a 50 per cent tariff reduction was envisaged, which by 2000 was to be further reduced to zero tariffs. Another important factor was rules of origin of goods in trade, which were to ensure that the maximum advantage was to be afforded to those exporting companies owned and managed by member states. Furthermore, multinational corporations (MNCs) had to be managed through majority national ownership, with a percentage of equity owned by foreign nationals that was not to exceed 40 per cent; nor could foreign nationals account for more than 60 per cent of the cost of materials. Because of external relations with foreign companies, this arrangement did not work for the PTA, as it meant a loss for businesses and new business partnerships; this arrangement was revised in the 1992 COMESA Treaty and later the 40/60 national ownership and foreign national model was completely abolished.

Open general import licences had been a major problem for the region since the 1970s. With exchange rates overvalued, Africa's states resorted to implementing import permits and quotas as a principal means of importation.[183] Transport had remained an important regional infrastructure issue, as moving goods around in the region was expensive owing to inadequate infrastructure. Access to finance for foreign exchange remained an enormous problem for the states of Africa, though the clearinghouse put in place by the PTA eased this burden considerably. But PTA member states became disgruntled, complaining that the contribution was not reflective of the actual economic strengths of member states. Mozambique noted on its part that it would only join PTA if the Treaty provided derogations with regard to member states' contribution to its budget, which PTA acceded to, adopting a resolution granting these derogations. This resolution paved the way for Mozambique's accession to the PTA in 1989.[184] From 1980 to 1989, total intra-PTA exports were $641 million, but went down to $579 million. Throughout the PTA, trade was significantly less than at its formation in 1978. While Kenya was the stronger economic state, it too experienced declining trade and between the period 1980–9: exports to other member states within PTA declined from $340 million to $218 million. Similarly, Tanzania's exports dropped from $56 million to $9.4 million. During the 1980s, total PTA trade with the rest of the world was 93–95 per cent and in 1989 totalled $25 billion.[185]

Like SADCC and other regions, the weak versus strong economies diverted trade for smaller infant industries against the more industrialised member states. Djibouti complained that reducing the tariffs had drastically reduced their revenue, given its dependence on revenue. For the period 1986, the total value added for manufacturing in Kenya was $709 million; Zimbabwe, $1,444 million; Mauritius, $284 million; Tanzania, $227 million; Uganda, $152 million; Burundi, $102 million; and Lesotho, $26 million. Exports from Kenya to PTA countries for the period 1982–7 totalled $1,236.2 million and imports from PTA to Kenya for the same period totalled $129.4 million.[186] Hence dissatisfaction with PTA intra-regional trade signalled the withdrawal of Mauritius at the beginning of 1986. Contributions by member states to the PTA organisation were based on the strength of member states' economies, defined in PTA Article 36 as well as member states' national budgets of GDP – 30 per cent; per capita national income – 40 per cent; and intra-PTA exports – 30 per cent. The PTA gave SACU member states (Lesotho and Eswatini) a ten-year exemption from any tariff cuts undertaken by the PTA (which was for the period from 1982, when the PTA treaty was signed, until 1992, when the PTA treaty was to be revamped into COMESA).[187] The starting range for these tariffs was to be from 30 per cent for food items to 70 per cent for capital goods (and manufactured and consumer goods), with particular emphasis placed on development.

COMESA's institutional architecture: Economic regional convergence

COMESA was formed in 1993 as the successor to the PTA. At this time the bloc consisted of seventeen member states: Angola, Burundi, Comoros, Djibouti, Ethiopia, Kenya, Lesotho, Malawi, Mozambique, Namibia, Rwanda, Sudan, Eswatini, Uganda, Tanzania, Zambia and Zimbabwe. Not much progress in trade liberalisation was made. COMESA was seen as a fulfilment of the PTA treaty to have a common market by 2000. By 1993, the COMESA bloc had nineteen member states: Burundi, Comoros, DRC, Djibouti, Egypt, Eritrea, Ethiopia, Kenya, Libya, Madagascar, Malawi, Mauritius, Rwanda, Seychelles, Sudan, Eswatini, Uganda, Zambia and Zimbabwe. COMESA had a vast geography of 4 million square kilometres, with 220 million people, and a GDP of US$66 billion.

COMESA and SADC aimed to achieve a free trade zone for its members to facilitate specialisation, elimination of barriers and establishing non-discriminatory practices among its members. As Jacob Viner points out in his customs theory of trade diversion and trade creation, free trade agreements and arrangements are made to remove all tariff and non-tariff barriers to trade among member states within a regional grouping. With SADC member states having to implement tariffs according to SADC FTA protocols, this impacted on COMESA member states by either diverting trade or creating trade. Furthermore, international agreements allowing access to Africa's markets, such as the Lomé Convention, had already been signed by COMESA member states, and began affecting trade for the small, vulnerable economies within the COMESA and SADC blocs.[188]

COMESA member states pursued a state-led market strategy with high tariff walls erected and supported by state subsidies, grants and protection from foreign competition. But COMESA's industries were not able to gain economies of scale, lacked competition, and produced goods of poor quality with low levels of foreign direct investment.[189] The apartheid South African government also affected and contributed to the low levels of growth in the COMESA region, notably within the member states of Angola, Malawi, Mozambique, Namibia, Zambia and Zimbabwe. High levels of borrowing ensued, with a lack of foreign direct investment to back it up.[190]

By 1993, COMESA member states negotiated a list of common goods and agreed to reduce and eventually eliminate customs duties and non-trade barriers. Initially the common list was effective from 1 October 1986 to 29 September 1992, with a 25 per cent reduction in tariffs every two years, but not all member states could meet this target. So in 1987 the 25 per cent reduction target was decreased to 10 per cent, meaning that tariffs on the list of common goods would be reduced by 50 per cent by 1996. The remaining 50 per cent was to be eliminated in two steps: 20 per cent in 1998 and 30 per cent in 2000. Non-tariff barriers pertaining only to the goods on the common list included quantitative restrictions, export and import licensing, foreign exchange licensing and stipulation of import services.[191] Each state had the liberty to negotiate and maintain its own regime of barriers against non-members, which meant that member states had their own set of tariff rates together with a built-in Most-Favoured Nation (MFN) rate, softening the blow for the small member states with infant industries. COMESA had to implement a common external tariff in 2004 of 0.5, 15 and 30 but was held back by the EAC common external tariff agreed between Kenya and Uganda of 0, 10 and 25 per cent.[192]

COMESA has institutionalised concrete steps to remove non-tariff barriers and to increase trade performance. Major remaining challenges include rent seeking by customs personnel, illegal roadblocks, and harassment of cross-border traders, activities that are not regularly reported by COMESA member states.[193] Important COMESA trade facilitation programmes that have been implemented include harmonisation of road traffic charges, introduced in 1991, and implemented in fifteen member states; final axle load limits are operational in sixteen member states; carrier licence and transit plates have been required in most member states since 1998; road transit declaration documents have been required since 1986; an advanced tracking system has been implemented to monitor the movement of cargo and equipment through ports, railways, roads and lakes; a yellow-card vehicle insurance plan, covering third-party liability and medical expenses, is used by twelve member states; a customs-bond guarantee scheme has been developed to eliminate unnecessary administrative and financial costs associated with national customs-bond guarantees for transit traffic; and an automated data management system (ASYCUDA) has been implemented to record statistics on customs declarations, customs accounting procedures, examination controls, warehousing, import and export licences and permits, and foreign trade processing procedures. As a result of this timely generation of trade and customs revenue statistics, goods are now cleared more quickly, more accurately and more reliably.

In addition to the harmonisation of trade standards among its member states, COMESA had also implemented a uniform system for classification of goods; customs declaration documents used for clearance, transit and warehousing of exports and imports have been simplified and standardised, replacing all declaration documents previously used by member states. A stance on common competition rules has been taken, and technical norms and certification procedures have been streamlined. In addition, business relations through strengthening of the Eastern and Southern African Business Organisation, chambers of commerce, and other trade promotion and business advisory groups have been enhanced.

COMESA's Regional Payment and Settlement System (REPSS) links member states' national payment systems to regional central banks to effect payment and settlement of trade, and includes banks in Asia and Europe as well as in Africa. REPSS is a complete and innovative online system with standards based on those of the Society for Worldwide Interbank Financial Telecommunication (SWIFT). The COMESA clearinghouse serves as the agent of the central banks in formulating bilateral agreements. All COMESA central banks are expected to facilitate payments for goods and services traded by transferring payments under the REPSS system. The dependence of COMESA and SADC member states on trade taxes is substantial and could be a major hurdle for liberalising tariff structures, since the majority of COMESA and SADC countries, aside from South Africa, are completely dependent on trade taxes to generate revenue. Eight countries are dependent on trade taxes for over 20 per cent of their revenue; only Rwanda, Uganda, South Africa and Tanzania generate less than 2 per cent of their GDP through trade taxes. Given COMESA and SADC's substantial dependence on trade-tax revenue, together with the 6 per cent decline in total revenue anticipated from the SADC free trade area – liberalisation of tariffs requires sound macroeconomic policies.[194] The regional payment mechanism would therefore benefit the region and serve as a support to those member states dependent on trade revenue, and contribute to their fiscus.

Rationalisation period of 1993 and 1994 of SADCC and PTA: A failed convergence

During the rationalisation process, in February 1991, when South Africa announced its decision to renounce apartheid governance and to embrace democracy, regionalism became centred on three regional schemes of the SACU, the FLS, and the PTA for eastern and Southern African States. The SADCC and PTA regional blocs were very closely linked in geography and colonial heritage.[195] South Africa's role became a major question for both PTA and SADCC, given the uncertainty about how it would conduct itself regionally and as a new player in the post-apartheid era. SADCC was grappling with the form and shape of a new South Africa and regional pressure concerned recent memories of the devastation of past disruption of regional trade routes.[196]

Fear played a role in the policy formulation and in the interactions of Southern African states, which were previously subject to military and economic domination by South Africa. Divergence and convergence literature on economic growth models suggests that for poorer countries to grow their economies, industrialisation as well as trade liberalisation policies should be implemented simultaneously to allow for advancing technology and development among other endogenous growth factors such as skills development, which are equally important for economic growth.[197]

While manufacturing in Southern Africa was dominated by South Africa during the 1980s,[198] South Africa's manufacturing sector was not so developed, as seen in Table 3.2, and had little value added to its manufactured products. Zambia had to rely on wire and cabling from South Africa for inputs into its copper manufacturing and electrical cabling. South Africa only scored the highest in percentage of manufacturing valued added composition as seen in ISIC Category 7 (non-metallic minerals) and

Table 3.2 Composition of manufacturing value added (MVA), 1987

Country	Percentage of composition of manufactured products per ISIC category (MVA), 1987									
	1 & 2 – Foodstuffs; beverages and tobacco	3 – textiles and clothing	4 – leather and footwear	5 – wood, wooden products, and furniture	6 – paper, printing, and publishing	7 – non-metallic minerals	8 – chemicals, rubber, and pharmaceuticals	9 – metals and metal products	10 – machinery and transport equipment	11 – other or not classified
Angola	30	18	–	7	4	12	6*	6	16	1
Botswana	54	9	–	–	2	6	–	4	2	23
Lesotho	71	12	1	2	1	6	2	3	–	2
Malawi	34	14	3	2	7	24	7	3	3	3
Mozam-bique	41	23	*	8	*	11	4	11	*	2
Namibia	65	6	3	4	4	7	6	2	1	2
Eswatini	58	2	*	2	12	10	4	1	9	1
Tanzania	34	17	4	3	8	13	1	7	11	2
Zambia	35	18	3	4	4	15	8	12	10	1
Zimbabwe	33	12	3	3	6	14	4	18	5	1
South Africa	14	7	2	3	9	22	5	18	19	1
Kenya	40	9	2	3	7	16	4	6	6	7
Mauritius	27	51	8	1	1	5	1	3	2	1

Notes: International Standard Industrial Classification (ISIC) categories: 1 = foodstuffs; 2 = beverages and tobacco; 3 = textiles and clothing; 4 = leather and footwear; 5 = wood, wooden products, and furniture; 6 = paper, printing, and publishing; 7 = non-metallic minerals; 8 = chemicals, rubber, and pharmaceuticals; 9 = metals and metal products; 10 = machinery and transport equipment; and 11 = other or not classified. * Excludes petro-chemicals accounting for almost 50 per cent of MVA.
Source: African Development Bank, *Economic Integration in Southern Africa*, vol. 2 (Oxford: Oxprint, 1993), pp. 249–71.

was on par with Zimbabwe in ISIC Category 9 (metals and metal products). Most of the other remaining categories, as shown in Table 3.2, demonstrate that Southern African states scored higher than South Africa in value added to manufacturing goods. South Africa's MVA was much lower than that of its neighbours, and comparatively its industrial base lacked sophistication and complexity.[199]

South Africa's reliance on manufactured exports had been much higher than that of its SADCC neighbours. This heavy reliance on the region, including the SACU member states, was a base from which to export its manufactured goods in extensively serving the needs of the domestic market. This had caused a decrease in the quality of South Africa's manufactured goods, unlike the higher-quality goods of its neighbours (foodstuffs and beverages; tobacco; textiles and clothing) as shown in Table 3.2. The following statistics should be considered in planning the future relations between COMESA, EAC and SADC in order to strengthen the trade framework and regional integration.

According to the World Bank,[200] the combined total manufacturing value-added (MVA) of SADCC and South Africa was $23 billion in 1989 – one-third that of Brazil and Spain, and less than half that of South Korea. Moreover, in 1988, SADCC and South Africa's manufactured exports constituted only 4.5 per cent of total production in SADCC and South Africa – compared with 11 per cent for all developing countries in the world, ranging from 16 per cent for all of Asia, and 8 per cent for all of Latin America and the Caribbean. MVA levels for SADCC and South Africa were largely attributed to substantial labour, skill, and resource deficiencies. Also 88 per cent of total exports in 1988 went from South Africa to SADCC. In the 1990s, Botswana, for example, lost to South Africa in a bid to host an auto assembly plant for South Korea's Hyundai Corporation.[201] SADCC states have not yet had the opportunity to address economic policies that could alter low levels of development and technology, and these have not remedied the region's weak economies either.

A SADCC review report on public and private sector cross-border investment projects observed that there was a huge skills deficit in technology and skills levels between SADCC and industrialised countries. Angola, Mozambique and Malawi had widespread skills shortages. The report also noted a general skills shortage observed in Botswana (with the exception of public administration, agricultural technology and mining engineering), Lesotho (with the exception of agricultural and metallurgical engineering), Eswatini (with the exception of mining engineering and agricultural research), and Zambia (with the exception of senior management and the financial sector).[202] Figure 3.3 shows that SADCC member states conducted trade in agriculture in fish and fish preparations ($65,493 million, mainly Malawi and Angola) and in cereals and cereal preparations ($147,490 million), textiles and wastes ($129,240 million) and ores and scrap metal ($228,223 million), constituting opportunities for future manufacturing and trade agreements in the region.[203] South Africa's accession into SADCC and later SADC was to allow for integration and economic convergence. But convergence was commensurate with policy implementation at the national level of the state. Such policies included domestic trade and regional policies, to improve on movement of goods and services by rail, road and port, but these policies that could determine growth were not implemented. As outlined by David Dollar,[204] effective

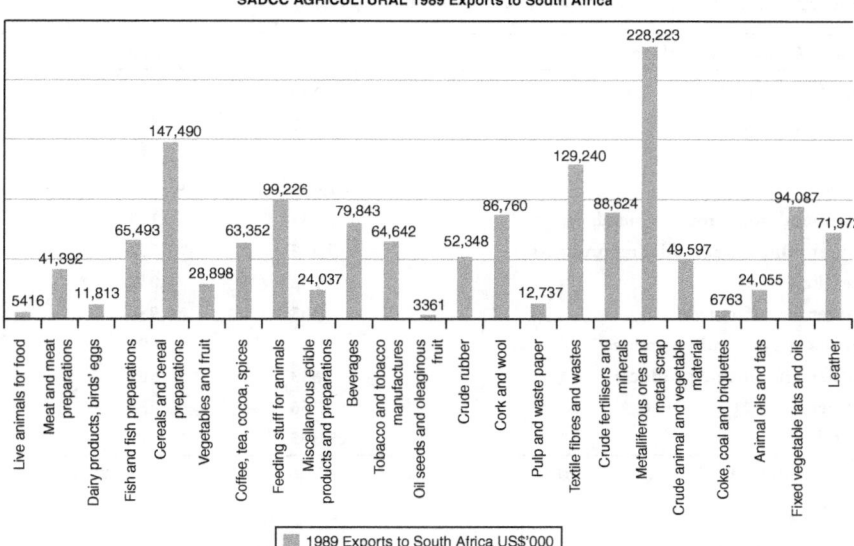

Figure 3.3 SADCC's agricultural exports to South Africa, 1989.

Source: African Development Bank, *Economic Integration in Southern Africa,* vol. 2 (Oxford: Oxprint, 1993), p. 90.

trade policies can promote convergence in trade openness. The implications for Africa's political economy have been due to monopolistic behaviours seen in the post-colonial era that was still linked to the African economy, which have been perpetuated and have opened avenues for exploitative practices and been exacerbated by the adoption of neoclassical economic approaches of liberal trade policies.[205]

While African states have pursued various models of economic development, the progression of economic structural adjustment programmes of the 1980s exacerbated the political and economic weaknesses of the state.[206] Khadiagala observed that the weakness of the state is central to the wealth of power. In 1987 SADCC states had a total GDP of $23 billion, an area of over 4 million square kilometres and a population of about 25 million people.[207]

In 1984 South Africa dominated most of the sectors of the Southern African economy, for example, trade import and exports (see Table 3.3). SADCC was most dependent on the region's transport infrastructure, and as observed by Khadiagala, South Africa was dependent on the region's leading export markets in 1990 with bilateral trade that was conducted mainly with Zimbabwe for its exports (see Table 3.4).

South Africa's trade to the rest of the world, shown in Table 3.5, was quite extensive in 1990, despite the imposition of Western sanctions because of its apartheid policies. A number of institutions in South Africa played an important role in its trade drive. Examples were the South African Foreign Trade Organisation (SAFTO) and its Chamber of Commerce.[208] During the rationalisation discussions and meetings there was a strong regional sentiment that was focused on the regional trade that a new

Table 3.3 South Africa's regional trade, 1984 (million rand)

South Africa's regional trade	Exports	Imports
Machinery	309	6,397
Transport equipment	169	2,653
Chemicals	672	1,785
Gold	11,684	–
Diamonds and precious metals	2,387	129
Other minerals and mineral products	5,515	1,721
Textiles	762	1,037
Other manufactures	808	2,980
Fruits, grains, and vegetables	480	996
Other agricultural products	833	801
Other	1,766	3,254
Total	25,395	21,717

Source: Joseph Hanlon, *Beggar Your Neighbours: Apartheid Power in South Africa* (London: Currey, 1986), p. 281.

Table 3.4 South Africa's leading export markets in Africa, 1990

Countries	1990 Exports (million US$)	1990 Imports (million US$)
Zimbabwe	403.5	167.8
Zambia	187.8	2.5
Zaire	172.1	8.2
Mozambique	164.2	11.5
Malawi	143.7	30.1
Mauritius	114.5	5.4

Source: African Development Bank, *Economic Integration in Southern Africa*, vol. 2 (Oxford: Oxprint, 1993), p. 29.

South Africa could integrate into SADCC, with equitable agreements put in place in respect of trade, transport and investment.[209]

As a start to the run-up to the rationalisation process, the 1991 SADCC Summit meeting deemed it important to establish a Joint Planning Committee (JPC) comprising Botswana (chairman), Mozambique, Zambia and Zimbabwe, and the ANC and the Pan-Africanist Congress (PAC).[210] The JPC commissioned two consultants,[211] and were tasked to identify, analyse and assess the interests and concerns of the SADCC member states. While the SADCC member states were contemplating how to incorporate South Africa into a new SADC, member states were also urged to refrain from contact with South Africa. The international community had placed sanctions on the South African government until a new political dispensation could be formed in the country.

With varying economic strengths among the SADCC members, the main concern was to provide an integration process that considered economic integration that encouraged development, while taking into account the differences in size of member states' economies. South Africa was in a different and much higher economic structure

Table 3.5 South Africa's trade to the rest of the world, 1990

Goods imported	Value 1990 (million US$)	Goods exported	Value 1990 (million US$)
Machinery and equipment	5,196.35	Machinery and equipment	542.88
Unclassified goods, mainly oil and arms	2,291.31	Unclassified (mainly gold, platinum, uranium, and arms)	9,733.62
Vehicles and transport equipment	2,225.07	Vehicles and transport equipment	439.41
Chemicals	1,865.95	Chemicals	736.32
Mining and quarrying (excluding precious stones and metals)	1,329.74	Diamonds and other	2,253.73
Agricultural products	939.94	Agricultural products	1,742.21
Textiles	781.68	Textiles (including wool)	628.68
Rubber and plastic	740.77	Base metal	3,538.47
Professional and scientific equipment	710.50	Machinery and equipment	542.88
Pulp and paper	486.88	Pulp and paper	642.95
Intermediate manufacturing materials	236.42	Intermediate manufacturing materials	443.00
Miscellaneous manufacturing articles	190.28	Other	231.70
Other	271.60		
Total	17,266.49	Total	21,475.85

Source: African Development Bank, *Economic Integration in Southern Africa*, vol. 2 (Oxford: Oxprint, 1993), p. 29.

than the other member states in SADCC. Simba Makoni, executive secretary of SADCC, expressed his position clearly, that 'a democratic South Africa, free of apartheid and the dream of economic and military hegemony over its neighbours would be welcome to join the Organisation'.[212] During the rationalisation period, SADCC was also faced with the challenge of huge food shortages of around 2.8 million tonnes recorded for the periods between 1991 and 1992. With the prospect of South Africa's joining post 1994, SADCC member states agreed that the current dominance of South Africa over the rest of the region would be both undesirable and unacceptable, and also undesirable even with a democratic South Africa as a member. During these deliberations, there was also uncertainty with regard to Namibia's ports and offshore islands. Namibia had gained its independence in 1990 and was still battling to retrieve Walvis Bay and the offshore islands from South Africa, which were integral to Namibia's economic development. SADCC stressed the need for the international community to pressure South Africa to restore sovereignty over Walvis Bay and the offshore islands to Namibia.[213]

With a new South African dispensation after 1994, the SADCC JPC recommended that the restructuring of SADCC's existing arrangements should be negotiated in 'baskets or calabashes of issues' with a strong coordinating mechanism to facilitate trade-offs across the different baskets (calabashes) and that ensured overall growth and development for the region as a whole.[214] The SADCC JPC's Macro-Framework Study Report was a broad policy and strategy document, which was seen as an important instrument to facilitate the smooth engagement of incorporating South Africa into future regional relations.

Makoni reiterated the importance of the Macro-Framework Study Report as a regional instrument to be taken into account and incorporated into future protocols or agreements envisaged by SADCC and its successor organisation, SADC. The importance of having a partner state was significant for the SADCC leaders. In 1989 for example, the average per capita GNP was $647 among SADCC states.[215] Local industries in several SADC member states were not well placed to compete against the increasing imports from South Africa's industries. A more comprehensive study conducted on income convergence that focused on twenty-eight regional integration agreements (RIAs) since the notification of the GATT/WTO, analysed the effects on trade liberalisation in South-South and North-North trade cooperation. This study was conducted by Fabrizio Carmignami and also included SADC, COMESA, and SACU RIAs. The results indicated no evidence for income convergence among COMESA countries, and weak convergence in the case of the SACU and the SADC blocs.[216] Lesotho, Malawi, Mozambique, Tanzania and Zambia had extremely low levels of per capita income in contrast with South Africa's $2,530.[217]

Besides the integration of a democratic South Africa into SADC, there were also discussions centred on the PTA and SADCC's restructuring role and how South Africa would impact on these two organisations. Open regionalism can be broadly defined as trade liberalisation that has easy market access in trade of goods and services, with a few exceptions for sensitive products. Open regionalism also has proponents of commitment to the MFN clause and principle as per the WTO rules for regional trade arrangements. Within the region, open regionalism, which signifies liberal trade, had reduced not only tariffs in trade, but also transaction costs at the borders. Deep integration goes beyond the mere issue of multilateral agreements. It means, first and foremost, an attempt at and willingness by Africa's leaders to integrate and to conduct trade. According to Nomvete,[218] implementation guidelines for deeper integration were already in force and agreed to by African leaders when UNECA was established. At the May 1963 meeting that inaugurated the OAU, leaders had viewed economic cooperation as a critical development strategy for addressing Africa's weak economies. Furthermore, at four OAU Summits in 1970, 1973, 1977 and 1979, it was decided that to establish an African Economic Community (AEC), five successive stages would be necessary: a Preferential Free Trade Area, Free Trade Area, Customs Union, Common Market, and Economic Community; these would begin at the regional level of Western, Eastern, Southern, Central and Northern Africa.[219] The EU integrationists did not adopt the strict linear progression model of region building that SADC and PTA was forced to embark through Europe's push – in making funding available – disguised in trade liberalisation at the regional level. Europe embarked on three phases:

Firstly a customs union was formed which eliminated tariffs and established a common external tariff between 1958 and 1968; then came a period of relative stagnation in the 1970s, when a number of non-tariff barriers prevented further progress; and thirdly, only much later in the 1980s, the single European market programme of 1992 was created.[220]

Africa's integration journey started in April 1980 at the first extraordinary OAU Economic Summit that was held in Lagos. At this summit, African leaders agreed to implement the guidelines adopted at the various OAU meetings during the 1970s and to incorporate a sound plan of action – the Lagos Plan of Action (LPA) where all African governments had to belong to regional economic communities by 1990. This would later be followed by an African Continental Community. For the PTA bloc, it meant that SADCC would naturally join the PTA organisation.[221] The decision to merge these two organisations was discussed in January 1992, at a PTA Summit meeting in Lusaka. PTA considered itself a 'better organised grouping'. PTA covered a geographic territory with a larger market and opportunities for economies of scale, and felt superior to SADCC in this regard. Previously, SADCC had been concerned about regional sectoral coordination; PTA, on the other hand, had concerns regarding regional trade liberalisation, and the two organisations' roles differed. But with SADCC taking on a trade role when it created SADC, major rivalries of competition and competing conflicts of interest in trade and investment were unleashed.

According to Peter Meyns, the SADC August 1992 Summit appeared to be a rushed decision, with the change of an old SADCC to a new SADC organisation, and from a ten-member state to a formal regional grouping. The old SADCC was largely concerned about how it would justify its existence and manage its donor agenda; it had concerns regarding donor fatigue in competing against the Eastern bloc countries of the PTA. As suggested by Meyns,[222] the erstwhile SADCC hastily formed the SADC and believed that it happened to have forestalled PTA (and the planned establishment of COMESA). Also noted by Meyns, was that an added factor to the precipitous transformation was the view that there had been no prior discussion of the SADC draft agreement among a broader public in the member states and hence it was believed that SADCC had decided to form the organisation without gauging public opinion.[223] There was also a major concern in an old SADCC to be seen competing for funds from donors and justifying its existence, programmes and goals in a new dispensation, since SADCC was no longer fighting for the liberation movements and against the apartheid regime in a post-apartheid South Africa. SADCC therefore needed a new raison d'être within a new SADC.

However, Makoni contended[224] that the transformation of SADCC to SADC occurred during the rationalisation process that considered two major issues (PTA and SADCC's merging, and South Africa's joining either organisation). It had less to do with donor funds, but rather wished to address how South Africa would fit into Southern Africa after its democratic elections. SADCC was largely concerned with the huge shortage of food in the region during this time.[225] At the SADCC

Windhoek Summit of 17 August 1992, the member states accepted the report of the Joint Council of Ministers on the re-formalisation of SADCC and agreed that the report adequately addressed the issues and concerns of the region with regard to South Africa's admission. The Summit agreed that the JPC report formed a sufficient basis to strengthen SADCC and provided the new SADC with appropriate legal status and other necessary instruments to create a REC of Southern African states. Hence the Windhoek Summit immediately approved and signed a new declaration, a treaty, and a protocol committing member states to more formal arrangements for cooperation and integration under the framework of a new organisation, SADC. The SADC Treaty specified six important factors and considerations.[226] The importance of South Africa's joining the organisation was reaffirmed at the 1992 Windhoek Summit. The Summit 'agreed that it was necessary to clarify that relations between SADCC and South Africa will be normalised only when a democratically elected government was in place'.[227]

The 1992 Windhoek Summit also approved a 1993 SADC Annual Consultative Conference, namely, 'SADC: A Framework and Strategy for Building a Community in Southern Africa', which articulated regional issues and proposed a timetable as well as the necessary steps required to build an economic community for Southern Africa. The Windhoek Summit in 1992 outlined clear objectives for the region's future engagements. It acknowledged that (i) the SADC Treaty should provide an agreement on protocols on specific areas of integration, which should set out principles and objectives for integration, and determine the rules under which member states were to conduct relations; (ii) member states were required to sign the follow-up plan of the Treaty, which provided a timetable for negotiations and protocols; (iii) priority had to be provided by member states for popular participation in ensuring that SADC citizens formed part of the regional integration process and were informed of the direction of the SADC integration process; (iv) movement of people within the region was to be facilitated and encouraged; (v) member states had to work toward progressively removing all barriers to the flow of capital, goods and services; and (vi) regional peace and security processes were to be prioritised by member states. These principles of engagement set the tone for member states for future engagement in regional integration. Also expressed at the 1992 Windhoek Summit was the hope that a democratic South Africa would join SADC in order to build a new economic order based on balance, equity and mutual benefit.[228]

Furthermore, the 1992 Windhoek Summit acknowledged the proposal of the authority of the PTA for Eastern and Southern African states that requested SADCC and PTA merge into COMESA. The SADCC member states at the 1992 Windhoek Summit objected to this proposal of PTA's calling for a merger, and reaffirmed their position that the two organisations, SADCC and PTA, had different objectives and mandates and should therefore continue to exist as autonomous but complementary entities.[229] In the end, and as documented in SADC's Windhoek Declaration of 1992, there was consensus that SADCC and the PTA conduct an independent commission to study SADCC and the PTA, and advise on how best to harmonise relations between the two regional communities, and also to address in the process and in going forward, how to establish the AEC.[230] Also, avoidance of duplication of efforts in the activities of the two organisations was to be an important consideration in the joint independent commission study.²³¹

At the 5 September 1993 SADC Summit in Mbabane, Eswatini, acknowledgement of the Macro-Framework Study, namely the JPC on Regional Relations Post-Apartheid,²³² and acceptance thereof by the SADC member states were made in agreeing to South Africa as the eleventh member state of SADC. The macro-framework study report was regarded as a broad policy and strategy document for future evolving arrangements for the smooth engagement of a democratic South Africa, and as an important input to planning for the integration of SADC member states, both for South Africa and the cooperating states and partners. The macro-framework study was seen as a resource to be used for future SADC discussion, analysis and policy formulation on future regional relations.²³³

Member states considered an SADC Resident Mission comprising diplomatic and trade missions of SADC countries in South Africa important, and this was established in Pretoria to monitor closely the events as they unfolded in achieving a democratic government in South Africa.²³⁴ There were regional fears that donor sympathies would become lukewarm post 1994, when South Africa joined.²³⁵ As noted by Fadzai Gwaradzimba, SADC faced three major options with regard to the new South Africa: South Africa could join SADC and assume its economic leadership role; South Africa's hegemony could be appealing to the Botswana, Lesotho, Namibia and Eswatini (BLNE) member states and as members of SACU; and SADC could also be faced with an FLS membership that might entail a redefinition of goals to address membership overlap with South Africa's bilateral deals.²³⁶ At the SADC Eswatini Summit in 1993, member states expressed their concern at the lack of funding for the SPA that initially had 518 projects, but had dwindled to only 464 by July 1993, and that required a budget of more than $8.8 billion.²³⁷ There were also growing concerns with regard to Angola, Botswana, Lesotho and Eswatini's emergency drought relief strategies. In 1994 Malawi, Mozambique, Tanzania and Zambia, were the worst hit by the adverse climatic conditions, with those regions experiencing huge food shortages and in particular a shortfall in cereal production.²³⁸

The rationalisation of SADCC and the PTA's existing regional mechanisms centred on 'what programme and approach to be adopted in building cooperation and integration and how organisational activities were to guide a rationalised regional organisation that takes into account different approaches of these two institutions'.²³⁹ At the meeting it was asked, 'Should a rationalization/merger be undertaken in anticipation of the entry of a democratic South Africa or should it be something that occurs in the process of or after South Africa's admission?'²⁴⁰ The timing of this debate was significant, happening just one year prior to both triumph and tragedy in April 1994 – the democratic elections in South Africa, the civil war in Burundi and the DRC that started in 1996 (involving seven African states: Angola, Burundi, Namibia, Rwanda, Uganda and Zimbabwe and also Chad), and the onset of the genocide in Rwanda. Angola and Mozambique were also emerging from domestic intra-state violent conflict and Angola from civil war. At the February 1993 meeting between SADC and the PTA, the PTA favoured a merger. As discussed earlier when talking about the PTA, Zimbabwe and Mozambique had doubts about the usefulness of the PTA (but they later joined). Botswana refused to join the PTA. The JPC also adopted the Council of Ministers in January 1994 – a strategy and policy framework for regional relations and cooperation post-apartheid.[241] During the SADC/COMESA rationalisation process, South Africa was going through its own rationalisation processes of its SANDF, its police force, and foreign and trade ministries. Democratic and political transformation, and socio-economic issues and security were more pressing issues for the country. The Southern African bank – and the Independent Development Trust (IDT) was also being transformed into the DBSA, to engage the region by helping address regional infrastructure development in particular.[242] South Africa had major setbacks in its socio-economic disparities in 1994 and these remained huge. A massive 80 per cent of South Africa's economy was still owned by four conglomerates from the apartheid era (Anglo American, Rembrandt, Sanlam and SA Mutual).[243]

South Africa was faced with domestic challenges and diverging interests in its own foreign policy – a dilemma that was confronted with a plethora of highly powerful business elite groups and conglomerates against a huge labour-intensive working class. South Africa was also simultaneously negotiating trade agreements with Europe. South Africa was eager to find the correct balance at the regional level to serve its national interests.[244] The post-apartheid government's national interests were dominant in its working class, who were strong supporters of its ANC party and trade union, Congress of South African Trade Unions (COSATU) that was formed in 1985.[245] South Africa also confirmed its standing and did not want to be saddled with a merger and focus on a joint COMESA, EAC and SADC when it was going through a difficult transition. It also had concerns around its military, police and security sector reform processes. During South Africa's deliberations, the government was presented with a political compromise in its regional role. It was also important to consider market cooperation as a regional approach that could benefit South Africa's business elite while also benefiting its own working class. These discussions were documented in Gavin Maasdorp's report on which way the pendulum swayed for South Africa's regionalism.[246] Rob Davies, South Africa's minister of trade and industry, was previously part of the Macro-Economic Research Group (MERG) and held views in support of COSATU and labour unions during the 1990s.[247] The decision makers in South Africa's regional developmental cooperation comprised the ANC-dominated government, guided by its Reconstruction and Development Programme (RDP);[248] COSATU, representing labour; South Africa's members of parliament, with the former chair of the trade and industrial policy group, Ben Turok; and Rob Davies, former chair of the portfolio committee on trade, also representing labour; also included were the Afrikaners, under the banner of the Afrikaanse Handelsinstituut (AHI) represented the Afrikaner business elite. The English business elite was represented by Anglo American, with Gavin Reilly as executive, and called for an ad-hoc regional integration approach as he noted that 'political reform in South Africa has opened up further opportunities for cooperation in the fields of tourism, transport, electricity supply, and the development and use of scare water resources ... sinews that bind ... the region ... need progress [and not] castles in the air'.[249] Trevor Manuel, former South African finance minister, advised that South Africa should steer away from joining any regional grouping.[250]

Furthermore, there were two parallel sets of trade negotiations happening simultaneously relating to SADC and the EU. South Africa's Industrial Development Corporation (IDC), reinforced by the DBSA, both opted for a SADC free trade area, since South Africa stood to gain and increase its GDP through total exports and manufactured exports. SACU countries were to fall short and be negatively affected in de-industrialisation trade processes. The Department of Trade and Industry (DTI) also supported the regional developmental approach led by former DTI minister, Alec Erwin, who noted, 'There is an acknowledgment that there are unequal starting points and that in the long run the benefits are better for all if the economically weaker partner is assisted to develop in the early stages.' Faizel Ismail, South African deputy director of the Department of International Relations and Cooperation (DIRCO) and former chief director of Foreign Trade Relations, noted that the South African delegation to the EU should be 'diplomats in service of development'.[251] Maasdorp's 1993 study outlined several problems that South African farmers within a SADC FTA could face, which related to 'sensitive agricultural subsidies and clothing imports from Zimbabwe specifically and for South Africa's textile and footwear industries that would be economically strained'.[252] With regard to Europe, the trade negotiators also highlighted strain on South Africa's labour-intensive industry in areas linked to textiles, cars, television assembly and parts, oil production from coal, footwear, small arms and ammunition, dairy products, beef and veal, and sugar. South Africa's alignment of its regional developmental approach with its own trade deals with the EU ultimately led to the Trade, Development and Cooperation Agreement (TDCA) in 1999. As one government official noted, 'We are not in the Father Christmas business ... surely, it is imperative that South Africa looks after its people who have suffered for centuries instead of bailing out corrupt bureaucrats who got freedom decades ago.'[253]

A report of the Joint Study on Harmonisation, Coordination and Rationalisation of the activities of the two organisations was studied[254] at the Gaborone SADC Summit of 29 August 1994, the decision was unanimous that the current PTA should be divided into two regions: (i) a PTA for the South comprising all SADC member states. Preferential trade arrangements in the South region were to be carried out under the auspices of SADC. The process of separating the two regions into North and South was to evolve over time, and the modalities regarding which area SADC member states would wish to belong to, had to be determined by individual member states as their sovereign right; and (ii) a PTA for the North comprising non-SADC countries.[255]

A decision was taken that SADC and the PTA should be split into North and South. The region that covered the geographical area of COMESA should be split into PTA North and PTA South, the latter comprising the current SADC member states. At the August 1995 Summit, however, SADC agreed to the proposal of the COMESA Authority for a joint SADC/COMESA Summit meeting on the future of the two organisations. In 1995 the PTA sent yet another proposal requesting to merge SADC with COMESA. Again it was agreed at the August 1995 meeting that SADC reaffirmed its previous position and decision to remain as separate institutions. Instead, a joint committee of ministers was appointed – five from each organisation, assisted by an equal number of officials from each side to address and recommend appropriate terms of reference for approval by the two chairpersons.[256] SADC's main concerns with regard to the merger were as follows:

> the many countries the PTA encompassed, and the geographical spread of the organisation, which made the PTA too complex and unwieldy to manage. The size and geographical spread of the organisation also made coordination and harmonisation of its activities very difficult. The situation would be compounded if the SADC member states maintained dual membership of both organisations. ... [The] Summit underlined ... the political, economic and cultural diversity of the countries which constituted the PTA. This factor made cohesion difficult; and cohesion was essential for meaningful and sustainable regional cooperation and integration.[257]

Furthermore, the SADC Summit heads of state had concerns about trade promotion within the PTA. The programme had not made satisfactory progress because member states were granted derogations from compliance under the provisions of the Treaty, principally to protect arrangements with third parties. This practice cast doubt on the viability of the trade programme in the PTA. SADC was equally concerned with dual membership, which was costly for member states in terms of time, human, material and financial resources. The international cooperating partners were also disillusioned because of uncertainty and lack of clarity on the future of the two organisations.[258] Members of SADC had to decide which organisation to join, and Seychelles and Mauritius (who attended their first SADC Summit with intentions of joining the organisation), were also given the option of which organisation to join.

The joint SADC/COMESA Ministerial Committee met in Harare from 31 July to 1 August 1996 to discuss and agree on an agenda and a programme for the Joint SADC/COMESA Summit. The SADC/COMESA Ministerial Committee was tasked to assess how best to harmonise relations between the two organisations and work towards the creation of an AEC as was outlined in the Abuja 1991 Treaty.[259] At the SADC Summit in Maseru, an agreement was reached among member states to allow the Joint SADC/COMESA Ministerial Committee complete its work, and for its report to be discussed once the work had been completed.[260]

Within the new SADC of 1992, and as a legal organisation, South Africa was afforded a regional investment and financial coordinating role. Since May 1995, South Africa within SADC had exerted a coordinating responsibility for financial integration and investment. SADC was looking at working towards a well-coordinated approach to link its financial markets. For SADC, a macroeconomic policy to work effectively for a regional grouping that could promote trade through compatible financial systems was deemed important to increase trade; however, this was too premature for the infant economies of SADC to implement.[261]

SADC was struggling to liberalise trade and address rules of engagement and equitable trade exchanges amidst infrastructure weaknesses, and was not yet at the stage of conforming to macroeconomic convergence. The Tripartite Common Monetary Area (between South Africa, Lesotho, Eswatini and Namibia) was seen as a means that could inform implementation of a unified exchange rate structure for SADC in the future. The Common Monetary Area (CMA) was viewed as a possible vehicle to facilitate financial integration for SADC member states and alleviate the debt burden and fiscal deficits. According to Maria Ramos, central to macroeconomic convergence for SADC would be careful consideration of five broad areas integral to the financial integration process.

These areas entailed financial reform and development that could stimulate the liquid financial markets, provide incentives for trade, attract surplus capital, and guarantee investments, with focused attention on both long- and short-term markets; increased supervisory powers to protect investors and consumers; a database to assist SADC in creating a regulatory framework; formal and informal mechanisms towards a coordination of fiscal policies; and greater investment in human resource capacity building as well as greater access to funds in international markets.[262] However, these processes appeared to be superficial for SADC member states as outlined by Ramos, given the huge disparity in economic size and varying trade ratios. Ramos suggested that for a monetary area to work, a redistributional arrangement to facilitate and expand trade and industry should complement regional integration.

At the 1997 SADC Summit in Blantyre, the Summit provided a report on SADC/COMESA relations and expressed satisfaction that COMESA (the sister organisation) had amicably reached a common understanding on the need to co-exist, while ensuring maximum coordination and harmonisation of their respective programmes of action. At the 1997 SADC Summit it was also noted that the SADC Secretariat would liaise with the COMESA Secretariat on areas of mutual interest to avoid duplication of efforts.[263] The year 1997 was also an important period for SADC, since it was the first time that OAU's AEC had met in Harare. SADC in particular had made huge strides towards developing closer relations with the AEC as well as with the OAU and other economic groupings, as part of its contribution towards the establishment of a continental economic community.[264]

The historical periods of the PTA and SADCC, shows that while trade was being conducted between these two blocs, the timing of the integration was not able to allow for convergence between the poorer and richer economies. Southern Africa's destroyed infrastructure of roads and railways was repaired at a snail's pace because of high costs. While lower labour costs could lead to an increase in economic convergence, industries were producing similar products with very little diversity.

The evolving Pan-African and regional integration processes that were linked to reviving Pan-Africanism, was seen as an ideology for achieving political solidarity and economic independence through the failure of the EAC and incorporating those countries into the PTA of 1981 and the SADCC of 1980. These two organisations were formed at a time when their members belonged to SACU as well as to a Common Monetary Area. SADCC took on a sector-led coordination approach to regionalism and the PTA took on open trade and liberalised markets in a step-by-step approach.[265] As Khadiagala noted, 'From the Mulungushi Club to the FLS and then SADCC, regionalism has been animated by the convergence of interests and decisions, among a core elite leadership.'[266] SADCC further demonstrated that in liberalising markets, smaller economies confronted economic setbacks with cheaper goods flooding smaller markets; this was explained and expanded on in the literature on divergence and convergence.

The events throughout the attempted region-building processes of PTA and SADC relate to approaches of power, state and wealth incorporated into Africa's states and economy. At times, external forces of trade liberalisation within the neoclassical economic framework of trade liberalisation policies of external actors like the Nordic countries with the aid for trade funding structures and in their relations with PTA and SADCC member states, did not strengthen these economies, but caused divergence for the members. The PTA's approach to regional integration was a functional approach in pursuing the self-interest of the state of trade liberalisation, which is associated with open markets and North-South trade liberalisation. The dissolving of the EAC resulted in member countries moving closer to COMESA. Similarly, a functional cooperation approach of SADCC, defined its sectoral coordination programme, and a developmental approach was adopted when it became SADC. South in the SADCC region with Africa's mercantilist policies, prior to South Africa's membership of SADC was largely dependent on the economies of SADCC. While there was a level of convergence of PTA and SADCC, member states were conducting trade among themselves and with external world partners. However, eastern and Southern African states were converging with their respective newly formed institutions – SADC and COMESA – and were not at a stage to converge trade policy to improve their economies by capitalising on their own comparative and absolute advantages and uniqueness of trade that could further boost manufactured goods. Both PTA and SADCC member states had memberships in both communities when COMESA was formed in 1993, and, for example, three SADCC members (Malawi, Zambia and Tanzania were active participants) before South Africa joined SADC in 1994, and Zimbabwe later joined as a COMESA member in 1998.

Similarly, in 1997 the SADC region was not in a position to merge with COMESA or sign any trade agreements owing to various internal and external factors and actors. It was also discussed that SADC was an organisation that was born out of the FLS and was formed to fight for the liberation of the region and against apartheid practices, and was unlike COMESA, which was created to conduct trade among its member states. During the rationalisation processes of PTA and SADCC, questions emerged with regard to South Africa's potentially negative impact on COMESA, on SADC, and on SACU. Lesotho, Namibia, Mozambique and Tanzania withdrew from COMESA because of the tariff settings of COMESA with which they could not conform. The position was that their economies were poorly equipped; this also led to SADCC's sectoral division of labour becoming more national than regional with a view to supporting the poor economies of SADCC. Zacarias also noted that the lack of cooperation beyond meetings and summits was associated with the poor institutional capacity of SADCC, which lacked political cohesion among member states. Member states were given a choice to join either organisation as their sovereign right.[267] SADC made regional integration membership easy for member states in allowing those member states with bilateral trade agreements to continue with such trade agreements. Eight SADC member states belonging to COMESA, namely, Angola, Lesotho, Malawi, Mauritius, Mozambique, Tanzania, Zambia and Zimbabwe, and management of multiple memberships, were raised by SADC. SADC became a full, legally binding institution when it incorporated South Africa into its fold. The only stringent rule that SADC stipulated was to sanction member states that reneged on their membership fees.[268] South Africa was a newcomer to the region and brought its own sets of domestic problems into the fraternity of SADC. South Africa joined SADC in 1994 during a period of socio-economic domestic problems, which placed some pressure on South Africa and on the region. South Africa's military power and its democratic transformation processes, fed into the divergence of the evolving regional position. South Africa took on a developmental approach that combined trade integration with infrastructural development to deepen regional integration and to derive benefits from such an integration process to assist its domestic socio-economic problems of poverty and underdevelopment through its DBSA funding institution.

4

The era of convergence: COMESA, EAC and SADC

This analysis of the COMESA-EAC-SADC Tripartite Agreement processes are critical to analyse since this Free Trade Area is active and running in parallel with the African Continental Free Trade Area (A-CFTA). The discussion expands thus on the Tripartite block to assess the extent of regional integration in the divergence and convergence debate in relation to Africa's major regional economic communities in their signing of a COMESA-EAC-SADC Tripartite Agreement in 2008. Furthermore, the analysis assesses how this convergence was managed towards achieving African integration of the COMESA-EAC-SADC Tripartite free trade bloc.

This chapter begins by first discussing the period 1998–2008, since the last decision to remain apart in 1997 was taken by COMESA and SADC. Assessed are the main actors, factors and the reasons that led to COMESA and SADC's decision to regroup in 2008 and sign a Tripartite partnership, which also included the East African Community (EAC), namely the COMESA-EAC-SADC 2008 Partnership Agreement, which was adopted at a summit heads-of-state meeting in Kampala, Uganda, in October 2008 by more than half of Africa's total fifty-five member states.[1] The intention among the three Regional Economic Communities (RECs) was a joint effort to create a free trade area. Secondly, the chapter discusses the unfolding events between 2008 (Tripartite Agreement) and 2015 (the first signing of the Tripartite Free Trade Agreement (TFTA) by the sixteen member states on 10 June 2015) to assess the extent of the convergence among the RECs: COMESA, EAC and SADC.

The chapter therefore poses the following questions: (1) What were the main events that occurred during the ten years (1998–2008)? Who were the main actors, and what were the main factors that led to the decision to regroup in 2008 and sign a Tripartite Agreement? What did this mean for the region, for the continent, and for the rest of the world? (2) Since the first signing of the free trade agreement (FTA) in 2015, what were proceeding relations and what have these three blocs – COMESA, EAC and SADC – managed to achieve with regard to the agreements and protocols outlined in their 2008 Tripartite Agreement for the period 2008–17 (before signing up to the Continental Free Trade Area (CFTA) in 2018)? Who were the main actors and what were the main factors that contributed to the progress of divergence and convergence?

The findings in this chapter distil examples that very carefully draw from the neoclassical economics approach that contends trade liberalisation is an important mechanism for convergence, since trade liberalisation that is not supported with the correct regional trade policies can be detrimental to economic growth, as this book shows. South Africa was also placed in a precarious position, which was to fill a regional security role, since their joining of SADC. The South African government wanted to show its commitment to 'changing hearts and minds' towards South Africa so that it was seen in a positive light in the region.[2] Christopher Clapham corroborated such views:

> The conversion of organisations for economic integration into providers of some kind of regional diplomatic framework for military intervention is not, however, as bizarre as it may seem. It is rather mirrored by changing orthodoxies in the analysis of the reasons for African economic failure. Whereas analysts once concentrated on the rival merits of capitalist as against socialist development strategies, and subsequently went on to argue over the advantages as against the defects of structural adjustment schemes, they are now virtually united in emphasising the importance of *political* developments in accounting for Africa's economic malaise.[3]

South Africa was an important actor in the convergence of COMESA, EAC and SADC in 2008 in signing the Tripartite Agreement. The country had the largest economy regionally, in terms of total GDP, of $128 billion in 2000; by 2010 it had reached a total GDP of $228 billion.[4] South Africa's market approach was to remedy its domestic issues, as South Africa's new government had major setbacks in terms of its socio-economic disparities.[5] South Africa's outward market approach with trade to Europe was extensive. In 2004, South Africa's exports to the European Union were R20.50 billion, and total imports were R26.82 billion. The total South African exports to Africa were R7.01 billion and the total imports from Africa were only R2.43 billion.[6]

Also considered is COMESA, EAC and SADC's competitive advantage in supporting endogenous growth factors of inputs of semi-skilled and unskilled labour in energy production, and unskilled labour in agriculture; these are considered potential opportunities for regional production chains and intra-regional trade that moves up the value chain, which are furthermore incentives for countries with smaller economies that encourage convergence in a trade bloc. The findings are presented in narrative, tabular and graphic format, and further evidence is supported by interviews conducted in the region in some instances, and relevant literature that further underpins the evidence. Since the rationalisation processes of COMESA, EAC and SADC between 1991 and 1997, various regional and extra-regional events have occurred between the blocs in a move towards a free trade arrangement. Next discussed is the period 1998–2008.

The period 1998–2008: Convergence of a Tripartite Agreement

Major events between 1998 and 2008 led to the 2008 Tripartite Agreement; these are issues that mainly concerned the Southern African region and SADC's member states.

During this period, COMESA's member states[7] were trying to liberalise trade tariffs and form a free trade area, which was formed in 2000. Old intra- and interstate conflicts emerged: the interstate conflicts in Ethiopia and Somalia's Ogaden Wars fought between 1977 and 1978 re-emerged.[8] Other conflicts included the Rwandan intra-state conflict during 1993–4 that led to a genocide in which eight hundred thousand people were killed in ethnic rivalry, the 1993 civil war in Burundi, the violent conflict in the Democratic Republic of the Congo (DRC) of 1997–8 and the border dispute between Eritrea and Ethiopia from 1998 to 2000, among others.[9] Millions of Africans were being killed because of intra- and interstate conflict-ridden state rivalries – but COMESA remained ruthless in realising its vision of forming an economic community towards a free trade area, and all eyes were focused on South Africa as the country was shedding its apartheid past for democracy. Regional security concerns were thus astonishingly neglected during 1993–4, which was a horrendous period with millions of lives lost in wars fought in the continent. Nevertheless, SADC signed its Trade Protocol in 1996, and it became effective only in January 2000 owing to the regional rivalry discussed here below.[10] SADC was also immersed in a restructuring of its Secretariat, concluded in 2009 and pushed by the European Union (EU) in ensuring that regional integration as a method to converging blocs and strengthening Southern Africa would be effective. But the trade packages imposed by Europe were part of its tactics to remain involved in Africa and security trade routes in the continent through its Economic Partnership Agreements (EPAs).

COMESA, on its part, was engaged in its own regional processes concerning trade, infrastructure, international financial institutions and migration. On SADC's part, member states were struggling with intra- and interstate conflicts as well as an organisational security vacuum that was evident in its structures, which lacked a security framework – the Organ on Politics, Defence and Security Cooperation (OPDSC)[11] became fully operational only in 2004, twelve years after SADC's formation.

Various conflicts flared up among the SADC member states, which warranted mediation and peacekeeping efforts. The earliest conflict was the border dispute over the island of Kasikili (Shedu) on the Chobe River between Botswana and Namibia, which ended in 1999 (having commenced in 1992), with a mediation intervention strategy by Zimbabwe's former president Robert Mugabe that eventually led to the signing of the 1999 agreement between the two countries and involved the International Court of Justice (ICJ) in the Hague.[12]

South Africa was eager to be seen as a good neighbour, given the apartheid past of regional destruction. But the controversial military intervention that led to the attack on the Lesotho Highlands Water Project by the South African National Defence Force (SANDF) undoubtedly left a bitter taste in the region. The attack resulted in the killing of fifty-eight members of the Lesotho Defence Force (LDF) and approximately forty-seven civilians.[13] Lesotho also served (which is currently still the situation) as a provider of water for the Gauteng province (encompassing Johannesburg and Pretoria) of South Africa, and it appeared that South Africa had a great deal to lose by the attempted military coup that was staged in Lesotho during that time.[14] This was the rationale for the push from South Africa to intervene militarily in Lesotho during 1998 with the assistance of Botswana.[15] The DRC conflict also erupted during the same period, which led to the formation of a mutual defence pact between Angola, Namibia and Zimbabwe in 1998.[16] The DRC conflict came to be known as Africa's 'First World War' in the Great Lakes region. The DRC was not yet a member state of SADC, but it was a member state of COMESA and turned to South Africa for military assistance. Civil war broke out in the DRC in 1996, and Tanzania was also involved in assisting to diffuse the conflict in the Great Lakes region and worked with the Burundian government in attempting to restore peace.[17] SADC's restructuring and regional mayhem of conflict and violence emanated from the organisation's inadequate security structures.[18] As Matlosa and Lotshwao have consistently argued, 'In part as a result of the paralysis of SNCs and the inherent weaknesses of the Secretariat in Gaborone, SADC lacks visibility at national level of its member states. Thus, its relevance for the promotion of democratic governance, peace, security and political stability became flawed.'[19]

SADC's member states experienced governance issues as well, with political elites of SADC viewed as a club of ruling parties whose main preoccupation was to provide political solidarity to one another, and who were not inclined to criticism in instances where authoritarian tendencies threatened democracy, constitutionalism and human rights.[20] This was evident in how SADC dealt with the Zimbabwe experience that had massive political and economic crises of land invasions that were sanctioned by Robert Mugabe's government, termed as 'fast track' land restitution.[21] The land programmes resulted in eviction of farm workers from farms that were predominantly white-owned. These events also brought about the collapse of the SADC Tribunal, since it became embroiled in the land disputes between Zimbabwe and the farmers. Former South African presidents Mbeki and Mandela opted to engage Zimbabwe through quiet diplomacy tactics, even though Zimbabwean activists called for stronger action to be taken against Mugabe.[22] In May 2000, Mandela had grown much closer to Mugabe since their difficult relationship in 1994 (discussed in Chapter 3) and spoke out in favour of Mugabe.

In defence of the quiet diplomacy approach adopted by South Africa, Mandela viewed this diplomatic stance as the best mechanism to resolve the violent political dispute over white land ownership in Zimbabwe.[23] Mugabe ignored the judgements handed down in favour of white farmers in Zimbabwe by the SADC Tribunal in 2008, which led to the effective dissolution of this body by the SADC heads of state in August 2011.[24] Nathan noted that the tribunal's demise had weakened the regional body's authority, which raised serious questions about SADC's commitment to the rule of law. Nathan also argued that the summit had little choice but to dissolve the court since its ruling for the farm owners fundamentally questioned the validity of a constitutional provision to confiscate land approved by Zimbabwe's parliament and courts, because of sovereignty of a member state taking precedence over the cause of justice.[25]

Chris Landsberg quoted Mandela as stating,

> It is no use standing on hilltops and shouting about such a highly sensitive matter. An approach through diplomatic channels without much publicity, is more likely to bring about a positive result ... I would personally support President Mbeki when he says we have diplomatic relations with Zimbabwe. Everything should be done through diplomatic channels.[26]

SADC's double standards were evident in how it chose to execute its duties: different standards were adopted for Zimbabwe, as for the DRC and for Madagascar. SADC leaders directly rejected the new Malagasy leadership in Madagascar's case, when Andry Rajoelina, a former mayor of Antananarivo, seized power through a military coup on 17 March 2009, which led to a military directive making him president of Madagascar, ousting President Marc Ravalomanana and forcing him into exile. This gave the High Transitional Authority (*Haute Autorité de la Transition*, or HAT) a monopoly of the economy and command of the island.[27] On the other hand, SADC had adopted a more casual approach in its intervention in Zimbabwe's security challenges, when at that time five million Zimbabweans were estimated to have suffered food shortages, and in some cases starvation, and Zimbabwe's inflation rate was at 619.5 per cent in 2001.[28] Huge food shortages were reported in Zimbabwe's Matabeleland and Masvingo areas in 2001, when Zimbabwe reneged on payments to foreign debtors to the amount of $4 billion and debt servicing fell behind by $690 million.[29]

Nelson Mandela also sought to facilitate a peace agreement and attempted to end Angola's thirty-year civil war. Further mediation efforts in the SADC region were conducted by SADC member states – Botswana, Mozambique, Namibia, South Africa and Zimbabwe – to assist in Lesotho's 2002 elections that turned violent.[30] Under Thabo Mbeki (former South African president after Mandela), South Africa negotiated the Sun City Agreement in Rustenburg in 2003, which cost the South African taxpayer $20 million.[31] Zimbabwe's domestic disputes re-emerged in 2002, and SADC mandated Thabo Mbeki to mediate between the Zimbabwean government and the opposition, the Movement for Democratic Change, and a government of national unity was installed in 2009.[32] Although the revised 2001 SADC Treaty[33] provides non-military powers of enforcement, such as sanctions, these have rarely been employed. Southern African economies are estimated to have lost more than $36 billion in potential investments in Zimbabwe as a result of its economic crisis between 2000 and 2008, which saw living standards and life expectancy fall more rapidly than anywhere else in the world. In addition, SADC countries provided $200 million of credit to Zimbabwe in 2009. In June 2011, Botswana agreed to a credit line of $76 million to assist struggling Zimbabwean companies, with an annual GDP of only $10.8 billion in 2012 and growth rates forecast at between 2.2 and 8 per cent in 2013.[34]

During this era (1998–2008), having joined SADC in 1994, South Africa had its own domestic situation in reforming its police force – an old guard force which presented many challenges for the South African government amid challenges of socio-economic inequalities.[35] Adebayo Adedeji[36] indicated that within South Africa's own backyard, a huge disparity between the rich and the poor (between the white majority and the black minority) still existed. In a report of the United Nations Development Programme (UNDP) he noted that under the Human Development Index (HDI), white South Africans averaged 0.878[37] (in the same league as the twenty-nine most industrialised countries globally, which, according to OECD rankings, included Italy, Spain and Portugal), whereas blacks in South Africa rated 0.462[38] (equivalent to an OECD league ranking similar to that of countries such as Botswana, Gabon, Eswatini, Lesotho and Zimbabwe).[39] With this mounting pressure,

South Africa had to act swiftly in its efforts to deliver on social development and the South African Social Security Agency (SASSA) dedicated R66.6 billion[40] in 2007-8 and R78 billion in 2009-10 to improve socio-economic issues.[41] During South Africa's land reform process, only 3.6 million of the 6.6 million hectares of farmland was transferred to black South Africans, with an official target of 30 per cent earmarked for land transfer by 2015.[42]

States, markets and developmental integration: 1998–2008, divergence or convergence

South Africa's tackling of domestic challenges led Tshwane to turn to regional integration. Regional integration was thus an avenue for socio-economic growth and to achieving policy implementation outlined in South Africa's New Growth Path (NGP), 2011, and its National Development Plan (NDP), 2030. These two policies outline an economic growth policy that includes infrastructure projects across Africa.[43] The National Industrial Policy Framework (NIPF) and the Industrial Policy Action Plan 2012/13–2014/15 sought to promote value-added trade and industrial production that build employment and to promote job creation, while the Trade Policy and Strategy Framework (TPSF) is an industrial policy instrument to support trade in favour of local manufacturing as well as to diversify the economy so that it is not so heavily dependent on commodities and non-tradable services.

South Africa's approach was twofold: first, a market-driven integration approach of bilateral trade agreements through SADC as a vehicle[44] and, second, a micro-regional development-led integration in using two of SADC's four Spatial Development Initiatives (SDIs). These two approaches entailed enhancing transport projects in a micro-region with Mozambique through the formation of the Maputo Development Corridor, and electrical power generation through the creation of the Southern African Power Pool (SAPP) created in 1995, which linked twelve SADC power utilities.[45] South Africa was also using the region creatively to solve Eskom's financial difficulties and improve its own domestic challenges of unemployment through SAPP, which became an important vehicle for the South African government.[46]

King-Akerele and Asiedu assert that micro-regions in regional integration can enhance growth and are innovative steps to grow the economies of least developing countries (LDCs); they are also a mechanism to withstand global competition.[47] For example, the Johor–Singapore–Riau Growth Triangle within the ASEAN bloc took advantage of Singapore's skilled labour and developed infrastructure, Johor's land and semiskilled labour and Riau's land and low-cost labour. Quebec's large industrialised economy was another form of a successful micro-region that became economically independent and technologically advanced.[48]

Similarly, South Africa's micro-regional approach was to make an effort in building on SADC's SDIs through SAPP, and the involvement of its parastatal, Eskom, which was providing power generation. Scholars like Tore Horve, Harry Stephan, Michael Power, Angus Fane Hervey and Raymond Steenkamp Fonseca noted that Eskom had financial difficulties and South Africa was attempting to address these problems by investigating

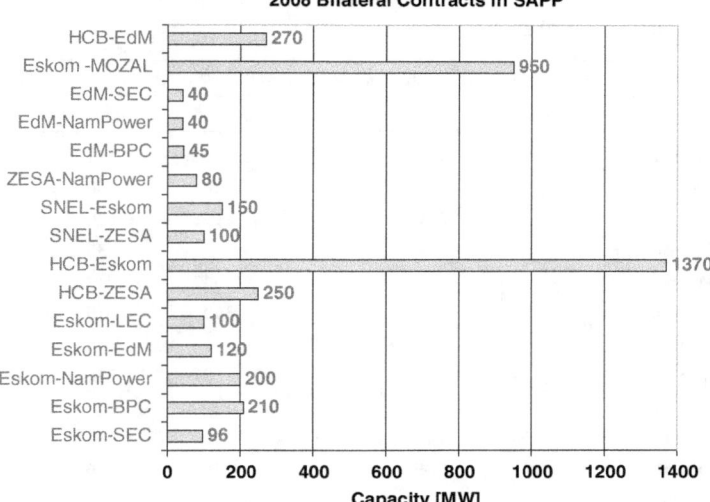

Figure 4.1 2008 bilateral contracts in SAPP.

Source: Alison Chikova, 'Power Generation and Projected Demand in Southern Africa beyond 2010', *The Southern African Power Pool (SAPP)*, www.sapp.co.zw.

means to remedy these difficulties. Figure 4.1[49] shows how micro-regionalism through energy generation formed strategic partnerships and created regional convergence among SADC member states.

Statistics in 1998[50] revealed that Eskom, South Africa's power utility, was the fifth-largest power utility globally and had annual sales of $4.8 billion, forty-thousand employees, a net income of $800 million, total assets of $14.4 billion, and a research and development department that was equivalent in size to the annual budget of many other power utilities in the Southern African region. In 2003, Eskom had a net loss of R719 million on revenues of R3.3 billion, in comparison with a R9 million profit on R2.9 billion revenues in 2002. In addition, Eskom had falling cash flows in operations, which declined from R324 million in 2001 to R285 million in 2003.[51]

The partnership created among power facilities in the SADC region in electricity generation grew from 1995 into a trade market in 2001. The new market – a short-term energy market – is in the form of a day-ahead market (DAM).[52] South Africa was also able to use this initiative for a number of domestic problems such as improving Eskom's economic stability and providing electricity for South African households. In the late 1980s, 85 per cent of households in South Africa had no electricity; however, by 2009, just about 85 per cent households in South Africa had electricity. The 1995 SAPP agreement revised in 2006–7[53] pledged full recovery of costs and equal sharing of profits among SADC members and also improved technology transfer in the region with the other power utilities. While there was convergence in the SAPP policy, it was not as equitable among its users. South Africa was the main consumer and consumed 78 per cent of installed power-generating capacity, 84 per cent of the regional peak

Table 4.1 SAPP's planned regional generation projects commissioned and funded up until 2017

No.	Country	Committed generation capacity, MW				
		2014	2015	2016	2017	Total
1	Angola	220	0	1,280	2,271	3,771
2	Botswana	150	-	-	-	150
3	DRC	-	580	-	240	820
4	Lesotho	-	-	35	-	35
5	Malawi	-	-	-	34	34
6	Mozambique	175	-	40	300	515
7	Namibia	-	-	15	-	15
8	RSA	4,836	1,805	3,717	1,918	12,276
9	Swaziland	-	-	-	-	-
10	Tanzania	450	240	660	250	1,600
11	Zambia	195	735	40	126	1,096
12	Zimbabwe	-	15	-	1,140	1,155
TOTAL		6,026	3,375	5,787	6,279	21,467

Source: SAPP, Annual Report, 2014, https:www.sapp.co.zw.

load and 85 per cent of the electricity distributed, among only 23 per cent of the overall Southern African population (1996).[54] SAPP envisaged an increase in SADC's total electricity generated by 42,000 MW between 2007 and 2027.[55] In 2007, SADC's combined electricity capacity was at 52,742 MW, of which 41,000 MW secured capacity was for consumer demand.[56] Table 4.1 outlines the progress that SAPP had made in the region's twelve committed and commissioned power utilities and the types of resources for electricity production and funding that were secured. SAPP, on the whole, had positive spin-offs for the region's economy, and South Africa's viable market created a pull factor for outside investment interests in the region. Eskom had thirty-four regional networks in 2006; it was the leading driver of SAPP and had technical and development expertise, as well as regional transmission systems and investments.[57]

Another example of the convergence leading to the Tripartite Agreement was the success of the Maputo Development Corridor (MDC) that was also spearheaded by South Africa through the Development Bank of Southern Africa and to which the government contributed $8 billion.[58] The MDC was able to facilitate trade between South Africa and Mozambique. Maputo became South Africa's largest trading partner in the region after Angola. Total trade increased from R899.5 million in 1992 to R7.4 billion in 2002, resulting in an exceptional regional spillover that increased Mozambique's economic growth from R47 million to R403 million over the same period.[59]

Figure 4.2 highlights South Africa's investment in the MDC and shows how the corridor was able to benefit Mozambique's economic growth through the bilateral trade from South Africa to Mozambique. This enhanced Mozambique's economic growth, and increased investment, which further contributed to its GDP growth. Jenkins

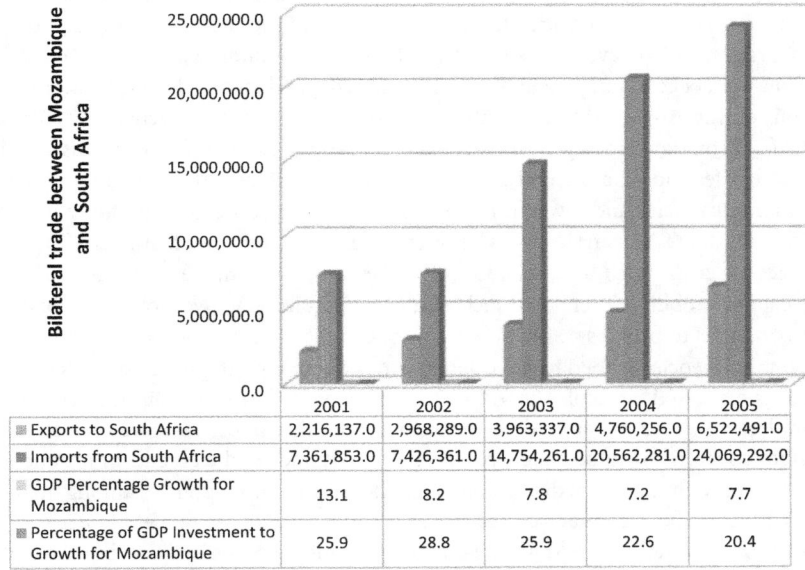

Figure 4.2 Growth in micro-regions: Mozambique and South Africa.

Source: SADC Mozambique report, http://www.sadctrade.org/files/Intra-SADC-trade-performance-review-2006-4-mozambique.pdf, pp. 86–7.

and Thomas argued that Southern Africa lacked a market for addressing factors for endogenous growth like technology and observed, 'For the smaller SADC economies, the domestic market is too limited to generate significant endogenous development.'[60] South Africa is a large economy compared with that of Mozambique, which allowed for economic growth for Mozambique as seen in Figure 4.2, through not only investments but also via a specific approach, which was to build a micro-region defined in the MDC. As shown in Figure 4.2, the exports of Mozambique had grown at an average of 20 per cent per annum for the period 2001–5.

Mozambique's trade had played a major role in its gross earnings from exports.[61] Over the last five years, Mozambique has experienced gross earnings from exports of MZN15.330 billion to MZN40.239 billion, and these earnings could have been higher. However, during this period, Mozambique also faced sharp increases in world market prices for unprocessed cashew nuts, sugar and tobacco (the primary products of Mozambique). Also, since 2000 there have been a number of reforms in Mozambique's trading patterns, where approximately twelve tariff lines, with an average weighted tariff rate of 18.4 per cent and a maximum tariff rate of 35 per cent, and a 40 per cent tax exemption on cashew exports were introduced.[62] Despite these challenges, SDIs show how micro-regions could be corrective measures to address market exploitation. As the neoclassical economics approach of open market-driven trade and trade liberalisation suggests, countries can grow in economic strength; however, as discussed here, public partnerships introduced in the formation of micro-regions have assisted in that economic growth. For example, the MDC further expanded into the Maputo Corridor and Logistics Initiative (MCLI) and required funds of R1.9 billion for upgrades, which have been shelved until 2030 when funding becomes available.

How market economies generate wealth is also dependent on effective trade policies. In considering Africa's economic integration processes, Arthur Hazelwood[63] purports that Africa's markets are largely driven through free trade that entails reductions in tariffs between states and other methods of lowering transaction costs between them, such as common currencies and lowered restrictions on labour and capital mobility within a region. Besides reductions in tariffs between states, there are other methods of lowering transaction costs, such as common currencies and lowering restrictions on labour and capital mobility. Therefore, such strategies require effective policy mechanisms for economies to progress. Similarly, Ibrahim Gambari underscores that conventional integration theories tended to focus largely on economic prerequisites such as gains in trade, as discussed by Jacob Viner,[64] and were largely a means to gain from exchanges in trade and led to either trade creation or trade diversion. Gambari indicates that economic factors, including the free movement of goods and elements of production, as well as the elimination of discrimination and discriminatory policies among member states, have not been conducive to Africa's economies and do not benefit LDCs.[65]

COMESA, EAC and SADC's regional integration processes have both adopted a market-led strategy of free trade and have made efforts to converge policy and implementation, with a functional coordinated approach (an incremental approach) adopted to execute trade liberalisation.[66] It was therefore a challenge to increase growth that could support projects for endogenous factors of technological spillovers and knowledge production, for example, in agricultural research that could affect economic growth and support the negative effects of trade within liberalised tariff settings. The timing of the step-by-step functional approach of incrementally reducing tariffs worked against the rapid speed of the market of free trade and trade liberalisation policies. While open trade was considered a regional benefit by COMESA, EAC and SADC in their individual approaches in converging their policies at their own organisational level, trade diversion was experienced owing to the external trade partnerships, with agreements between South Africa and Europe leaving member states with little control over the market, and with goods flooding their markets through openness of trade. These experiences of trade diversion for weaker economies in COMESA, EAC and SADC made convergence and future deliberations between the two organisations difficult and created future challenges, as will be discussed later. Gains and benefits in a regional scheme are important considerations for states, depending on what the gains and benefits are. Andre Gunder Frank identifies in world systems theory the 'core' as feeding off the periphery, which distorts trade, but regional trade agreements are believed to help address such conflicting objectives of distorted trade through policy formulation and implementation, as Hazelwood and Gambari posit.[67] In 1999, South Africa, as the strongest economy in the region, also signed an agreement with Europe, the EU–SA Trade, Development and Cooperation Agreement (TDCA). This happened after four years of negotiations in an attempt to be accepted by Europe as a developmental country under the Lomé Convention.[68] South Africa was also a signatory to the SADC FTA in 1996.[69]

South Africa was conducting open trade with both SADC and Europe and, with Europe being much wealthier than SADC states, consequently Europe's finished agricultural trade goods flooded the Southern African markets.[70] Southern Africa was no match for Europe, since half of the European Economic Commission's (EEC's) budget of 126 billion euros was for subsidising and supporting a farming sector that employed only 5 per cent of the working population of 70 per cent of farm workers in Africa's regions.[71] Moreover, the Organisation for Economic Co-operation and Development (OECD) spent $265 billion on farm subsidies in 2008 and only $4 billion on aid for agriculture in developing countries.[72] Europe's Common Agriculture Policy (CAP) was 55 billion euros (31 per cent of the EU's total budget) in 2013.[73]

Hence the 1999 EU–SA TDCA agreement created divergence in trade for COMESA, EAC and SADC blocs in the clothing and textile sectors and in agricultural sectors such as beef and sugar.[74] COMESA warned South Africa that it would take action and prevent South Africa from trading in the region if trade were distorted by the South African market.[75] Zimbabwe's calculation was that it had a better competitive advantage over its regional COMESA partners than it had in SADC, which also led to the Zimbabwe government's decision to align itself with COMESA.[76] The EU–SA FTA rules of origin for apparel had a two-stage conversion rule that required garments in South Africa to be manufactured from only South African or EU-produced fabric.[77] South Africa's FTA offer to SADC evoked concern from the clothing and textile sectors that had a labour working force of 215,000.[78] South Africa's textile market was not spared by its own experiences of similar negative trade patterns with the African Growth and Opportunity Act (AGOA) trade agreement that it signed in 2000.[79] South African Textile Federation spokesman Brian Brink noted that the South African textile industry was also affected by Europe's FTA agreement with South Africa, as well as by the AGOA trade agreement with the United States, seen in the negative growth and drop in textiles, from $562 million in 2000 compared with $392 million in 2001, which dropped further to $95.6 million in 2007.[80] Ron Sundry at the Trade Law Centre also noted that although exports of apparel from South Africa to the United States grew by 38 per cent in the first year after the AGOA agreement was introduced in 2001, export growth was limited owing to the barriers of restrictive rules of origin introduced by neighbouring countries in COMESA, EAC and SADC, like the DRC, and once buyers diminished, interest declined.

When South Africa joined SADC, the South African government was invited in by SADC to oversee its infrastructure and financial and investment regional clusters as it was thought that it had the expertise to do so. South Africa had not only promoted SADC economically but had also sought to provide a peacekeeping environment regionally and to allow for a stable market that was attractive to foreign investors.[81] Since joining SADC, South Africa had invested regionally with its own foreign direct investments. In 2001–2 the South African investments entailed $20 million (South African Airways); $6 billion (Eskom for the Inga project in the DRC, and in November 2011 the governments of South Africa and the DRC signed an memorandum of understanding (MOU) that led to an October 2013 treaty under which South Africa agreed to buy 2,500 MW of the Grand Inga III's expected 4,800 MW of hydroelectric output);[82] $56 million (Sun International Hotel in Zambia); $142 million (Vodacom in Tanzania); and $53 million (Portland Cement in Zimbabwe, which was a merger business investment activity). These investments did not bode too well with the region since South Africa's MNCs favoured their businesses and not the region entirely.

As Soko suggests,

> Regional integration in Southern Africa will not succeed unless South Africa, [which is] by far the largest and most diversified economy in the region, discharges its responsibilities in accordance with its hegemonic status. Whether South Africa can assume a hegemonic role will depend on three considerations: first, the extent to which the political elites are able to balance the country's regional obligations against domestic pressures; second, the manner in which the country deals with the legacy of apartheid South Africa's historical destabilisation of the region, and third, the degree to which the country's leadership credentials are accepted by other regional states.[83]

To benefit from trade and diversification, the United Nations Conference on Trade and Development (UNCTAD) 2012 report noted that global trade inequality warrants that developing countries are encouraged to diversify more and produce final products as exports instead of exporting raw materials.[84] What UNCTAD also noted was that offshore finished goods require particular attention. Countries should therefore consider the increase in oil prices, which translates into increased costs in logistics and transportation. Therefore, developing countries should assess the supply-chain risks and management costs and reconsider manufacturing goods. Agriculture could be equally beneficial to small economies for advancing regional integration. One such approach is the sugar industry in the region. For example, smaller economies could benefit from South Africa's agriculture market, which was $209.7 billion in 2011.[85]

Figure 4.3 shows the quantity of sugar produced by the major countries over the period 1996–2010. Production involved several rounds of negotiations to agree on a sugar protocol and rectify the impact of outside external trade agreements (trade between the EU and South Africa).[86]

The cheapest and most efficient producer of sugar is Zimbabwe, but South Africa is the largest producer. Simply having Zimbabwe refine the sugar will not be beneficial to South Africa, since in South Africa 130,000 people are directly employed in the sugar industry and in related production factories, as shown in Figure 4.4.

Member states could benefit from a regional sugar protocol that benefits the region instead of exporting raw sugar to Europe's sugar refineries. Since SADC and COMESA member states with the EAC are concentrating on a framework to liberalise tariffs, a sugar agreement should be ratified that is able to contribute to economic growth regionally.[87] While Southern Africa has the potential to industrialise and enhance its comparative position in production, agriculture could be a significant convergence point for regional trade. Agriculture accounts for 18 per cent of Africa's GDP (compared with 7 per cent for Asia and Latin America, 2 per cent for Europe, and 1 per cent for the United States), but Africa produces only 3.5 per cent of the world's food exports.[88]

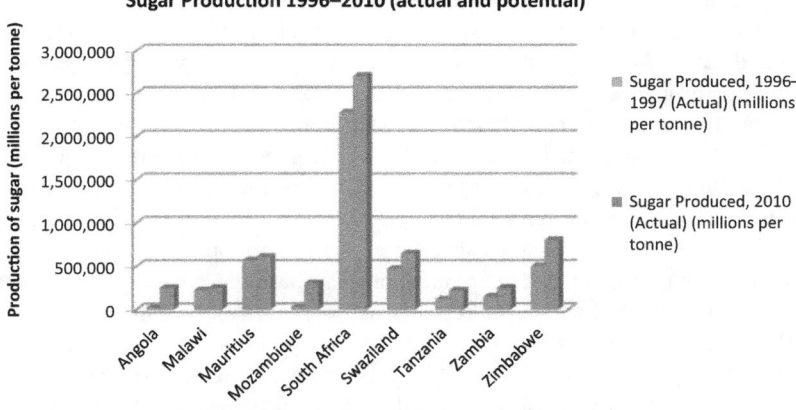

Figure 4.3 Major sugar producers in COMESA, EAC and SADC.

Source: Adopted from Margaret C. Lee, *The Political Economy of Regionalism in Southern Africa* (Boulder, CO: Lynne Rienner, 2003), p. 122.

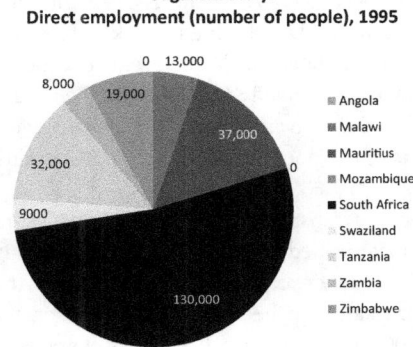

Figure 4.4 Direct employment in the sugar industry (COMESA, EAC and SADC member states).

Source: Adopted from Margaret C. Lee, *The Political Economy of Regionalism in Southern Africa* (Boulder, CO: Lynne Rienner, 2003), p. 122.

COMESA, EAC and SADC's diplomatic efforts of the main summits and meetings: The period 1998–2008

To spearhead the process of cooperation and harmonisation, the chairpersons of the COMESA Authority and SADC Executive played a significant role in those efforts in regrouping COMESA, EAC and SADC sparked by the drive made by the OAU's decision to revive the Yamoussoukro Declaration (YD),[89] which was reinstated in 1999 and signed in 2000 with a view to fully liberalising Africa's airspace market by 2002.[90] The harmonisation of regional policies is guided by the Abuja Treaty created in 1991, which outlines the need for a fully integrated, internationally competitive regional economic community through an airspace-driven liberalised market strategy, for free movement of people, goods and services and for RECs to harmonise regional policies.[91] COMESA, EAC and SADC were invited to join the YD arrangement in 1999, but the EAC joined six years later, in 2005. To comply with the Yamoussoukro Declaration, COMESA, EAC and SADC had to form a joint legal protocol and harmonise implementation of guidelines for a liberalised regional airspace, as well as harmonise their provisions and procedures for regulating airline competition. The harmonised policies were based on their own individual air transport liberalisation programme treaties: Article 87 of COMESA's Treaty;[92] Article 9 of the SADC Protocol on Transport, Communications and Meteorology;[93] and Article 92 of the EAC Treaty.[94] The harmonisation process involved several meetings between 2001 and 2005. The fact that a number of states were members of COMESA, EAC and SADC presented a challenge for the harmonisation of policies in the YD process. To spearhead the process of cooperation and harmonisation, the chairpersons of the COMESA Authority and SADC Executive met in Egypt in 2004 and agreed to set up a joint COMESA-SADC Bilateral Task Force at the Secretariat level to discuss and agree on the harmonisation of programmes for an airspace market, initially for the organisations COMESA, EAC and SADC.[95]

The 2008 COMESA-EAC-SADC Tripartite Agreement was further propelled by funding provided by the African Development Bank (AfDB) of $3.5 billion, and also with funding from the United States due to the events that occurred in implementing an African airspace. COMESA received $443,000 from the US Trade and Development Agency (USTDA) for a market-driven airspace.[96] The offer given to the two RECs was an attractive one because of the poor road and transport conditions in the COMESA, EAC and SADC regions.

Inefficient and inadequate transportation in Africa impedes trade logistics, and poor infrastructure services have impeded both interregional and intercontinental trade. COMESA, EAC and SADC rely excessively on international trade, which constitutes up to 80 per cent of their total trade, because of poor infrastructure. At the continental level, for the period 2000–10, intra-African imports averaged 14.2 per cent of total annual African imports, and intra-African exports averaged 10.4 per cent of total annual African exports.[97] These low levels of continental and regional trade are directly linked to the costs associated with conducting trade in the region. For example, as of 2014, the cost to ship a standard 20-foot container from Durban, South Africa, to Lusaka, Zambia, was $5000, compared with $1,500 from Japan to Durban. For a trader in Juba, Sudan, it costs $9,500 to import a standard container through the port of Mombasa, Kenya, in addition to a two-month wait for the goods to reach Juba.[98] To comply with the Yamoussoukro Declaration, COMESA, EAC and SADC had to form a joint legal protocol and harmonise implementation guidelines for a regional airspace, as well as harmonise their provisions and procedures for regulating airline competition.

These harmonised policies involved several meetings over a period of time between 2001 and 2005. During the meetings, the two organisations were confronted with multiple membership difficulties and the fact that a number of states were members of

COMESA, EAC and SADC, which presented a challenge in harmonising policies and working towards the YD process. In an attempt to address those challenges of multiple memberships, the secretary general of the COMESA Authority and the executive secretary of the SADC Summit met in Cairo, Egypt, in 2004 and agreed to set up a joint COMESA, EAC and SADC Task Force at the Secretariat level to discuss and agree on how to harmonise the programmes of the two organisations.[99] EAC, which had a competitive airline, Kenyan Airways, showed interest in being part of the YD processes and was invited to the meetings with COMESA and SADC; this became significant to the COMESA–SADC integration process in 2005, when EAC joined, as it paved the way as a first step towards convergence of regional policies of the COMESA, EAC and SADC blocs. The Joint Commission and Task Force eventually led to the 2008 COMESA-EAC-SADC Tripartite Agreement.[100] This cooperation led to the emergence of the full-fledged COMESA-EAC-SADC Tripartite Task Force (TTF), which focused on harmonisation of programmes for the YD process. The task force met several times under the guidance of the chief executive officers (CEOs) to address how to collaborate and harmonise regional programmes.[101] To address the issue of multiple memberships, the COMESA-EAC-SADC CEOs also tasked the TTF overseeing the YD to additionally oversee the harmonisation of programmes and establishment of an institutional framework for cooperation that could move into deeper integration. Such deeper integration measures entailed creating an FTA and, later, a customs union, as it was hoped that this would also deal with the issue of multiple memberships.[102] The three RECs commissioned a study in 2005, undertaken by an independent consultant from Leiden University, which helped COMESA, EAC and SADC to jointly develop terms of reference and guidelines for implementing provisions and rules of procedure for external relations for consumer protection.[103] To discuss the Leiden report and recommendations therein, a joint meeting of COMESA-EAC-SADC aviation and legal experts was convened in 2006 in Lusaka, Zambia; in Johannesburg, South Africa; and in Zimbabwe at Victoria Falls. The Joint Competition Authority (JCA) for a liberalised airspace was formed for the three RECs. The JCA was to oversee the full implementation of the YD for air transport in the three RECs, as well as for the harmonisation of programmes in the areas of trade, customs, free movement of people and infrastructure development.[104]

In November 2006, the TTF CEOs called a meeting with the COMESA, EAC and SADC ministers of transport to adopt the guidelines, provisions and procedures for the implementation of the competition regulations and to discuss how to launch the JCA for a liberalised airspace. These regulations were circulated to the member states through their respective Secretariats. Regional integration programmes for trade and economic development were also adopted, which received political endorsement and direction for the process of cooperation and harmonisation. The JCA guidelines were adopted in 2007 by the policy organs of COMESA, EAC and SADC, and at individual Secretariat levels. The recommendations were accepted by the COMESA Secretariat in May 2007, by the EAC Secretariat in June 2008 and by the SADC Secretariat in August 2008. Thereafter, the JCA was formalised at the first COMESA-EAC-SADC Tripartite Summit of Heads of State and Government meeting in October 2008 in Kampala, Uganda, to which the discussion now turns.

Diplomatic efforts: A move towards establishing the COMESA, EAC and SADC Tripartite free trade area

The progress made towards economic convergence by COMESA, EAC and SADC in connecting its regional policies was the signing of the 2008 Tripartite Agreement. The landmark meeting of 20 October 2008 was the first Tripartite Summit with COMESA, EAC and SADC heads of state. The 2008 COMESA-EAC-SADC Tripartite Summit binds the Tripartite group with an MOU and outlines the harmonisation of trade and investment regimes. Article 2 of the MOU includes the following:

1. Establishment of an FTA among COMESA, EAC and SADC.
2. Enhancement of inter-REC economic cooperation.
3. Enhancement of cooperation with multilateral and bilateral partners.
4. Coordination of negotiations on multilateral issues.
5. Promotion of industrialisation.
6. Enablement of intra-regional investment.[105]

COMESA, EAC and SADC include twenty-six of Africa's fifty-five countries, with a combined population of approximately 632 million people (which is 57 per cent of Africa's population) and a GDP of $1.3 trillion as of 2014 (which contributes 58 per cent of Africa's GDP).[106] All three RECs were identified by the African Union's 2000 Constitutive Act, and the Abuja Treaty, as the building blocks of the African Economic Community. Decisions of the COMESA-EAC-SADC Tripartite are made at the summit level. The Tripartite MOU came into force on 19 January 2011 and was tabled at the second Tripartite Summit on 12 June 2011.[107] The MOU defines the free trade process and membership agreements. Article 1 of the MOU outlines the following: (i) approval and expeditious establishment of an FTA encompassing the member/partner states of the three RECS (COMESA, EAC and SADC) and an ultimate goal of establishing a single customs union (though no timeframe had been outlined) and (ii) that the three RECs (COMESA, EAC and SADC) undertake a study incorporating, among others, (a) a roadmap for establishing an FTA which would take into account the principle of variable geometry and (b) a legal and institutional framework to underpin the FTA.

A Tripartite Summit of Heads of State and/or Government must sit once every two years, as an interim measure of the pending MOU. The 2008 Tripartite Summit established (a) a Tripartite Council of Ministers to meet at least once every two years; (b) a Tripartite Sectoral Ministerial Committee on Trade, Finance, Customs, Economic Matters and Home/Internal Affairs; (c) a Tripartite Sectoral Ministerial Committee on Infrastructure; and (d) a Tripartite Sectoral Ministerial Committee on Legal Affairs. It also made provision for any other ministerial committees as established by the Tripartite Council of Ministers, which must meet at least once a year. Furthermore, the 2008 Tripartite Summit

1. approved extraordinary meetings of the Tripartite Summit and Tripartite Council of Ministers to be held as and when necessary;
2. established a Tripartite committee of senior officials and experts, which must meet at least once a year; and

3. finalised and ratified the TTF of the Secretariats of the three RECs that meet at least twice a year.

The 2008 Tripartite Summit officially ratified the JCA on air transport liberalisation to oversee the full implementation of the YD on air transport in the three RECs, commencing in January 2009 as was discussed above. The JCA comprises seven members: two members each from the participating RECs and a rotating chairperson. To promote air transport liberalisation, the 2008 Tripartite Summit directed the RECs to put in place a joint programme for the implementation of a single seamless upper airspace within one year.

Transport barriers are one of the major impediments to regional trade, and rectifying infrastructure problems could considerably boost intraregional and intracontinental trade. For example, South Africa's Richards Bay port, which primarily concentrates on coal shipments, had been experiencing huge problems in handling shipment volumes.[108]

Figure 4.5 provides an overview of the major air markets for COMESA, EAC and SADC, and their total passengers in 2011. Traffic statistics are drawn from the 2011 World Airport Traffic Report.[109] An airspace market in Africa has the potential to develop 7 million jobs, including 257,000 direct jobs, which are worth about $67.8

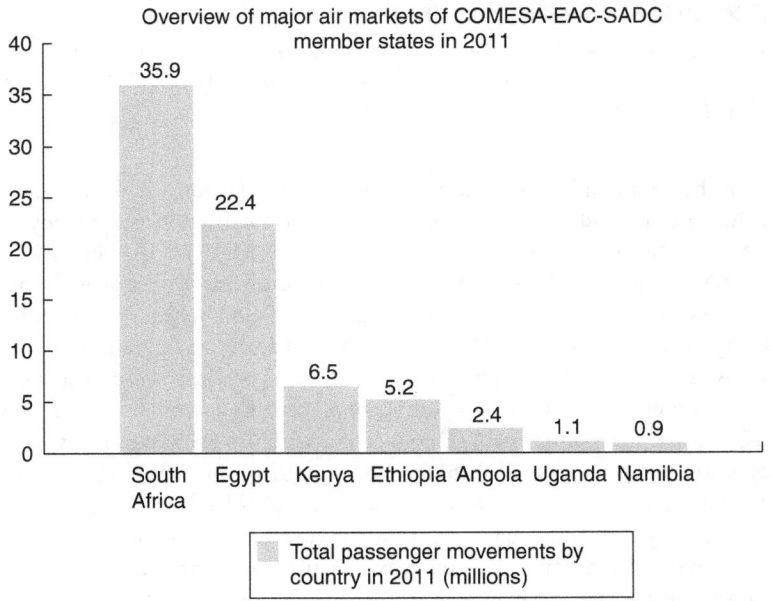

Figure 4.5 Overview of air markets of COMESA, EAC and SADC member states (2011).

Source: InterVISTAS Consulting, 'Transforming Intra-African Air Connectivity: The Economic Benefits of Implementing the Yamoussoukro Decision' (July 2014), pp. vi, 54. (Data adopted from source to provide table data.)

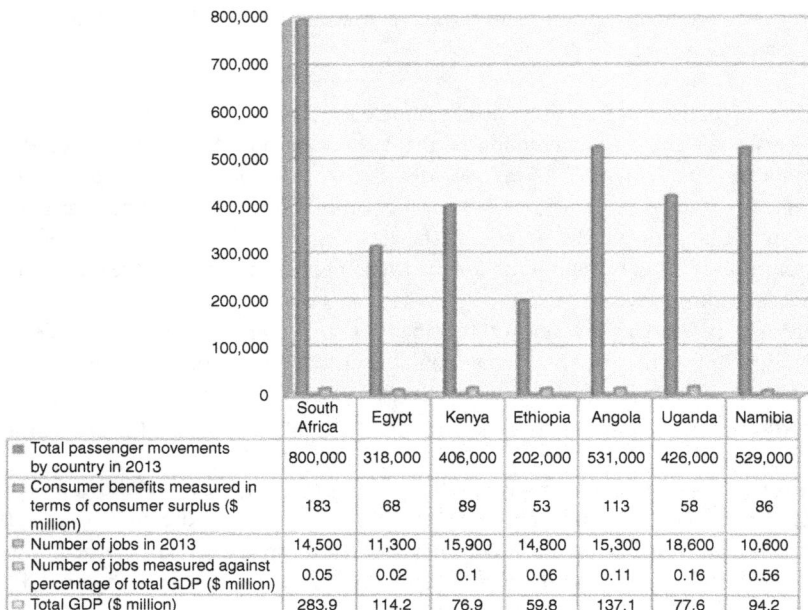

Figure 4.6 Total economic impact stimulated by airspace market liberalisation in COMESA-EAC-SADC member states (2013).

Source: InterVISTAS Consulting, 'Transforming Intra-African Air Connectivity: The Economic Benefits of Implementing the Yamoussoukro Decision' (July 2014), pp. vi, 54. (Data adopted from source to provide table data.)

billion of the continent's GDP. Progress made on the YD was discussed at the 2011 Tripartite Summit, and the JCA reported that it had finalised its main study on the unification of the Upper Flight Information Region (UFIR).[110] Although low-cost carriers have begun operating in Africa, intra-African airline service growth has been stifled because of a lack of liberalisation policy formulation between Africa's member states. Figure 4.6 shows the total economic impact from air operations in 2013 of COMESA, EAC and SADC member states and the benefits accrued in terms of consumer surplus, job creation and number of passengers against percentage of GDP.

EAC had set the lead in establishing a civil aviation safety and security oversight agency and exchanged protocols with member states that could help to establish similar agencies for COMESA, EAC and SADC. Progress has also been slow on an accelerated, seamless interregional ICT broadband infrastructure network, a joint programme for implementation of a harmonised policy and regulatory framework that will govern ICT, and infrastructural development in the three RECs, owing to pledged funding initiatives that were not received.[111] Infrastructure bottlenecks such as roads, ports, railways and borders are major impediments to economic growth. The YD process was eventually finalised and launched the continent's first Single African Air Transport Market (SAATM) in January 2018.[112]

The benefits of migration are job creation, technology transfer and skills development, and it has huge potential for economic growth. Economic convergence requires the movement of both goods and people to achieve success. The divergence of economic integration is largely associated with the ability for people to move and the necessary conditions available to do so. In July 2016, at a Kigali Summit, the African Union launched the first African passport for its ambassadors with a view of all Africans being able to access the African passport by 2020.[113]

Progress of the Tripartite MOU towards convergence

In 2008, the TTF finalised a regional integration strategy paper (RISP) and held several consultative meetings.[114] These meetings included discussions with Britain's Department for International Development (DFID) in London in January 2010, where an MOU was signed between the TTF and DFID in support of transport corridors and trade facilitation towards the Tripartite FTA. Funding had been secured for programmes, including £400,000 for administrative and logistical support for Tripartite meetings.[115] Furthermore, DFID announced continued funding for the COMESA-EAC-SADC Tripartite initiative over a period of an additional three years, from 2011 to 2014.[116]

The Tripartite merger and progress of the free trade area roadmap

The Tripartite Summit in October 2008 directed the TTF of the three Secretariats to develop a roadmap for the implementation of this merger for consideration at the June 2011 summit meeting.[117] The Tripartite free trade area had incorporated an approval process and a roadmap towards the operationalisation and implementation of the FTA within the bloc. The roadmap entailed four stages. First came a preparatory period for consultations at the national, regional and Tripartite levels that began early in 2010. Second, member states would discuss how to incorporate the legal and institutional frameworks from the draft roadmap as a basis for creating a single FTA. Third, each REC would submit concrete recommendations for discussion. Finally, on signing the agreement, member states would have six to twelve months to finalise national processes for ratifying the agreement as well as establish the required support institutions and adopt customs procedures and instruments.[118] The Tripartite alliance is also examining how to incorporate a customs union for its member states at a much deeper level of regional integration. Within the customs union, member states will define a common process of abolishing tariff and non-tariff barriers among themselves, and in addition agree on a common external tariff for non-members.

Each REC must also address its individual macroeconomic policies, since a monetary union for the Tripartite bloc requires macroeconomic convergence criteria to be considered that entail a number of processes. Such processes include the formation of one FTA; harmonising of policy instruments and trade policies, processes and procedures, internal and external tariffs, rules of origin and customs documents for exporters and importers; consideration of phytosanitary health measures and safety;

and elimination of tariff barriers. COMESA addressed macroeconomic convergence for its bloc. Its criteria entail consolidation of existing instruments of monetary cooperation and implementation of policy measures; an overall budget deficit against total GDP of not more than 5 per cent; an annual inflation rate not exceeding 5 per cent; minimising central bank financing of a budget deficit of zero per cent; and external reserves of not less than four months of imports of goods and non-factor services. COMESA's member states have to achieve and maintain stable real exchange rates, market-based real interest rates and growth rates of real GDP that are not less than 7 per cent; a full monetary union by 2018 was envisaged at the regional level. These plans have not yet been concluded.[119] EAC is at a more advanced stage in moving towards a monetary union as a bloc. For EAC, fiscal discipline is one of the most important elements as outlined in the EAC Treaty, the 'Development Strategy 2006–2010', and its 'Common Market Protocol'. EAC's most fundamental principle entails implementing continued cooperation in the monetary exchange rate field during the period ahead of a monetary union.

The East African Central Bank (EACB) has been implementing an institutional framework for an East African Monetary Union (EAMU). The East African Monetary Institute has been established as the preparatory stage and framework for an EAMU.[120] On its part, diversification of SADC member states' economies to make them more resilient would require coherent policies and reforms aimed at how best to diversify their economies. The challenge of regional trade liberalisation that calls for harmonisation of a common external tariff should also be addressed. In 2011 the SADC region recorded an average real GDP growth of 4.7 per cent; in 2010 it was 5.5 per cent. The current account deficit of the balance of payments improved marginally from 8.8 per cent of GDP in 2010 to 8.3 per cent of GDP in 2011; the average fiscal deficit deteriorated to 4.8 per cent of GDP in 2011, while it was 3.2 per cent in 2010. SADC's member states' debt remained at a level of 39 per cent of GDP.[121]

However, Jenkins and Thomas note in their discussion on macroeconomic convergence that emphasis should be placed on economic and trade policy reforms at national level first before considering regional efforts. At the regional level, medium-term coordination should be underpinned by the direct effects of cross-border transactions.[122] On the other hand, other regional groupings, such as in Europe, had huge problems with smaller economies pegged to its monetary union during the global financial crises and the EU could not support the market shocks. As Fingleton, Garretsen and Martin have observed, within the Eurozone, regions of the core closely connected with the economic powerhouse of German regions suffered less in terms of employment loss in contrast with the states of the peripheral regions (Ireland, Spain, the Baltic states and Greece), fared worse during the great recession of 2008–9 and experienced greater divergence. A monetary union could lead to regional divergence and greater disparity in regional vulnerability. Such underlying aspects are also informed by the theory on optimum currency areas, which Fingleton, Garretsen and Martin observed were not part of the EU's monetary framework. The optimum currency area (OCA) theory highlights the importance of incorporating symmetry, flexibility and integration as key variables that ought to be considered in a monetary union.[123]

COMESA-EAC-SADC member states are still at the stage of harmonising trade policies. SADC member states have been very slow in moving towards reducing tariffs. Attempting to converge regional economic interests conforming to one trade treaty within a free trade area has been difficult. This is outlined in key objectives of trade in services, free movement of businesses, free movement of people, free movement of goods in trade and removal of all tariff and non-tariff barriers in trade between COMESA, EAC and SADC member states. Under this framework, member states are also able to negotiate and maintain their own tariffs in trade against non-members. Each member state is also at liberty to apply its preferred regime of tariff rates to third countries, customarily referred to as the most-favoured nation (MFN) rate, and also involving complicated international agreements with external partners.

The 12 June 2011 summit noted that while the FTA negotiations were underway, efforts were being made to complete the negotiations for a free trade area by June 2014 (that was within six months of the roadmap, but transpired a year later – discussed below). The COMESA executive secretary, Sifiso Ngwenya, noted that the FTA roadmap presupposed that the twenty-six countries would need to engage in negotiations; it was also recognised that these countries already had preferential trade and free trade agreements in place. The COMESA-EAC-SADC TFTA is guided by a variable geometry approach: incremental liberalisation and MFN treatment.[124]

Efforts towards the establishment of a Tripartite free trade area

On 9 February 2015, the Tripartite Trade and Customs Committee (TTCM) held its third meeting in Lusaka and provided a progress report on the movement of business people.[125] The Tripartite Technical Committee on Industrial Development (TTCID), established in accordance with the directive handed down by the second Tripartite Summit in June 2011, noted that it had developed a work programme and a Tripartite Industrial Development Roadmap. The TTCID also developed a draft modalities framework on cooperation in industrial development, which would foster value addition and improve production capacity. These issues were tabled and discussed at the third Tripartite Summit in June 2015 in Egypt. Negotiations for the FTA were launched in June 2011 after the second Tripartite Summit, and in December 2011 negotiations on Phase 1 (the Market Integration Pillar) began, focused on trade in goods.[126] Five out of seven meetings of the Tripartite Committee of Senior Officials (TCSO) were held. Ten meetings of the Tripartite Trade Negotiating Forum (TTNF) and eighteen meetings of the Tripartite Technical Working Groups (TTWGs), established by the TTNF to assist in clarifying specific technical negotiating issues, were held.

In October 2014, the draft TFTA was agreed to but not finalised by all member states, and only sixteen member states signed on 10 June 2015. The preamble and two articles – Article 1 on interpretations and Article 28 on dispute settlement – were finalised at the TTNF extraordinary meeting in Egypt and at the third Tripartite Summit by half of its members.[127] Since the signing of the 2008 Tripartite Agreement, annexures have been concluded on non-tariff barriers (Annexure 3), customs cooperation (Annexure 5), trade facilitation (Annexure 6), transit (Annexure 7), technical barriers to trade (Annexure 8) and sanitary and phytosanitary measures

(Annexure 9). Annexures on tariff schedules (Annexure 1), trade remedies (Annexure 2) and rules of origin (Annexure 4) are still under negotiation. Tariff officers had been prepared by sixteen of the twenty-six countries as of the tenth meeting of the TTNF, in Bujumbura, Burundi, in 2014. Since then, the Southern African Customs Union (SACU) bloc has offered to open up 60 per cent of tariff lines on which duties will be reduced to zero, while 15 per cent of tariff lines will be reduced gradually over a period of five years. The 2015 meeting of the TTCM also noted that all the trade offers for a Tripartite FTA had involved fourteen out of fifteen COMESA member states only; thus launching the TFTA with only these members would not yield a true Tripartite FTA, but that a COMESA 'plus' is what is required (since the member states were mainly from the COMESA bloc).[128]

Fostering cooperation through establishing institutional arrangements and harmonisation of programmes is important to the member states of the three RECs, and the 2008 Tripartite Summit also directed the chairpersons of the Councils of Ministers of the RECs to ensure that Secretariats participate in, coordinate and harmonise positions on the Economic Partnership Agreement negotiations with the EU, the World Trade Organization (WTO), Doha Development Round and other multilateral negotiations. There was no movement at the summit and Councils of Ministers levels but only at the member-state level. Member states are negotiating on their own terms, as seen in South Africa's negotiations within SACU and the EPA that Mozambique concluded with Brussels, which was finalised in October 2016.[129]

While maintaining their own regional protocols, mandates and time frames for free trade areas and customs unions, COMESA, EAC and SADC in October 2008 signed an important MOU on interregional cooperation and integration to accelerate their efforts as underpinned by a legal and institutional framework for this Tripartite body.[130] However, national interests of member states override regional interests. Power and resources have determined the economic policy of member states, and such economic policies are historically linked to African states associated with sovereignty.[131] At the earlier stages of negotiations, South Africa refused to sign the FTA for the Tripartite bloc and felt that it was not ready to commit to such an agreement of zero tariff settings.[132]

At the February 2015 TTCM meeting, an analysis of rules of origin was tabled that demonstrated that Tripartite imports in 2012 were worth $323 billion, of which $42 billion were intra-Tripartite imports and $280 billion were extra-Tripartite imports. After revising the agreed number of chapters to eighteen and headings to thirty-nine, the total Tripartite imports for the eighteen chapters in 2012 were $27.52 billion, accounting for 8 per cent of Tripartite imports. The intra-Tripartite imports were $4.04 billion and accounted for 9 per cent of the total intra-Tripartite trade, while the extra-Tripartite imports were $23.5 billion, accounting for 8 per cent. Furthermore, the thirty-nine headings for total Tripartite imports were $6.5 billion, accounting for 2 per cent of the total Tripartite imports. The intra-Tripartite imports were $1.7 billion, which accounted for 4 per cent of the total intra-Tripartite imports, and the extra-Tripartite imports were $4.7 billion, accounting for 2 per cent of the total extra-Tripartite imports. This analysis showed that the intra-Tripartite trade for the agreed chapters were still low and accounted for 9 per cent and 4 per cent, respectively, of the total intra-Tripartite imports.¹³³

Therefore, an interim arrangement was discussed at the February 2015 TTCC meeting to address rules of origin for the COMESA-EAC-SADC bloc, and recommendations included the following: (a) to use agreed common rules and the value addition rule of 35 per cent ex-works cost as an interim measure to be launched at the third Tripartite Summit in Egypt and (b) to use the agreed common rules for the launch of a partial TFTA, which was recommended for adoption at the third Tripartite Summit in Egypt. The TTCC prepared their recommendations (which were tabled at the third Tripartite Summit and heads-of-state meeting), and it was envisaged that the Tripartite member states will sign the TFTA, adopt the Post-Signature TFTA Implementation Roadmap and launch Phase 2 negotiations that concern trade in services, competition policy, intellectual property rights and cross-border investment. The following recommendations were also prepared ahead of the third Tripartite Summit in Egypt and included the following: (a) the Tripartite free trade area to be launched in 2015 based on the principles of variable geometry; (b) on rules of origin, a general value addition rule of 35 per cent ex-works cost to be used when the TFTA is launched, while the work on the Customs Union to be negotiated under the built in Agenda; (c) on Part Five (Trade Remedies) of the draft TFTA, the following approach would be endorsed by COMESA: (i) Detailed procedures on trade remedies to be discussed as part of the Built in Agenda, that is, Annexure 2, (ii) Existing REC provisions to apply within RECs and WTO provisions to apply across RECs in the interim, and (iii) the feasibility of developing a preferential safeguard as part of the current negotiations to be considered; (d) on dispute settlement, the Annexure 10 to be adopted as finalised by the fourth (4th) technical working group on trade remedies and dispute settlement; (e) the Phase 2 negotiations (Built in Agenda) to be launched by the end of 2015, and the TTNF to be allowed to begin preparatory processes and convene a meeting to launch the negotiations; (f) the industrial pillar work programme and roadmap, as well as the draft Modalities on Cooperation in Industrial Development, to be adopted by the senior Tripartite organs; (g) COMESA member states to have made tariff offers under the TFTA; and (h) the Secretariat to organise a consultative meeting for member states to determine a common COMESA position prior to the first extraordinary meeting of the TTNF, on 21–24 February 2015 in Lilongwe, Malawi. ¹³⁴

The February TTCC further reaffirmed their commitment to launch the TFTA during the third Tripartite Summit in Egypt in 2015 on the principle of variable geometry. The ministers also agreed that Phase 1 issues that were not exhaustively negotiated over the last two years would be concluded after the launch of the TFTA. To this end the TTCM had prepared a provision that was included into the draft TFTA for continued negotiation. The TTCM also reaffirmed that because of Zimbabwe's non-availability as the former presiding chair at the third Tripartite Summit that was supposed to have been held in December 2014, there was a need for further consultations with SADC before the rescheduled third Tripartite Summit in June 2015 (an expanded discussion on variable geometry is provided in more detail in Chapter 5). At the July 2017 Tripartite Summit, it was clear that member states had still not signed all the instruments necessary for a free trade area. Since the launch of the TFTA in Egypt, Phase 2 negotiations related to trade in services and rules of origin have not been concluded. An impressive twenty-four countries of the twenty-six Tripartite COMESA-EAC-SADC bloc have signed the declaration showing interest in the TFTA, with only Libya and Eritrea in limbo. The Tripartite Council of Ministers urged COMESA, EAC and SADC member states to sign and ratify the TFTA, and by April 2019 only four states ratified the TFTA – Egypt, Kenya, South Africa and Uganda. The TFTA can only come into force when fourteen member states have ratified it.[135]

Regional transport master plan

This section discusses the progress that the Tripartite bloc had made in regional infrastructure projects besides the regional airspace market discussed above. The most important aim in building Africa's regional infrastructure is to exploit regional growth for larger markets, particularly for Africa's landlocked states, through better-managed water resources and electricity production and by establishing linkages for goods to reach both markets and people.[136] Such initiatives inevitably lead to job creation and poverty eradication: effective transport lowers transport costs, and effectively generated energy facilitates agricultural production, industry, mining and communications and is therefore conducive to intraregional trade.[137]

Specialisation and infrastructure linkages have been viewed as important factors in economic integration. COMESA, EAC and SADC, through their Tripartite Agreement, held a conference that addressed regional infrastructure for the Tripartite bloc, in Lusaka, Zambia, in April 2009 and focused on the North-South Corridor. A second conference on the topic of development corridors was held in Nairobi, Kenya, in October 2010. The Tripartite Summit of Heads of State is to meet every two years. These governments, with their Secretariats, met again in Johannesburg, South Africa, on 12 June 2011 to assess achievements since the 2008 Tripartite Summit. Progress made with regard to the objectives has been very slow. Therefore, the 2011 Tripartite Summit urged the donor community to support the Aid for Trade Programme that was developed for the major corridors in the region. This support was further promoted at the Tripartite's infrastructural development programmes and has been implemented at the Tripartite and IGAD Infrastructure Investment Conference on 29–30 September 2011 held in Nairobi.

The African Regional Transport Infrastructure Network (ARTIN) is also addressing trade corridors to expand Africa's overall trade from 13 per cent of total trade in 2009 to 18 per cent by 2040.[138] Africa's transport costs are the highest globally. The African Union's heads of state and government launched the Programme for Infrastructure Development in Africa (PIDA) in Kampala in July 2010, followed by the New Partnership for Africa's Development (NEPAD) Priority Action Plan (PAP), adopted by Africa's states in January 2012.[139] PIDA is projected to cost $360 billion by 2040. PIDA projects would create 37,300 kilometres of modern highways, 30,200 kilometres of modern railways, 1.3 billion tons of added port capacity, 61,099 megawatts of hydroelectric production, 16,500 kilometres of interconnecting power lines, 21,101 cubic hectametres of new water storage capacity and six terabits of broadband internet capacity.[140] Short-term policy frameworks have also been implemented by NEPAD, largely to promote intra-African trade, reduce transaction costs and improve regional competitiveness. NEPAD contributed $2.27 billion in 2007 to multinational projects in Africa, $2.46 billion in 2006 and $2.78 billion in 2007.

As of 2011, the World Bank ranked Southern Africa 149th out of 183 regions in terms of cross-border trade.[141] On average, cargo takes thirty-five days to be exported from Southern Africa and forty-two days to be imported. The estimated cost to import a 20-foot container of non-sensitive goods ranges from $1,899 to $2,410. On average, eight documents are required for export, and nine for import. Therefore, AfDB had committed $52 billion to regional development in transport, energy, and information and communications technology.[142]

Convergence in infrastructure is evident in the North-South Corridor, jointly owned by COMESA, EAC and SADC, which is also Africa's busiest and most congested corridor for freight under a single umbrella, boosting and revamping reforms to customs, border management, infrastructure and transport regulation. Eight countries are benefitting from this initiative: Tanzania, the DRC, Zambia, Malawi, Botswana, Zimbabwe, Mozambique and South Africa.

In August 2011 the SADC summit launched its Regional Infrastructure Master Plan in Luanda, Zambia. At the individual REC level, EAC has prioritised plans to develop roads, ports, railways, transmission lines, and oil and gas infrastructure over the next decade in its 2015–25 strategy paper. EAC is improving handling capacity and efficiency at the ports of Dar es Salaam and Mombasa. In SADC, the Regional Infrastructure Development Master Plan is a major component of the Regional Indicative Strategic Development Plan.[143] The master plan has synergies with PIDA and the Tripartite free trade area among the three RECs: COMESA, EAC and SADC. This plan was signed by member states at the SADC Summit in August 2012 and will be implemented over three 5-year intervals: short-term (2012–2017), medium-term (2017–2022) and long-term (2022–2027).

Funding from external donors will greatly assist regional infrastructure, and the Tripartite bloc is awaiting earmarked funds from Europe totalling 110 billion euros pledged for infrastructure development. While funding is a challenge, there are other creative ways in which to address infrastructure challenges. For example, the Deloitte and Touche auditing firm offers a creative project funding methodology that can support governments in major infrastructure projects by including new pools of infrastructure investors and financiers to deliver the required infrastructure needs.[144] SADC was looking at $100 billion to finance its projects by 2015. Investment in the energy sector will require $47 billion over a period of five years; road projects, up to $26 billion; ports and inland waterways, $18 billion; and information and communications technology, postal systems, and meteorology and water projects, $9 billion.[145] South Africa contributed $6.2 billion in 2012 towards investment through the Industrial Development Corporation in forty-one projects across seventeen African countries in mining, industrial infrastructure, agro-processing and tourism.[146]

The MDC was further developed in 2014 by South Africa's Transnet for port and rail operators in Eswatini and Mozambique. The aim of the Maputo Corridor Joint Operating Centre (JOC) is to increase the MDC's rail freight capacity. The JOC is a major milestone among the three countries: Eswatini, Mozambique and South Africa. The rail freight corridor runs from Mpumalanga in South Africa through Eswatini to the Port of Richards Bay in South Africa and the Port of Maputo in Mozambique. In operation since 2013, turnaround time for trade was reduced from 118 hours on road to 62 hours with an average of ten to eighteen trains running per week on this corridor. As discussed earlier, the MCLI required funds of R1.9 billion for upgrades and road freight has been costly – on average, rail is 75 per cent cheaper than road transport.[147] South Africa's Transnet's market demand strategy is moving cargo from road to rail and includes a R312-billion seven-year infrastructure investment programme starting from 2013.[148]

Throughout Africa, exploitable energy resources like hydropower, coal, gas, oil and uranium – both new and renewable resources – are in abundance. While both northern and western Africa have an abundance of oil and gas reserves, Southern Africa has large coal deposits. The SAPP grid and the East African Power Pool (EAPP) grid, as well as planned power interconnections for five corridors and planned power-generation projects in Ethiopia, Sudan, the DRC, Kenya, Uganda and Tanzania, are positive developments. In Southern Africa, challenges for power generation of cleaner energy sources (such as solar, hydro, wind and nuclear) compared to fossil fuels such as coal, as identified in the Renewable Energy Strategy and Action Plan, remains a challenge.[149] Hydropower potential is evident in the Nile, Congo, Niger, Senegal, Volta, Orange and Zambezi river systems. Geothermal resources are found in the Red Sea Valley and Rift Valley, and solar energy enterprises can be harnessed in Southern Africa (such as through South Africa's coastal wind farms). Public–private partnerships are one mechanism that has been used to bridge the funding gap in infrastructure, as was discussed in the micro-regionalism section further above in the assessment of the MDC. South Africa had proposed a plan through Eskom to have independent power producers within twenty-eight projects between 2012 and 2025 to secure procurements under the Renewable Energy Independent Power Producer Programme (REIPPP).[150] The REIPPP project assumes the following: a baseload capacity of 2,500 MW of coal-fired generation by 2024; 2,652 MW of gas power by 2025; 2,609 MW of hydroelectric power imports by 2024; 9,200 MW of wind generation; 1,200 MW of concentrated solar power; 8,400 MW of solar photovoltaic production; 9,600 MW of nuclear capacity; 4,930 MW of open-cycle gas-turbine peaking plant capacity; 2,370 MW of combined-cycle gas-turbine capacity; 11,332 MW of pumped-storage scheme; 2,659 MW of imported hydropower; and 465 MW of renewable technology.

South Africa's Integrated Resource Plan (IRP) of 2010–13 further confirms a rolling renewable and procurement programme with 3,200 MW added to projects for development by 2020, as well as 3,725 MW in renewable capacity projects, valued at R100 billion.[151] Such agreements could bring about significant convergence among the Tripartite bloc member states. Although the airspace market was finalised, which is a first step to this integration process, the integration partnership between African member states, however, requires further development of the infrastructural policies and institutional capacities of both of these regional economic communities for viable economic growth.[152]

Concluding remarks

This discussion examined the extent to which convergence had occurred in regional trade agreements in providing a detailed account of the progress of COMESA, EAC and SADC's Tripartite Agreement in relation to its roadmap, by assessing their trade protocols and timeframes. This provides an adequate account of how much convergence had occurred within COMESA, EAC and SADC. These findings were presented and directly aligned with the theme: situating regional integration in the divergence and convergence debate. The findings on regional integration and convergence were particularly relevant to this chapter as they provided the contextual basis for understanding the major issues before and after the formation of the 2008 Tripartite Agreement of COMESA, EAC and SADC, adequately assessed and discussed in this chapter. These major factors constitute the principal issue of the book, to connect regional integration with liberalisation of regional trade arrangements linked to economic growth. Findings on this theme also revealed that while COMESA, EAC and SADC were faced with open markets of trade, regional integration could be exploited positively through micro-regionalism to support weaker economies, as in Mozambique. The importance of building infrastructure to conduct effective regional trade was discussed. The chapter also considered COMESA, EAC and SADC's competitive advantage to support endogenous growth factors of inputs of semi-skilled and unskilled labour in energy production. SAPP is an example of how electricity in trade had assisted the Southern African region. Also at the early stages of integration, the impact of South Africa was considered, who, as a stronger economy and with the most advanced parastatal, Eskom, was able to contribute to the region's infrastructure development and electricity generation favourably, while also creatively managing to address some of its own socio-economic domestic challenges. Competition and competitive trade in agriculture was expanded on when examining how convergence could be improved among the three RECs through agriculture. An example of a COMESA-EAC-SADC sugar protocol in agriculture was provided to address several challenges of trade competition, skills enhancement and technology development. The findings were presented in narrative form and in tables and graphs, and were supported by evidence that was at times based on interviews conducted in the region. In most instances relevant literature was used to support such evidence.

The chapter also fully assessed the major events that occurred during the ten years (1998–2008) and expanded on the main actors and factors that led to the 2008 Tripartite Agreement.[153] The chapter outlined how it happened that these three RECs, COMESA, EAC, and SADC, met again and merged in 2008, since their last gathering in 1997, which had been directly linked to facilitating infrastructure to enhance trade through the YD for air travel. The chapter interrogated what COMESA, EAC and SADC have managed to achieve with regard to their agreements and protocols outlined in the 2008 Tripartite Agreement for the period 2008–15, as well as the actors and factors that retarded their progress. The COMESA-EAC-SADC free trade area will be running in parallel to the African Continental Free Trade Agreement, which is discussed in further detail in Chapter 6.

5

Convergence and consolidation of multiple memberships: An attempted convergence

The focus of this chapter is on the management of multiple memberships of the Common Market for Eastern and Southern Africa (COMESA), the East African Community (EAC) and the Southern African Development Community (SADC) member states, which belong to various regional economic communities of free trade areas (FTAs) and customs unions.

The discussion assesses the management of multiple memberships by both regional economic communities (RECs) and member states with a view to assess the implications of convergence for the bloc and will expand the discussion on South Africa's and the Southern African Customs Union's (SACU's) relations. Trade is largely being conducted with powerful external trade schemes such as the African Growth and Opportunity Act (AGOA), the Brazil-Russia-India-China-South Africa (BRICS) and the European Economic Partnership Agreements (EPAs).

As a starting point the chapter posits that the success of convergence of the Tripartite FTA is linked to the achievement of real economic gains and benefits for all member states, and these benefits may not be equal. Moreover, convergence of the Tripartite bloc can only occur with a hegemonic presence – a strong member state/s with a strong economy/ies, and the hegemonic state must achieve real economic gains, while smaller economies must obtain economic growth, particularly socio-economic growth. This convergence does not advocate for market exploitation by the powerful hegemonic state, as was discussed in Chapter 3, but what is shown in this chapter is how economic convergence can be achieved with a hegemonic state (powerful economy) within a regional bloc with smaller economies, while being considerate of sensitive trade.

In order to contextualise the discussion, on the management of multiple memberships, the chapter notes as a starting point that the genesis of multiple memberships are owing to the 1997 rationalisation processes of COMESA and SADC, as was discussed in Chapter 3. Also explained in Chapter 3 under the rationalisation process of the two blocs, COMESA and SADC agreed to divide the two regions into a Preferential Trade Area (PTA) for Southern Africa that comprised all SADC member states. Preferential trade arrangements in the southern region were to be carried out under the auspices of SADC.[1] The process of separating the two regions into North and South was to evolve over time, and the modalities regarding which region COMESA and SADC member states would want to belong to had to be determined by individual member states as their sovereign right. The EAC countries remained in COMESA, while Tanzania also joined SADC. Also agreed was that there should be a PTA for the North, which comprised non-SADC countries, and member states from both blocs could choose which REC they wished to join.

Second, the 2008 Tripartite Agreement allowed member states to liberalise tariffs according to their individual preparedness, namely the variable geometry approach that had been adopted by the Tripartite bloc. Furthermore, the same approach was also adopted at the individual REC levels of SADC, COMESA and the EAC, where member states were given considerable flexibility in terms of timing and liberalisation of tariffs. This chapter argues that the dilemma for the Tripartite bloc now is that its decision to implement a variable geometry approach – allowing for member states of a regional grouping to cooperate separately from other members, as well as for flexible progression in cooperation in a variety of areas and at different speeds – was an attempt to help manage the multiple memberships of member states.[2] But the chapter also argues that the variable geometry approach has hampered economic convergence for the bloc since the reality of globalisation is that markets operate freely.

Having that said, when the 2008 Tripartite Agreement was signed, member states were also allowed to continue with or create external trade and enter into bilateral agreements, for example, with Europe and the United States. The COMESA-EAC-SADC bloc is also running parallel free trade agreements (FTAs) with the African Continental Free Trade Area (which is discussed in Chapter 6).

The findings in this chapter will demonstrate that due to rules of origin (ROOs) specified in trade commodities in external trade agreements – such as in the AGOA agreements and with Europe, for example –these arrangements have further complicated the management of multiple memberships for the Tripartite bloc. The chapter therefore shows that given the fact that the Tripartite bloc has not finalised its own policies concerning ROOs (which is a work in progress), trade liberalisation that is reflective of open markets is causing polarisation of smaller markets and industries.[3]

The bilateral agreements of AGOA are examples of the polarising nature of trade, and the chapter thus shows the extent of trade between AGOA schemes and the Tripartite bloc member states and the extent of trade divergence. Moreover, this chapter notes that globalisation dictates open markets and trade, which creates a contradiction for the Tripartite Agreement's regional integration approaches. These contradictions are not adequately supported within the neoclassical economic approach theory of open trade and regional integration divergence and convergence debates, as was discussed in the literature reviewed in Chapter 2. Therefore, the discussion examines, in the first main argument in this chapter, convergence defined as neoclassical economic regional integration, which will help in supporting the findings provided here in this chapter. The theory of neoclassical economic regional integration[4] is focused on converging regions through a regional economic integration lens, which is applied in this chapter to help explain how long-run convergence in a regional grouping can be achieved and is applied to the case of South Africa and the SACU.

South Africa unfortunately succumbed to Europe's diversion move, and since the 2000 Cotonou EU-ACP trade agreements, Tshwane had begun distancing itself from the Caribbean and the Pacific countries. Such moves Europe successfully orchestrated when it evoked South Africa's developed economic status and denounced its least-developing-state profile.[5]

Management of multiple memberships

The purpose of the discussion is to contribute to the core focus of the book: convergence and divergence of the Tripartite bloc and convergence of Pan-African economic integration (see Chapter 6). Fourteen of COMESA's nineteen member states participated in the COMESA FTA it established in 2000. The exceptions are Ethiopia, which has liberalised only 10 per cent of its trade; the Democratic Republic of the Congo (DRC), which has liberalised none of its trade and is still charging duty on all goods entering the country; Uganda, which has liberalised 80 per cent of trade; and Eritrea, which has liberalised only 10 per cent of trade. Eswatini, as a SACU member state, is under derogation and not liberalising tariffs.[6] The EAC, besides being member states of COMESA and Tanzania in SADC, is creating its own zone of free trade and has achieved 100 per cent liberalisation of trade, as well as formed its own customs union.[7] Under Article 31 of the SACU Agreement (revised in 1969 and 2002), 'Eswatini as a COMESA member sought derogations from granting trade preferences to its COMESA trade partners due to its SACU membership'.[8] South Africa, as the largest economy in the Tripartite FTA bloc, belongs to one free trade area (SADC's) and one customs union (SACU's). Of the African Union's (AU's) fifty-five member states, twenty-six are members of two RECs and twenty are members of three RECs. The DRC belongs to four RECs. Of the fourteen regional integration groupings in Africa, there are two or more groupings in other subregions (e.g. both in SADC and COMESA).[9]

The Grand Ethiopian Renaissance Dam (GERD) has also exacerbated tensions with Ethiopia's government remaining wary of Egypt's moves.[10] The Ethiopian government has had several disputes with Egypt, such as that over the Nile River dam (as discussed in Chapter 7). Egypt's deployment of troops in South Sudan and signing of a bilateral cooperation agreement with it have further estranged Ethiopia from South Sudan.[11] Table 5.1 seeks to show what the factors are that are prohibiting the convergence of the bloc and what conditions led to the signing of the June 2015 TFTA. By 2015, Ethiopia had still not reached a position of trust or the ability to conduct and liberalise tariffs when security and political tensions have been looming large over the region; Addis Ababa only signed the TFTA in July 2017 after several rounds of summit meetings, and only four countries ratified the TFTA by May 2019, namely, Egypt, Kenya, South Africa and Uganda – fourteen member states are required to ratify the TFTA for it to be implemented (an agreement lapsing by the end of 2019).

In SADC, fourteen of sixteen member states are in the SADC FTA, excluding Angola and the DRC. There are also tensions that relate to historical relations among the Tripartite bloc's member states. The DRC conflict flared up again in 2011, and in 2016 over third-termism of its president going against the country's constitution, leading to violent intra-state conflict preceded by an election and a new DRC president, Félix Tshisekedi, elected in January 2019, but working with politicians

Table 5.1 Membership in RECs and FTAs in the Tripartite bloc

COMESA	EAC	SADC	COMESA FTA	EAC FTA and Customs Union	SADC FTA	Membership in other RECs	Tripartite FTA (10 June 2015)[a]
Burundi	Djibouti	Angola	Burundi	Djibouti	Botswana	Angola (ECCAS)	Angola
Comoros	Kenya	Botswana	Comoros	Kenya	Lesotho	Burundi (CEPGL)	Burundi
Djibouti	Rwanda	DRC	Djibouti	Rwanda	Madagascar	Djibouti (CEN-SAD)	Comoros
DRC	South Sudan	Lesotho	Egypt	Tanzania	Malawi	DRC (CEPGL)	DRC
	Tanzania						
Egypt	Uganda	Madagascar	Kenya	Uganda	Mauritius	Egypt (CEN-SAD)	Djibouti
Eritrea		Malawi	Libya		Mozambique	Eritrea (CEN-SAD)	Egypt[b]
Ethiopia		Mauritius	Mauritius		Namibia	Eritrea (CEN-SAD)	Kenya[b]
Kenya		Mozambique	Rwanda		Seychelles	Libya (CEN-SAD)	Malawi
Libya		Namibia	Seychelles		South Africa	Rwanda (CEPGL)	Namibia
Madagascar		Seychelles	Zambia		Eswatini	Somalia (CEN-SAD)	South Africa[b]
						Sudan (CEN-SAD)	
Malawi		South Africa	Zimbabwe		Tanzania		Rwanda
Mauritius		Eswatini			Zambia		Seychelles
Rwanda		Tanzania			Zimbabwe		Sudan
Seychelles		Zambia					Tanzania
Sudan		Zimbabwe and Comoros					Uganda[b]
							Eswatini
Tanzania							Ethiopia (joined in 2017)
Uganda							Zimbabwe
Zambia							
Zimbabwe							

Note: ECCAS = the Economic Community of Central African States; CEPGL = the Economic Community of the Great Lakes Countries; CEN-SAD = the Community of Sahel-Saharan States.
[a] Carlos Lopes, 'Mega Trade Agreement a Step Forward for the Continent', *UNECA*, 12 June 2015, http://www.uneca.org/stories/mega-trade-agreement-step-forward-continent-%E2%80%93-carlos-lopes. See also Gerhard Erasmus, "The Tripartite FTA: Technical Features, Potential and Implementation', *Tralac* (18 June 2015), https://www.tralac.org/news/article/7574-tralac-s-daily-news-selection-19-june-2015.html.
[b] TFTA ratified by only four states.
Source: United Nations Economic Commission for Africa (UNECA), *Study on the Establishment of Inter-RECs' Free Trade Areas in Africa Drawing on Lessons from the COMESA-SADC-EAC FTA Experience*, 2 May 2011, http://www.uneca.org/sites/default/files/uploaded-documents/CTRCI-VII/Tripartite_comesa_eac_sadc_fta-study-final-report.pdf, pp. 14–20.

from the old guard[12] of the former DRC president Joseph Kabila. Also, the Rwandan-backed March 23 (M23) rebel group movement occupying some of the territory in the DRC caused much regional mayhem and violence (see Chapter 7 for a detailed discussion of these). Porous borders and poor governance have also contributed to the Tripartite's bloc's own set of challenges in obtaining regional convergence.[13] As indicated in Table 5.1, there is extensive overlap, with most member states belonging to more than one REC. Political and economic tensions and examples of divergence are evident. Rwanda and Uganda's conflicts in the DRC have kept the DRC from joining or sharing a zone of trade initially with these member states. Rebel groups supported by Rwanda and Uganda in the DRC[14] have been the centre of an intermittent but long-standing conflict since 1998. However, while the conflict situation in the Great Lakes region has caused regional divergence, since the move of South Africa, Malawi and Tanzania in coordinating military efforts, in assisting the Great Lakes region by militarily deploying a three-thousand-strong Force Intervention Brigade (FIB) in eastern Congo, the regional dynamics have changed.

The tense political situation in the Great Lakes region did initially create divergence among the member states of the EAC, but as discussed above, it has also caused the convergence of these members' economic policies in trade due to the FIB and its success in combating the M23 rebel movement. Evidently, on 10 June 2015, the DRC, Tanzania, Rwanda, Uganda and Burundi were all part of those who signed the Tripartite Grand Free Trade Agreement. This meeting took place in Egypt and was signed by only sixteen member states, mainly of the COMESA bloc, based on variable geometry.[15] The sixteen member states and signatory to the Tripartite FTA included Angola, Burundi (EAC), Comoros, the DRC, Djibouti, Egypt, Kenya (EAC), Malawi, Namibia, Rwanda (EAC), Seychelles, Sudan, Tanzania (EAC), Uganda (EAC), Eswatini and Zimbabwe.[16] South Sudan also joined the EAC in 2015 and has received strong support from Uganda during its conflict with Khartoum (discussed in Chapter 7).

On its part, the SACU Secretariat pointed out that it had no intentions of joining the Tripartite FTA;[17] however, two of its member states signed it: Namibia and Eswatini. Namibia was among the countries that initially bitterly complained about South Africa's relationship with the European Union (EU). There were major losses in agricultural produce due to quota-free market access for fish, beef and grapes.[18]

Namibia also complained that South Africa's stringent ROOs have been a further impediment to intraregional trade for Southern Africa and that South Africa has prohibited the importation of live animals from Namibia; as a result, costs to the Windhoek government were estimated at R30 billion in establishing agro-processing schemes such as feed-loads and abattoirs to create an environment conducive to trade.[19] Namibia became signatory to the Tripartite FTA on 10 June 2015.[20] On its part, Eswatini is hoping to benefit from the AGOA trade within a larger Tripartite FTA and also signed the TFTA, since the United States stopped its trade relations with Eswatini (discussed later on in this chapter). Eritrea and Ethiopia have remained wary of joining the COMESA FTA and initially feared revenue losses, trade divergence on sensitive products and loss of protection of their key industries. Ethiopia's fears also concern mainly the country's manufacturing sector, and it envisages substantial job losses since it lacks competitive advantages.[21]

Cordial relations also started to exist among Sudan, Ethiopia[22] and Kenya in particular, with the 4 March 2012 official opening of Lamu Port in Kenya by the former Kenyan president Mwai Kibaki and the successful completion of the Lamu Port for Southern Sudan–Ethiopia Transport (LAPSSET) corridor. In July 2013, at the 12th Annual Ethiopian–Djibouti Joint Commission Ministerial Meeting, agreements on trade investment and infrastructure, as well as security and other issues, were reached. These two countries were already executing joint mega-projects, including rail and road infrastructural development and new ports, power and water services. Ethiopia exports 65 megawatts of electricity and clean water to Djibouti in a multimillion-dollar new railway project between Addis Ababa and Djibouti.[23] Only two years later in July 2017 did Ethiopia sign the TFTA but has not ratified the TFTA to take effect.

In the case of SADC, trade liberalisation takes on an asymmetrical structure in SADC, which means that the sixteen countries are classified into three groups: SACU; least developed countries, or LDCs (Angola, the DRC, Madagascar, Malawi, Mozambique, Tanzania, Zambia and Zimbabwe); and developing countries (Seychelles and Mauritius). With the adoption of the SADC trade protocol and moving towards an FTA, SADC like COMESA also took on a variable geometry approach. SADC's non-SACU members decided to front-load their tariffs within five years of adoption of the trade protocol and bring the tariffs to zero with the exception of a few sensitive products. The developing countries agreed to start their tariff reductions earlier than other non-SACU members, while LDCs were allowed to backload their reduction commitments.[24]

Variable geometry and the Tripartite bloc

This section provides a brief account of how COMESA, EAC and SADC (as both institutions and member states) manage multiple memberships. In the area of trade, customs and economic integration, the Tripartite Summit at Kampala, Uganda, on 22 October 2008[25] and the Tripartite memorandum of understanding (MOU) that came into force on 19 January 2011[26] defined the free trade process and membership agreements (as was discussed in Chapter 4). In Article 1 of the MOU, the 2008 Tripartite Summit agreed that in establishing the FTA it would take into account the principle of variable geometry and provide a legal and institutional framework to underpin the FTA. Since the signing of the June 2015 TFTA, these legal instruments are still being negotiated and are still to be concluded, as has been explained above.[27]

The Tripartite bloc's decision to implement variable geometry, which is a principle that allows member states of a regional grouping to cooperate in separation from other members as well as flexibility for progression in cooperation in a variety of areas and at different speeds, was an attempt to help manage the overlapping REC memberships of member states.[28] The Tripartite bloc has also adopted a trade liberalisation framework that is reflective of open markets.[29] Trade liberalisation through bilateral trade agreements further hampers the principle of variable geometry and appears to contrast with trade protection and incremental integration, since the pace of integration varies between these two approaches.

As Gathii contends, variable geometry is a time-tabled approach committing member states to different speeds of economic ability to serve the interests of members belonging to a regional bloc, which provides them with the flexibility to trade. The Tripartite bloc is attempting to harmonise regional policies in trade undertaken for regional economic convergence. Krugman and Martin[30] note that regional economies dependent on export clusters held together by local Marshallian-type[31] external economies allow states to reap benefits from specialised labour of technological spillover, which also lead to increasing economic returns that further benefit those member states within a regional grouping and place such states in a competitive advantage.[32] States should therefore consider how to build on total factor productivity to boost jobs and skills.

Furthermore, Krugman suggests that 'regional trade can benefit in technology and skills transfer in those export clusters (poorer economies) that conduct trade with more advanced economies. Such benefits include a shift in the production of goods to countries which can produce them most competitively and efficiently; improvement in socio-economic welfare due to consumer surplus resulting from lower prices from competitively produced goods; an increase in employment and job creation; and more importantly, comparative advantages and being able to produce and manufacture goods that reflect these advantages, which in turn have the potential to create economies of scale.'[33] What this means is that for the Tripartite bloc to become more technologically advanced and competitive, it should not only focus on internal interregional trade and value-added and industrialisation-driven policy but also consider conducting trade outside of the bloc with external partners that benefit from its own integration. The qualities of competing and becoming competitive have been lacking for the Tripartite bloc, which stifles economic growth with industries not advancing as outlined by both Krugman and Martin.[34]

This chapter analyses how the Tripartite member states are conducting trade with external partners like AGOA trade schemes that have challenged the ROOs associated with similar trade, as with the Tripartite bloc. Gathii contends that trade liberalisation policies have complicated ROOs that are attached to goods linked to external trade agreements and conflict with internal settings of ROOs.[35] He notes,

> African RTAs [regional trade arrangements] are trade-plus regimes that reflect a broad set of goals and are not simply trade treaties. Seeing African RTAs as regimes adds to the argument that countries that are members of more than one RTA may well regard treaties establishing RTAs as providing a framework for cooperation, but not necessarily as treaties creating binding obligations.[36]

Africa's states have the liberty to form multiple memberships, which states see as offering them the flexibility to retain their sovereignty and accrue benefits.[37] COMESA, EAC and SADC's economic integration practices allow further openness of their markets.[38]

According to trade and legal expert Gerhard Erasmus,

> The signing of the FTA Agreement [10 June 2015] is indeed an important development ... it will take time before this Agreement will enter into force. The

remainder of the negotiations [also discussed in more detail in Chapter 4] include Phase 1 (the built-in-agenda); Annex 1 – the Elimination of Customs Duties; Annex II on Trade Remedies and Annex IV on Rules of Origin.[39]

Nyong'o[40] posits that it would not be possible for COMESA, EAC and SADC FTAs to accommodate multiple memberships within a common external tariff and within a customs union. This is not a norm and would be in violation of the General Agreement on Tariffs and Trade (GATT) Article XXIV.[41] All preferential agreements covering trade in services must also be reported under Article 5 of the World Trade Organisation (WTO), regardless of membership. However, Article 5 is less relevant for Africa's RECs, since their trading arrangements generally focus on trade in goods. Africa's RECs experience great difficulty with the wide-open nature of the enabling clause. COMESA, for example, is considering reporting under Article 24 to protect itself from complaints concerning displacement of imports. Sri Lanka, for instance, has contended that its tea exports into Egypt have been displaced by Kenyan exports benefiting from COMESA preferences. Hence, under the enabling clause, Sri Lanka can claim that it is entitled to compensation since Egypt has a tariff agreement on tea that was undermined by the preferences.[42] This means that African governments, through their RECs, have designed compensatory mechanisms to ensure that losses arising from liberalisation commitments are recovered and given to the disadvantaged parties. As Gathii posits, 'by foregrounding variable geometry and distributional equity concerns, African RTAs have correspondingly distanced themselves from non-discriminatory free trade'.[43] As Arvind Panagariya notes, the complexity of regional integration is daunting even in the absence of trade barriers and 'crisscrossing FTAs lead to a replacement of non-discriminatory most-favoured nation (MFN) tariffs by a spaghetti bowl whereby tariffs vary according to ostensible origin of the product'.[44] Jagdish Bhagwati coined the increase in the number of bilateral and regional trade agreements as the 'spaghetti bowl'.[45] Jenkins, Leape and Thomas identify the generally poor regional frameworks that have been created as regional trade initiatives that have achieved very little.

> In spite of their political appeal ... [m]any schemes were designed without taking into account members' divergent interests and the conflicting obligations stemming from overlapping [multiple] membership of different regional arrangements; without considering the feasibility of implementation for participating countries; and without assessing members' incentives to comply and their scope for substituting non-tariff barriers for tariffs.[46]

On the other hand, Europe is replacing its 1999 EU–SA TDCA agreement with South Africa and is negotiating under the SADC EPA with Southern African countries, mainly Botswana, Lesotho, Namibia, Eswatini, Mozambique and South Africa. On 22 July 2014 the first round of negotiations with Europe addressed key trade areas which had negatively impacted Botswana, Lesotho, Namibia and Eswatini (BLNE) markets in the past during the 2000s. The renegotiated agreement was scheduled for conclusion by October 2016.[47] The SADC EPA, as the EU's largest trading partner, consists of six out of sixteen members of SADC (Comoros is the latest member state) (SACU plus 1 (Mozambique)). Europe's exports have dwindled somewhat since South Africa joined BRICS. The 2013 EU exports to Southern Africa totalled 33 billion euros, and Southern Africa's main trade to the EU in 2013 totalled 31 billion euros and comprised chiefly Botswana (diamonds), South Africa (diamonds; platinum; agri-food sector, including wine, sugar, citrus, table grapes and other fruit; precious stones, metals and uranium), Namibia (fish) and Eswatini (sugar, fruit and nuts).

The new SADC EPA agreement includes shielding sensitive sectors from European competitors in their domestic market. In the new negotiations, the EU had to make a commitment and refrain from subsidising its agricultural exports to the region. This the South African negotiators have enforced as a condition for signing the EPA agreement in 2016 and it has since been initialled and under observation.[48] A list of 251 EU and 105 South African geographical indications has been agreed to.[49] Trade can only be to the benefit of the Tripartite bloc economies when the lists of the SADC EPA, the trade lists of the AGOA scheme and the trade list of the TFTA are taken into consideration jointly and carefully balanced so that the Tripartite FTA benefits the most, which must conclude its own ROOs trade policy in order to derive maximum benefit. As outlined in Chapter 4, a pilot study should be considered in trade that considers the comparative advantage of the Tripartite bloc in sugar, leather and steel.

Rules of origin and external trade agreements: AGOA and EPAs

In building on the overall divergence and convergence debate of the book, this section expands on how external bilateral agreements with the EU and the United States impact on multiple memberships of the Tripartite bloc member states.

Trade with the EU's EPAs and the United States' AGOA liberalisation policies have complicated ROOs attached to their goods.[50] The goal of non-discriminatory trade under the GATT/WTO ROOs, a ten-year assessment known as the Sutherland report, is inconsistent with regard to ROOs in multiple regional trade agreements, which hamper trade flows.[51] In the case of COMESA-EAC-SADC, each REC, namely, the FTAs of COMESA, EAC and SADC, has its own ROOs, which vary across products and transition phases; hence there are several different tariff rates complying with the tariff rates assigned to the products. The lists of sensitive products in SADC, for example, came to the fore when South Africa signed the Trade Development and Corporation Agreement in 1999 with the EU.[52]

The requirements in SADC are, for example, that garments must be produced from regionally produced textiles, fabric must be made from regionally produced yarn, and yarn must be made from un-carded, uncombed fibre or from chemical products.[53] Multiple memberships diminish trade capacity, since the Tripartite bloc has to conform to various ROOs under various regional economic communities' requirements. ROOs are to protect trade and therefore restrict trade within a liberalised trade regime of the Tripartite bloc. These rules have become major obstacles to convergence and the

COMESA-EAC-SADC bloc has not completed the negotiating process, which has been a continuous one since the TFTA was signed by only sixteen member states and Annex IV of the TFTA on ROOs had not been finalised in 2015; only recently, in July 2017, a total of twenty-four countries signed, but it still requires ratification by fourteen countries to come into effect, as explained in Chapter 4.[54]

SADC's own trade protocol objectives were particularly strained during the slow progress in ratifying the ROOs for clothing, textiles and cane sugar. South Africa had excluded a list of sensitive products from duty-free entry into its market, including dairy; wheat and wheat products; sugar and sugar confectionery; cotton, knitted or crocheted fabrics, and knitted or crocheted clothing; leather footwear; and motor vehicles. These were classified under Category C of sensitive products. Moreover, multilateral and international trade agreements offer the MFN tariff to only one trade partner, and to date such clauses have benefited European agreements in the main, leaving regional arrangements vulnerable.[55] Brenton, Flatters and Kalenga note,

> Rather than facilitating development through trade, the Trade Protocol will replace transparent and declining tariff barriers in important sectors with complex and more restrictive input sourcing requirements that will diminish trade, increase transactions costs, reduce flexibility of producers and make the region a less attractive place to invest. Restrictive rules of origin might be in the interests of particular producers that wish to avoid new competition in their domestic markets. By the same token, however, such rules will make it impossible for them to compete in other regional markets, make it difficult if not impossible to benefit from attractive sourcing opportunities in the region and elsewhere, and will deprive downstream users, both producers and final consumers of the benefits of preferential tariff reductions.[56]

Figure 5.1 demonstrates the levels of trade with AGOA markets as an example of how trade with various ROOs is causing difficulties in the management of multiple memberships for the Tripartite bloc. COMESA and South Africa's trade with AGOA also outlines AGOA's main export markets. The figure also shows South Africa in the top category alongside those of Egypt and Libya. Top US export markets with COMESA member states and South Africa in 2013 were Egypt – $5.2 billion; Libya – $812 million; Ethiopia – $678 million; Kenya – $651 million; and Djibouti – $170 million. South Africa was the United States' thirty-ninth-largest supplier of imported goods, with total imports from South Africa at $8.5 billion in 2013, and AGOA's exports to South Africa totalled $7.3 billion in 2013. The major economies like South Africa, Kenya and Egypt have continued to conduct more trade with external partners like the United States and the EU than with its regional partners, and external trade with external businesses and trading partners is progressively pursued, as seen in the AGOA trade imports and exports.[57] Brenton, Flatters and Kalenga have also noted that trade agreements conducted outside of the blocs, as in the case of the Tripartite bloc, distort trade. ROOs specify when a product qualifies for duty-free movement within a regional trade agreement and the proportion of value to be added if it originates within the trade bloc, or whether it is required that a product undergo

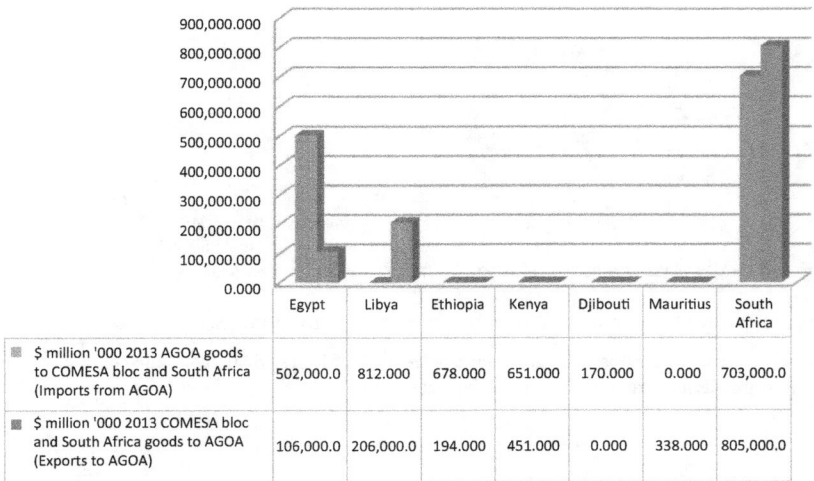

Figure 5.1 Major partners of COMESA and South Africa with the AGOA market in 2013.

Source: Adapted from https://ustr.gov/countries-regions/africa/regional-economic-communities-rec/common-market-eastern-and-Southern-africa-comesa.

a substantial amount of transformation to allow it as a product for trade as per the stipulated requirements.[58]

Figure 5.2 shows the top export commodities from AGOA markets to COMESA: machinery ($1.2 billion), aircraft ($1.1 billion), wheat ($714 million), vehicles ($551 million) and oil ($549 million).

Figure 5.3 shows the major export goods in 2013 from COMESA to AGOA: mineral fuel and crude oil ($2.7 billion), woven apparel ($829 million), knitted apparel ($564 million), spices, tea and coffee ($253 million) and fertilizers ($172 million).[59]

The primary products exported through the AGOA agreement, besides the extensive list of 316 tariff lines, are also based on the primary products of the COMESA-EAC-SADC Tripartite members' trade with the United States, and directly impact on the fabric origin rule for apparel. The third-country fabric provision had changed, with textiles in Lesotho decreasing from 21 per cent in 2006 to 12 per cent of total textile trade with AGOA.[60] The AGOA Committee on Ways and Means and trade committees focus largely on US preference programmes. US imports of private commercial services (excluding military and government) were $1.9 billion in 2012 for travel, while the other private services (business, professional and technical) accounted for most of US services imports from South Africa.[61] Former US president Barack Obama had extended his private sector budget proposal and AGOA trade fund for another fifteen years from September 2015 to September 2030. According to Stephen Lande, president of Manchester Trade, and commonly known as the 'father of the Generalized System of Preferences of GATT', the extended AGOA agreement indicates that although AGOA provides duty-free access for 97.5 per cent of all tariff lines, there are still 316 tariff lines, mostly in agriculture, that are not currently included under the second AGOA.[62]

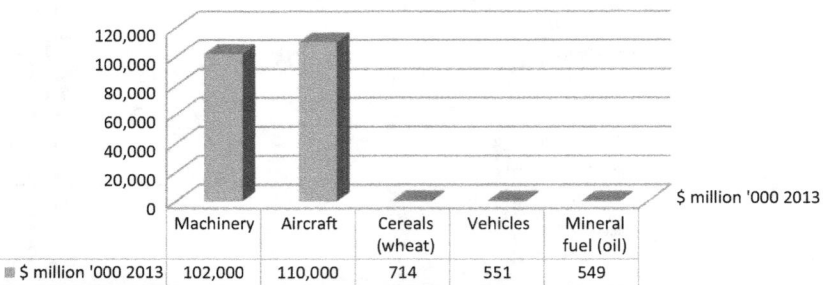

Figure 5.2 Five top export commodities from AGOA to COMESA in 2013.

Source: Adapted from https://ustr.gov/countries-regions/africa/regional-economic-communities-rec/common-market-eastern-and-Southern-africa-comesa.

	Mineral fuel and oil (crude)	Woven apparel	Knit apparel	Spices, tea and coffee mostly coffee	Fertilisers
$ million '000 2013	207,000	829	564	253	172

Figure 5.3 Major export goods from COMESA to AGOA in 2013.

Source: Adapted from https://ustr.gov/countries-regions/africa/regional-economic-communities-rec/common-market-eastern-and-Southern-africa-comesa.

With the EAC, the United States had $1.8 billion in total goods during 2013. Exports totalled $1.2 billion and imports totalled $597 million. US trade exports to the EAC in 2013 were $1.2 billion: Kenya – $651 million, Tanzania – $420 million, Uganda – $125 million, Rwanda – $25 million and Burundi – $17 million. US exports of agricultural goods to EAC countries totalled $127 million in 2013. These included pulses ($23 million) and coarse grains ($22 million).

US goods imported from the EAC countries totalled $597 million in 2013, with partners Kenya ($451 million), who is also a major trading partner of the United States, as noted earlier in Figure 5.1; Tanzania ($70 million); Uganda ($47 million); Rwanda ($24 million); and Burundi ($4 million). Goods exported from the EAC to the United States were knitted apparel ($171 million), woven apparel ($148 million), spices, coffee and tea ($119 million), edible fruit and nuts ($31 million) and precious stones ($22 million). EAC agricultural exports to US markets in 2013 comprised unroasted coffee ($111 million) and tree nuts ($31 million).[63]

Panagariya provides an illustration of the spaghetti-bowl concept in FTAs as opposed to customs unions:

> Member countries fear that imports from outside countries destined to a high-tariff member may enter through a low-tariff member ... or entrepreneurs in the

low-tariff country may import a product in almost finished form, add a small value to it and export it to the high tariff country free of duty.[64]

Therefore, to avoid trade diversion, FTAs need to take into account the ROOs and specify such rules 'according to which products receive the duty-free status and only if a pre-specified proportion of value added in the product originates within the union'.[65]

Regional arrangements in multiple memberships: Hindrance or promotion?

The first purpose of the discussion in this section is to show that multiple memberships are linked to real economic gains for all parties irrespective of economic strength.[66] If there are real economic benefits derived in another regional trade agreement/ scheme, there will be divergence in the TFTA. The second purpose of this section is to demonstrate economic benefits derived over a long-run convergence period in a regional trade agreement, and states can come on par with the stronger economy. The discussion on SACU indicates that although economic convergence of the bloc is achieved, such economic growth is attained through a funding envelope of 98 per cent of generated revenue primarily through South Africa's trade contribution, which is divided among the BLNE countries – a lucrative package made possible by South Africa as a member state in the SACU customs union. However, very little socio-economic benefit is being achieved by BLNE countries owing largely to the oligopolistic and monopolistic practices of South Africa's business in regional relations that trump political governance of the SACU arrangement.

Currently, South Africa's dominant multinational corporations and parochial practices in the region have exploited smaller industries. South Africa's socio-economic transformation processes have not transpired as yet and hence the country's wealth rests in the hands of, and is still owned by, a minority group of its population attached to an apartheid past.

Having said that, the purpose of this chapter, however, is to show how economic convergence can be achieved over a long-run economic convergence (gaining in economic strength) period with emphasis placed on converging (coming together) of a regional bloc. These findings will help the Tripartite FTA in its trade relations as the twenty-six-member bloc attempts to converge and should take the lessons that are positive for generating growth and development. Furthermore, these findings further show that if real economic growth is derived in a regional scheme, relations among member states will be strengthened in such a scheme. It must also be noted that the flipside of this debate is that due to the convergence of SACU, its member states have been more at liberty to choose which regional scheme they wish to join based on real economic growth. Hence, greater economic benefits experienced in one scheme could diverge integration in another – and in this instance divergence will be seen in the Tripartite FTA – if trade and conditions are not addressed for smaller economies within the negotiations of the TFTA. This section also shows that greater economic benefits in a regional scheme can only be achieved with the presence of a strong partner or hegemonic state in a regional scheme and the willingness for the hegemon to be a 'paymaster'. The discussion further outlines that in order for the integration process to work, the hegemonic state incentivising the regional group must therefore also experience real economic gains and derive real economic benefits. This section will also provide effective ways and means of how the Tripartite bloc could better manage multiple memberships and guard over the member states as South Africa has been guarding over SACU countries, which is further explained below.

Multiple memberships have been compounded at the individual REC levels of COMESA, EAC and SADC. Member states are still faced with the difficulties of negotiating with stronger member states like South Africa. There are various interpretations as to why South Africa is attached to SACU. According to Brendan Vickers, former official in the Policy Research Unit at the South African Department of Trade and Industry, South Africa is enlarging its market to place itself in a position to deal effectively with domestic challenges, which is a key objective of its regional developmental approach.[67] However, South Africa also protects its markets and productive firms through implementing high domestic entry barriers in the various sectors and protecting imports, which preserves market shares of less productive and less innovative firms in some sectors; this is believed to place regional firms at risk.[68] These policies are also viewed negatively by regional partners and are seen as impacting on trade, making it a challenge and hurdle to trade competition policies as well as a high regional trade barrier. For example, at the 34th SADC Heads of State and Government Summit in August 2014, Zimbabwe's former president Robert Mugabe noted,

> We appeal to South Africa, which is highly industrialised, to lead us in this [industrialisation] and work with us, and cooperate with us and not just regard the whole continent as an open market for products from South Africa. We want a reciprocal relationship where we sell to each other [and] not just receiving products from one source.[69]

At the same August 2014 SADC summit, South Africa was not in a position to sign the SADC Trade Protocol Services Agreement, and Namibia similarly refused. At the SADC level, Robert Mugabe, presiding in the chair, expressed his disappointment at South Africa's one-sided trade practices at the SADC summit at Victoria Falls in August 2014.[70] Zimbabwe, in a 'tit-for-tat' political move, went on to sign a $533 million power project with China and a further $3 billion deal with Russia to jointly mine platinum in Zimbabwe, with Moscow providing the investment funds. This was a countermove by Mugabe, based on South Africa's one-sided deals in excluding Zimbabwe from the platinum deal.[71] Hence, from the Tripartite bloc perspective, SACU/South Africa has been changing the negotiating mood in the Tripartite bloc. As the SACU Secretariat officials have pointed out,[72] they are looking at how to attract 'swing countries'[73] in widening their negotiation reach for strategic reasons such as population size, which provides a larger market, GDP and natural resources.

In considering economic growth linked to benefits of regional schemes, this section focuses on the theory of Anthony Venables which suggests that trade liberalisation with external partners in north–south regional trade agreements can bring about economic development and growth in per capita gross national income for poorer economies in a regional trade agreement. Venables observes that in an FTA that has a member with a high income relative to that of the rest of the world, the lower-income members are likely to converge with the high-income partner and benefit from the FTA. Venables therefore suggests that developing countries are likely to be better served by north–south than by south–south FTAs. This discussion takes into account economic convergence over a long run of nine years (2005–13).[74] A neoclassical economic approach should predict that open trade will produce convergence.

Barro and Sala-i-Martin provide a further understanding of economic growth convergence as a result of trade liberalisation by describing two levels of convergence in their model: beta-convergence or absolute convergence (also called the 'catch-up' process) and sigma-convergence, when the dispersion among a group of countries decreases over time.[75]

States' preservation of their membership in SACU, while also being member states of the Tripartite bloc, exacerbates the problem of managing multiple memberships.[76] The SACU Secretariat has already stated that the region has no intention of joining a COMESA-EAC-SADC FTA, because of the extensive tariff adjustments required.[77] But as we can see, Eswatini and Namibia both signed the TFTA on 10 June 2015.

South Africa was also trading more with BRICS and slowly reducing trade with Europe because of the severity of the agricultural trade subsidies of Europe's farmers on the Southern African market. Though Europe's trade with South Africa is still more than China's, it is declining. Hence, from 2000 to 2012, South Africa's exports to other BRIC members (Brazil, Russia, India and China) rose from 5 to 19 per cent of its total exports. Over the same period, the EU's share of South African exports declined from 60 per cent to 21 percent. South Africa's exports to East Asia were R10.96 billion and total imports were R12.16 billion.[78] During the financial crises of 2009–10, South Africa formalised its relationship with China, mainly through BRIC.[79] South Africa attempted to take advantage of the industrialised markets; its exports exploded and did exceedingly well, as was noted by the World Bank in their economic update report on South Africa.[80] The report noted that South Africa should adopt an inward-looking trade strategy. Its finding was that the lower competitiveness in Africa's markets and regional export markets was ineffective and could not compete against an outside market. South African firms stood a better chance in the region, since African markets are less likely to demand high standards and superior quality of exports from South African firms than European markets would demand.[81] South Africa is also determined to remain attached to SACU because of the awkward position it was put in when listed as a 'developed' country during the Uruguay Round of WTO negotiations (1986–94).[82] Since then, South Africa has been negotiating at the WTO to be recognised as a special case requiring additional flexibility related to its membership of SACU.[83]

Venables addresses income convergence in trade liberalisation in free trade agreements with a high-income member.[84] This chapter is concerned with trade growth, which will have spillover effects and benefits for smaller economies and poorer countries over the long run. If countries discern benefits over time, they will remain in a regional grouping and thus economic convergence in the grouping will occur, as it did in the case of SACU.

Two variables are therefore relevant here: total trade as a percentage of GDP and growth of total trade over a long-run period of nine years. Growth in trade in the BLNE countries is of critical importance and will lead to overall GDP growth. The economic gap between these countries and those with stronger economies is so great that attainment of economic parity is highly unlikely; for instance, in 2013, South Africa had a GDP of $366 billion compared with Lesotho's $2.3 billion.[85]

Figure 5.4 shows that growth in trade as a percentage of total trade of poorer countries has improved relative to growth in trade as a percentage of total trade of South Africa, particularly for Lesotho and Eswatini. The convergence between Lesotho, Eswatini and South Africa in total trade as a percentage of GDP provides evidence for beta-convergence over the long-run period of 2005–13. Whereas Botswana and Namibia have experienced growth in trade, this does not indicate divergence but instead demonstrates that these two countries have grown more as smaller economies belonging to an FTA with a strong partner (namely South Africa). Figure 5.4 also shows that South Africa's trade growth as a share of GDP is smaller than trade growth for some countries in the BLNE group during this period. Botswana in particular experienced 12 per cent growth for the period 2012–13, while South Africa had 3 percent. Eswatini's growth increased by 2 per cent for the same period; Lesotho had no growth, because of political violence during this period, particularly in 2013.[86]

As Venables's theory postulates, conducting trade with a stronger economic partner that trades more with stronger external economies can benefit smaller economies within a regional grouping. To demonstrate the total trade growth of individual SACU members and whether there are benefits for poorer countries belonging to an FTA with a wealthy partner, Figure 5.5 analyses total trade over the same nine-year period, 2005–13. Figure 5.6 shows convergence in trade growth.

Figure 5.7 shows the trade growth of Botswana and South Africa, and the trade growth convergence point for these two countries, for the period 2005–12.

Figures 5.8 to 5.10 show the convergence points, respectively, for Lesotho (2008–9), Namibia (2006 and 2008–9) and Eswatini (2006, 2008 and 2010) with South Africa.

These convergence points illustrate when the smaller economy's trade begins to achieve parity with that of the rich partner in a regional trade grouping and shows that over a long-run period, the trade growth of poorer countries increases. It also shows that poorer partners are growing faster than South Africa. Various external factors explain why trade growth in the SACU bloc differs among its members. Consider South Africa and Eswatini. For South Africa, between 2009 and 2011, both the global economic recession and the strikes at South Africa's platinum mines severely damaged the country's trade. The violence and strikes, commencing in 2011 at South Africa's Marikana mine, and which continued into 2014 at the Impala, Amplats and Lonmin mines, resulted in losses of R24.1 billion in revenue, 440,000 ounces of platinum and twenty-thousand jobs.[87] South Africa's shortages seen in its electricity supply severely hampered its economic progress (which is also further discussed in Chapter 6 in providing the linkages of economic and security complexities), with South Africa losing R400 billion to its economy during the period 2008–15.[88]

Eswatini, on the other hand, experienced reduced trade after the United States ejected it from the AGOA regime in January 2015. US Trade Representative Michael

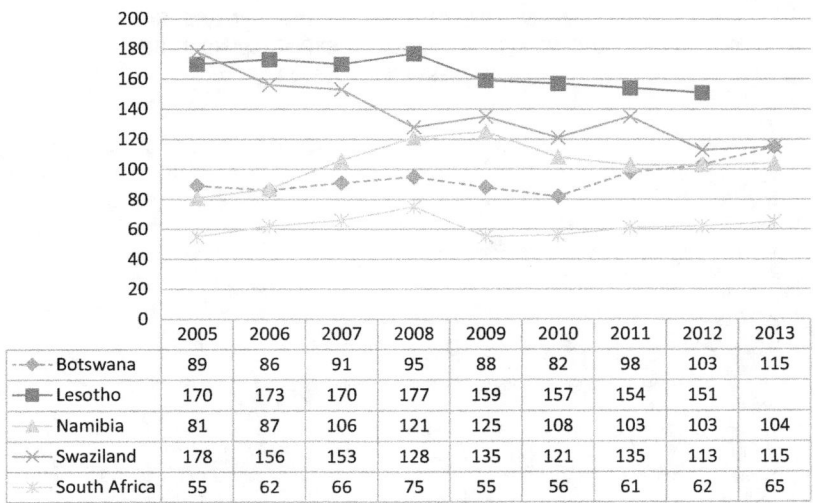

Figure 5.4 SACU trade as a percentage of GDP, 2005–13.

Source: World Bank, 'Trade (%of GDP)', http://data.worldbank.org/indicator/NE.TRD.GNFS.ZS.

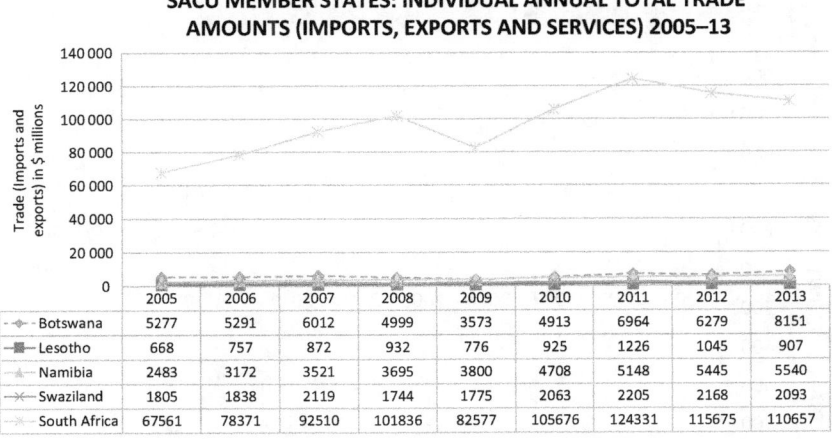

Figure 5.5 Total trade of SACU member states, 2005–13.

Source: United Nations Conference on Trade and Development (UNCTAD) statistics database, http://unctadstat.unctad.org/wds/ReportFolders/reportFolders.aspx?sCS_referer=&sCS_ChosenLang=en.

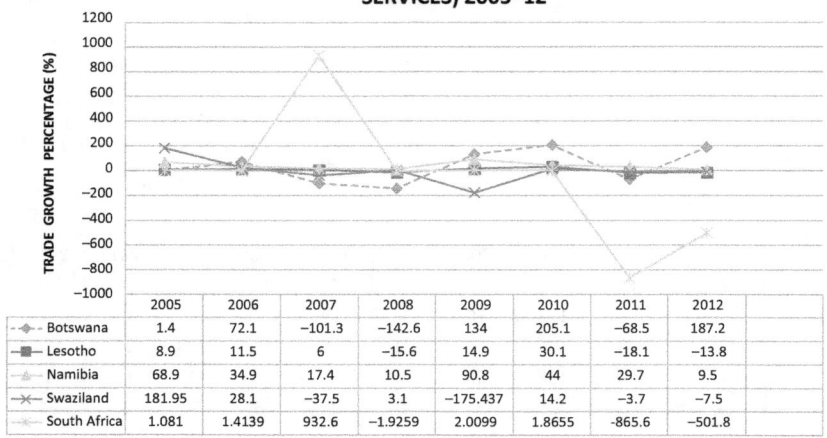

Figure 5.6 Trade growth of SACU member states, 2005–12.

Source: UNCTAD statistics database, http://unctadstat.unctad.org/wds/ReportFolders/reportFolders.aspx?sCS_referer=&sCS_ChosenLang=en.

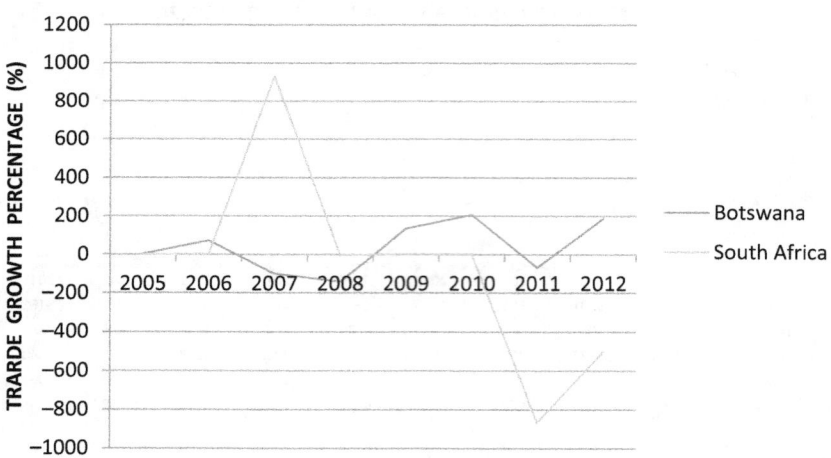

Figure 5.7 Trade growth convergence of Botswana and South Africa, 2005–12.

Source: UNCTAD statistics database, http://unctadstat.unctad.org/wds/ReportFolders/reportFolders.aspx?sCS_referer=&sCS_ChosenLang=en.

Convergence and Consolidation of Multiple Memberships 137

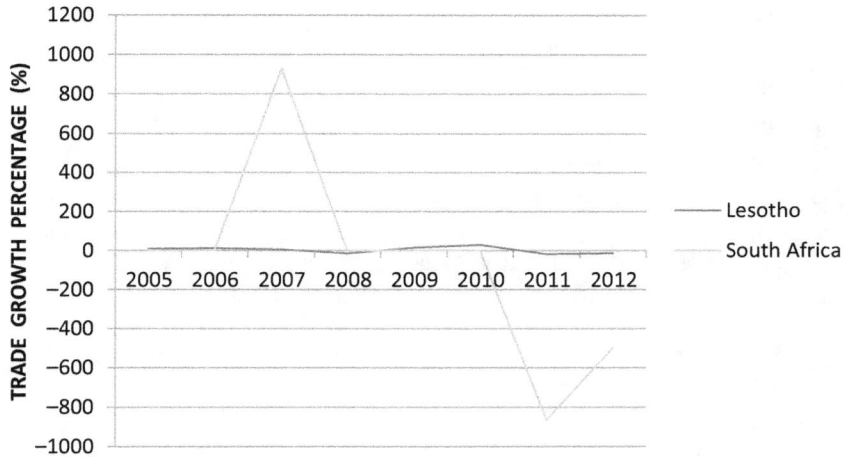

Figure 5.8 Trade growth convergence of Lesotho and South Africa, 2005–12.

Source: UNCTAD statistics database, http://unctadstat.unctad.org/wds/ReportFolders/reportFolders.aspx?sCS_referer=&sCS_ChosenLang=en.

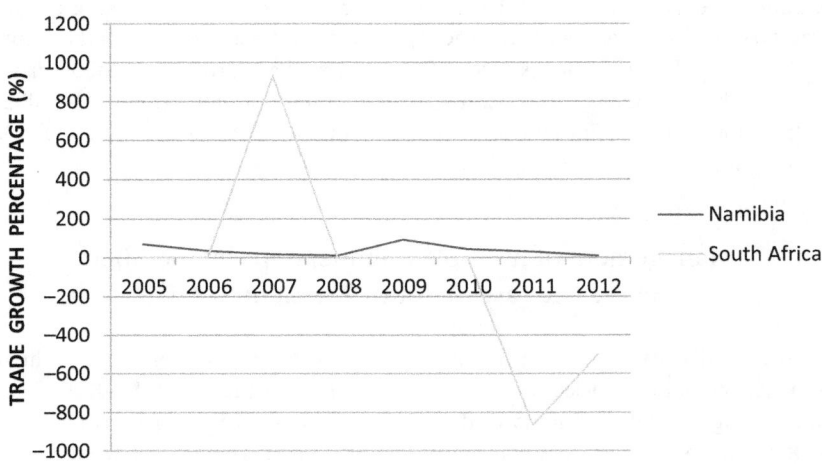

Figure 5.9 Trade growth convergence of Namibia and South Africa, 2005–12.

Source: UNCTAD statistics database, http://unctadstat.unctad.org/wds/ReportFolders/reportFolders.aspx?sCS_referer=&sCS_ChosenLang=en.

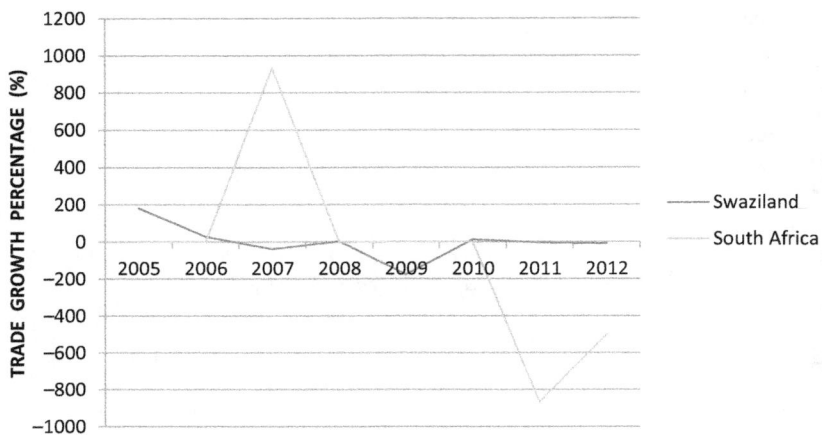

Figure 5.10 Trade growth convergence of Eswatini and South Africa, 2005–12.

Source: UNCTAD statistics database, http://unctadstat.unctad.org/wds/ReportFolders/reportFolders.aspx?sCS_referer=&sCS_ChosenLang=en.

Froman explained, 'Our concerns [are] clear to Eswatini … and we engaged extensively on concrete steps that Eswatini could take to address the concerns. … [W]e hope to continue our engagement with the Government of the Kingdom of Eswatini on steps it can take so that worker and civil society groups can freely associate and assemble and AGOA eligibility can be restored.'[89] Eswatini was the 173rd-largest goods trading partner with the United States in 2013, with $82 million in total trade ($23 million in US exports to Eswatini and $59 million in imports, with a US trade deficit of $36 million).[90]

Management of multiple memberships by member states: The case of South Africa in SACU

This section discusses the main findings of this chapter and addresses the reality of the major stumbling blocks of some of the members of the COMESA-EAC-SADC Tripartite Agreement leading up to the signing of the 2015 FTA in Sharm El Sheik, Egypt. The major divergence explained in this book is clear: as long as SACU experiences growth (as was demonstrated) with a stronger member it will hinder convergence of the Tripartite FTA and complicate the management of multiple memberships. The findings show that South Africa has carefully managed the relations in SACU to promote economic integration for member states in a regional scheme and considered a four-pronged approach. The first element of the approach is to factor in a 'paymaster'. South Africa, as a malign hegemonic state, manages the multiple memberships of the SACU bloc by incentivising poorer economies through the trade revenue generated in the bloc. This has benefited the smaller BLNE economies in SACU only as far as revenue is generated from the customs union; the downside is that regional trade is skewed and leans more in favour of the hegemon. The reality is that a hegemon with powerful parochial regional interests can converge the economies of a regional bloc and grow the economies of smaller countries. Having said that, Walter Mattli notes that a 'paymaster' can provide benefits that promote economic convergence in a regional grouping.[91] South Africa is guarding its BLNE trading partners because their markets matter. According to a 2013 International Monetary Fund report on SACU-generated revenue as a percentage of GDP, Botswana, Lesotho, Namibia and Eswatini are accruing enormous incomes from the customs union.

In 2013, current account receipts constituted only 28 per cent of GDP for South Africa, compared with over 37 per cent in Botswana, more than 55 per cent in Namibia and over 100 per cent in Lesotho.[92] Gathii and Panagariya argue that the pace of regional integration is defined by and linked to the benefits of regional integration, and this explains why African countries join different regional schemes.[93] According to the SACU agreement, SACU's present revenue-sharing formula requires that South Africa contribute 98 per cent of generated revenue to the revenue pool, which is shared according to intra-SACU trade or imports. South Africa has agreed to this formula because it dominates intra-SACU trade, accounting for over 75 per cent of Botswana's and Namibia's total trade and over 90 per cent of Eswatini's and Lesotho's trade.[94] To balance its domination in trade, South Africa's approach includes a second element.

The second element of the approach is a market-led approach in recognising the importance of increasing intraregional trade while balancing external trade. The region is important to South Africa, which this chapter outlines as crucial in the convergence debate as was indicated in the conceptual framework in Chapter 2 when discussing Robert Putnam's two-level game theory.

Putnam argued that at the national level, 'domestic groups pursue their interests by pressuring the government to adopt favourable policies, and politicians seek power by constructing coalitions among these groups'.[95] 'At the international level, national governments seek to maximise their own ability to satisfy domestic pressures, while minimising the adverse consequences of foreign developments.'[96] South Africa was facing pressure with low unemployment and poor manufacturing (as was shown in Chapter 3, Figure 3.2). According to the World Bank's 2014 report, and in assessing the iron and steel value chain, South Africa's exports seem to have been moving in the opposite direction – towards basic production and lower quality. Similarly, the United Nations Economic Commission for Africa (UNECA) had also observed that the quality of South Africa's manufactured products was inferior to that of its neighbouring states. In order for South Africa to participate in higher value-added segments, it would require

> investment in research and skills, access to raw materials, reliable and cost-effective electricity, access to imported technologies, and effective transport flexible enough to reach global export markets. However, amid high transport costs for non-commodities, rising cost and declining reliability of electricity, and import parity pricing on key inputs, the economics of adding value would not add up for South Africa.[97]

Hence, South Africa changed its approach in manufacturing and moved towards the region by conducting more trade, and in so doing addressed its semi-skilled labour, as well as flooding the region with iron ore of a lower-value segment. Evidently, in 2000, level-1 products (iron ore and concentrates) accounted for just 18 per cent of exports (by value), but by 2012, their share had more than tripled to 57 per cent. By contrast, the share of level-2 products (ferroalloys) and level-3 products (semi-finished/finished steel) in exports declined dramatically, with level-3 products falling from a 44 per cent share to just 13 per cent.[98] On the other hand, these manufacturing levels could also be positive for regional growth if the correct policy is applied to spearhead economic growth. Thus, in considering Steve Dowrick and Duc-Tho Nguyen's total factor productivity (TFP) as a catch-up variable for downstream industries, smaller industries have an opportunity to input into the value chain. Therefore, the Tripartite bloc should consider trade agreements that take into account endogenous factors of growth, such as technology, research and inputs into trade that links ROOs, to spur real growth. Such initiatives can also expand on endogenous growth factors in industrialisation and value addition of interregional trade.[99]

External trade has led to a larger revenue pool generated from total trade, which benefits the BLNE countries, as shown in Figure 5.11 for the period 2005–13. South Africa conducted trade with Europe long before this period; in 1999, for example, South Africa and the EU signed a trade development agreement, as already noted.

Furthermore, South Africa has conducted trade not only with the BRICS bloc since 2010 but also with Asian and Chinese markets long before the 2005–13 period. As Carolyn Jenkins and Lynne Thomas argue, South Africa must look beyond the region to enhance economic growth for poorer economies.[100]

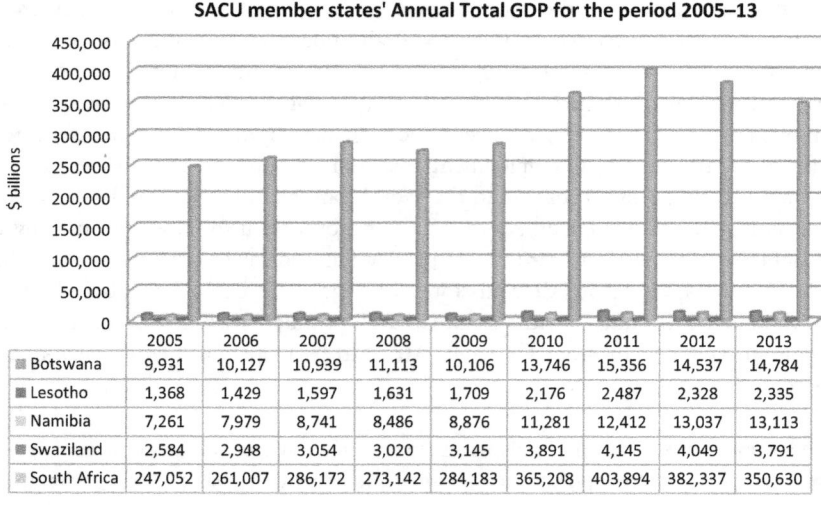

Figure 5.11 Total GDP of BLNE member states, 2005–13.

Source: UNCTAD statistics database, http://unctadstat.unctad.org/wds/ReportFolders/reportFolders.aspx?sCS_referer=&sCS_ChosenLang=en.

Greater trade and enlarged markets have increased the SACU revenue pool and strengthened the SACU region; for example, South Africa's 2011 merger with the BRIC states – a grouping of the world's fastest-growing economies – was potentially positive for Southern Africa as a whole, by providing greater trade prospects (for the period under review).

South Africa has been reaping the benefits of intra-SACU trade ever since the 1910 SACU trade agreement (revised in 1969 and again in 2002). Even though South Africa has conducted trade with Chinese and Asian markets prior to the merger, the BRICS agreement has provided a more formalised relationship for its trade with African markets, resulting in increased trade among the BRICS bloc between 2010 and 2014, with 2013 showing the greatest trade, as seen in Figure 5.12.

The third element of the approach is development-led regional integration. South Africa has taken the lead in infrastructure development. It has approached infrastructure development through SADC's spatial development initiatives and through the Southern African Development Bank (as was discussed in Chapter 4). The neoclassical growth model also stresses the importance of governments' focus on physical investment to expand national outputs. Investment in equipment is just as important as investment in transport infrastructure, since equipment is critical for technological advancement.[101]

Kenya's rapid growth, for example, is linked to its growth in banking and telecommunications services (which have expanded to the middle class), urbanisation, and investment in infrastructure and railways. Uganda's growth is supported by increased activity in the construction, financial services, transport and telecommunications sectors.[102]

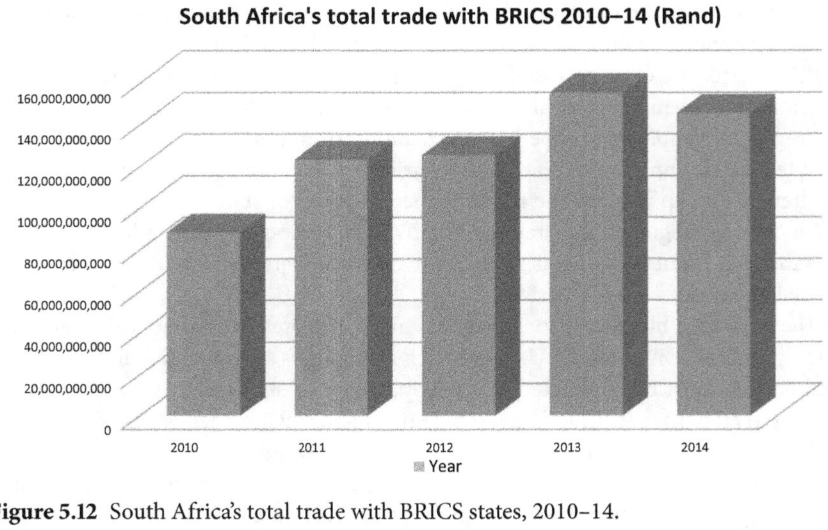

Figure 5.12 South Africa's total trade with BRICS states, 2010–14.

Source: Trade database of the South African Department of Trade and Industry (DTI), http://tradestats.thedti.gov.za/ReportFolders/reportFolders.aspx?sCS_referer=&sCS_ChosenLang=en.

The fourth element of the approach is to strengthen regional institutions. SACU is not recognised as a regional economic community by the Abuja Treaty of 1991 or by the AU. Rather, it is one of the regional mechanisms promoting convergence on the continent because of its negotiation skills; its access to BRICS, the EU, and the United States; and its strong security mechanism, which is well endowed through South Africa's support. Currently, SACU is in negotiations with all the larger markets with which it does not share an FTA. Notably, these include Egypt in COMESA and Kenya in the EAC.

Concluding remarks

In concluding this chapter, the findings claim that multiple memberships have not been adequately managed by the Tripartite bloc. Multiple memberships, however, did benefit the political and economic circumstances of some member states, as pointed out in Table 5.1 in infrastructure projects. In examining regional trade agreements in Africa, the neoclassical economic approach is relevant to understanding regional integration, divergence and convergence and provides a context for understanding the issues after the 2008 Tripartite Agreement among COMESA, the EAC and SADC, and the benefits of multiple memberships for poorer economies in a regional integration process. However, this chapter has highlighted that the pace of globalisation dictates open markets and trade, which creates a contradiction for the Tripartite Agreement's regional integration approaches of variable geometry and liberal tariff settings. These contradictions were not adequately supported within the neoclassical economic approach theory of open trade and regional integration and divergence and convergence debates, as discussed in the literature reviewed in Chapter 2. A new theory was deployed in support of this discussion, defined as a neoclassical economic regional integration which supported the findings provided in this chapter. In this regard, the chapter also discussed the dilemma for the Tripartite bloc in its decision to implement a variable geometry approach – allowing for member states of a regional grouping to cooperate in separation from other members, as well as for flexible progression in cooperation in a variety of areas and at different speeds – as an attempt to help manage the multiple memberships of states.[103] But this approach has hampered regional integration. The Tripartite bloc has also adopted a trade liberalisation framework that is reflective of open markets and is causing polarisation of smaller markets and industries.[104]

The Tripartite bloc has also allowed its member states to conduct external trade, notably with AGOA and the EU. While such agreements are important for generating wealth, they must be negotiated at the Tripartite level to ensure that ROOs do not hamper regional trade. The findings in this chapter claim that ROOs specified in trade commodities in external trade have caused divergence of regional trade and further hamper the spillover effects of endogenous factors of growth concerning technology, research and skills. The findings identify this as a gap in the theory of Krugman's accounting index, who does not take into account the impact of ROOs in his discussion that concerns inputs of production. As Krugman suggests, growth accounting needs to calculate explicit measures of 'increases in the output per unit of input. ... Increases in knowledge can be positive for growth convergence. However, growth measurements must be considered in the process of economic growth. The view is that per capita income can only occur if there is a rise in output "per unit of input".[105] Restrictive ROOs might also be in the interests of particular producers who wish to avoid new competition in their domestic markets. These rules will then make it impossible for smaller industries to compete in other regional markets and keep downstream users from inputting into products to benefit value addition industrialisation.[106]

This chapter noted that trade agreements must take into account endogenous factors of growth, such as technology, research and inputs into trade, that link ROOs to spur real growth. The chapter also expanded on endogenous growth factors in industrialisation and value addition of interregional trade, as defined by Dowrick and Nguyen's TFP as a catch-up variable for downstream industries.[107] Therefore, in looking ahead, as the COMESA-EAC-SADC Tripartite FTA negotiates its ROOs (Annexure 4), synchronisation of trade agreements of member states' national policies is of vital importance and must be carefully aligned with that of the COMESA-EAC-SADC Tripartite FTA as well as at individual REC levels. Bhagwati and Gathii have noted that African regional trade agreements provide a framework for cooperation, but because of the non-existence of legal binding agreements, Africa's states have the liberty to form multiple memberships, which states see as offering them the flexibility to retain their sovereignty and also accrue benefits.[108] Multiple memberships have hindered progress in the Tripartite FTA. Since SACU members are deriving benefits from the SACU configuration, it has not signed the TFTA and hindered progress in this regard. Therefore, core trade must be conducted intracontinentally and carefully balanced against external trade.

Gathii contends that instead of using intraregional trade to expand trade in the region and as a framework for growth, it should be swung around and the framework of industrial growth should inform intraregional trade and market diversification.[109] Trade with competitive advantage should be built in the Tripartite bloc and potential for value-add possibilities to build Africa's industrialisation should be actively pursued.

The findings of this chapter for the period under research (2005–16) were intended for the specific purpose of demonstrating how much convergence occurred in the COMESA-EAC-SADC FTA. South Africa's relations with the BRICS countries was also considered, and the events that evolved in September 2015 were taken into account in relation to China's economic slowdown, when leading economists like Jason Muscat and Mthuli Ncube outlined China's recent economic downturn as worrisome for Africa. During August and September 2015, economists were alarmed when China's Shanghai Composite index, a proxy for the Chinese equity market, fell by 30 per cent after a 150 per cent increase over the previous year (2014). According to Goldman Sachs, '$225 billion of capital flowed out of China between April and June 2015'.[110] Various articles in *Finweek* noted that what this means for South Africa as a major trading partner to China is that the decades-long commodity super cycle is effectively over. With that comes slower economic growth, or worse – outright recession. For the rest of the world, slower Chinese growth translates into weaker demand for commodities: Brent crude oil was down by half to $54 a barrel since 2012, while tin, copper and iron ore dropped 40 to 60 per cent. Countries that are rich in commodity resources will also be heading into a recession – Canada, Australia, Brazil, Venezuela, Peru, Russia, Nigeria, Angola, Chile and Indonesia. According to Muscat, senior industry analyst at First National Bank, South Africa, two sectors of the South African economy that will be worst affected by China's slow growth are mining and manufacturing. Muscat notes,

> This is obviously very bad news for South Africa as it means a material decrease in export revenue and prevents a faster narrowing of the current account deficit. Fortunately for our economy, the lower oil price is rescuing the import bill and offsetting what would otherwise have been a far worse deterioration in terms of trade. Even so, our expectations are for the current account deficit to narrow very slowly, which should keep the rand under pressure, raising inflation and interest rate concerns.[111]

To mitigate the negative downturn, Ncube suggests that African governments will also need to focus more on implementing 'cross-border infrastructure programmes and raising intra-regional trade to mitigate the effects [with China's] of the slowdown'.[112] Economists also indicated that Africa will have to increase intraregional trade and strengthen its economic policies.

While it was an important actor leading up to the convergence of COMESA, EAC and SADC in 2008 in signing the Tripartite Agreement, South Africa will need to conduct more intraregional trade and will need to consider increasing its infrastructure project development contributions for spearheading regional trade, as was outlined and discussed in this chapter.[113]

The growth convergence of BLNE members in the SACU bloc could also have been accelerated by mineral-rich countries, which were expected to build on their momentum and accelerate from an average of 3.4 per cent GDP growth in 2014 to 4.1 per cent in 2015. These include countries in the Southern African region, such as Angola (coal), Botswana (coal, copper and diamonds), Namibia (diamonds and uranium) and Zambia (copper). Southern Africa's GDP growth was expected to accelerate from 2.9 per cent in 2014 to 3.6 per cent in 2015, with Angola, Mozambique and Zambia expected to be the fastest-growing economies in 2015.[114] These growth poles were 'mainly driven by an increased investment in the non-diamond sector in Botswana, private consumption recovery in South Africa, and an increase in mining and natural gas investment and exploration in Mozambique'.[115] The reality, though, is that South Africa, the major economic power in Southern Africa, with an ailing electrical supplier, Eskom, had its economy on its knees, crawling to 0.8 per cent in 2018.[116] In the EAC, GDP growth is expected to continue to increase from 6.5 per cent in 2014 to 6.8 per cent in 2015, which will make East Africa the fastest-growing African subregion. Kenya and Uganda were the key drivers in 2014 and 2015, as indicated by the UN's 2015 economic outlook report.[117] SACU is hoping that Angola will join the 2016 Southern African EPA agreement and that the DRC will join the SADC FTA in order to enlarge the SACU trade market.[118]

As discussed above, Europe's relations with Africa have caused much trade diversion for the bloc. While economic integration has been central to the Tripartite bloc for improving economic growth, the management of multiple memberships is critical for convergence. Moreover, this book is of the view that without regional security, economic prospects will also remain bleak.

6

Pan-African economic integration

What the Pan-African economic integration theory shows is that the African Continental Free Trade Area (CFTA) has used the 26-member-state Tripartite free trade area (FTA) (comprising of the COMESA-EAC-SADC Tripartite Agreement) as a springboard for economic convergence. The COMESA-EAC-SADC FTA process is being concluded with the deadline for their Free Trade Area lapsing in 2019. In the meanwhile, the African Union (AU) established a CFTA in March 2018, which means that there are separate agreements running on parallel tracks alongside the COMESA-EAC-SADC Tripartite FTA.[1] The CFTA was signed by twenty-two countries that deposited instruments for ratification including Chad, Côte d'Ivoire, the Democratic Republic of Congo (DRC), Djibouti, Egypt, Eswatini (formerly known as Swaziland), Ethiopia, Gambia, Ghana, Guinea, Kenya, Mali, Mauritania, Namibia, Niger, Rwanda, the Saharawi Republic, Senegal, Sierra Leone, South Africa, Togo and Uganda. On its part, Zimbabwe has received parliamentary approval for ratification but is yet to deposit its ratification instruments.[2]

The reality, though, is that the Tripartite FTA is negotiating separate trade protocols and, on the other hand, the CFTA is negotiating its own set of trade protocols, which is a dilemma for achieving Pan-African economic integration. The Tripartite FTA is liberalising 100 per cent of tariff lines by converging the EAC, which is a customs union, and the Southern African Customs Union (SACU) into the TFTA in line with its principle of acquis. Prior to the signing of the grand FTA on 10 June 2015, in a January 2015 report by COMESA secretary general Sindiso Ngwenya, he provided a detailed account of the failed negotiations towards an FTA (leading up to the free trade agreement being concluded and the legal binding treaties that have not been concluded):

> Some of the main challenges and pitfalls on the Tripartite FTA have been ambitious tariff liberalisation threshold. The 60 per cent to 85 per cent liberalisation threshold is less than trade liberalisation thresholds attained under the three REC FTAs, and the failure to respect the principle of *acquis* fully in this respect. The apparent contradiction between some principles, notably between variable geometry, which would allow countries that are ready to make progress while allowing slower countries to join later … the principle of decision-making by consensus …

resulted in slow progress as countries that were not ready could not allow others to proceed.³

The COMESA-EAC-SADC Tripartite Agreement is based on the principle of acquis – meaning that the agreements are binding. This means that everything that the three RECs had agreed to cannot be undone. According to the African Development Bank, the compromise required for successful convergence is a special and differential treatment (SDT) for least developed countries (LDCs) – a paymaster to compensate integration costs – which countries such as South Africa strongly opposed.⁴ South Africa is already in a similar scheme as a paymaster in SACU (discussed in Chapter 5). The Tripartite FTA was thus not incorporated into the CFTA owing to the difficulties in the negotiations and the necessity to preserve the acquis. The CFTA has two phases outlined for negotiation. Phase 1 consists of three protocols: trade in goods, trade in services and procedures on the settlement of disputes with associated annexes. Phase II also comprises three protocols: competition policy, intellectual property and investment. The CFTA envisages a market size of fifty-five African countries by 2030 that include 1.7 billion people with estimates of $6.7 trillion. The major agreement concerning the rules of origin (ROOs) has not being finalised under the CFTA. The legal instruments of the CFTA are still a work in progress since the agreement was implemented on 30 May 2019 and only came into force in July 2019. It is thus premature to critically assess trade progress at this time. Similarly, within the Tripartite FTA the variable geometry approach (see Chapter 5) allows flexibility among the member states to cooperate with the TFTA at different speeds, complementary to the principle of acquis. The TFTA negotiations failed to come to an agreement on sensitive products including sugar, maize and spirits, among others, and with this hanging in balance, the CFTA set up a new FTA.⁵ However, Africa's stronger economies such as Egypt, Kenya and South Africa should conduct less trade with Europe, the United States, China and India, who are large economies with mega industries. Nigeria is one of Africa's strongest economies, but Abuja did not initially commit to the CFTA, with the Nigerian president Muhammadu Buhari refusing to allow Nigeria to become a dumping ground of finished goods due to trade distortion by powerful external trade partners such as Europe and China.⁶ President Buhari has only recently consented to joining the CFTA in July 2019 with strong prospects for increasing intracontinental trade; with Nigeria's population size at 130 million, it provides a huge market force to Africa's integration prospects.⁷

The CFTA agreement was eventually signed at an AU-held special extraordinary summit on 21 March 2018 in Kigali, Rwanda – the Rwandan president Paul Kagame is a fervent integrationist with a view to finalise the legal instruments – and with Nigeria joining on 7 July 2019, twenty-three of fifty-five African member states signed the CFTA.⁸

The Pan-African economic integration theory claims that for economic convergence to occur, the implementation of effective policies of the Tripartite FTA and the CFTA, with both their member states currently belonging to existing and various regional blocs, should carefully and sparingly consider the impact of external international agreements that appear to favour regional trade, and instead consider forging stronger

African trade partnerships that can benefit trade growth such as agro-industrialisation-driven commodities and the blue economy. The theory also underscores that regional policies should consider value-driven industrialised manufacturing that includes endogenous factors of growth – such as technology, research and inputs of smaller industries and economies into the outputs of stronger economies and industries – and strengthen Africa's efforts within the Fourth Industrial Revolution (4IR). Production of regional trade should link clear, agreed-to ROOs with a view to spurring real economic growth, and incentivising poorer economies of member states could create the necessary economic conditions for achieving Pan-African economic integration.

The theory, therefore, advocates that global economic inequality warrants that Africa's governments and regional communities adopt stronger partnerships among African states and specifically have trade relations with those economies that are on a more equal socio-economic footing, such as countries from the Caribbean and the Pacific, and that are development-orientated, namely the Africa, Caribbean and Pacific (ACP) group of states.

Intraregional trade: An agricultural comparative advantage

But what does the CFTA's relationship mean for the Tripartite FTA, and how can Africa grow its economies? Regional agreements have not worked in favour of trade opportunities. For example, the impact of external trade agreements on sugar producers also affected and distorted trade in the region for COMESA, EAC and SADC member states from 1998 to 2008. Economists like Krugman, MacMillan and Rodrik have proposed that economic growth convergence in trade liberalisation has to consider production structures that first assess the risk and mitigate costs associated with labour, manufacture, high-productivity and low-productivity jobs and the impact of outputs versus inputs.[9] For example, sugar is the cheapest commodity to produce in the SADC region for nine member states, some of which are COMESA member states as well. Sugar producers in the SADC and COMESA blocs, for example, should capitalise on and benefit from the agricultural products in future trade agreements in the continent. Agricultural trade has been sorely lacking in the African continent. Agriculture is the most important sector in Africa, with 70 per cent of its population employed in the sector – but the agro-processing business model as a subset of agriculture is flawed. Take leather in Africa, for example. The role of agro-processing is viewed as a critical transformation process of agricultural raw materials to produce value-added intermediate or finished products for achieving socio-economic development, regarded as increasingly important in the continent. South Africa has an inward-looking approach to safeguarding its own leather value chain. It might thus need to reconsider its current policy of goods wholly produced by South Africa and South African inputs only and broaden its policy to include regional industry inputs into overall output commodities in the textile and leather industries – one that does not minimise the effects of achieving greater industrialisation potential in the leather industry but rather softens the protectionist nature of its current policy.[10]

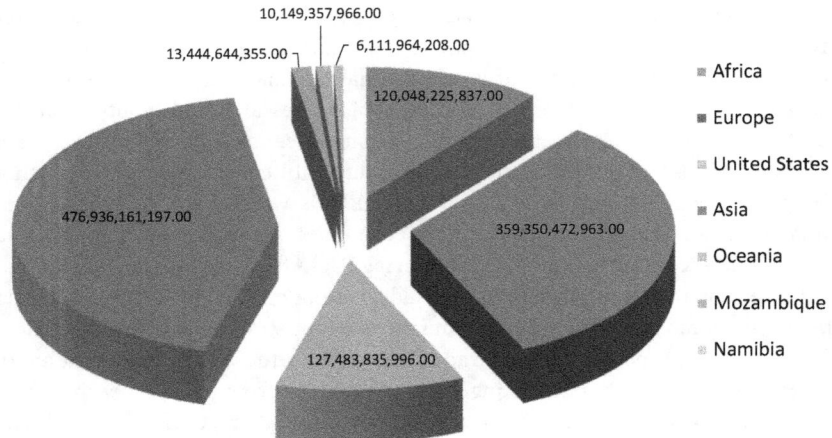

Figure 6.1 South Africa's total import trade with main partners, January–December 2016 (R billions).

Source: Adapted from South African Revenue Services (SARS), http://www.sars.gov.za/ClientSegments/Customs-Excise/Trade-Statistics/Pages/Merchandise-Trade-Statistics.aspx.

Such a move would allow for industrialisation and also see the potential for economic growth in the country's raw hides and skins in particular, which require inputs from downstream industries within the region and from the African continent as a whole. South Africa's trade with the international market as a trading partner for sourcing leather goods should thus be done sparingly, particularly with Europe, and become more circumspect as an AU member state to ensure that government policies support the AU's *Agenda 2063* that pursues a developmental agenda to transform Africa's agro-based sectors and move more towards regional trade growth.

On the whole, intra-COMESA trade remains very low. While sugar and leather are examples of how the African states can converge agricultural policies that could lead to economic growth and can derive benefits, other examples should also be considered, for example, in textiles and electricity. South Africa has a healthy export and import sector, as shown in Figures 6.1 and 6.2, but more importance could be placed on the types of commodities traded from the region, considering that the business sector seeks to achieve more regional benefit within a value-added, industrialisation-driven market through regional business partnerships as a means. The lack of attention placed on the quality of commodities traded among businesses can also be largely attributed to the inappropriate business policy throughout Southern Africa.

The Tripartite FTA and eventually the CFTA can only succeed with strong economies such as South Africa, Kenya and Egypt conducting viable African continental trade relations – and trading more with the ACP bloc with a view to moving its economies from remaining in the under-periphery of the world to the semi-periphery.

South Africa has a vibrant vehicle manufacturing and assembly industry for cars, but the leather hides that are required for its car seats still predominantly come from

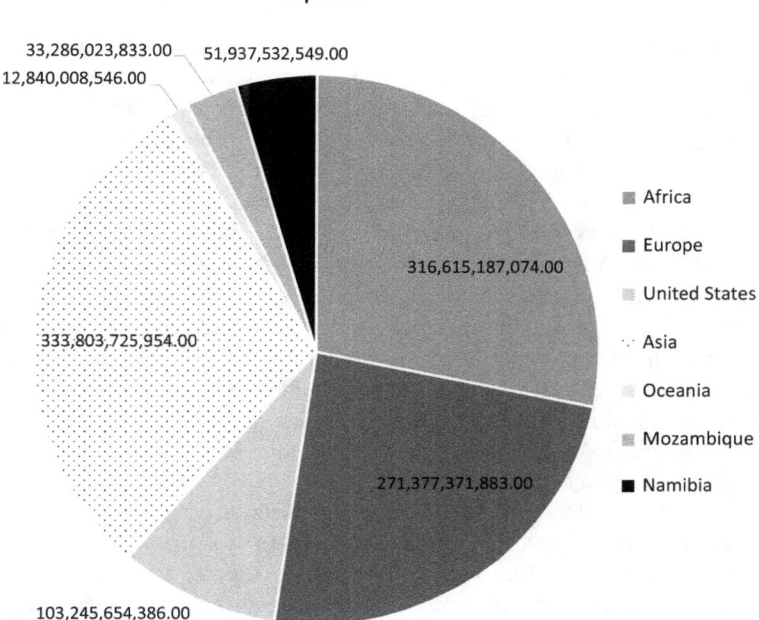

Figure 6.2 South Africa's total export trade with main partners, January–December 2016 (R billions).

Source: Adapted from SARS, http://www.sars.gov.za/ClientSegments/Customs-Excise/Trade-Statistics/Pages/Merchandise-Trade-Statistics.aspx.

international markets. South Africa's total trade for leather and raw hides in 2016 was R2 billion with Europe and R1.4 billion with Asia, compared to a meagre R790 million with the rest of Africa.[11] These discrepancies in trade totals for the leather/hide commodity show that not much consideration has been given to drawing trade from Southern Africa's regional states first, or to attempting to make trade conditions attract regional business and benefit from research, design, and technology and skills transfer from the African continent.

South Africa is the largest exporter of ostrich leather globally, but the skills in this sector are fast dwindling. The African continent on its part is currently the largest producer of raw hides and skins as semi-processed leather. But the entire continent contributed only a meagre $4 billion in 2015 out of the total global leather industry that is currently worth $120 billion annually. Major markets instead come from the direction of Asia: China, India, Pakistan, Thailand and Vietnam. If global value chains are what Southern African governments and the continent at large are wanting to achieve, then governments must come to terms with the realist perspective that major markets and states are likely to show less compassion towards supporting Africa's achievements of value additions or in gaining a competitive global edge.

According to Ethiopian economist and scholar-diplomat Mwinyikione Mwinyihija,[12] the leather sectors should look at 'trickling down' effects and towards mainstream leather value chains, which include strong producers from the markets of Ethiopia, Kenya, Rwanda, Sudan, Zambia and Zimbabwe. There has also been a significant decline in the leather industry of 'wet-blue' chemicals in South Africa, which has resulted in the closure of several tanneries.[13] These industries have been forced to shift to new growth sectors and towards the footwear leather industry. While there is a growing demand for exotic leather and other leather products such as handbags and shoes, as well as leather clothing such as saddles and belts, among other things, tanners and manufacturers, for whom inputs such as wet-blue chemicals for hides to tan leather are necessary, have succumbed to the pressures of accessing these products locally. According to the South African Skin, Hide and Leather Council,[14] cattle farmers have also not been able to produce quality hides due to the damage caused to hides by barbwire fencing and due to taxidermy, among several other things that are also related to the ease of accessing finance for smaller business industries. African governments ought to put more effort into accessing raw materials and building a viable regional market, as well as making available the necessary conditions for financing these sectors, with hassle-free credit facilities.

Unlike the 1980s and 1990s when South Africa had a weak manufacturing base, this young-democracy South Africa – hardly over two decades old – has made significant progress in value additions to protect its automotive industry. According to the Department of Trade and Industry's (DTI's) 2015–16 annual report, the country saw a growth in total manufacturing value addition of R5 billion between 2007 and 2015. South Africa's automotive industry consumes the bulk of the leather produced in the country, and the success that the automotive industry has attained, as noted by the DTI in its 2015–16 annual report, has largely been achieved through export of vehicles. The DTI reports that the automotive industry was the major contributor to this significant growth, owing to the South African government's Automotive Production and Development Programme (APDP).[15] In 2016, South Africa was ranked twenty-first out of the top fifty-three production countries globally. Since the leather of car seats is attached as an input into the automotive sector, South Africa's leather producers could make entry difficult for local and regional suppliers with tariffs being high, and the APDP should take these issues of their impact on the regional leather market into account.

New Partnership for Africa's Development's (NEPAD's) Infrastructure and Investment Desk underscores the crucial importance of creating the conditions necessary for export credit facilities for business ventures that might help them gain access to markets due to unavailability of funds.[16] In 2014, South Africa exported key automobile components, including seats and stitched leather, worth R1.3 billion to markets in the European Union (EU), Africa, the United States, Brazil, Japan, Australia, South Korea, India and China. But the inputs used for producing the vehicle seats for South Africa's automobiles are imported mainly from Brazil, India and Italy. The negotiation of tariffs within intra- and extraregional trade agreements must be carefully considered so that commodities tap into benefits from both national and regional trade. In particular, trade barriers such as ROOs placed on leather products must be considered by governments in tariff negotiations so that the adequate conditions for regional business ventures are created and not restricted, with a view to creating further possibilities conducive for a regional trade market, one in which businesses gain easier access and one that does not hamper furtherance of socio-economic growth and promotion of employment.

Most socio-economic growth models cannot obtain equality of winners; however, there must be winners throughout the model, even though varied. There must also be a paymaster and a driver for achieving convergence within the regional leather agro-processing sector and for business sectors to secure business ventures within the region that are beneficial for Southern Africa and Africa as a whole. There must be a more regional approach being adopted towards technology and innovation with a view to merging regional technology and design to achieve global competitiveness and value addition.

In the East African region, for example, Kenya is the third-largest livestock holder in Africa, behind Ethiopia and Sudan. Kenya's total livestock population in 2016 was 127.5 million, and thus agro-processing as a means of value-driven industrialisation is of critical importance to that government – but agro-processing has been strained in the leather sector. In 2014, Kenya on average produced only 2.46 million hides (cattle) and 8.22 million skins (sheep and goats), of which 14 per cent hides, 34 per cent sheep and 29 per cent goat skins remained uncollected from abattoirs with losses estimated at $2.1 million for cattle hides at an average loss of $6 per hide, and a total loss of $1.315 million for skins estimated at a retail trade price of $0.5 per skin. The reasons for the uncollected Kenyan hides and skins include poor infrastructure of roads prohibiting the free access to collection centres, insufficient tanneries that are operating at over 50 per cent below installed capacity due to the lack of hides and skins for producing intermediaries, among several other factors. Up to 70 per cent of hides and skins were being exported in their raw form, leaving the industry without adequate raw materials to enhance value-additions commodities owing to the disinterest shown in the leather industry by Kenyan farmers and producers due to the low prices attached to hides and skin – leaving only 30 per cent for manufacturing. In 2014, Kenya only earned a total of 10 billion Kenyan shillings (approximately $96.4 million) for a total of 10 million hides, skins and semi-processed (wet-blue) leather products.

In comparison, globally, hides, skin and leather products generated a total amount of $5.2 billion; semi-processed leather, $3 billion; finished and crust leather, $10 billion; footwear, $47 billion; and leather goods and products, $12.3 billion. South Africa's total livestock herd, on the other hand, was recorded at 13.7 million total livestock herd, of which cattle hides and skin exported were 23,313 tonnes in 2015, but lacking in finished products. Similarly, Kenya's leather sector could produce 140,000 jobs, but only 14,000 people were employed, and 10,000 informally emloyed. Creating economies of scale and increasing consumer surplus have the potential of reducing prices of competitively produced goods and could further allow for an increase in employment and job creation as well as boost economic growth spurts – but the international market is way ahead of Africa.[17]

At the global level, the most lucrative global leather industry is the EU market. For example, currently the EU has a market value of about 41 per cent in leather footwear;

the EU leather-goods sector comprises about thirty-six thousand enterprises, generates a turnover of €48 billion and employs around 435,000 people.[18] China is among several other international markets to have managed to become a global competitor in leather goods because Beijing conducts value additions in regional partnerships that are not constricted to silos as seen in the case of Southern Africa.

While there is a considerable African market for agro-processing opportunities in Africa, the sector is stifled by some prohibitions. Such defects require rectifying: access to capital and investments, providing appropriate research and technology, and accessing infrastructure including electricity, water, road and rail. Comparative advantage and cost locations must form an integral part in regional integration. For example, Zambia is a significant hide producer but does not have the market for trading hides. The region can tap into Zambia's market and contribute to trade and value additions with Kenya and Ethiopia providing research and innovation for technical skills.

On its part, South Africa's National Development Plan (NDP) target is to create eleven million jobs by 2030 and, in so doing, reduce poverty and inequality with the unemployment rate falling to 6 per cent or less, which stood at 27 per cent overall in 2016 (and closer to 50 per cent among youth). Tshwane is determined in meeting the target of creating eleven million jobs by 2030, but South Africa's economy will have to produce about six hundred thousand jobs annually to meet this target. According to a 2016 World Bank report,[19] South Africa's pace in creating employment and jobs has been remarkably slow. It managed to produce only 310,000 jobs per year for the period 2005–15, comprising 260,000 jobs in the private sector and 50,000 jobs in the public sector.[20] One of the significant impediments here is the government's lack of knowledge and initiative for job creation, attributed mainly to the decline observed in total capital productivity within relevant sectors such as agriculture, manufacturing, construction and trade, as well as the unavailability of finance for business industries.[21]

The consequences of a region lacking a clear vision are indicative of a weak regional integration plan. Currently, South Africa injects a yearly amount of R150 billion to social grants, of which, for example, 60 per cent of social grantees can be employed in entrepreneurial sectors. There is thus a case to be made for the government to critically assess the grant-making structure and set up some of the grantees in small business cooperatives and reverse economic dividends that benefit the economy. If leather is the medium, then the quality of the product should be placed within the industry across the region and adhere to quality assurance, which is also critical to promoting global value chains. The leather sector must have a regional focus and knowledge of the global state of the market and recognise that within the agro-processing sector there are different laws and regulators. There should, therefore, be a buffer created across the region to cooperate with regional trade unions and increase levels of production to achieve value chains, such as the Southern African Trade Union Coordination Council (SATUCC).

Southern African governments on the whole must, therefore, learn from the international community and create the necessary conditions for businesses to work together regionally and reap the benefits of comparative advantage from specialised labour and technological spillover. On its part, South Africa must tap into regional benefits of technology and skills transfer to enhancing its skills development and training, with a view to creating precise shifts in the production of goods to spur the country's growth from the region and to build a regional hub in partnership with regional states. South African companies are also misinformed regarding the production of agro-processed leather in a way that can enhance economic growth for downstream industries from the region and Africa as a whole. At the regional level, Eastern and Southern Africa's leather firms have stifled their own growth prospects owing to the stiff competition in this sector among its producers and thus diminished any attempts at keeping abreast with industrialisation or producing quality leather products, which becomes a lost opportunity. Technical services to South Africa's government, business community and education sectors must make use of regional training and expertise in leather from Ethiopia and Kenya.[22]

The leather sector must develop an ownership model and create a paradigm shift. Within the ostrich industry a profit-sharing model must be well thought through; given the sensitive nature of the shortage of skills within the industry, a business model thus ought to consider and ensure that supervisory performance is not overstretched. South Africa has a lot to lose in revenue generation through trade as it grapples with changing the direction of the textile and leather sectors towards effecting socio-economic growth and protecting the automotive industry, where leather as input plays a significant role in the manufacturing of car seats. But as shown in Figure 6.3, South Africa is struggling to complete the leather value chain. Unfinished leather products are still predominantly being exported as raw materials to international markets with no processing done in South Africa for its leather products. While there is a significant regional skills base, the major weakness in the leather trade is the lack of the overall regional training capacity. Since 1998, South Africa made inroads in addressing the skills gap in the leather industry and implemented critical institutional programmes. These included the implementation of several infrastructural institutions representing the rights of workers such as the National Bargaining Council for the Leather Industry (NCBLI), the Clothing and Textile Workers Union (SACTWU) and the National Union of Leather and Allied Workers. The South African government, furthermore, strengthened its 1998 Sector Education and Training Authorities (SETAs) and enacted its national skills agencies to implement the government's National Skills Development Strategy (NSDS) to encourage credible training to better serve the leather sector with suitable training programmes.

The leather that is attached to the car seats in the automotive sector is thus essential to protect the market since 70 per cent of South Africa's vehicles are sold in international markets with a substantial workforce, with approximately R60 billion injected into the industry by its government. Tshwane, therefore, can ill afford to diminish production of automotive manufacturing – and the quality of leather for this industry is important for value additions, notwithstanding foreign currency that is generated as a massive contribution to the government's economy. Having said that, the reverse could also happen and dampen prospects for enhancing a business model for black businesses. The major beneficiaries of the R60 billion injected into the motor trade industry are oligopolies; such businesses are highly competitive and protective over their industries. According to South Africa's minister of trade Rob Davies, 'Getting smaller companies, particularly black-owned companies, involved in

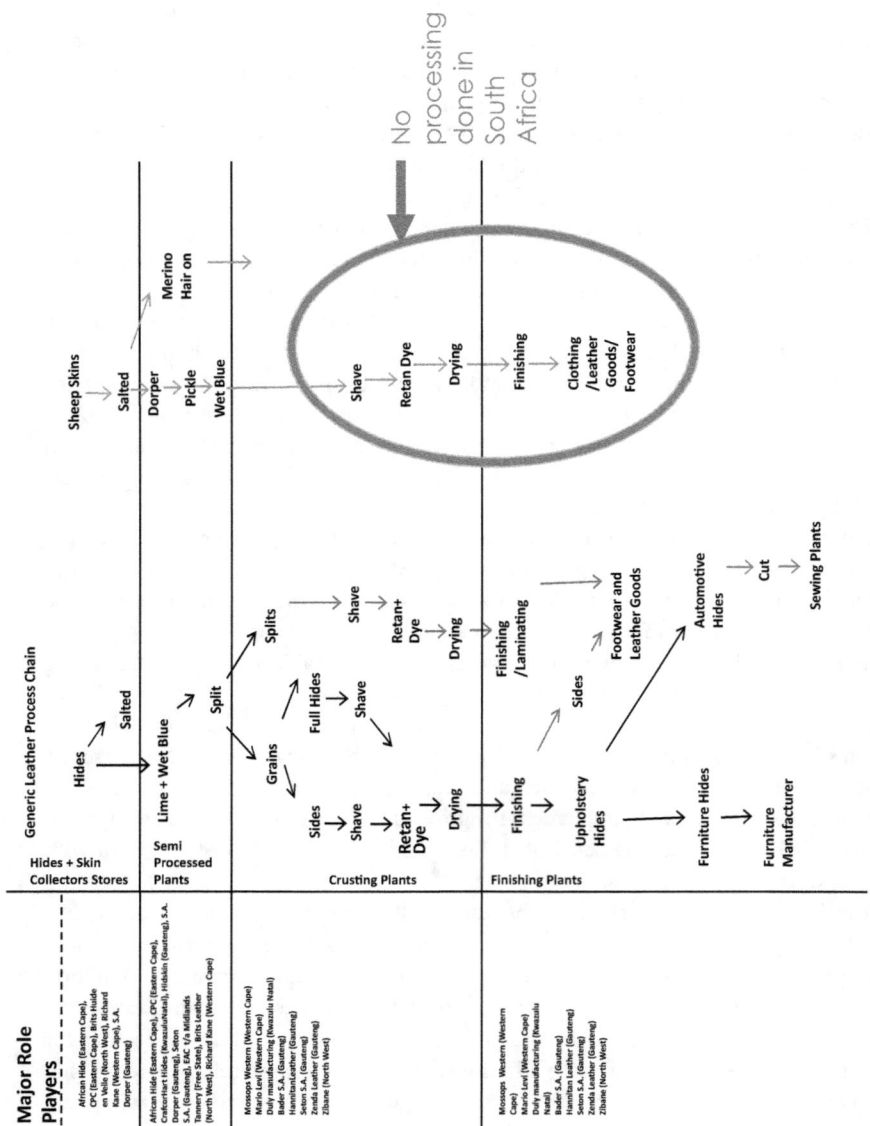

Figure 6.3 South Africa's generic leather processing chain.

Source: Adapted from the South African Skin, Hide and Leather Council (SHALC), 2017.

component manufacturing will require some particular tools. One of them is that if we're going to provide incentives to big companies, and we expect a quid pro quo in terms of black economic empowerment, some of that has to be implemented now in what's called supplier development.'[23] If this is the position taken by South Africa, then the critical importance of achieving socio-economic transformation in South Africa – particularly in the business sector of creating black businesses in the leather sector that matters to the region – will never happen and remain rhetoric.

It is for these reasons that it is imperative that Davies put forward policy and laws and a legally binding commitment for implementation from the South African government to major monopolies in the leather sector, among several others, that force monopolistic and oligopolistic practices among white conglomerates, enforcing them to stick to business principles of socio-economic transformation and trade laws. In the meanwhile, however, immediate action plans are necessary as the dwindling of specialised skills throughout the leather industry is evident. Southern African governments' inability of generating globally competitive knowledge in domestic leather products, mainly ostrich leather, bovine hides and game skins, should be addressed. Exorbitant costs of locally produced chemicals for tanning and dying, specifically those of wet and blue chemicals, compound the problem of inadequate skills. South Africa's total livestock herd was recorded at 13.7 million and cattle hides and skin exported were 23,313 tonnes in 2015, lacking in finished products. Similarly, essential approaches ought to be adopted immediately. South Africa's smaller business industries and emerging entrepreneurs must be granted a safety net that is supported by a strong government policy.

The government, and more substantially businesses, must consider implementing a four-pronged approach. The first approach should enhance South Africa's Economic Transformation Programme to engage and create the space for existing and new African entrepreneurs. This method must apply the DTI's supplier–demand model that is indicative of incentivising big industries intending to build national and regional smaller businesses through law and policy implementation. The second approach ought to implement a government policy that binds leather industries to regional markets intending to access beneficiation of regional downstream products, which could create further employment potential. While governments and prominent leather businesses implement policy and loyalty, they should create conditions for smaller enterprises that afford knowledge sharing and also that allow for inputs from smaller companies to benefit the regional value-addition leather chain.

Moreover, the first and second approaches offered above favour both political will by the government and businesses – the commitment from larger industries within the leather sector to create a platform for smaller companies to enter the industry – with a view to forming the desired job creation. But while businesses are concerned with balancing the books and governments with policies and protecting industries, there are no guarantees that emerging leather industries will ultimately benefit from the leather market as these approaches are central to 'political will' and 'business commitment'. Therefore, a business critique model is suggested here, as a third approach.

A third approach is essential to involve the South African government's Ministry of Agriculture, and the agro-processing sector in particular, to making provisions available in financing sponsored learnership programmes for young entrepreneurs. The youth should also be involved in such plans since eleven million youth were unemployed in Africa in 2016. Graduate academic research courses and practical training in leather processing offered by the University of Nairobi's Leather Science and Technology Training Programmes should be made use of. A fourth approach should involve small, medium and micro enterprises (SMMEs): micro companies should make up a group of emerging and small leather entrepreneurs with a view to becoming 'self-efficient and go-it-alone' industries, as Kenya has implemented, and form cooperatives. Accessing investors both locally – in the continent – and internationally should be part of the mission of the cooperatives.

In the case of Kenya, with the government increasing export taxes on raw hides and skins in 2016 – a moratorium was also placed on 40–80 per cent of raw hides traded with international partners with a view to discouraging cheap exports and encouraging value addition of the leather products – the economy is reaping substantial benefits in leather trade. In the meanwhile, the Kenyan government institutionalised the country's Leather Science Institute and the academic programme was closely supported by collaboration efforts between Kenya and UK-based Northampton Leather Academic Research Institute, where training was undertaken by Kenyan scholars in the UK. Kenya has thus developed an international quality assurance standard for its leather. The Nairobi Research Institute developed the acumen for producing quality hides with veterinary academic practice as its base; hides are therefore treated from the calf stage. Since 2012, the University of Nairobi produced forty-three graduates in the Leather Science and Technology Training Programme: twenty graduate diplomas, twenty Bachelor of Science degrees and three students with master's degree. In 2017, the University of Nairobi further enrolled 120 students for Bachelor of Science degrees in the Leather Science and Technology Training Programme, while a further five students pursued their postgraduate studies in the programme. The Kenyan government is thus reaping the benefits from the leather training institute seen in the critical skills sector. Eastern and Southern Africa should work closely with Nairobi and ensure that academic training at the University of Nairobi's Leather Science and Technology Training Programme is being accessed by governments. For example, the South African government's Ministry of Agriculture and the agro-processing sector can enable financing sponsored learnership programmes for young entrepreneurs in leather institutes such as Nairobi's Leather Science Technology Institute and Ethiopia's Leather and Science Institute.

Information and technology systems control: Achieving value addition

Quality assurance is a crucial element in achieving value addition and obtaining global reach through trade. Thus, products must be traceable for leather products, and the complete hierarchy of retailers' supply chains must be available to all traders as well. The information should include the condition of the product from the initial raw material stage (original condition), with the product traceable to the original producer. The system of tracking and tracing is thus crucial in the leather industry and requires an effective database that is able to capture such information and is reliable for Southern Africa and Africa at large. Proper systems must be in place if South Africa's producers are to position a leather market up the value chain. Partnerships must be more results-driven to accelerate the pace of value addition through industrialisation, and thus having such a database capture national and regional industries for easy access should also be considered. These information portals should be able to provide the necessary knowledge, particularly of smaller industries, if such industries are to gain access to and tap into larger firms' outputs (downstream industries). This should go both ways. Aside from the role that trade has had in the convergence debate, the Secretariats of COMESA, EAC and SADC and their executives similarly had a significant influence in the events leading up to finalisation of the CFTA as they had in the 2008 period leading up to its convergence.

The second main finding of this book, therefore, applies the new theory of Pan-African economic integration that considers Africa's trade relations with the Caribbean and Pacific countries and the impact of external powerful trade partners such as EU on these relations.

The theory therefore claims that conducting trade among Africa's countries with similar economies to the Caribbean and Pacific countries can create the necessary conditions to achieve Pan-African economic integration and, ultimately, economic growth. Some elements of Jan Tinbergen's gravity theory of trade, which underscores that 'relative economic size attracts countries to trade with each other, while greater distances could weaken the attractiveness', could be considered by African states.[24]

The preferences of Africa's governments have erroneously leaned more towards entertaining exploitative and oppressive powerful international actors including Beijing, Brussels and Washington – such powerful economies have no match in Africa's peripheral economies. What is instead required is the boosting of trade relations within the ACP bloc (bearing in mind that the 2000 ACP–EU Cotonou Trade Agreement comes to an end in 2020) with a view to growing Africa's economies with developing states.

For example, the ACP has a total gross domestic product (GDP) that includes the following: Africa – \$2,074,447 million, the Caribbean – \$74,163 million and the Pacific – \$1,472,938 million, which are in trade relations with the twenty-seven-member EU that had a total GDP of \$16.6 trillion in 2016.[25] Such huge GDP discrepancy undoubtedly warrants for a critical analysis. Such analysis must thus consider, more critically, Europe's relations with the ACP bloc with a view to unearthing the real geopolitical reasoning underpinning relations among realist states.[26]

The EU's relationship with the ACP bloc has largely been driven by realism in pursuing Europe's parochial needs through neo-liberal and neocolonial spheres of power. The benefits derived through parochial needs linked to a zero-sum game exposes the extent of the dysfunctional nature of the ACP–EU relationship. For example, since the signing of the Lomé Convention of 1975, international cooperation between the ACP and the European Economic Commission (EEC) and the tangible gains of trade as an instrument to aid development for the ACP bloc have been disappointing. The ACP bloc, with a population of 2.2 billion people across seventy-eight countries including South Africa, contributes to only 4.7 per cent of global trade and accounts for only 1.9 per cent of total global GDP of $1,075 trillion as of 2014, slightly less than the 2 per cent for the latter in 1975.[27]

The November 2017 EU Multiannual Financial Framework (MFF) (2014–20) is currently under review. The EU's future ambitions and challenges are linked to this midterm MFF review, and a report was made available to the EU council and parliament in December 2017. A renewed MFF is currently under review for the period 2021–7[28] Central to Europe's realities are the protracted conflicts, migration and refugee flows it faces, which have placed added pressure on Europe's external financing instruments. The European Consensus on Development has become intertwined with the goals of a post-Cotonou agenda, as well as with the sustainable development goals (SDGs) and delivering on the 2030 Global Agenda. Europe therefore seeks to focus spending for the ACP bloc on private-sector involvement and investment through development, and it is making several attempts to keep migrants at home.

One such EU strategy is private investment – not a novel idea; EU member states have been involved in private investments in Africa since the 1970s. Between 1975 and 1985, major oil-trading partners and private businesses were operating in Angola, including Belgium's Petrofina, Italy's Agip, France's Total and Elf Aquitaine, Spain's Hispanoil, the UK's British Petroleum (though the UK in 2016 signed a referendum to exit the EU), Germany's Diminex and Brazil's Petrobras.[29] These are mainly investments of oil and petroleum. Investment gaps should instead be directed by the ACP bloc, in a way that serves the investment needs of the bloc. The European Commission's preferred scenario is to move from multilateral to bilateral relations reflecting the ACP bloc in three separate chapters, having more of a regional package with Africa instead of separate packages for Africa and its RECs. Thus, what is considered is merging the Joint Africa-EU Strategy (JAES) and other funding envelopes into a regional package and focus.[30]

Africa's regional economic communities also receive separate funding envelopes from Europe. The EU's 11th Development Fund entails support across regional priorities, with an overall amount of €1.3 billion funded within regional envelopes from January 2015. Regional infrastructure priority areas of €600 million will be used to support 'hard' and 'soft' regional infrastructure projects, with €450 million to be split among Africa's RECs to implement regional initiatives. SADC receives €90 million of this fund, while COMESA and EAC each receives €85 million.

Europe's strategy on its part has always been one of divergence of the ACP, except where convergence mattered to the EU. Brussels identified South Africa as one of its top ten strategic partners globally. South Africa joined the ACP bloc in April 1997, with limited access later to the Cotonou Agreement of 2000, since it was viewed by Europe as a developed state and its agriculture and textile exports could damage sensitive EU sectors. After several rounds of negotiations over a two-year period, South Africa conceded to join the Lomé Convention but under a separate protocol. Thus, while Tshwane is in the ACP bloc geographically, it is not really part of the bloc as it does not align to Cotonou. In March 1999, the EU–South Africa Trade, Development and Cooperation Agreement (TDCA) was eventually finalised. The EU has continued its dumping of highly subsidised beef, has continued to pay its wheat farmers $103 per tonne production subsidy, and in addition applies a wheat import tariff of 73 per cent against zero protection. South Africa also receives a contribution fund from the EU separately from that of SADC. This separation of South Africa from the rest of the bloc has caused trade diversion for the rest of the members of the ACP bloc, particularly in Africa, given South Africa's hegemonic status on the continent. This divergence of South Africa has thus allowed the EU easy entry into the ACP markets.

The EU floods the ACP bloc's market with manufactured goods. The EU mainly imports from the Caribbean countries: fuel and mining products, notably petroleum gas and oils; bananas, sugar and rum; minerals, notably gold, corundum, aluminium oxide, hydroxide and iron ore products; and fertilisers. The main imports into the Caribbean from the EU include boats and ships, cars, constructions vehicles and engine parts, phone equipment, milk and cream, and spirit drinks. In 2016, total exports from Europe to the Caribbean market exceeded EU imports from the Caribbean countries by $3.4 billion (see Figure 6.4).[31]

On 16 October 2014, the EAC (Burundi, Kenya, Rwanda, Tanzania and Uganda) finalised their negotiations for an economic partnership agreement with the EU. The economic partnership agreement (EPA) covers both trade in goods and development cooperation. It also contains an extensive chapter on fisheries, which reinforces the future cooperation prospects of fisheries within the ACP bloc. Ironically, the continent remains a net importer of agriculture produce, despite the fact that 70 per cent of its population is working in the agriculture sector and yet Africa produces only 3.5 per cent of the world's food exports.[32]

The EU is currently negotiating a comprehensive EPA with all fourteen countries of the Pacific region: the Cook Islands, Fiji, Kiribati, the Marshall Islands, Micronesia, the Federated States of Nauru, Niue, Palau, Papua New Guinea, Samoa American and

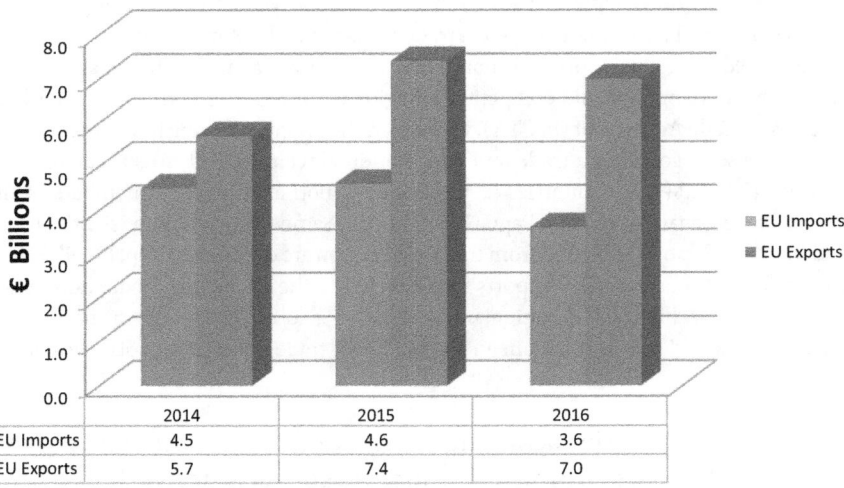

Figure 6.4 EU–Caribbean countries: Total trade in goods, 2014–16.

Source: Adapted from European Economic Commission, 'Overview of Economic Partnership Agreements', http://ec.europa.eu/trade/policy/countries-and-regions/development/economic-partnerships.

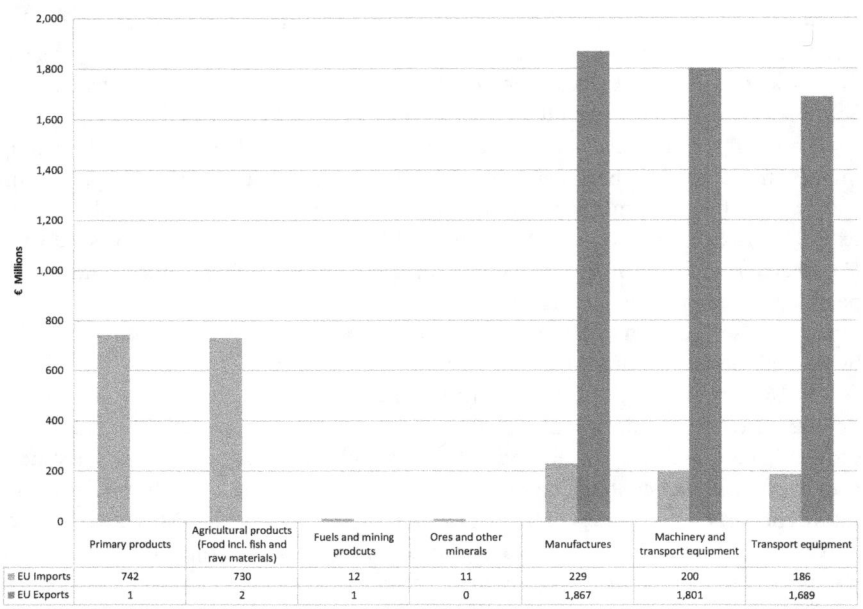

Figure 6.5 EU–Pacific trade flows in main commodities, 2016.

Source: Adapted from EU Commission on EPAs, http://ec.europa.eu/trade/policy/countries-and-regions/regions/pacific (accessed 30 August 2017).

Samoa Western, the Solomon Islands, Tonga, Tuvalu and Vanuatu.[33] The comprehensive agreement would cover trade in goods, trade in services, development cooperation and trade-related issues like food health and safety, technical barriers to trade, agriculture, sustainable development and competition. Regional trade is based on the Pacific Island Countries Trade Agreement (PICTA), which is in the process of being implemented. The region is also negotiating a trade and cooperation agreement with Australia and New Zealand (PACER+). Six countries in the Pacific region are currently members of the World Trade Organisation: Fiji, Papua New Guinea, Samoa, the Solomon Islands, Tonga and Vanuatu. Exports to the EU from the Pacific region are dominated by palm oil, coffee, coconut, and fish and caviar. Imports from the EU to the Pacific region are dominated by electrical machinery and equipment. Machinery and equipment from the EU (see Figure 6.5) should be sourced from an all-ACP intra-trade agreement post-Cotonou.

Comparative advantage and economic growth for Africa's geostrategic economic convergence with the Caribbean and Pacific

The governments of the ACP group of states must converge policy in key trade commodities in which they have a comparative advantage, with a view to fostering economic growth and socio-economic development. The success of a post-Cotonou trade partnership lies in the ability of governments to streamline policies to build stronger interregional trade relations. It is thus crucial that Africa address effective growth for its agriculture sector. Another area of concern that could be addressed within the ACP bloc based on interregional (intra-ACP) cooperation and trade is diversification of trade. Consider fertilised land. In Africa only 9 kilograms of fertiliser is used per hectare per year, compared to 157 kilograms of fertiliser per hectare in Asia, and an average of 99 kilograms per hectare globally. More staggering is that each fertilised hectare in Africa produces a market value of only $85;[34] though the Caribbean group of states have an abundance of fertiliser, it largely exports its fertiliser as a main trade commodity to the EU. Rather, the direction of fertiliser from the Caribbean should be pointed towards Africa's markets. Africa also accounts for 60 per cent of arable land globally, yet only 6 per cent of this land is irrigated annually. In contrast, 34 per cent of Asia's arable land is irrigated annually.

A key condition for successful intra-ACP relations would require that the ACP group draw on the numerical strength of its seventy-nine member states to become economically stable. Sound market liberalisation policies along with effective macroeconomic policies are crucial for economic growth – to counter the continuous export of primary commodities with low or no value added and subsequent import of those same goods back into the ACP bloc as manufactured goods. The ACP bloc must address how to add value to key trade commodities in agriculture, for example, and this based on comparative advantage, including palm oil in the Pacific region and West Africa, tuna in the Pacific region and Cape Verde (West Africa), sugar in the SADC region and the Caribbean, and coffee in the Pacific region and Ethiopia and Kenya (East Africa).

Blue economy: The Africa, Caribbean and Pacific Bloc

The ACP governments must address how to keep labour within the bloc and place less emphasis on the EU's migration woes, in the process creating the necessary conditions for cross-border initiatives within the ACP bloc. Europe is already involved in the Pacific's deep-sea mining, for example, to obtain resources. The SDGs most relevant to the 'blue economy' concept is the fourteenth goal (SDG 14), which stipulates, 'By 2030 to increase the economic benefits to Small Island Developing States and least developed countries (LDCs) from the sustainable use of marine resources, including through sustainable management of fisheries, aquaculture and tourism.'[35]

This goal has great relevance for the ACP bloc, since thirty-seven of the fifty-seven small island developing states (SIDS), and twenty-seven of the thirty-two LDCs, are also member states of the ACP group. The ACP coastal and island states cover 32 square kilometres of maritime space, and thus concrete processes are being formulated to develop the blue economy as a critical pillar for economic growth and development. However, a fuller partnership is necessary to accelerate growth of the blue economy of the ACP group and address constraints on trade, investment, technological advances and innovation.[36] The ACP states should collaborate in their efforts to build stronger technologies and innovated systems for unlocking the bloc's blue economy as defined in SDG 14 and work with both United Nations Economic Commission for Africa (UNECA) and Economic Commission for Latin America and the Caribbean (ECLAC). Both of these organisations have created specialised knowledge centres, for example, in mining production, politics, gender and climate change, as well as model institutional frameworks for the SDG implementation agenda.[37] The AU has developed a 2050 Africa's Integrated Maritime (AIM) strategy for governments in support of maritime challenges and opportunities. A post-Cotonou process should define a common maritime policy for the ACP bloc. Africa has the potential to unlock $1 trillion per year in total maritime commerce.[38]

In light of climate change and erratic rainfall patterns particularly in Africa and cyclones in the SIDS, 'who grows and who produces' is an important consideration for deliberation in an all-ACP developmental framework. ACP countries with excess fertiliser should thus consider trading more with Africa, with a view to increasing fertilised land areas. Within the ACP group, the bloc also has an extensive fishing agricultural market, notwithstanding the Pacific Island countries' vibrant fishing industry. For example, in 2015 the tuna market of the Pacific Island countries represented 60 per cent of the global tuna catch, valued at $4.8 billion, which created more than twenty-five thousand jobs and contributed to 40 per cent of government revenue in the countries of the Pacific region. 'Who produces and who manufactures' is another important consideration for expanding intra-ACP trade relations. Inputs into final products, such as the canning of tuna, should be considered in furtherance of the intra-ACP developmental framework.

With regard to airline safety and air transport, Africa is responsible for 20 per cent of all accidents in the world but accounts for only 3 per cent of global traffic.[39] Such initiatives should be developed further in future ACP relations. Infrastructure of airports should be addressed in order to expand the airspace market. For example, the airspace market in Africa has the potential to develop seven million jobs, including 257,000 direct jobs, worth about $68 billion of the continent's $1 trillion total GDP.[40] The aviation sector is thus vital for socio-economic development. Conducting more trade among the ACP states also needs to take into account the geography of the ACP bloc. The closest distance between a Pacific country and Africa is between Mauritius and Papua New Guinea, at over 9,000 kilometres; the distance from Trinidad and Tobago to Cape Verde, for example, is over 4,000 kilometres. Flying time from Trinidad and Tobago to Namibia is approximately 11 hours, over a distance of 5,000 nautical miles. Africa's interregional cooperation in the aviation sector has made some progress in regional integration, and thus an airspace market and airline partnerships among the ACP group should be exploited and viewed as an opportunity for economic growth.

Aside from infrastructure to facilitate cross-border trade, infrastructure is just as important in adapting to the effects of climate change. The Pacific Island countries are some of the most vulnerable in the world to the effects of climate change and natural disasters. Five Pacific countries are among the top twenty in the world with the highest average annual disaster losses scaled by GDP. Sustained development progress will require long-term cooperation between governments, international development partners and regional organisations. More broadly, greater economic integration, more equitable natural resource agreements and more open labour markets, all with an eye towards adaptation to climate change, could be vital for the long-term future of the ACP bloc post-Cotonou.[41] Hurricane Irma on 6 September 2017 in Antigua of the Caribbean attests to such challenges.[42] The UN's 2016 *World Risk Report*[43] outlines the crucial importance of workable infrastructure as well as properly built structures, particularly in high-risk climatic zones. Dilapidated transport routes, unsafe power grids, and buildings in a state of disrepair have major negative consequences for local populations and are also contributors to disaster risk management and challenges that could be confronted by relief organisations during logistical support. Without workable infrastructure, an extreme natural event such as a hurricane can become an unmanageable disaster. The report provides an analysis of disaster risk for 171 countries calculated on the basis of the vulnerability of a society by taking into account exposure to natural hazards – cyclones, droughts, earthquakes, floods and sea-level rise – and coping and adaptive capacities. The fifteen countries at most risk globally (from most at risk to less at risk) include Vanuatu, Tonga, Philippines, Guatemala, Bangladesh, Solomon Islands, Brunei Darussalam, Costa Rica, Cambodia, Papua New Guinea, El Salvador, Timor-Leste, Mauritius, Nicaragua and Guinea-Bissau. Infrastructure is central not only to trade routes but also to managing high climatic risks. Five of the Pacific countries – Kiribati, Papua New Guinea, Solomon Islands, Tonga and Vanuatu – are among the most at risk globally with extreme natural disasters.[44]

The most important aim of building ACP regional infrastructure is to exploit regional growth for larger markets, on its part – for Africa's landlocked states – through better-managed water resources and electricity production and by establishing linkages for goods to reach both markets and people. Such initiatives inevitably lead to job creation and poverty eradication; effective transport lowers transport costs; and effectively generated energy facilitates agricultural production, industry, mining and communications. All of these results are conducive to intraregional trade. Moreover, Pan-African economic integration can therefore only be achieved when more focus is placed on strengthening internal trade and conducting external trade with Caribbean and Pacific countries – along with whom Africa is in a bloc, the ACP bloc. Moreover, forming trade relations with developing states means that more amicable trade relations within the 79-member-state ACP bloc will be achieved, lessening opportunities for market exploitation and power imbalances. Less external exploitation in trade relations with external partners could further result in transforming the socio-economic conditions for Africa's over one billion people and an opportunity to achieve 'economic growth and development', as Immanuel Wallerstein accurately notes.[45]

Current trade relations among members of the ACP bloc are weak with no convergence of the seventy-nine member countries. Moreover, for trade blocs to succeed, it is imperative that a strong presence drives the economic integration while serving the interest of the bloc such as Egypt in COMESA, Kenya in the EAC and South Africa in SADC, as Europe had done when it formed its trade bloc in 1957 – Belgium, France, Italy, the Netherlands, West Germany and Britain joined eighteen years later – the main integrationists that led to its success and the formation of the EU in 1993. As the convergence and divergence literature explained in Chapter 2, powerful economies in a regional bloc can thus lead to convergence of a trade bloc (coming together). It is for this important economic reason among several others that Europe distanced South Africa from the ACP bloc and in so doing ensured the divergence of the ACP bloc, while gaining easy entry into Africa's markets.

7

Pan-African security convergence: The evolution of collective security

The national interests of states have set the pace for the continental peace and security agenda, particularly those of the African Standby Force (ASF), and not the African Union (AU) – the architect of the African Peace and Security Architecture (APSA). Such interests have derailed policy implementation of the ASF and have been misguided by the state's parochial domestic conditions, yielding a nationalist approach to dealing with external affairs. Africa's continental peacekeeping has also become squarely linked to the economic interests of the state, with security issues coming to be viewed by governments through the lens of realism and trumped by concerns of political economy over regional and human security.

In other words, a regional hegemonic power – a state with immense political clout and authority within a regional bloc, but bound by the need to address its own domestic socio-economic concerns – will set the rules of the game for its own benefit. Moreover, such a state will have the political will to militarily intervene in support of other states in its region to achieve regional security, and only do so when this is linked to its own national interests. This also means that national-level challenges, particularly in the case of regionally powerful states, will tend to filter into the continental-level aim of achieving convergence of regional security mechanisms.[1]

Therefore, the theory of Pan-African security convergence claims that it will only occur based on the extent of economic convergence associated with trade in the Continental Free Trade Area (CFTA) and, similarly, the extent of intracontinental trade undertaken by powerful states who would militarily intervene with a view to protecting their vested interests, which will advantage continental security.

The CFTA was ratified by powerful member states such as South Africa, Kenya and Egypt, thus demonstrating their commitment to conducting intracontinental trade, and therefore, a heightened continental economic commitment of states will guard over such interests, which will ultimately result in more commitment being shown towards securing intracontinental trade and attain Pan-African security convergence.

The CFTA has only been recently adopted in March 2018, and therefore, it would be premature to gauge the extent of such security convergence. This chapter assesses the past patterns of security convergence at regional levels of COMESA, EAC and SADC to help better gauge and test the theory of Pan-African security convergence. But in support of the Pan-African security convergence theory, the analyses will assess the past roles of powerful states with regional interests like South Africa in efforts of achieving collective security.

While South Africa has provided military support, as is discussed in this chapter, it has also acted as a malign hegemon that has self-interest as its principal gain; hence realists' analyses of self-interest associated with dominance and mercantilist strategy are able to support the analysis provided in this chapter.

The chapter further expands the discussion on how COMESA, EAC and SADC manage security in their respective regions by providing specific case studies confined to the period 2008–19. Since overall the book aims to assess the growing convergence between COMESA, EAC and SADC in the economic arena towards Pan-African economic integration (see Chapter 6), the discussion on security is thus important to assess the growing convergences between COMESA, EAC and SADC in their security roles, with the objective of securing trade.

A regional security complex framework theory assists in providing a detailed analysis regarding security issues and also helps understanding security complexities. Buzan and Wæver's writing on regional security (as was discussed in the conceptual framework in Chapter 2) outlines 'the possibility of systematically linking the study of internal conditions, relations among units in the region, relations between regions, and the interplay of regional dynamics with global acting powers'.[2] However, security dynamics at the interregional level can override the regional dynamic through support gained from a single great power, which in turn can create more complexity such as super-complexes (with one or more great power at their core) and further redefine and reshape the interregional level into a super-region.[3]

General Carl von Clausewitz noted, 'War has increasingly become the continuation of economics by other means.'[4]

Regional security is complex and has various dimensions not solely defined as military and security dimensions but involving economic, military, political, social and international dimensions. Eastern and Southern African states, in their drive for power within a regional security complex framework, appear to have played one region off against another, and one state against another, and these practices have filtered into the security of the region.[5]

Buzan and Wæver also suggest that where there are instances in which great powers can override the regional imperative, there will also be small powers present in such a security dynamic that tend to reinforce it. Thus penetration into regions occurs when external actors intervene in conflict and establish security mechanisms with states. In building on Buzan and Wæver's regional security complex theory, this chapter assesses the main conflict drivers and the conflict-prone and problem countries in the three regional economic communities (RECs), within the convergence years of COMESA, EAC and SADC since 2008.

Africa's attempts of achieving collective security

The idea of a continental security arrangement goes as far back as the late 1950s and early 1960s.[6] Steeped in Pan-Africanism, Ghanaian leader Kwame Nkrumah believed in the importance of seeking a political union for the continent. Other newly independent African states, though, sought functional regionalism through the creation of subregional organisations that they envisaged would become economically and politically independent through freer trade and interlinking customs unions. Nkrumah raised the idea of an African High Command for discussion at the 1958 All-African Peoples' Conference, but it dissipated, with African leaders divided on the issue. There were two major factions that developed on the issue of African integration: the Monrovia group and the Casablanca group. The Monrovia group – comprising Benin, Burkina Faso, Cameroon, the Central African Republic (CAR), Congo-Brazzaville, Côte d'Ivoire, Gabon, Liberia, Madagascar, Mauritania, Niger, Nigeria, Senegal and Togo – called for the gradual establishment of a joint defence command instead, so as to allow for time and space to strengthen the political and economic bases of African states, whereas the Casablanca group – Algeria, Egypt, Ghana, Guinea, Libya, Mali and Morocco – had called for the establishment of a joint high command as expeditiously as possible.[7] With states jealously guarding their newly established sovereignty and steering away from any form of supranational power, Nkrumah's idea did not take root. Since its creation, the AU, which replaced its predecessor, the Organization of African Unity (OAU), in 2002, has undertaken major missions including those in Burundi (2003–4), Sudan's Darfur region (2004–7) and Somalia (since 2007). The history of Africa's RECs in peacekeeping dates further back.[8]

The African Standby Force was conceived at the AU's 2002 Durban summit and established as part of the union's protocol related to the Peace and Security Council (PSC), which came into force in December 2003. In addition to the PSC and the ASF, the protocol also provided for the creation of a Continental Early Warning System (CEWS), a Panel of the Wise and a Special Fund (the Peace Fund). All these together form the main pillars of the APSA. The protocol also provides for the establishment of a Military Staff Committee. The ASF is arguably the most critical element of the APSA, and the standby force must be able to undertake interventions timeously and robustly. Crucially, such interventions will require the political will of its member states.

Since 1992, peace operations have been conducted by African RECs such as the Economic Community of West African States (ECOWAS), SADC and the Economic Community for Central African States (ECCAS). There is thus considerable experience among these regional bodies to feed into the operationalisation of the regional brigades in East, West, Southern and Central Africa. In Eastern Africa, the Intergovernmental Authority on Development (IGAD) oversaw the region's initial efforts to establish its standby brigade. In September 2004, the first meeting of the Eastern African Standby Brigade (EASBRIG) – later renamed the Eastern Africa Standby Force (EASF) – adopted a draft policy framework establishing the standby brigade. In September 2005, the chiefs of defence staff met to discuss the operationalisation of the AU Roadmap and Planning Element (PLANELM), the skeleton brigade headquarters and the establishment of an independent coordination mechanism, with the operationalisation of the logistics base deferred until the AU had finalised the logistics concept for the ASF. By 2007, the EASBRIG structure had made fair progress, with the establishment of the East African Standby Force Coordination Mechanism (EASFCOM) (previously EASBRICOM) in March of that year.[9] The status of EASFCOM was elevated to that of a full secretariat in 2014 by the Eastern Africa Council of Ministers of Defence and Security. The regional PLANELM was adopted in July 2005 and located in Nairobi, while the logistics base and the command headquarters of the EASF are in Addis Ababa. As of 2017, the active membership of the EASF comprised ten countries: Burundi, Comoros, Djibouti, Ethiopia, Kenya, Rwanda, Seychelles, Somalia, Sudan and Uganda.[10] It is worth noting that the EASF was set up amid several severe regional conflicts, including the aftermath of the Ethiopia–Eritrea border conflict of 1998–2000, the electoral crisis in Kenya in 2012, the ongoing conflict in Somalia, the Ethiopia–Sudan Nile River water dispute[11] as well as the water conflict between Tanzania (EAC and SADC member) and Malawi (SADC member) over Lake Malawi.[12]

The PLANELM serves as a roadmap for the five brigades – a framework to guide their operationalisation based on six mission scenarios. Scenarios 1 to 4 are aimed at deployment within thirty days from a mandating AU resolution. More specifically, Scenario 1 describes AU/regional military advice to a political mission; Scenario 2, an AU/regional observer mission co-deployed with a UN mission; Scenario 3, a stand-alone AU/regional observer mission; and Scenario 4, an AU/regional peacekeeping force for peacemaking and preventive deployment missions. Scenario 5 involves the deployment, within thirty to ninety days, of an AU peacekeeping force for complex multidimensional peacekeeping missions. Scenario 6 calls for deployment in a situation of genocide, where the international community has failed to act promptly, with the AU envisaged to have the capability to deploy a robust military force within fourteen days. Furthermore, the first phase of operationalisation (Scenarios 1 and 2) was expected to have been completed by June 2005, and the second phase by June 2010 (a missed deadline). By this time, it was conceived that the AU would have developed the capacity to manage complex peacekeeping operations, while the different regions continued to develop their capacities to deploy a mission headquarters for Scenario 4 involving AU/regional peacekeeping forces.[13] The nomenclature has changed over time as the development of the ASF has progressed. It took Africa nearly five decades after independence to consider the establishment of a continental peacekeeping force. As the 'military pillar' of the APSA developed by the AU, the ASF is one of the most important mechanisms for addressing Africa's conflicts.[14] As mentioned, the ASF has missed two deadlines – 2010 and 2015 – for achieving full operational capacity. At the time of writing, progress remains slow, and this standby force is closing in on the two-decade mark since its 2002 conception and is still not brigade-ready. In the meantime, external actors such as France and the United States are setting up operations in the Horn of Africa and guarding over their interests there. For example, Djibouti matters to the United States, and to France with regard to military operations. Djibouti's Camp Lemonnier houses two thousand US troops and is also a vital link to the war on terror in the Horn of Africa ever since the 11 September 2001 attacks occurred in New York. In the case of France, their fighter planes are stationed at Djibouti's Ambouli airport.[15]

Regional security complex framework: Evolving domestic actors and factors

This section builds on the discussion in Chapter 3 which highlights that despite violent conflict and the wars of the apartheid regime that ended in 1994, the COMESA, EAC and SADC regional blocs have become a regional community with complex security issues that have forced these RECs to work together. This section also expands on the complexity of regional security, which also concerns economic reasons and the further difficulties that COMESA, EAC and SADC were confronted with in their attempts of managing complex regional security scenarios.

Buzan and Wæver note, 'A regional security complex [RSC] cannot be applied to any group of countries ... [but] in order to qualify as a RSC, a group of states or other entities must possess a degree of security interdependence sufficient both to establish them as a linked set and to differentiate them from surrounding security regions.'[16]

What distinguishes states within a RSC framework is their security interconnectedness, and their indifference. These factors also distinguish them from global powers that produce a set of complications, anomalies and difficulties that have elements of both external involvement and border concerns between regions.

Many states with legitimate regimes have also faced territorial insecurity within the first few decades of independence such as border conflicts. These are evident in the cases of Burundi, Uganda, Rwanda and the Democratic Republic of the Congo (DRC). The liberal view of the state leans more on individual responsibility and on the freedom of state political and economic structures.[17] Illiberal regimes feature at times as established democratic states but, in essence, are autocratic regimes that are partially free and straddle between democracy and authoritarianism (also defined as quasi-democratic, semi-authoritarian or hybrid regimes), where democratic rights are either not upheld or not institutionalised.[18] Such regimes see regional organisations as a mechanism to serve their own self-interests, because of historical and past legacies. Regional security has become a polarised system between the international and regional levels.

Furthermore, within a regional security complex is a clear security complex framework found in an alliance formed at the subregional level. Pertinent examples are the roles of South Africa in SADC, and Malawi and Tanzania in COMESA, EAC and SADC, in forming a security complex of peacekeeping troops and trying to remedy the conflict in the DRC and the Great Lakes region.[19] COMESA was not designed as a security organisation and does not have a brigade as SADC does. Member states with strong military presence assisted in managing the regional conflicts. Resource-based conflicts have many dimensions and actors. Actors could include national armies, rebels, insurgents, private militias, warlords, mercenaries, private security companies and multinational corporations. These actors often accumulate wealth by gaining direct and indirect access to resource-rich areas such as the DRC with its diamonds, cobalt, oil, zinc, copper and gold, and South Sudan with its oil.

Out of desperation in April 2013, the AU set up an African Capacity for Immediate Response to Crises (ACIRC).[20] This brand-new military intervention tool sought to create a rapid deployment capability. Though seen as a temporary measure, the robust military force would have integrated combat units of 1,500 troops with many specialist capabilities. The main idea behind ACIRC was to prevent atrocities and war crimes by armed rebel forces, crimes against humanity and genocide, with the main imperatives to save lives, protect democratic governance, and establish and maintain the rule of law. The delay in operationalising a continental brigade had resulted in African states improvising interventions.

The major issue of non-support for the AU by the United Nations (UN) has also been argued by former Kenyan foreign minister Moses Wetangula: 'The practice in the past two years seems to indicate an undesirable trend that appears to be selective on the part of the Security Council and that seems to disregard full consideration of the position and/or recommendations of the AU or its organs.'[21]

Buzan and Wæver also suggest that violent conflict explains the complex nature of intervention that requires a multidimensional approach of governmental, intergovernmental and development agencies, alongside non-governmental organisations and state and non-state agencies, which are both internally and externally connected. In assessing regional security, various dimensions need to be considered. These include the poverty dilemma (the deprivation of basic needs) and the mismanagement of resources that spill over into various levels of society and cause violent conflict. Protests by DRC civilians have persisted since conflict erupted in the Congo in 2011. The parties to the conflict have been the Allied Democratic Forces (ADF), the Armed Forces of the DRC, the Democratic Forces for the Liberation of Rwanda (*Forces démocratiques de libération du Rwanda*) (FDLR) and the DRC government. In February 2013, eleven African states signed a peace, security and cooperation framework agreement for the DRC, to restore peace in the Eastern Congo.

In the absence of a continental brigade, South Africa, Tanzania and Malawi, as well as the AU, scrambled together resources in support of the DRC. Their initiative spurred the UN Department of Peacekeeping Operations (DPKO) into action. Only later did the UN Security Council authorise its first ever offensive UN force in April 2013 with the key responsibility of neutralising armed groups, namely the Force Intervention Brigade, which was created when UN Resolution 2098 was passed. It provided a 19,815-strong intervention brigade.

> Resolution 2098 condemned M23, the Democratic Forces for the Liberation of Rwanda, the Lord's Resistance Army, and all other armed groups for their continued acts of violence and atrocities committed that impacted on the human rights of citizens. It tasked the new brigade with carrying out offensive operations, either unilaterally or jointly with the Congolese armed forces, in a robust, highly mobile and versatile manner to disrupt the activities of those groups.[22]

Conflicts involving armed militia groups use civilians as a tool of war, and the most vulnerable groups of society are often targeted. Examples are the rape of women and recruitment of children as soldiers.[23] COMESA, EAC and SADC member states are mainly developing states, plagued by weak governance structures such as parliamentary and electoral systems, inadequate security and justice systems, public administrations that are either absent or dysfunctional, and debilitating poverty evident in post-election conflicts in countries such as Madagascar, Zimbabwe and, more recently, Burundi and Lesotho. These are key ingredients that lead to conflicts that can spiral into violence which inevitably leads to lawlessness and the collapse of states. Africa overall is still confronted with corrupt governments inadequately delivering (and sometimes failing to deliver) the most basic social services for their citizens.

COMESA, EAC and SADC member states – Burundi, the DRC, Rwanda and Uganda – have also been equally involved in a complex security web. Regional disputes have been largely driven by mutual threats to security and domestic politics. Since 1997, the conflict in the DRC has largely been linked to diamond and cobalt plundering, and over two decades later later in 2019, the DRC was still trying to address the same issue with Burundi, Rwanda and Uganda. The conflict style of most African leaders, when resources and state apparatus are threatened, is to use force through military action, and by fuelling rebel groups and inciting violence.

In the case of Uganda, ADF and the National Army for the Liberation of Uganda (NALU) have had a continued presence in the DRC, dating back to the 1980s. Sudan's refugees were hosted in Uganda and formed the Sudan People's Liberation Army (SPLA) and fought the Khartoum government from Uganda's soil. Uganda also assisted Rwanda, with many refugees harboured there since the early 1960s. In 1982, when Rwandans were expelled from Zaire, close to three thousand Rwandese joined Museveni's Bush War.[24]

By 1986, the number of Rwandans in the National Resistance Army (NRA) had increased to about eight thousand troops. Moreover, from 1998 to 2003, Uganda became involved in the violent conflict in the DRC and backed militia groups in Kisangani in the Eastern DRC.[25] The UN accused Ugandan commanders of unlawfully extracting the DRC's mineral resources, and in 2005 the International Court of Justice ordered Uganda to pay reparations.[26]

In the north-east of the DRC, Uganda has also played a dual role of both 'arsonist and fireman with disastrous consequences for the local population'.[27] Uganda's continued political feuds among Congolese party leaders sparked violence among the local ethnic groups, and these heightened their plundering of resources and furthering their own interests at the expense of the DRC government while occupying its territory. In December 2009, the Lord's Resistance Army/Movement (LRA) rebels killed over 300 people and abducted 250 more over four days in Makombo, in the north-east of the DRC. Several reports have blamed Uganda's presence in the DRC and linked it to the plundering of the Congo's resources. Museveni's own domestic track record has also been viewed as poor. Domestic politics in Uganda have become commercialized, with the president carrying bags of money and distributing money to Ugandan citizens in an attempt to gain favour.[28] The political instability and the upcoming elections led to 144,000 refugees fleeing Burundi to Tanzania, Rwanda, the DRC, Uganda and Zambia by June 2015.[29]

Burundi is chiefly dependent on agriculture and grows coffee and tea, and in 2014 it had a gross domestic product (GDP) of $3.037 billion and a population of 9.201 million people. Coffee plantations employ 90 per cent of the population, with eight hundred thousand farmers dependent on employment in this sector, directly followed by tea production. In the mining sector it has the world's second-largest coltan reserve (coltan is a dull metallic ore, used extensively in almost all cell phones, laptops, pagers and many other electronic devices) and 6 per cent of the world's nickel reserves.[30] But Burundi is one of the poorest countries in Africa. In April 2015, it faced a constitutional crisis that centred on the question of Burundian president Pierre Nkurunziza's bid for a third term. Regardless of its constitutional laws, Nkurunziza was controversially re-elected as president on 20 August 2015.[31]

With regard to Rwanda, since its genocide in 1994, which killed eight hundred thousand people, the country has seen real improvements in economic growth. In 2014, Rwanda's total GDP was $7.5 billion versus a total GDP of $753 million in 1994. It boasted one of the highest economic growths on the continent in 2014, at 7.5 per cent,[32] and has developed its military capacity largely due to the donor support that it received – totalling $4.2 billion – between 2005 and 2012.[33] Although Rwanda had troops in the DRC until 2002, Rwanda's FDLR rebel group is stationed in the east Kivus region of the DRC and has invaded the DRC four times.

The tide started turning against Kagame in 2012, when evidence emerged that Rwanda was supporting the March 23 (M23) rebel group movement. After this revelation, several donors suspended aid to Rwanda, and Kigali started becoming more circumspect in its actions.[34]

Burundi, Rwanda and Uganda have been embroiled in regional conflict, given the resources in the DRC that have much greater importance, as shown in Figure 7.1.[35] A 2012 UN report made allegations against Uganda for deploying six hundred troops to help rebels prepare offensives against the DRC government. Uganda has vehemently denied the accusations and portrayed its role as a regional mediator that was attempting to facilitate dialogue between Kinshasa and the rebels. In its attempts to portray the UN reports as inaccurate, during this time, Uganda became actively involved in supporting the DRC in disarming the M23 rebel group alongside South Africa and Malawi. Three tonnes of minerals mined in the DRC have been smuggled across borders to Burundi (and Rwanda and Uganda), including gold, diamonds, cobalt and copper. Other smuggled resources include fish, ivory, timber and charcoal.[36] Uganda exported seven tonnes (7,000 kg) of gold in 2006, which was 318 times the official production figure of only 22 kg that year. During this same period Uganda also assisted in deploying its military troops to assist the South Sudanese president Salva Kiir Mayardit against the opposition leader, Riek Machar, a rebel leader of the Sudan People's Liberation Movement in Opposition (SPLM-IO) and a former vice president who was sacked by President Kiir.[37]

According to an April 2015 United Nations Environment Programme (UNEP) report, transnational organised crime syndicates have benefited greatly from the conflicts in the Great Lakes region, and in the DRC in particular.[38] The report noted that 'illicit natural resource exploitation in Eastern DRC amounted to between $722 to $862 million per annum, and these amounts excluded illicit diamond exploitation. Of this amount, 10 to 30 per cent (approximately $72 million to $426 million per annum) goes to organised transnational criminal groups'.[39] The report further reveals that

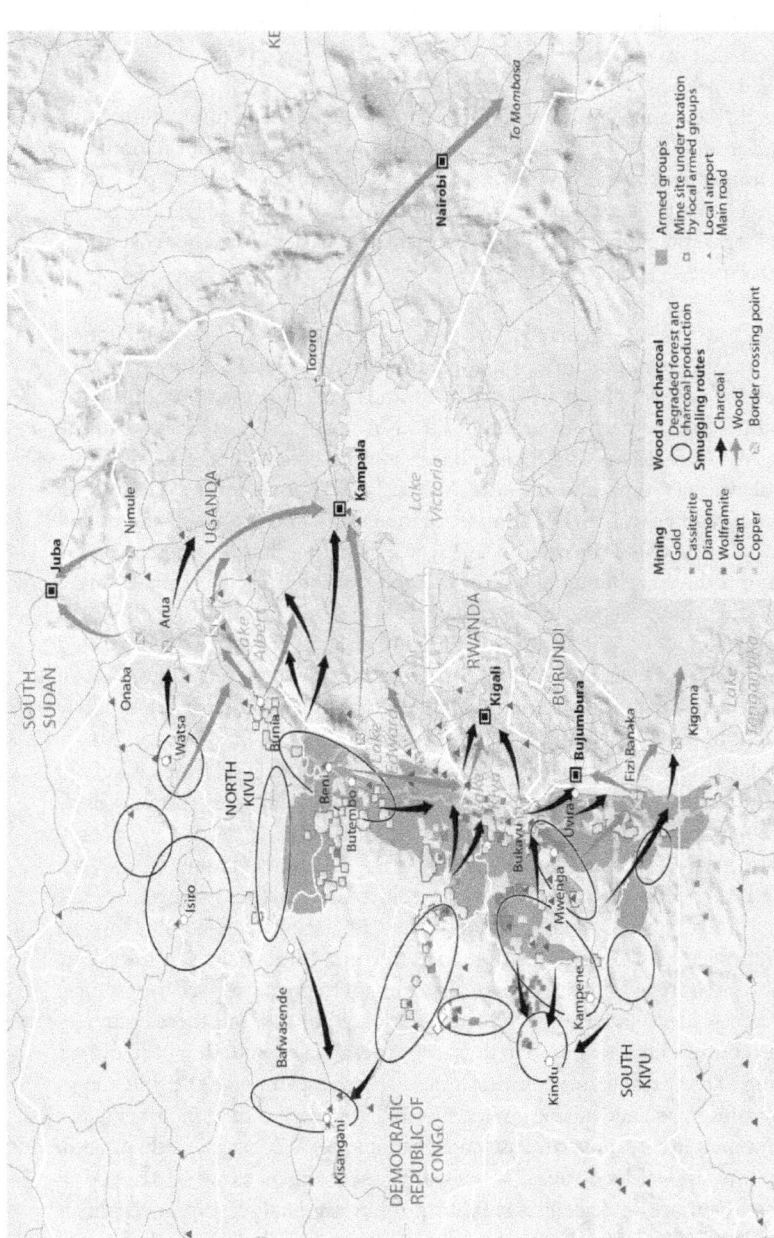

Figure 7.1 Smuggling by transnational organised crime syndicates from the Eastern DRC to criminal groups, companies or individuals in Uganda, Rwanda and Burundi.

Source: United Nations Environment Programme (UNEP) and the Mission des Nations Unies en République Démocratique du Congo (MONUSCO), 'Experts' Background Report on Illegal Exploitation and Trade in Natural Resources Benefitting Organized Criminal Groups and Recommendations on MONUSCO's Role in Fostering Stability and Peace in Eastern DR Congo', 15 April 2015, https://postconflict.unep.ch/publications/UNEP_DRCongo_MONUSCO_OSESG_final_report.pdf.

illicit resources were derived from deals in gold ($40 million to $120 million); timber ($16million to $48 million); charcoal ($12 million to $35 million); 3T minerals (cassiterite [tin], wolframite [tungsten], coltan [tantalum]), cobalt, and copper ($7.5 million to $22.6 million); diamonds sourced mainly from outside of the DRC ($16 million to $48 million); and wildlife, including ivory and fisheries; local taxation schemes; cannabis; and other resources ($14.3 million to $28 million).[40]

'Ninety-eight per cent of the net profits were from illegal natural resource exploitation, particularly of gold, charcoal, and timber, which went to transnational organised criminal networks operating in and outside of the DRC. Armed groups retained around two per cent (approximately $13.2 million per year) of the net profits from illegal smuggling, which also represents the basic subsistence cost for at least 8 000 armed rebel fighters per year.[41]

Furthermore, the revenue generated from illegal natural resource exploitation finances about twenty-five armed groups that continue to destabilise the Eastern DRC. Minerals are carried across borders to Uganda, Rwanda and Burundi and other parts of the DRC. Tantalum is largely produced and sold in north Katanga, Rubaya in the Masisi territory of north Kivus and Shabunda in south Kivus. Tantalum smuggling occurs from Rubaya via Goma into Rwanda. Militia in Shabunda control the mining and distribution of cassiterite. Official estimates of the DRC's gold produced and traded were 150.58 kg in 2014 and 180.76 kg in 2013, which is less than 2 per cent of the actual total gold produced. The remainder of the gold was smuggled, estimated at 10 tonnes in 2013 at a value of about $391 million to $418 million. In 2014, the DRC produced up to 40 tonnes of gold for the year, and illicit gold exports were estimated between $118 million and over $1.8 billion. Burundi officially exported two tonnes of gold in 2008, of which one tonne originated in the DRC, and Rwanda exported nearly twice its production, although only 38 kg was mined in 2008.[42] In February 2014 a COMESA meeting of the Council of Ministers[43] commended the DRC for its efforts to restore peace and security in the Eastern DRC and the victory of the *Forces armées de la République démocratique du Congo*/Armed Forces of the DRC (FARDC) – greatly assisted by South Africa, Tanzania and Malawi – over M23 rebel factions. COMESA urged Kinshasa to expedite the regional peace, security and cooperation framework commitments of disarmament, demobilisation and reintegration of ex-combatants. At the same summit meeting, COMESA commended Burundi for its efforts to resolve its land disputes and encouraged the Burundian government to create a space for political actors coming from exile to participate in formal national politics. But these countries are experiencing continuous corruption in their countries with exploitation of resources and undermining of their respective constitutions.[44] These gestures by COMESA shows that regional communities have turned a blind eye to bad governance of member states as well as non-adherence to government constitutions. SADC, on the other hand, was set up from the start of its creation as a security mechanism, as was discussed in Chapter 3, and is at a more advanced stage in terms of its regional security mechanism than COMESA. The SADC Summit launched the SADC Brigade in Lusaka, Zambia, in August 2007, as a regional and multidimensional peace support operation.

Towards Pan-African security convergence

Convergence of COMESA, EAC and SADC in managing regional security has been possible with the presence of a hegemonic power like South Africa. In discussing the complex security scenarios, this section also provides examples of security convergence between the two blocs and includes member states of the EAC. South Africa as a regional hegemonic power has been an important player in the convergence of security due to its own self-interests. In the absence of the ASF, a major challenge for regional brigades is to address the peacekeeping gap of the UN launching interventions timeously in Africa's conflicts.

In further guarding over national interests, South Africa's former president Jacob Zuma's administration was also investing hugely in regional peacekeeping operations and has been assisting the countries in recent conflicts in the Great Lakes region. Neorealists define the hegemonic state as a powerful, strong economy that sets the rules of the game, has a greater advantage over its partner states and exerts power.[45] South Africa has taken on a leading role in security issues in the COMESA, EAC and SADC blocs. From 2008 to 2010, South Africa, with the strongest economy and military component, assisted with funding of military equipment and provided troops. Its African Renaissance and International Cooperation Fund (ARF) of 2001 prescribes in its legislature that its mandate is to identify and fund projects and programmes aimed at the promotion of democracy, conflict prevention and resolution, socio-economic development, humanitarian assistance and human resource development in Africa.[46] These moves are outlined in its 2014 Defence Review policy that shows R44 billion, equivalent to 1.6 per cent of South Africa's 2015 GDP, made available for military deployment.[47] The South African government has over the past decade and a half (2000–15) deployed its National Defence Force (SANDF) of about five thousand personnel to UN-led regional peacekeeping missions. With South Africa remaining constrained by its domestic challenges such as accessing reliable electricity, which affects its economic growth and has various other spin-offs such as job losses, it has increasingly turned towards the region. The South African government lost billions of dollars due to electricity shortfalls, which drained its economy, and at the time of writing the failed power utility Eskom has crippled South Africa's economy, draining it by R4 billion per day during Stage 4 load-shedding (4000 MW of power is removed from the Eskom grid).[48] According to the US Central Intelligence Agency (CIA), 'South Africa's economic growth has decelerated in recent years, slowing to just 1.5 per cent in 2014. ... The rolling black outs were the worst the country faced since 2008. ... Economists judge that growth cannot exceed 3 % until electrical supply problems are resolved.'[49]

Tshwane's electricity is generated by its parastatal Eskom and operates coal plants. Hydroelectricity will be a key alternative source in assisting Tshwane's strained parastatal. In assisting the government in its dilemma, South Africa begun securing regional investments in Lesotho and in the DRC, both militarily and economically. In Lesotho, South Africa invested R11.2 billion to build a hydropower plant. In the DRC, Tshwane had tried since 2010 to secure links with the DRC government in trying to gain access to its water resources in the Grand Inga Dam.[50] South Africa adopted a more firm approach towards the DRC government, having invested hugely militarily, with more clout in doing so. In mid-2015 South Africa secured a 2,500 MW hydroelectricity contract with the DRC government for electricity generation from the Grand Inga 3 project in the DRC.[51]

While South Africa had been providing regional security, it had also been expanding its arms exports. For example, South Africa's arms exports totalled R2.98 billion in exports in 2014, R3.2 billion in 2013 and R10.6 billion in 2012, as outlined in a South African National Conventional Arms Control Committee (NCACC) report.[52] From 2008 to 2015, South Africa assisted the DRC in its perennial conflicts.[53] As shown in Table 7.1, South Africa assisted Comoros (the newest SADC member state since

Table 7.1 State interventions in conflict areas from 2008 to 2015

Conflict states	Date of intervention/ deployment	State intervention
Burundi	2009 2010 2013	Mozambican and South African troops deployed alongside AU and later UN hybrid missions.
Sudan	2008–2010 2010	South Africa assisted Sudan in a hybrid multinational mission (AU/UN) and also provided a component of security sector reform in Sudan with assistance from Sweden. Peace-support operations and military deployment.
The DRC and the Great Lakes region	2008–2010 2010–2015 (present)	MONUC (involvement of South Africa's troops). FARDC SSR (involvement of South Africa and requested by the AU's Post-Conflict Reconstruction and Development Programme (PCRD))[a]. South Africa's ARF provided financial assistance of R101 million. *SSR – South Africa's involvement with Sweden. *Peace support operations and military deployment.
Zimbabwe	2008–2009 2010–2013	South Africa's ARF project provided financial assistance of R613 million for PCRD projects in Zimbabwe.[b]
Comoros (Grande Comore and Moheli Islands) and Anjouan Island	2008	Elections – involvement of South Africa. Comorian and AU forces (800) deployed to restore constitutional rule on Ajoujan.[c]
Rwanda	2008–2010	SSR – South Africa's involvement with Sweden.
Uganda	2010	Peace support operations – military deployment.
Madagascar	2009–2013	Track Two Diplomacy – mediation.
Libya	2011	Peace diplomacy – South Africa's support of the UN Resolution 1973 (calling for a no-fly zone, an arms embargo and an asset freeze of the Gaddafi regime).

[a] African Union Peace and Security, 'Post-Conflict Reconstruction and Development Programme', *AU*, http://www.peaceau.org/en/page/70-post-conflict-reconstruction-and-development-pcrd.
[b] Anthoni van Nieuwkerk, 'A Review of South Africa's Peace Diplomacy since 1994', in Chris Landsberg and Jo-Ansie van Wyk (eds), *South African Foreign Policy Review* (Johannesburg: IGD, 2012), p. 96.
[c] van Nieuwkerk, 'A Review of South Africa's Peace Diplomacy since 1994', p. 94.
Source: Dawn Nagar, 'Towards a New Pax Africana: The Politics of Peacekeeping in Africa', CCR seminar paper (August 2013).

2017) in 2008 with elections and also deployed eight hundred forces to restore the rule of law there. In Rwanda, South Africa assisted the Rwandan government with setting up a security sector reform programme. South Africa was involved in Madagascar between 2009 and 2013, and the then South African president Zuma tried to mediate but failed.

South Africa's outward-looking regional strategy is an approach that has been adopted to address inward-looking problems. South Africa intervened militarily in Lesotho in 1998, and it has ever since been involved in mediating efforts in Lesotho's political affairs. Lesotho, thus, matters to the South African government since Maseru provides water to South Africa's Gauteng province with a population of thirteen million people. While Lesotho was experiencing political conflict in 2015, following post-election disputes, South Africa agreed to mediate there. This request emanated from the 3 July 2015 SADC Double Troika Extraordinary Summit that met in Tshwane and included presidents from Zimbabwe (SADC chair), Botswana (incoming chair), Malawi (outgoing chair), South Africa (current OPDSC chair), Lesotho (incoming OPDSC chair) and Namibia (outgoing OPDSC chair) during this period.

The meeting focused on how to remedy the ongoing violence in Lesotho. The main cause of the violence was linked to Lesotho's elections and also to the brutal killing of Brigadier Maaparankoe Mahao on 25 June 2015 – a key political figure and a former Lesotho Defence Force commander. The South African president Cyril Ramaphosa (as then deputy president) was asked by its government to be the SADC facilitator and to mediate between the various political stakeholders in Lesotho.[54] South Africa also assisted Sudan's government and the SPLM in forming its Comprehensive Peace Accord (CPA) of 2005, aimed at crafting a government for South Sudan as well as a central government for Khartoum.[55]

Prolonged periods of the human rights atrocities and abuses by both governments and warring parties and groups – in Africa's most resourced region, the Great Lakes countries, having faced the same conflict conditions since the 1960s, and with such prolonged human rights violations – inevitably lend themselves to lawlessness and statelessness, and corrupt governments challenge security.

The persistence of rebel groups in the DRC and South Sudan, among several countries in Africa, have largely been due to the lack of economic growth and lawlessness alongside aid for trade packages designed with China and the European Union (EU). Moreover, the continent's security concerns have been more centred on the violent groups and rebel movements that have begun threatening Africa's pursuit of peace, including the insurgent groups of the Central African Republic's Séléka, the DRC's Mai-Mai groups and Mali's Ansar Dine.

The Great Lakes region's woes were also infiltrated by several other African states fighting proxy-fuelled wars in pursuit of greed, including Angola, Burundi, Rwanda and Uganda. Superpowers aided the states that were leveraging the necessary support to further their own interests. For example, in the case of Sudan, the United States, Europe and China were forced to change their game plan in 2010, to tread more carefully given the realisation that Sudan's Comprehensive Peace Agreement (CPA), signed in January 2005 by the government of Sudan and the Sudan People's Liberation Movement/Army (SPLM/A), had reached a critical stage that potentially risked major investments of these superpowers. In the run-up to the 2011 South Sudan referendum, Washington therefore became the biggest contributor of humanitarian aid to Sudan, with such assistance exceeding $1.2 billion in 2011.[56] Therefore, as noted, strengthening trade relations with neutral actors such as the African, Carribean and Pacific bloc would create the necessary conditions for engendering economic growth and minimize opportunities for corruption and exploitation of Africa's resources, thus increasing socio-economic growth which contributes to peace and security.

Unlike other subregional organisations (see Figure 7.2 outlining COMESA's profile), COMESA was intended to be a purely trade- and investment- oriented organisation. However, a Committee on Peace and Security has been formed, which meets once a year. Article 3 of COMESA's treaty is aligned with the Abuja 1991 Declaration of Political Principles. COMESA had tried adopting an approach of inclusivity by involving all of its member states in its security framework and through partially managing to align converging national policies with its regional peace and security frameworks. However, conflicts have persisted within the region and have been difficult to resolve (also, as discussed below, in the case of Zimbabwe).

COMESA member states are committed to a number of principles, and among them are the recognition of human and peoples' rights in accordance with the African Charter on Human and Peoples' Rights, also known as the Banjul Charter, which was established in 1987 and adopted in 1988 (and came into force on 25 January 2005);[57] the maintenance of regional peace and stability; and peaceful settlement of disputes. In September 1998, COMESA signed two agreements with United States Agency for International Development and received $6 million

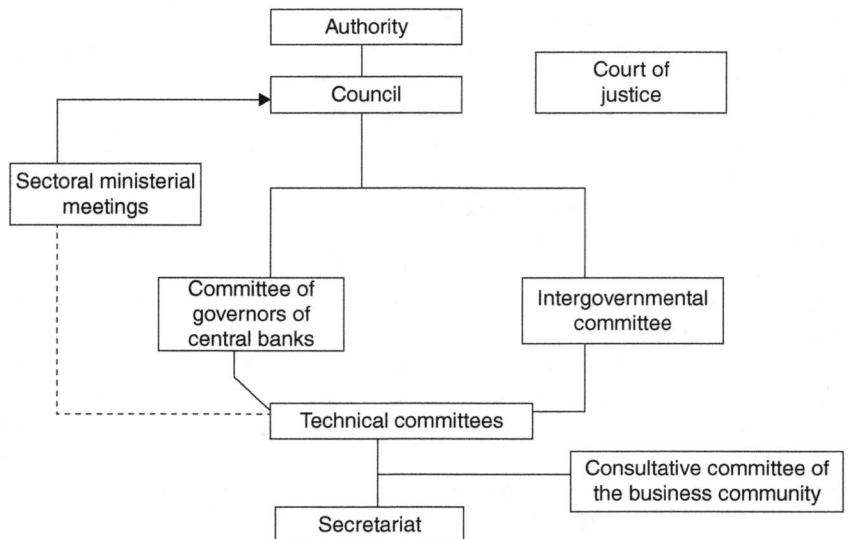

Figure 7.2 COMESA profile.

Source: https://www.comesa.int/comesa-institutions/.

towards democracy/conflict management and regional economic integration for the benefit of its member states.[58]

COMESA established good relations with IGAD, the Indian Ocean Commission and the EAC. It had signed a cooperation agreement with IGAD and ECOWAS. In November 1999, COMESA's Intergovernmental Committee addressed member states to explore efforts for a security framework specifically for post-conflict reconstruction. The next year, in March 2000 at a meeting of member states, the COMESA bloc made the decision to put together a legal framework on peace and security, based on the widespread violence and conflicts experienced among its member states, the DRC, Rwanda, Uganda, Ethiopia, Eritrea and Sudan.

Regional communities are trying to create greater cohesion among member states. For example, just prior to the 2008 Zimbabwe elections, the then president Robert Mugabe's government was awaiting a shipment of arms from the Chinese vessel *An Yue Jiang*. The ship was turned away from South Africa and was not able to dock.[59] Likewise Angola, Mozambique and Namibia refused the vessel entry to their ports. Zambia's then president Levy Mwanawasa urged nations in the region to bar the Chinese ship carrying arms destined for Zimbabwe from entering their waters and noted that this shipment would aggravate the conflict and violence in Zimbabwe.[60] Nevertheless, three million rounds of assault rifle ammunition, three thousand mortar rounds and 1,500 rocket-propelled grenades were offloaded in the Congolese port of Ponta Negra and airlifted by freight charter to Zimbabwe.[61]

Member states have also used the regional economic community to their advantage. For example, on 31 July 2013, COMESA instead of SADC was asked to intervene in Zimbabwe's election at the request of Zimbabwe to monitor the country's elections. As Zimbabwe is a COMESA, EAC and SADC member state, it expressed its dissatisfaction with South Africa's approach under SADC. This was so when COMESA sent an election monitoring team to Zimbabwe consisting of Ambassador Bethuel Kiplagat and twenty-seven observers drawn from COMESA member states (Ethiopia, Kenya, Malawi, Mauritius, Seychelles, Uganda and Zambia), including civil society organisations accredited to COMESA.[62] In 2014, COMESA's regional electoral monitoring team led successful observer electoral missions, among others, to Malawi in May 2014. The legal framework in Malawi was based on COMESA's international, continental and regional standards, governing the conduct of democratic elections. COMESA has been working closely with the AU's 2002 Principles of Governing Democratic Elections and the African Charter on Democracy, Elections, and Governance, as well as adopting SADC's Principles and Guidelines in Governing Democratic Elections.[63]

COMESA worked extensively with the Intergovernmental Authority on Development by drawing support from IGAD to resolve conflicts in South Sudan, Egypt and Ethiopia, while adopting its own conflict early warning system. These systems are still a work in progress.

The conflict styles adopted by most African leaders, when resources and state apparatus are threatened, use force through military actions, fuelling rebel groups and inciting violence.[64] For example, in 2013, former Egyptian president Mohamed Morsi invited state leaders from Ethiopia and Sudan to discuss a tripartite Egypt–Ethiopia–Sudan commission in Ethiopia's efforts to build a hydropower dam of $4.2 billion to produce electricity. The source of the water was from the Blue Nile River, which both Sudan and Egypt depend on for water.[65] Egypt had plans of sabotaging the hydro dam in Ethiopia by aiding rebels inside Ethiopia.[66] But since the dam constituted no serious threat to the flow of water reaching Egypt and Sudan, leaders could resolve their water conflict amicably. The hydro dam construction is Africa's biggest producer of electricity.[67]

COMESA had been battling to attract funding for its governance programme and therefore could not continue the work in this area.[68] COMESA's secretariat, like SADC's, is largely dependent on donor funding and is only able to implement programmes that attract funding. Funding assistance is critical for the COMESA-EAC-SADC bloc to be effective in continued efforts to fight piracy on the shores of especially Kenya, Seychelles, Madagascar and Mauritius.[69] COMESA believes that maritime security can significantly benefit integration for the entire region.[70] COMESA, EAC and SADC's member states' maritime security framework was provided with the assistance of donor funds from the EU in March 2013.[71] The International Maritime Organization (IMO) reported 237 attacks on ships in 2011, 75 attacks on ships in 2012 and 13 incidences of piracy for the first three quarters of 2014.

The decrease in incidences and attacks on Africa's shores are believed to be due to the implementation of 'Best Management Practices for Protection against Somalia-Based Piracy'.[72] Maritime security is important for both the United States and the EU. For example, the United States has up to 90 per cent of regional trade volumes transmitted by maritime transport and that is linked to its African Growth and Opportunity Act trade relations with COMESA, EAC and SADC. The UN spends $139 million to counter each attack on sea, and the estimates from 2011 to 2014 were $3.2 billion.[73] Security was also imperative to secure Europe's trade in goods by sea. COMESA was able to launch a programme to fight piracy with EU pledged funds of 37.5 million euros to implement a comprehensive programme to fight piracy in the Indian Ocean.[74]

Concluding remarks

The theory of Pan-African security convergence adequately assessed the ability of the continent to converge security apparatuses, given the protection warranted by powerful states in minimising conflicts and in securing an expanded continental free trade area, namely the CFTA.

The discussion provided an analysis regarding the security issues in security complexities and expanded on the main conflict drivers in the two regions over recent years (2008–15), the convergence years of COMESA, EAC and SADC. The chapter further expanded on the conflict problem countries which were confined to three RECs: COMESA, EAC and SADC. Rwanda, Uganda and Burundi are member states of COMESA and the EAC, while the DRC is a member state of COMESA. These three regions, including member states of the EAC, were able to galvanise efforts and form a peacekeeping initiative against the violence in their regions. The chapter then discussed how COMESA, EAC and SADC managed security issues in their regions and provided specific case studies confined to the recent regional conflicts. The chapter outlined the importance of the hegemonic state in security convergence and South Africa's role; even though at times its regional support was due to state self-interests and it acted as a malign hegemon, the reality is that South Africa was able to prevent hundreds of thousands of women and children being violated, particularly in the Great Lakes conflicts.

8

Analysis and normative proposals: Pan-African convergence theories

The book is largely concerned with actors and factors that can move Africa towards Pan-African economic integration and security convergence. Although globalisation dictates open markets and trade, it creates a contradiction for the Tripartite Agreement's regional integration approaches of variable geometry and those of the Continental Free Trade Area (CFTA). African countries have remained staunch in their practice of building extensive trade relations with powerful external actors and giving in to such woes, regardless of the African continent facing continuously poor economic growth, with South Africa, for example, achieving 1 per cent economic growth in 2018, total intracontinental trade standing firm at 16 per cent and industries shutting down (see Chapters 4 and 5). Powerful external economies, and the world's largest economies, have remained involved in Africa's economic and security issues.

Therefore, the theory of Pan-African economic integration claims that Africa's conducting stronger trade among its countries (taking into account value-driven industrialisation and comparative and absolute advantage principles) with similar economies like those of the Caribbean and Pacific countries can create the necessary conditions for achieving Pan-African economic integration and ultimately economic growth, and to conduct carefully considered trade with external partners that does not distort Africa's trade.

But the preferences of Africa's governments have erroneously leaned more towards exploitative and oppressed powerful international actors including Beijing, Brussels and Washington, viewed largely by Africa as the saviour to achieving economic growth for the African continent, albeit countless examples and decades of experiences of trade diversion. Africa has also ignored the importance of the Caribbean and Pacific countries and should critically implement policies that enhance trade with the bloc as the 2000 African, Caribbean and Pacific (ACP) Cotonou agreement comes to an end in 2020.

Africa's powerful economies (Kenya, Egypt and South Africa) are important actors for viable trade relations and for Africa achieving Pan-African economic integration with a view to moving its economies from the under-periphery of the world to the semi-periphery. In the case of South Africa, the European Union (EU) had also effectively evoked Tshwane's developed economic status and denounced its least developed country (LDC) profile, adding to the trade dilemma.[1]

The parochial interests of rogue blocs like the EU's economic partnership agreements (EPAs) have never been of any benefit to Africa and its regions, as is explained in discussions of multiple international trade agreements in this book.

Rules of origin

This book identified the gaps in the rules of origin (ROOs) of the Tripartite bloc in light of its fourteen articles that are being negotiated under its roadmap and has not yet been fully completed.[2] Moreover, a CFTA, and the participation of COMESA-EAC-SADC in the CFTA, adds an additional conundrum of trade policies. International relations and political economy students and scholars could possibly interrogate how ROOs could work to benefit the Tripartite and CFTA's future trade negotiations. The recently negotiated EPA configurations also have agreements with prescribed texts regarding Africa's sensitive products and tariffs amid its own free trade configurations, further complicating ROOs and derailing the success of African economic integration. With regional economies not performing as well, several smaller economies have become dependent on other forms and ways of economic growth to protect their infant industries, which have further entrenched the notion of multiple memberships with member states trying to protect their economies and infant industries. These distortions in trade were adequately explained by Gathii, Panagariya and Bhagwati.[3] Distorting mechanisms included signing external trade agreements with the United States (African Growth and Opportunity Act (AGOA) trade agreements) and the EU (EPAs). Similarly, external trade agreements have also proven to challenge economic growth. According to Panagariya, states are also simultaneously trying to circumvent or replace the non-discriminatory most-favoured nation (MFN) tariff associated with the World Trade Organisation (WTO) regulations.[4] External trade agreements have their own ROOs that have exploited COMESA, EAC and SADC's markets and affected trade negatively within the Tripartite bloc. Price distortions and market inflations hinder competitiveness of downstream industries in adding value into products and for companies dependent on inputting into larger firms' outputs.[5] Moreover, trade policies that reduce the profitability of exporting and that favour established industries and firms raise the costs of inputs for downstream sectors.

Total factor productivity

Manufacturing that fosters endogenous growth factors like technology transfer, skills development, research and education is important to enhance trade, since African countries invariably gained independence with economies that spent a large part of their resources on the production of export commodities, which is currently still the practice. Lesotho, for example, has only been exporting clothing to the United States under the aegis of AGOA, with no other diversification of goods. The view from some leading economists is that rise in per capita income can only occur if there is a rise in output 'per unit of input', a point which Krugman makes.[6] Krugman's expansion on total factor productivity (TFP) similarly outlines that because capitalist growth is based on growth in both inputs and efficiency, efficiency is therefore the median to raise per capita income, and therefore it is per capita income that will show an increase through output per unit of input. In expanding on endogenous growth factors in industrialisation and value addition of interregional trade, Dowrick and Nguyen's TFP as a catch-up variable for downstream industries is to be considered in the CFTA negotiations. Hence, aligning such processes within Africa will lead to technological advances and TFP. For example, and as was discussed earlier, the World Bank's 2014 report outlined that South Africa has increased its trade in iron and steel – with a share of level-2 products – from 18 per cent in 2000 to 57 per cent in 2012, all traded to Africa's markets with the largest share of iron ores (ferroalloys) to Southern African Customs Union (SACU) markets.[7] To enhance regional value-addition industrialisation, the book notes that this is an opportunity for the CFTA negotiations to consider addressing, at policy level, how smaller industries could input into South Africa's semi-manufactured level-2 products in the region and benefit from TFP, thus benefiting smaller economies. Hence, the Tripartite bloc could then consider how 'downstream industries can add value into iron and steel products and input into larger firms' outputs'.[8]

Protecting Tripartite member states' industries is much more than just variable geometry, free trade and the principle of acquis

A grand continental free trade area (FTA) and customs union have further positive spinoffs, which an enlarged market could bring about, such as increased economies of scale, as well as greater political and negotiating leverage at international forums. However, benefits for smaller economies will only occur on the basis that more trade is conducted and regional hegemons like Kenya and South Africa accept more exports from smaller economies into their markets that also support smaller industries. The approach of variable geometry implemented by the Tripartite bloc is to provide a mechanism for smaller, vulnerable member states to come on board at a slower pace than other members while protecting their markets. The variable geometry approach is also envisaged to enhance interregional trade with a view to expanding trade, but while protecting smaller economies. However, the approach will not be helpful for smaller African economies, since Africa's strong economies like South Africa, Kenya and Egypt conduct more trade with Europe. Therefore, it is imperative that African countries conduct less trade with Europe and more with African governments over a period of time. African governments must also put forward a thoroughly negotiated trade deal with the EU's economic partnership agreements, which distorts trade for smaller economies and industries. The book identified that variable geometry and trade tariff liberalisation are two approaches that are not conducive to the convergence of Pan-African economic integration. The variable geometry approach has not sufficiently helped the Tripartite bloc in assisting poorer economies to converge on tariff adjustments and would be similarly cumbersome in the CFTA. The openness of trade liberalisation allows international trade to flood the markets of the Tripartite bloc, with no coping mechanism for small, vulnerable industries to withstand the economic shocks associated with loss of industry. Africa's governments ought to be more firm in trade negotiations with external actors.

For example, South Africa refused to sign the new SADC EPA initially with Europe, should Brussels not forgo its agricultural subsidies and those on goods that it will trade within the new SADC EPA – the EU has now agreed to this. South Africa has been very firm in negotiations with the EU because of negative experiences where the Botswana, Lesotho, Namibia and Eswatini (BLNE) bloc was negatively affected by the 1999 SA–EU Trade Development and Corporation Agreement resulting in negative growth in several South African industries. South Africa is adamant not to repeat the past. The Tripartite bloc should learn from this negotiation experience and deploy similar strategies when negotiating trade agreements and in finalising the new regional EPAs. The book proposes a key recommendation here, that trade protocols and agreements should put in place a legal framework that fines member states belonging to the blocs for violating the current trade preferences of the Tripartite bloc. Member states that jeopardise the trade liberalisation of agreed goods should also be sanctioned. There has been commitment shown by the EU of abandoning subsidies, however. Trade agreements that favour and protect regional trade in both goods and services must be negotiated, as the EU has done by protecting its own industries through agricultural subsidies since the 1950s. As discussed in the book, a total of 251 EU geographical indications and 105 South African geographical indications have been negotiated.[9] While external trade is important to grow smaller economies in a regional scheme (as was discussed in SACU), this requires a clearly defined and articulated negotiated agreement that does not exploit smaller industries within the BLNE bloc.

To promote Pan-African economic integration, a five-pronged approach is recommended:

1. Strong economies in a regional grouping must conduct trade with global partners carefully, taking into account trade diversion, while progressively conducting more trade with similar developing countries from the Caribbean and Pacific. Phillip O Nying'uro argues that global trends in the political and economic global order had been mainly associated with free-market-driven liberalisation processes. Similarly, O Nying'uro holds the view that the capitalist global order has been more diverging than converging.[10] The effects of both economics and security have further entrenched multiple memberships, since states have become more focused on guarding their industries. Both France and the UK have already made their 2018 foreign policy clear – with the UK anchoring Zimbabwe, outlining their intentions in Africa, as former prime minister Theresa May's predecessor Margaret Thatcher had done – however, nothing good has ever come from Africa–US, Africa–EU and Africa–BRICS relations.[11] Africa has also ignored the importance of the Caribbean and Pacific countries for greater opportunity in enhancing trade with the bloc, as the 2000 ACP Cotonou agreement comes to an end in 2020.

2. The second element of the approach is to factor in a paymaster. There must be a compensating trade mechanism, such as SACU's trade revenue disbursement mechanism, with a view to compensating smaller economies in the Tripartite FTA and the CFTA, so that there is a benefit for smaller economies to belong to a trade scheme. Such benefits could also consider the implementation of a payment mechanism to assist member states in facilitating trade such as COMESA's Regional Payment and Settlement System (REPSS), created to make trade conducive for its member states. REPSS links member states' national payment systems to regional central banks to effect payment and settlement of trade; it includes banks in Asia and Europe as well as Africa and is viewed as an innovative online system with standards based on those of the Society for Worldwide Interbank Financial Telecommunication. The COMESA clearinghouse serves as the agent for the central banks in formulating bilateral agreements that could assist interregional trade among the member states.
3. Both the Tripartite FTA and the CFTA have been implemented for the sake of reaching artificial timeframes. If more amicable relations with more intraregional trade are to occur, then larger economies must relax its stringent domestic industrial policies and trade protectionism.[12] For instance, Botswana's hide and leather market is of great value to South Africa's motor industry for the manufacture of car seats, and South Africa should continue to guard over such relationships. Kenya, Egypt and Ethiopia have strong leather markets, and implementation of trade policy that factors in endogenous growth must be seriously addressed at summit meetings and at the state level.
4. The fourth element of the approach is that development-led regional integration must be a dual benefit for both stronger economies and smaller economies in a trade bloc. For example, during the 1980s, South Africa's manufacturing products (as noted in Chapter 3; see Figure 3.2) were not conducive for the global market, and therefore, it conducted more trade in the region. This increased production traded regionally and similarly advantaged semi-skilled labour in South Africa, which it has an abundance of for its regional trade, for example, of iron and steel. Trade agreements should therefore consider how smaller industries from within the bloc can input into strategic products, while carefully formulating policies concerning ROOs to make such value-added trade possible for its member states.
5. Fifthly, regional transport linkages that are effectively managed are similarly trade-enhancing factors and clear policy-implemented. Barro and Sala-i-Martin outline the importance of linkages for trade convergence and the increased economic integration that follows from trade liberalisation; reduced transport and transaction costs lead to greater 'spatial agglomeration' as well as specialisation.[13] South Africa has done so in the Maputo Development Corridor, since poor infrastructure capacity inevitably affects trade.[14] While workable infrastructure is critical in pursuing region-building and regional integration, equally important is the concentration of holders of the transport infrastructure monopoly, where South Africa plays a key role in its Transnet (freight railway carrier) structure. The country has several areas of monopoly over regional transport areas. For example, the South African government's tariff pricing for freight is still reflective

of support for import substitution and cross-price subsidisation. Freight prices are similarly seen to place smaller labour-intensive industries at a disadvantage. According to the World Bank's 2014 report, 'Port tariffs on containers were 360 per cent of the global average in 2012, while on bulk commodities they were 19–43 per cent below the global average. [However], [r]ail freight tariffs on iron ore were below US prices while those on general freight businesses are 4–7 times higher.'[15]

What has been foregrounded is that within the individual regional economic communities, regional political dynamics and fragmentation among member states are prevalent. These divergences have affected a convergence within the Tripartite bloc, and it is unlikely that the CFTA would have a different result. The takeaway of the Pan-African economic integration theory is that for Africa to converge and conduct more trade, it should strengthen trade relations with the Caribbean and Pacific countries – and the end of the 2000 Cotonou Agreement in 2020 must act as a major stepping stone for Africa to use Brussels initiatives to its advantage.

Multiple memberships

In explaining the multiple roles of a hegemonic state, the book expanded on Robert Putnam's 'two-level game' model (as was outlined in Chapter 2's conceptual framework). This model helped explain how state capital of hegemonic states influenced the pace of economic and regional growth. This model was able to assist the discussion in expanding on the inward-looking and regionally focused policies of South Africa. Similarly, John Friedmann's theory in the conceptual framework, outlined in Chapter 2, helped the book to conceptualise the debate on the unequal nature of growth defined in his world systems theory. This theory highlighted the fact that the core could be seen to be dependent on the periphery through market exploitation, creating a periphery of the periphery (with poor, vulnerable and resource-depleted economies).

The book noted that a hegemonic state must be able to derive benefits from integration so that it is able to continue supporting the integration process, but not through oligopolistic principles. As was discussed in the book, at the beginning of 2000, an estimated 60 per cent of South Africa's total exports went to the Organisation for Economic Co-operation and Development (OECD) markets and constituted mainly trade with Europe. But in the next decade, from 2000 to 2010, South Africa's exports to the EU and to OECD members slowly started stagnating and exports from the South African market went to Africa's markets. South Africa's inward-oriented approach and the shift to concentrate more on Africa's market was outlined by the findings of the World Bank in 1988 concerning the quality in its manufacturing (as was shown in Figure 3.2 in Chapter 3). The book built on this discussion and the assessment made sixteen years later in the World Bank's 2014 report (discussed in Chapter 4). The 2014 report suggested that since South Africa is a major minerals producer and exporter of metal-based manufactured goods, it has opportunities for export expansion and for offering scope to countries in moving to higher quality (and thus higher value) and greater variety, both across and within stages of production which could build industries across the region.

The pace and intentions of regional integration of the Tripartite bloc – COMESA-EAC-SADC – provide an indication of how regional integration will fare. Moreover, such factors include skills and education, labour migration, infrastructure such as transport and communications, and trade and finance, among others. Therefore, Panagariya outlined that the complexity of regional integration is daunting even in the absence of trade barriers and crisscrossing FTAs lead to a replacement of non-discriminatory MFN tariffs by a spaghetti bowl, whereby tariffs vary according to ostensible origin of the product.[16]

Infrastructure gaps

With ten landlocked member states within the Tripartite bloc, infrastructure gaps have remained a challenge for the bloc.[17] Trade is not the only means of binding states to agreements, since without workable infrastructure for landlocked countries particularly, it is equally impossible to achieve economic growth if there is no viable means of transport to conduct trade. Transportation costs for trade facilitation are also expensive for the member states of the COMESA-EAC-SADC Tripartite bloc. States may see benefits in having more than one trade agreement. Gathii indicated the importance of accessing commodities through waterway transportation, as the largest river basins globally are found in Africa. Multiple memberships therefore provide alternative access to landlocked countries. Regional trade agreements shift to where the benefits are. Gathii has noted, 'African RTAs also serve as institutions of basin management demonstrating the entwined relationships among trade, environment, and security aspects of international river basins.'[18] Therefore, numerous trade agreements are related to the limited access of trade routes for landlocked countries and the competition in relation to transport costs in regional trade in Africa. Similarly, as had been claimed by Paul Kalenga,[19] trade barriers in the COMESA-EAC-SADC Tripartite bloc have also contributed to the lack of effective trade. These trade barriers included 451 different technical barriers to trade (TBTs) reported in April 2013, such as lengthy and costly customs procedures, issues related to ROOs, costly road user charges and other issues related to phytosanitary issues.

Security convergence

Security remains a challenge for COMESA, EAC and SADC. The new wave of regional integration has become complex, with various dynamics of state and border conflicts, involving intra- and interstate conflicts, piracy in East Africa and the emergence of rebel groups. There has been a resurgence of violence and abuse against women and children, as well as an influx of child soldiers in Eastern and Southern Africa. These violent conflicts have precipitated changes to the traditional methods of peacekeeping and leaving regional economic communities (RECs) fending for themselves in the light of an absent continental African Standby Force (ASF). While South Africa had taken the lead in implementing subregional peace and security, its former mediation strategy in the 1990s did not always bear fruit. Middle powers like Zimbabwe, Namibia and Angola bypassed South Africa in 1998 and militarily intervened in the Democratic Republic of the Congo (DRC) conflict. The national interests of states have set the pace for the continental peace and security agenda, particularly those of the ASF, and not the AU – as the architect of the African Peace and Security Architecture. Such interests have derailed policy implementation and are misguided by the state's parochial domestic conditions, yielding a nationalist approach to dealing with external affairs. Africa's continental peacekeeping has become squarely linked to the economic interests of the state, with security issues coming to be viewed by governments through the lens of realism and trumped by concerns of political economy over regional and human security. In other words, a regional hegemonic power – a state with immense political clout and authority within a regional bloc, but bound by the need to address its own domestic socio-economic concerns – will set the rules of the game for its own benefit. Moreover, when such a state has economic interests in a region, it will be more inclined to to militarily intervene in support of other states in its region with a view to securing its own interests. Such interventions also mean that military interventions conducted regionally by powerful states will tend to filter into the continental-level aim of achieving convergence of African security.[20]

9

Conclusion

COMESA, EAC and SADC have been largely driven by the diplomatic efforts of their Secretariats. The success of these diplomatic efforts bore fruit with the first Tripartite Summit that took place in Uganda on 20 October 2008. Even though the EAC joined the 2008 Tripartite Agreement, it nevertheless established its own regional trade mechanism among its member states and still sets its own tariffs with a customs union and likewise Southern African Customs Union (SACU). The Continental Free Trade Area (CFTA) also has its own free trade area (FTA). African states at the subregional level have also undertaken a linear approach of economic integration that comprises suppressing some form of discrimination through removal of trade barriers. As Pascal Lamy suggested (see Chapter 2), there is a tendency among academics to apply analytical frameworks and linear models that are fifty years out of date.[1] Such models prove that regional integration processes begin with an FTA and proceed to a customs union, a common market and a monetary union, which then lead to a political union. The linear models do not correspond to today's world, hence there are various processes and degrees of integration globally.

'Doubling up' of efforts compound regional integration efforts for the Tripartite and CFTA bloc. The same processes are repeated at the continental level with the CFTA. While it is important to have regional integration policies that are aligned at the national, subregional and Tripartite levels, the implementation of an FTA at individual regional economic community (REC) levels are too duplicating efforts and distracting from the CFTA.[2] In the case of the CFTA, a specific recommendation is to be more attractive in negotiations with stronger incentives put forward by trade negotiators and trade economists to attract member states to the bloc. For example, trade negotiations within the CFTA must be elevated beyond the generation of lists of sensitive trade items and tariff adjustments. But what is warranted is a stronger trade agreement that provides a list of specific value-addition-driven trade items negotiated and agreed to, with a view to enhancing Africa's industrialisation and agro-industrialisation among member states. Such trade relations among Africa's states within the CFTA must conduct trade that is based on comparative advantages, which will make trade attractive to member states and ultimately advantageous for boosting economic growth, thus making everybody a winner.

Furthermore, to achieve Pan-African security convergence, mechanisms for strengthening the linkage between national, regional and continental efforts in conflict prevention and mediation should also be considered at the African Union (AU) and REC levels. Thus, a regional structural conflict prevention framework is recommended to enhance regional and continental leadership for the maintenance of peace and security. This initiative would be a key opportunity to harmonise regional experiences and complementary action by national governments and construct consensus-building processes.[3] While there have been instances where countries relapse into war and conflict such as in Burundi, the Democratic Republic of the Congo and Sudan, peacekeeping initiatives should find effective strategies of involving the United Nations (UN) in effective post-conflict reconstruction efforts and peace-building interventions that address the root causes of conflicts and that deal with such triggers effectively. Such strategies include setting up good governance and institutional structures and assisting building infrastructure; assisting to address humanitarian assistance; refugees; repatriation; political, economic and social structures; and, most importantly, disarmament, demobilisation, disintegration and reintegration of ex-combatants and militia groups into their communities.

On its part, the Caribbean and the Pacific have been relatively stable with regard to conflict; the regions are susceptible to climatic disasters, as mentioned earlier. This requires humanitarian management and resources, towards which the UN has a critical role to play. Thus on the international level, the African, Caribbean and Pacific (ACP) Ambassadorial Group and the AU Africa Group should address strengthening their efforts and expanding their working framework with a view to creating a joint body at the UN. The Africa Group is the largest bloc at the UN and has been an important platform through which African states have coordinated their positions and influenced the decisions of the world body, including resolutions of the UN Security Council. Africa has already created strong relations with the UN that could be beneficial in post-Cotonou relations between the ACP and AU secretariats. For example, the AU Peace and Security Council and the UN Security Council hold annual consultative meetings to assess cooperation between the two councils in the areas of conflict prevention, conflict resolution, peacekeeping and peacebuilding in Africa.[4] The consultative meetings also explore ways in which the partnership between the AU and the UN could be strengthened. Such platforms should be expanded in post-Cotonou relations among the ACP countries.

This book has addressed key issues that will help shape the future of Pan-African economic integration and security convergence. It is hoped that the book will strengthen future studies in this area on topics pertinent to these Pan-African objectives towards Africa's achieving sustained and solid economic growth and security. Although this is the first full research study on this topic that I am aware of, it is recognised that this book has not covered every topic of this broad area. More analyses are required in assisting the processes of convergence of the Tripartite Free Trade Area and the Continental Free Trade Area, and this will have more meaningful analyses with increased African trade with similar economies such as the Caribbean and Pacific countries. Academics and students in Africa's think tanks and universities should assess, address and/or expand on the lacunae in this book. The conclusions of this study are relevant for the academic community, policymakers, trade negotiators within ACP, COMESA, EAC, SADC and SACU, secretariats and their governments, regional security mechanisms, as well as African Peace and Security Architecture institutional bodies; other beneficiaries are IGAD, ICGLR and ECCAS; Africa's continental bodies, like the AU; important African bodies like Africa's Human Rights Institutions, New Partnership for Africa's Development, the African Development Bank, the Development Bank of Southern Africa and the United Nations Economic Commission for Africa; the European Union; the United States; and donor communities and civil society actors.

Notes

1 Introduction: Pan-African integration

1 See African Union (AU), 'Accelerating Intra-African Trade and Boosting Africa's Trading Position in the Global Market by Strengthening Africa's Common Voice and Policy Space in Global Trade Negotiations', https://au.int/en/cfta; and https://au.int/en/pressreleases/20180321/list-african-countries-signed-establishment-african-continental-free-trade.
2 See Brookings Report by Joshua Miller, 'African Continental Free Trade Agreement Meets Ratification Threshold for Approval', *Brookings Report*, 6 April 2019, https://www.brookings.edu/blog/africa-in-focus/2019/04/06/africa-in-the-news-african-continental-free-trade-agreement-updates-algerias-president-resigns-and-vodacom-tanzania-executives-face-criminal-charges/. See also United Nations (UN) Department of Global Communication, Kingsley Ighobor, 'Africa Set for a Massive Free Trade Area', *Africa Renewal*, November 2018, https://www.un.org/africarenewal/magazine/august-november-2018/africa-set-massive-free-trade-area.
3 Dawn Nagar, 'Strengthening Policy Development on Inter–Regional Cooperation between the ACP and the AU', *Concept Note*, African Caribbean and Pacific (ACP) Secretariat, Brussels (November 2017).
4 Dawn Nagar, 'The Politics and Economics of Regional Integration: COMESA and SADC, 1980–2015', doctoral thesis, Wits University, 2016, pp. 175–6, http://mobile.wiredspace.wits.ac.za/bitstream/handle/10539/22225/20160716_Nagar%20final%20thesis%20PhD.%20Wits_clean%20version.pdf?sequence=2&isAllowed=y. See also Dawn Nagar, 'Pillars of Africa's Peace and Security Architecture: The African Standby Force', in Tony Karbo and Kudrat Virk (eds), *Towards a New Pax-Africana* (New York: Palgrave Macmillan, 2018).
5 This chapter and the two theories developed and deployed in this book has been authored based on the author's completed doctoral thesis in international relations, submitted to the University of the Witwatersrand (Wits), South Africa: Nagar, 'The Politics and Economics of Regional Integration: COMESA and SADC, 1980–2015', pp. 175–6; and See also Nagar, University of Cape Town (UCT) master's thesis, 'Towards A *Pax Africana*: The Southern African Development Community's Architecture and Evolving Peacekeeping Efforts, 1996–2009'.
6 This theory was coined by the author in a doctoral thesis, 'The Politics and Economics of Regional Integration: COMESA and SADC, 1980–2015', pp. 175–6.
7 Nagar, 'Pillars of Africa's Peace and Security Architecture: The African Standby Force'.
8 Douglas G. Anglin, 'Economic Liberation and Regional Cooperation in Southern Africa: SADCC and PTA', *International Organization*, vol. 37, no. 4 (Autumn 1983): 681–711. See also Samuel K. B. Asante, 'The Years of Preparation: Adedeji and the ECA', in Samuel K. B. Asante, *African Development: Adebayo Adedeji's Alternative Strategies* (Lagos: Spectrum, 1991), p. 21.
9 Danso Kwaku, 'The African Economic Community: Problems and Prospects: the Politics of Economic Integration in Africa', *Africa Today* (Fall, 1995).

10 United Nations Economic Commission for Africa (UNECA), 'Assessing Regional Integration in Africa V', 2012, pp. 13–16. See also Fin24 and Bloomberg, 'Ramaphosa Sign Declaration on African Free Trade Region', 21 March 2018, https://www.fin24.com/Economy/sa-signs-african-free-trade-agreement-20180321.
11 See AU, 'Indication of Legal Instruments to Be Signed at the 10th Extraordinary Session of the Assembly on the Launch of the ACFTA', March 2018, Kigali, https://au.int/sites/default/files/pressreleases/34033-pr-indication20of20signing20author ity20-20updated20final20final20docx.pdf.
12 See also Southern African Development Coordination Conference/Southern African Development Community (SADCC)/(SADC) Summit Communiques, http://www.sadc.int/files/3913/5292/8384/SADC_SUMMIT_COMMUNIQUES_1980-2006.pdf.
13 See Nagar, 'Promoting Dialogue on South Africa's Regional Integration Role in Southern Africa', *Policy Brief*, Centre for Conflict Resolution (CCR) (July 2017).
14 Nagar, 'The Politics and Economics of Regional Integration: COMESA and SADC, 1980–2015', pp. 175–6.
15 Walter Mattli, *The Logic of Regional Integration: Europe and Beyond* (Cambridge: Cambridge University Press, 1999).
16 Anthony J. Venables, 'Regional Integration Agreements: A Force for Convergence or Divergence?' *Policy Research Working Paper*, no. 2260, World Bank (December 1999).
17 Steve Dowrick and Duc-Tho Nguyen, 'OECD Comparative Economic Growth 1950–85: Catch-Up and Convergence', *American Economic Review*, vol. 79, no. 5 (December 1989): 1010–30. See also Dan Ben-David, 'Trade and Convergence Among Countries', *Journal of International Economics*, vol. 40 (May 1996): 279–98.
18 The 2000 Cotonou Agreement will be revised or scrapped, see European Union, 'ACP – Cotonou Agreement', https://ec.europa.eu/europeaid/regions/african-caribbean-and-pacific-acp-region/cotonou-agreement_en.
19 This discussion is premised on research conducted and a concept note created by the author based on a request by the Secretary General, Patrick Gomes of the ACP Secretariat in Brussels in September 2017 (unpublished paper).
20 Jan Tinbergen (ed.), *Shaping the World Economy: Suggestions for an International Economic Policy* (New York: Twentieth Century Fund, 1962).
21 José Antonio Ocampo and Joseph E. Stiglitz (eds), *Capital Market Liberalization and Development* (New York: Oxford University Press, 2010), pp. 125–6.
22 Barry Buzan and Ole Wæver, *Regions and Powers: The Structure of International Security* (London: Cambridge University Press, 2003).
23 Amitav Acharya, 'Regional Security Complexes in the Third World: Stability and Collaboration', *National University of Singapore: Department of Political Science* (unpublished essay) (1992), www.amitavacharya.com (written permission by email granted by author to the researcher to use article, accessed 20 March 2015).
24 See also David Balaam and Michael Veseth, *Introduction to Political Economy* (Upper Saddle River: Pearson Prentice Hall, 2001), pp. 110–27.

2 The evolution of Pan-Africanism: Regional integration theories and approaches

1 See Nagar, 'The Politics and Economics of Regional Integration: COMESA and SADC, 1980–2015', pp. 175–6.

2   Dawn Nagar, 'Strengthening Policy Development on Inter-Regional Cooperation between the ACP and the AU', *Concept Note* (African Caribbean and Pacific Secretariat, Brussels November 2017).
3   See Nagar, 'The Politics and Economics of Regional Integration: COMESA and SADC, 1980–2015', pp. 175–6.
4   See also discussion paper by Chris Alden and Maxi Schoeman, 'South Africa's Symbolic Hegemony in Africa', London School of Economics, London; and University of Pretoria, South Africa (2015) http://repository.up.ac.za/dspace/bitstream/handle/2263/51617/Alden_South_2015.pdf?sequence=1&isAllowed=y.
5   Dawn Nagar, 'Pillars of Africa's Peace and Security Architecture: The African Standby Force'; and Nagar, 'South Africa's Role 20 Years Post-Apartheid', *Journal Für Entwicklungspolitik,* vol. xxix, no. 4 (2013).
6   See Permanent Mission of France to the United Nations in New York, G-5 Sahel Joint Force, https://onu.delegfrance.org/G5-Sahel-Joint-Force-10433.
7   See https://www.globalcenter.org/events/engaging-civil-society-actors-in-the-rehabilitation-and-reintegration-of-individuals-associated-with-and-affected-by-terrorism/.
8   John Pinder and Simon Usherwood, *The European Union: A Very Short Introduction* (Oxford: Oxford University Press, 2007).
9   Pinder and Usherwood, *The European Union.* See also Pascal Lamy, 'Regional Integration in Africa: Ambitions and Vicissitudes', *Notre Europe Policy Paper,* no. 3 (2010).
10 Mattli, *The Logic of Regional Integration.*
11 Mattli, *The Logic of Regional Integration,* p. 41.
12 Ibrahim A. Gambari, *Political and Comparative Dimensions of Regional Integration: The Case of ECOWAS* (Atlantic Highlands: Humanities Press International, 1991).
13 Nagar, 'Strengthening Policy Development on Inter-Regional Cooperation between the ACP and the AU'.
14 Karl W. Deutsch, *Political Community and the North Atlantic Area: International Organisation in Light of Historical Experience* (Princeton, NJ: Princeton University Press, 1957).
15 Deutsch, *Political Community and the North Atlantic Area.*
16 Ernest Haas, *The Uniting of Europe* (Stanford, CA: Stanford University Press, 1958); Leon N. Lindberg, *The Political Dynamics of European Integration* (Stanford, CA: Stanford University Press, 1963).
17 Haas, *The Uniting of Europe;* Lindberg, *The Political Dynamics of European Integration.*
18 Mattli, *The Logic of Regional Integration,* p. 25.
19 David Mitrany, *A Working Peace System* (Chicago, IL: Quadrangle Books, 1966).
20 Mitrany, *A Working Peace System,* p. 99. See also David Mitrany, 'A Functional Approach to World Organization', *Royal Institute of International Affairs,* vol. 24, no. 3 (1948): 350–63.
21 The AU Strategy for regional integration, 'Towards a Common Market for Agricultural Products', Charter of the organization of African Unity and the AEC Treaty, Article 3(c) and (d), http://www.au2002.gov.za/docs/key_oau/sirte.pdf.
22 Anglin, 'Economic Liberation and Regional Cooperation in Southern Africa', pp. 681–711.
23 John Ravenhill, 'The Future of Regionalism in Africa', in Ralph I. Onwuka and Amadu Sesay (eds), *The Future of Regionalism in Africa* (London: Macmillan, 1985), pp. 205–24.

24 Lamy, 'Regional Integration in Africa: Ambitions and Vicissitudes'. See also Arthur Hazelwood, 'The End of the East African Community: What Are the Lessons for Regional Integration Schemes?', in Ralph I. Onwuka and Amadu Sesay (eds), *The Future of Regionalism in Africa* (London: Macmillan, 1985), pp. 172–89. See also Peter Robson, *Economic Integration in Africa* (Evanston: Northwestern University Press, 1968).
25 UNECA, 'Assessing Regional Integration in Africa V', 2012, http://new.uneca.org/aria/aria5.aspx. The African Union identified the following RECs and states: the Economic Community of West African States (ECOWAS) – formed in 1975 – Benin, Burkina Faso, Cape Verde, Cotê d'Ivoire, Gambia, Ghana, Guinea, Guinea-Bissau, Liberia, Mali, Niger, Nigeria, Senegal, Sierra Leone and Togo; the Arab Maghreb Union (AMU) formed in 1989 – Algeria, Libya, Mauritania, Morocco and Tunisia; the Preferential Trade Area of Eastern and Southern Africa, now Common Market for Eastern and Southern Africa (COMESA) formed in 1993 – Burundi, Comoros, the DRC, Djibouti, Egypt, Ethiopia, Kenya, Libya, Madagascar, Malawi, Mauritius, Rwanda, Seychelles, Sudan, Swaziland, Uganda, Zambia and Zimbabwe; the Economic Community for Central African States (ECCAS) formed in 1983 – Angola, Burundi, Cameroon, Central African Republic, Chad, the DRC, Congo, Equatorial Guinea, Gabon, Republic of the Congo, São Tomé and Príncipe; the Intergovernmental Authority for Development (IGAD) formed in 1996 – Djibouti, Eritrea, Ethiopia, Kenya, Somalia, Sudan and Uganda; SADC formed in 1992 Angola, Botswana, the DRC, Lesotho, Madagascar, Malawi, Mauritius, Mozambique, Namibia, Seychelles, South Africa, Swaziland, Tanzania, Zambia and Zimbabwe; Community of Sahel–Saharan States (CEN–SAD) formed in 1998 – Benin, Burkina Faso, Cape Verde, Central African Republic, Comoros, Cotê d'Ivoire, Chad, Djibouti, Egypt, Eritrea, Gambia, Ghana, Guinea-Bissau, Guinea, Kenya, Liberia, Libya, Mali, Mauritania, Morocco, Niger, Nigeria, São Tomé, Príncipe, Senegal, Sierra Leone, Somalia, Sudan, Togo and Tunisia; the East African Community (EAC), formed in 1919 from Kenya, Tanzania and Uganda and in existence even before independence but dissolved in 1975, has now been reactivated and expanded with the addition of Burundi, Rwanda and South Sudan (as its latest member) – six members). There are two French government – sponsored RECs – Western African Economic and Monetary Union (UEMOA) formed in 1994 and the Central African Economic and Monetary Community (CEMAC) also formed in 1994 by ECOWAS and ECCAS respectively.
26 Hazelwood, 'The End of the East African Community', p. 172.
27 Ahmed Aghrout, 'Africa's Experiences with Regional Cooperation and Integration: Assessing Some Groupings', *Istituto Italiano per l'Africa el'Oriente (IsIAO)* (1992).
28 Samuel K. B. Asante, *African Development: Adebayo Adedeji's Alternative Strategies* (Lagos: Spectrum, 1991), pp. 18–21.
29 Overseas Development Institute (ODI), 'Sanctions and South Africa's Neighbours', *Briefing Paper* (May 1997).
30 Lynn Mytelka, *Regional Development in a Global Economy: The Multinational Corporation, Technology and Andean Integration* (New Haven, CT: Yale University Press, 1979).
31 Gambari, *Political and Comparative Dimensions of Regional Integration*.
32 Gerald M. Meier, 'The Old Generation of Development Economists and the New', in Gerald M. Meier and Joseph Stiglitz (eds), *Frontiers of Development Economics: The*

Future in Perspective (Oxford: Oxford University Press, 2001). See also Ali Abdel Gadir Ali, 'The Rediscovery of the African Alternative Framework to Structural Adjustment Programmes', in Amos Sawyer, Afeikhena Jerome and Ejeviome Eloho Otobo (eds), *African Development in the 21st Century: Adebayo Adedeji's Theories and Contributions* (Johannesburg: Wits University Press, 2015), pp. 29–52.
33 Lamy, 'Regional Integration in Africa: Ambitions and Vicissitudes'.
34 See also Margaret Legum, 'Nyerere's Challenge', in Adekeye Adebajo and Helen Scanlon (eds), *A Dialogue of the Deaf: Essays on Africa and the United Nations* (Johannesburg: Jacana, 2006), pp. 167–81. See also the Organization of the Petroleum Exporting Countries (OPEC) and its establishment in 1960, http://www.opec.org/opec_web/en/about_us/24.htm. See also Edmondson, 'Africa and the Developing Regions', p. 868.
35 Richard Peet, *Unholy Trinity, The IMF, World Bank, and WTO*, 2nd edn (London: Zed Books, 2009). The establishment of OPEC and the oil price hike. OPEC was established in 1960 and was set up to coordinate the policies and prices of petroleum among member states, including Algeria, Iran, Iraq, Saudi Arabia, Kuwait, the United Arab Emirates, Libya, Nigeria, Venezuela and Qatar, and to offset pressure from major Western oil companies. The 1973 oil crisis was sparked by OPEC's refusal to ship oil to Western countries that had supported Israel in its Yom Kippur war.
36 Gambari, *Political and Comparative Dimensions of Regional Integration*, pp. 2–3.
37 Mitrany, 'A Functional Approach to World Organization'.
38 Joseph S. Nye and Robert O. Keohane, 'Transnational Relations and World Politics', *International Organization*, vol. 25, no. 3 (Summer 1971): 329–49.
39 Robert O. Keohane, 'International Institutions: Two Approaches', *International Studies Quarterly*, vol. 32, no. 4 (December 1988): 379–96.
40 Andrew Moravcsik, 'Negotiating the Single European Act: National Interests and Conventional Statecraft in the European Community', *International Organization*, vol. 45 (Winter 1991): 21.
41 Margaret C. Lee, *The Political Economy of Regionalism in Southern Africa* (Cape Town: University of Cape Town (UCT) Press, 2003), p. 30.
42 Samuel K. B. Asante, *Regionalisation and Africa's Development: Expectations, Reality and Challenges* (London: Palgrave Macmillan, 1997), p. 20.
43 Alex Warleigh-Lack, 'Towards a Conceptual Framework for Regionalisation: Bridging "New Regionalism" and "Integration Theory"', *Review of International Political Economy*, vol. 13, no. 5 (December 2006): 750–71. See also Björn Hettne and Fredrik Söderbaum, 'Theorising the Rise of Regionness', *New Political Economy*, vol. 5, no. 3 (December 1999): 457–72; and James H. Mittelman, 'Rethinking the "New Regionalism" in the Context of Globalization', *Global Governance*, vol. 2, no. 2 (May–August 1996): 189–213.
44 John Akokpari, 'Dilemmas of Regional Integration and Development in Africa', in John Akokpari, Angela Ndinga-Muvumba and Timothy Murithi (eds), *The African Union and Its Institutions* (Johannesburg: Jacana, 2008), p. 87. See also Richard S. Mukisa and Bankole Thompson, 'Prerequisites for Economic Integration in Africa: An Analysis of the Abuja Treaty', *Africa Today*, 4th Quarter, vol. 42, issue 4 (1995): 56–80, http://www.jstor.org/stable/pdf/4187066.pdf.
45 Marianne H. Marchand, Morten Bøås and Timothy M. Shaw, 'The Political Economy of New Regionalisms', *Third World Quarterly*, vol. 20, no 5 (1999): 897–910.
46 Akokpari, 'Dilemmas of Regional Integration and Development in Africa', pp. 86–90.
47 Akokpari, 'Dilemmas of Regional Integration and Development in Africa', p. 87.

48 Gilbert M. Khadiagala, *Allies in Adversity: The Frontline States in Southern Africa Security 1975–1993* (Athens: Ohio University Press, 1994); and Brendan Vickers, 'South Africa's Economic Diplomacy in a Changing Global Order', in Chris Landsberg and Jo-Ansie van Wyk (eds), *South African Foreign Policy Review, Volume 1* (Johannesburg: Africa Institute of South Africa and Institute for Global Dialogue (IGD), 2012), pp. 112–34.
49 Mills Soko, 'The Political Economy of Regional Integration in Southern Africa', *Notre Europe* (2007).
50 Fredrik Söderbaum and Ian Taylor, *Afro-Regions: The Dynamics of Cross-Border Micro-Regionalism in Africa* (Stockholm: Elanders Sverige, 2008), pp. 36–42.
51 Gregg Mills, *Why Africa Is Poor and What Africans Can Do about It* (Johannesburg: Penguin Books, 2011).
52 Ian Taylor, 'Globalization and Regionalization in Africa: Reactions to Attempts at Neo-Liberal Regionalism', *Review of International Political Economy*, vol. 10, no. 2 (May 2003): 315.
53 Mittelman, 'Rethinking the "New Regionalism" in the Context of Globalization', p. 190. See also Warleigh-Lack, 'Towards a Conceptual Framework for Regionalisation', pp. 750–71. See also Hettne and Söderbaum, 'Theorising the Rise of Regionness'; and Björn Hettne, András Inotai and Osvaldo Sunkel (eds), *Globalism and the New Regionalism*, Volume I (London: Palgrave Macmillan, 1999).
54 Carl G. Rosberg, Jr, 'The Federation of Rhodesia and Nyasaland: Problems of Democratic Government', *Annals of the American Academy of Political and Social Science*, vol. 306 (July 1956): 98–105.
55 John Ravenhill, 'Regional Integration in Africa: Theory and Practice', Paper presented on Region-Building and Regional Integration in Africa (Cape Town, South Africa: Centre for Conflict Resolution (CCR)) (April 2014).
56 Björn Hettne and Fredrik Söderbaum, 'The New Regionalism Approach', *Politeia*, vol. 17, no. 3 (1998): 6–21.
57 Söderbaum and Taylor (eds), *Afro-Regions*, pp. 36–42.
58 Söderbaum and Taylor (eds), *Afro-Regions*, p. 35.
59 Söderbaum and Taylor (eds), *Afro-Regions*, p. 35.
60 Nikki Slocum-Bradley, 'The Zambia–Malawi–Mozambique Growth Triangle (ZMM-GT): Discursive Region-Building in Africa and Consequences for Development', in Fredrik Söderbaum and Ian Taylor (eds), *Afro-Regions: The Dynamics of Cross-Border Micro-Regionalism in Africa* (Stockholm: Elanders Sverige, 2008), p. 90.
61 Olubanke King-Akerele and Kojo Boafo Asiedu, *Accelerating Africa's Integration through Micro-Regionalism: The Case of Zambia-Malawi-Mozambique Growth Triangle and Its Impact* (Tema: Digibooks, 2013).
62 John Ravenhill, 'Understanding the "New East Asian Regionalism"', *Review of International Political Economy*, vol. 17, no. 2 (May 2010): 173–7.
63 Ravenhill, 'The "New East Asian Regionalism": A Political Domino Effect', *Review of International Political Economy*, vol. 17, no. 2 (May 2010): 178–208.
64 Bela Balassa, *The Theory of Economic Integration* (Homewood: Richard D. Irwin, 1961), p. 2.
65 See the European Commission's Economic Partnership Agreements (EPAs), http://www.eusa.org.za/en/trade/EPA.htm.
66 John Friedmann, *A General Theory of Polarized Development* (1972), cited in Robert Gilpin, *The Political Economy of International Relations* (Princeton, NJ: Yale University Press, 1987), p. 21.

67 Justin Malewezi, 'Regional Integration: The Path to Prosperity?', in Christopher Clapham, Gregg Mills, Anna Morner and Elizabeth Sidiropoulos (eds), *Regional Integration in Southern Africa: Comparative International Perspectives* (Cape Town: South African Institute for International Affairs (SAIIA), 2001), pp. 19–26.
68 Harry Stephan, Michael Power, Angus Fane Hervey and Raymond Steenkamp Fonseca, *The Scramble for Africa in the 21st Century: A View from the South* (Cape Town: Renaissance Press, 2006), pp. 224–5.
69 Stephan, Power, Hervey and Fonseca, *The Scramble for Africa in the 21st Century*, pp. 226–7.
70 Robert D. Putnam, 'Diplomacy and Domestic Politics: The Logic of Two–Level Games', *International Organization* (Summer, 1988), cited in Stephan, Power, Hervey and Fonseca, *The Scramble for Africa in the 21st Century*, 2006.
71 Ian Bremmer, 'State Capitalism Comes of Age: The End of the Free Market?', *Foreign Affairs*, vol. 88, no. 3 (May/June 2009): 40–55.
72 The thirteen largest oil companies in the world, measured by their reserves, are owned and operated by governments: Saudi Arabia's Saudi Aramco; the National Iranian Oil Company; Petróleos de Venezuela, S.A.; Russia's Gazprom and Rosneft; the China National Petroleum Corporation; Malaysia's Petronas. These state-owned companies own more than 75 per cent of global oil reserves and production.
73 Bremmer, 'State Capitalism Comes of Age: The End of the Free Market?', p. 51.
74 See also Lisa Martin, 'Interests, Power and Multilateralism', *International Organization*, vol. 46, no. 4 (Autumn 1992): 765–92.
75 Lynn Mytelka, 'Building Partnerships for Innovation: A New Role for South-South Cooperation', in Réal Lavergne (ed.), *Regional Integration and Cooperation in West Africa* (Trenton, NJ: Africa World Press, 1997), pp. 131–50.
76 Ron Martin, 'EMU versus the Regions? Regional Convergence and Divergence in Euroland', *ESRC Centre for Business Research*, Working Paper no. 179 (September 2000).
77 Gerald M. Meier, 'The Old Generation of Development Economists and the New', p. 19; see also Ali, 'The Rediscovery of the African Alternative Framework to Structural Adjustment Programmes', pp. 29–52.
78 Martin, 'EMU versus the Regions? Regional Convergence and Divergence in Euroland'.
79 Martin, 'EMU versus the Regions? Regional Convergence and Divergence in Euroland'. See also Robert Solow, 'A Contribution to the Theory of Economic Growth', *Quarterly Journal of Economics*, vol. 70, no. 1 (February, 1956): 65–94.
80 Paul Krugman, 'The Myth of Asia's Miracle', *Foreign Affairs*, vol. 73, no. 6 (November/December 1994): 62–78.
81 Solow, 'A Contribution to the Theory of Economic Growth'.
82 Paul A. Samuelson, *Economics: an Introductory Analysis* (New York: McGraw-Hill Company, 1948). See discussion in Gilpin, *The Political Economy of International Relations*, p. 310.
83 Gottfried Haberler, 'Some Problems in the Pure Theory of International Trade', *The Economic Journal*, vol. 50, no. 238 (June 1950): 227.
84 Theodore W. Schultz, *Transforming Traditional Agriculture* (New Haven, CT: Yale University Press, 1964), cited in Gilpin, *The Political Economy of International Relations*, p. 311.
85 Gilpin, *The Political Economy of International Relations*, p. 307.
86 See discussion in Gilpin, *The Political Economy of International Relations*, p. 308.
87 Alexander Gerschenkron, 'Economic Backwardness in Historical Perspective', in Bert F. Hoselitz (ed.), *The Progress of Under-developed Areas* (Chicago, IL: University of

Chicago Press, 1952), cited in William J. Baumol, 'Productivity Growth, Convergence, and Welfare: What the Long-Run Data Show', *American Economic Review*, vol. 76, no. 5 (December 1986): 1072–85.
88 David Cass, 'Optimum Growth in an Aggregate Model of Capital Accumulation', *Review of Economic Studies*, vol. 32, no. 3 (1965): 233–40.
89 Dimitri B. Papadimitriou (ed.), *Contributions to Economic Theory, Policy, Development and Finance: Essays in Honor of Jan A. Kregel* (London: Palgrave Macmillan, 2014), pp. 1–18.
90 See discussion in Legum, 'Nyerere's Challenge', pp. 167–81.
91 Paul Krugman, 'The Myth of Asia's Miracle', *Foreign Affairs*, vol. 73, no. 6 (1994): 62–78.
92 Robert Lucas, 'On the Mechanics of Economic Development', *Journal of Monetary Economics*, vol. 22 (1988): 3–42. See also Nicoli Nattrass, Jeremy Wakeford and Samson Muradzikwa, *Macro Economics Theory and Policy in South Africa*, 3rd edn (Cape Town: David Philip, 2003), pp. 31–3.
93 Paul M. Romer, 'Increasing Returns and Long-Run Growth', *Journal of Political Economy*, vol. 94 (1986): 1002–37.
94 Romer, 'Increasing Returns and Long-Run Growth', p. 1003.
95 Edward C. Prescott, 'Robert M. Solow's Neoclassical Growth Model: An Influential Contribution to Economics', *Scandinavian Journal of Economics*, vol. 90, no. 1 (March 1988): 11.
96 Prescott, 'Robert M. Solow's Neoclassical Growth Model: An Influential Contribution to Economics'. See also Garry D. Hansen, 'Indivisible Labor and the Business Cycle', *Journal of Monetary Economics*, vol. 16 (1985): 309–27.
97 Prescott, 'Robert M. Solow's Neoclassical Growth Model: An Influential Contribution to Economics'.
98 Lucas, 'On the Mechanics of Economic Development', p. 40.
99 Walter Edwin and Orondo Orchoro, 'Trade and Industrial Development in the EAC', in Rok Ajulu (ed.), *The Making of a Region* (Johannesburg: Institute for Global Dialogue, 2005), pp. 127–34.
100 UNECA, '*The Mutual Review of Development Effectiveness in Africa: Promise and Performance*' report (Addis Ababa: United Nations Economic Commission for Africa' (2013), p. 6.
101 Robert J. Barro and Xavier Sala-i-Martin, 'Convergence across States and Regions', *Brookings Papers on Economic Activity*, 1 (1991): 107–82.
102 Barro and Sala-i-Martin, 'Convergence across States and Regions'.
103 See discussion by Rob Davies, 'South Africa in Southern Africa Seminar Report', *Centre for Conflict Resolution* (November 2012): p. 25.
104 Dowrick and Nguyen, 'OECD Comparative Economic Growth 1950–85: Catch–Up and Convergence'. See also Ben-David, 'Trade and Convergence Among Countries'.
105 Dowrick and Nguyen, 'OECD Comparative Economic Growth 1950–85: Catch–Up and Convergence', p. 1010.
106 Oded Galor, 'Convergence? Inferences from Theoretical Models', *The Economic Journal*, vol. 106, no. 437 (July 1996): 1056–69. See also Romer, 'Increasing Returns and Long-Run Growth'; Robert J. Barro, 'Economic Growth in a Cross Section of Countries', *Quarterly Journal of Economics*, vol. 106 (1991): 407–501; Gregory N. Mankiw, David Romer and David N. Weil, 'A Contribution to the Empirics of Economic Growth', *Quarterly Journal of Economics*, vol. 107, no. 2 (1992): 407–37; Robert J. Barro and Xavier Sala-i-Martin, *Economic Growth*,

2nd edn (Cambridge: MIT Press, 2004); Steven N. Durlauf and Paul A. Johnson, 'Multiple Regimes and Cross Country Growth Behaviour', *Journal of Applied Econometrics*, vol. 10, no. 4 (October–December 1995): pp. 365–84, cited in Galor, 'Convergence? Inferences from Theoretical Models'; Danny Quah, 'Convergence Empirics across Countries with (Some) Capital Mobility', *Journal of Economics Growth*, vol. 1 (1996): 95–24; also see an earlier version by Quah, 'Convergence Empirics across Countries with (Some) Capital Mobility' (1995), http://eprints.lse.ac.uk/2257/1/CEP_Convergence_Empirics_Across_Economies_with_(Some) Capital_Mobility.pdf.

107 Galor, 'Convergence? Inferences from Theoretical Models', pp. 1056–69.
108 Matthew J. Slaughter, 'Trade Liberalization and per Capita Income Convergence: A Difference-in-Differences Analysis', *Journal of International Economics*, vol. 55 (2001): 203–28.
109 Richard Griffith, 'The Dynamics and States of European Construction, 1945–1995, SADC–EU', Seminar on the Regional Integration Process (1995): 78.
110 Richard Griffith, 'The Dynamics and States of European Construction'.
111 Ben-David, 'Trade and Convergence among Countries'.
112 Francisco Rodriquez and Dani Rodrik, 'Trade Policy and Economic Growth: A Skeptic's Guide to the Cross-National Evidence', *National Bureau of Economic Research (NBER) Macroeconomics Annual 2000*, vol. 15 (January 2001): 261–338.
113 Krugman, 'The Myth of Asia's Miracle', pp. 62–78.
114 Krugman, 'The Myth of Asia's Miracle', p. 66.
115 Krugman, 'What's New about the "New Economic Geography"?,' *Oxford Review of Economic Policy*, vol. 14, no. 2 (1998): pp. 7–17. See also Martin, 'EMU Versus the Regions?', pp. 23–4.
116 Alfred Marshall, *Principles of Economics* (London: Macmillan, 1920), cited in Nicoli Nattrass, Jeremy Wakeford and Samson Muradzikwa, *Macro Economics Theory and Policy in South Africa*, 3rd edn (Cape Town: David Philip, 2003), p. 15. Marshallian-type economies refer to many of the assumptions which are similar to the foundational models for macroeconomic and neoclassical models. These are: 'price adjustment in individual markets ensures that no surpluses or gluts prevail; wage adjustment ensures full employment; and the interest rate fluctuates in order to bring savings into line with investment; and typically it is assumed that under conditions of perfect competition, the operation of market forces will ensure that all resources are optimally allocated. Markets are assumed to be perfectly competitive and characterised by many buyers and sellers, homogeneous products, perfect knowledge and perfect factor mobility. The value of the economy is therefore measured by nominal and real values (the equilibrium values of real [real values are obtained by deflating nominal values by a price index] variables [employment, output] are determined in the labour and goods markets, whereas nominal [nominal values are e.g. wages, and output] variables [current prices] are determined in the money market). Given that real variables are not affected by changes in the money supply in such a model, money is then neutral. Hence this generates two parts to the theory: (i) a theory of how equilibrium output and employment are determined, and, (ii) a theory of how the aggregate price level is determined.'
117 Martin, 'EMU versus the Regions? Regional Convergence and Divergence in Euroland', pp. 51–80.
118 Krugman, 'The Myth of Asia's Miracle', p. 67.

119 See also Frank Flatters, emeritus professor at Queens University Canada on SADC Rules of Origin, See discussion in Southern African International SAIIA SADC Barometer issue 1 (March 2003): 21–2.
120 Orchoro, 'Trade and Industrial Development in the EAC', pp. 127–34.
121 Orchoro, 'Trade and Industrial Development in the EAC', pp. 127–34.
122 Orchoro, 'Trade and Industrial Development in the EAC'.
123 Carolyn Jenkins and Lynne Thomas, 'The Macro-economic Frameworks', in Carolyn Jenkins, Jonathan Leape and Lynne Thomas (eds), *Gaining from Trade in Southern Africa: Complementary Policies to Underpin the SADC Free Trade Area* (London: Palgrave Macmillan, 2000), pp. 1–23.
124 United Nations Economic Commission for Africa, 'Macroeconomic Convergence in African RECs 'Assessing Regional Integration in Africa', 2008, http://www.mcli.co.za/mcli-web/downloads/ARIA4/aria3/chap5.pdf, p. 137.
125 David Dollar, 'Outward-Oriented Developing Economies Really Do Grow More Rapidly: Evidence from 95 LDCs, 1976–85', *World Bank Economic Development and Cultural Change*, vol. 40, no. 3 (April 1992): 523–44.
126 Ogochukwu Nzewi, 'The Challenges of Post-1990 Regional Integration in Africa: Pan-African Parliament', *Centre for Policy Studies Policy Brief*, vol. 57 (Johannesburg: Centre for Policy Studies (CPS), April 2009), p. 7.
127 Nzewi, 'The Challenges of Post-1990 Regional Integration in Africa: Pan-African Parliament', pp. 1–11.
128 UNECA report, 'Macroeconomic Policy and Institutional Convergence of Member States in the Southern African Development Community' (Addis Ababa: UNECA), http://www.uneca.org/sites/default/files/publications/report_macroeconomic-policy.pdf (accessed 10 January 2015).
129 Bernard Fingleton, Harry Garretsen and Ron Martin, 'Shocking Aspects of Monetary Union: The Vulnerability of Regions in Euroland', *Special Issue of Journal of Economic Geography* (2015), pp. 1–28.
130 Fingleton, Garretsen and Martin, 'Shocking Aspects of Monetary Union', p. 23.
131 Jonathan Gould and John O'Donnell, 'ECB Launches 1 Trillion Euro Rescue Plan to Revive Euro Economy', *Reuters* (22 January 2015), http://www.reuters.com/article/2015/01/22/us-ecb-policy-idUSKBN0KU2ST20150122.
132 Gould and O'Donnell, 'ECB Launches 1 Trillion Euro Rescue Plan to Revive Euro Economy'.
133 Fingleton, Garretsen and Martin, 'Shocking Aspects of Monetary Union', p. 5. 'The symmetry condition means that economies should be roughly similar and synchronised so that shocks are symmetrical where all countries are roughly affected the same.'
134 Fingleton, Garretsen and Martin, 'Shocking Aspects of Monetary Union', p. 7.
135 Bernardo Venturi, 'Africa and Italy's Relations After the Cold War', in Dawn Nagar and Charles Mutasa (eds), *Africa and the World: Bilateral and Multilateral International Diplomacy* (New York: Palgrave Macmillan, 2018), pp. 169–88.
136 Jenkins and Thomas, 'The Macro-economic Frameworks', pp. 24–57.
137 Jenkins and Thomas, 'The Macro-economic Frameworks', pp. 24–57.
138 Keith R. Jefferis, 'The Process of Monetary Integration in the SADC Region', *Journal of Southern African Studies*, vol. 33, no. 1 (March 2007): 83–106.
139 Jefferis, 'The Process of Monetary Integration in the SADC Region', p. 87.
140 Fingleton, Garretsen and Martin, 'Shocking Aspects of Monetary Union', p. 5.

141 Thabo Mbeki, 'Foreword', in AU and UNECA Report of the High Level Panel on Illicit Financial Flows From Africa, *Illicit Financial Flows Report*, February 2012, p. 2, www.uneca.org/sites/default/files/PublicationFiles/iff_main_report_26feb_en.pdf. See also Nagar, 'Promoting Dialogue on South Africa's Regional Integration Role in Southern Africa', *CCR Policy Brief*, May 2017.
142 Jenkins, and Thomas, 'The Macro-economic Frameworks', pp. 24–54.
143 Jenkins, and Thomas, 'The Macro-economic Frameworks', p. 7.
144 Richard Gibb, 'Rationalisation or Redundancy? Making Eastern and Southern Africa's Regional Trade Units Relevant', *Brenthurst Foundation* (2006), p. 5.
145 Gibb, 'Rationalisation or Redundancy?', p. 5.
146 Barro and Sala-i-Martin, *Economic Growth*, pp. 16–21.
147 Nzewi, 'The Challenges of Post-1990 Regional Integration', p. 7.
148 James T. Gathii, 'Neo-Liberal Turn in Regional Trade Agreements', *Albany Law School Legal Studies, Research Paper Series*, no. 40 (2010–2011). See also Gathii, *African Regional Trade Agreements as Legal Regimes* (London: Cambridge University Press, 2011), pp. 1–50.
149 Gathii, 'Neo-Liberal Turn in Regional Trade Agreements', pp. 647–48. See also Arvind Panagariya, 'The Regionalism Debate: An Overview', *World Economy* 22, no. 4 (1999): 1–60.
150 Rodriquez and Rodrik, 'Trade Policy and Economic Growth'. This article is a selection of an out-of-print volume from the National Bureau of Economic Research, *NBER Macroeconomics Annual 2000*, vol. 15 (January 2001): 261–338.
151 Gilpin, *The Political Economy of International Relations*, p. 11.
152 Haarløv, *Regional Cooperation in Southern Africa: Central elements of the SADCC Venture* (University of Bonn, Centre for Development Research (CDR), 1988). See also Lee, *The Political Economy of Regionalism in Southern Africa*, p. 23.
153 Anthony J. Venables, 'Regional Integration Agreements: A Force for Convergence or Divergence?', Policy Research Working Paper, no. 2260 (December 1999).
154 Ravenhill, 'The "New East Asian Regionalism"', p. 191.
155 Ravenhill, 'The "New East Asian Regionalism"', pp. 178–208.
156 Panagariya, 'The Regionalism Debate', pp. 1–60.
157 Phillip O Nying'uro, 'The EAC's Prospects on the Global Stage', in Rok Ajulu (ed.), *The Making of a Region* (Johannesburg: Institute for Global Dialogue, 2005), pp. 31–44.
158 United Nations Conference on Trade and Development (UNCTAD) Trade and Development Report, *Policies for Inclusive Development and Balanced Growth* (2012), http://unctad.org/en/publicationslibrary/tdr2012_en.pdf, pp. 103–4.
159 UNCTAD, 2012.
160 Deutsche Welle (DW), 'G20 Summit "a disappointment for Africa"', *DW News*, Germany (5 September 2016), http://www.dw.com/en/g20-summit-a-disappointment-for-africa/a-19528089.
161 See Germany's Federal Ministry of Finance, 'G20 Compact with Africa' policy document, 30 March 2017, https://www.compactwithafrica.org/content/dam/Compact%20with%20Africa/2017-03-30-g20-compact-with-africa-report.pdf.
162 Dani Rodrik, 'An African Growth Miracle?', *National Bureau of Economic Research*, Working Paper no. 20188 (June 2014): p. 8. See also Amadou Sy, 'Convergence or Divergence: Discussing Structural Transformation in Africa during the G20', *Brookings Institution*, http://www.brookings.edu/blogs/africa-in-focus/

posts/2014/11/14-convergence-divergence-structural-transformation-africa-g20-sy.
163 Baumol, 'Productivity Growth, Convergence, and Welfare', pp. 1072–85.
164 Gene M. Grossman and Elhanan Helpman, 'Endogenous Innovation in the Theory of Growth', *Journal of Economic Perspectives*, vol. 8, no. 1 (Winter 1994): 23–44.
165 Robert E. Baldwin, 'Openness and Growth: What's the Empirical Relationship?', in Robert E. Baldwin and L. Alan Winters (eds), *Challenges to Globalization: Analyzing the Economics* (Chicago, IL: Chicago University Press, February 2004), pp. 499–525.
166 Baldwin, 'Openness and Growth: What's the Empirical Relationship?', p. 511.
167 Baldwin, 'Openness and Growth: What's the Empirical Relationship?', p. 517.
168 Robert O. Keohane and Joseph S. Nye, *Power and Interdependence*, 3rd edn (New York: Longman, 2001), pp. 20–32.
169 Peter Willetts, 'Transnational Actors and International Organizations in Global Politics', in John Baylis and Steve Smith (eds), *The Globalization of World Politics*, 2nd edn (Oxford: Oxford University Press, 2001), pp. 356–86.
170 Willetts, 'Transnational Actors and International Organizations in Global Politics', p. 358.
171 Balaam and Veseth, *Introduction to Political Economy*, pp. 110–27. See also Nordiska Afrikainstitutet, *Regionalism and Regional Integration in Africa: A Debate of Current Aspects and Issues, Discussion Paper 11*, Uppsala, Sweden (2001).
172 See also Jack Snyder, *Myths of Empire: Domestic Politics and International Ambition* (Ithaca, NY: Cornell University Press, 1991).
173 Gideon Rose, 'Neoclassical Realism and Theories of Foreign Policy', *World Politics*, vol. 51, no. 1 (October 1998): 144–72. See also Kathleen Thelen and Sven Steinmo, 'Historical Institutionalism in Comparative Politics', in Sven Steinmo, Kathleen Thelen and Frank Longstreth (eds), *Structuring Politics: Historical Institutionalism in Comparative Analysis* (Cambridge: Cambridge University Press, 1992), p. 11.
174 Thomas M. Callaghy, 'The State and the Development of Capitalism in Africa: Theoretical, Historical, and Comparative Reflections', in Donald Rothchild and Naomi Chazan (eds), *The Precarious Balance: State and Society in Africa* (Boulder, CO: Westview Press, 1988), pp. 67–99.
175 Robert B. Strassler (ed.), *The Landmark Thucydides: A Comprehensive Guide to the Polepennesian War* (New York: Free Press, 1996).
176 Rose, 'Neoclassical Realism and Theories of Foreign Policy', p. 147.
177 Agostinho Zacarias, 'SADC: From a System to Community of Security?' *African Security Review*, vol. 7, no. 6 (1998): 44–61.
178 Zacarias, 'SADC: From a System to Community of Security?', p. 44.
179 Edward Mansfield, 'Effects of International Politics on Regionalism in International Trade', in Kym Anderson and Richard Blackhurst (eds), *Regional Integration and the Global Trading System* (New York: Harvester Wheatsheaf, 1993), pp. 199–17. See also Edward Mansfield and Helen V. Milner, 'The Domestic Politics of Preferential Trade Agreements in Hard Times', *Department of Political Science* (Philadelphia: University of Pennsylvania, 2014), pp. 1–40, http://web.stanford.edu/group/sssl/cgi-bin/wordpress/wp-content/uploads/2014/03/Mansfield-and-Milner-PTAhard-times-03292014.pdf.
180 I. William Zartman, 'African Regional Security and Changing Patterns of Relations', in Edmond J. Keller and Donald Rothchild (eds), *Africa in the New International Order: Rethinking State Sovereignty and Regional Security* (London: Lynne Rienner, 1996), pp. 52–70.

181 Zartman, 'African Regional Security and Changing Patterns of Relations', p. 55.
182 Zartman, 'African Regional Security and Changing Patterns of Relations', p. 57.
183 Rok Ajulu, 'African Security: Can Regional Organisations Play a Role?', in Shannon Field (ed.), *Peace in Africa: Towards a Collaborative Security Regime* (Johannesburg: Institute for Global Dialogue, 2004), pp. 265–80.
184 John Siebert, 'R2P and the IGAD Sub-region: IGAD's Contribution to Africa's Emerging R2P-oriented Security Culture', in Hany Besada (ed.), *Crafting an African Security Architecture* (Burlington: Ashgate, 2010), pp. 89–108.
185 Siebert, 'R2P and the IGAD Sub-region: IGAD's Contribution to Africa's Emerging R2P-oriented Security Culture', pp. 89–108.
186 Hany Besada, Ariane Goetz and Karolina Werner, 'African Solutions for African Problems and Shared R2P', in Hany Besada (ed.), *Crafting an African Security Architecture* (Burlington: Ashgate, 2010), pp. 1–14.
187 Peter Vale, *Security and Politics in South Africa: The Regional Dimension* (Cape Town: Cape Town University Press, 2003) p. 175.
188 Vale, *Security and Politics in South Africa*, p. 175.
189 Deutsch, *Political Community and the North Atlantic Area*, pp. 7–8.
190 Barry Buzan and Ole Wæver, *Regions and Powers: The Structure of International Security* (London: Cambridge University Press, 2003).
191 Buzan and Wæver, *Regions and Powers*, p. 52.
192 Khadiagala, *Allies in Adversity*, p. 8.
193 Khadiagala, *Allies in Adversity*, p. 8.

3 Pan-Africanism's birth, burial – reincarnate: A historical trajectory of divergence and convergence

1 Guy Martin, *African World Politics: A Pan-African Perspective* (Trenton: Africa World Press, 2002). See also Nagar, 'Pillars of Africa's Peace and Security Architecture: the African Standby Force'; and Nagar, 'South Africa's Role 20 Years Post-Apartheid' *Journal Für Entwicklungspolitik*, vol. xxix, no. 4 (2013).
2 Samuel K. B. Asante and David Chanaiwa, 'Pan-Africanism and Regional Integration', in Ali A. Mazrui and C. Wondji (eds), *General History of Africa VIII: Africa Since 1935* (Paris: United Nations Educational, Scientific and Cultural Organization (UNESCO), 1993).
3 See Immanuel Wallerstein, 'Regional Unity and African Unity', in Immanuel Wallerstein (ed.), *Africa: The Politics of Independence and Unity* (Lincoln: University of Nebraska Press, 2005). See also Kasaija Phillip Apuuli, 'The African Union and Regional Integration in Africa', in Daniel H. Levine and Dawn Nagar (eds), *Region-Building in Africa: Political and Economic Challenges* (New York: Palgrave Macmillan, 2016), pp. 143–56.
4 The years that African states gained independence from their colonial masters: Liberia 1847; South Africa 1910 (and from apartheid rule 1994); Egypt 1922; Libya 1951; Morocco, Sudan and Tunisia 1956; Ghana 1957; Guinea 1958; Ethiopia (also the first century of the Christian era), Benin, Burkina Faso, Cameroon, Central African Republic, Chad, Congo Brazzaville, Côte d'Ivoire, Gabon, Madagascar, Mali, Mauritania, Nigeria, Senegal, Somali, Togo and Zaire 1960; Sierra Leone and Tanzania 1961; Algeria, Burundi, Rwanda and Uganda

1962; Kenya and Zanzibar 1963; Malawi and Zambia 1964; Gambia 1965; Angola, Botswana, Equatorial Guinea and Lesotho 1966; Mauritius and Swaziland 1968; Guinea-Bissau 1973; Cape Verde, Comoros, Mozambique, São Tomé and Príncipe, and Western Sahara 1975; Seychelles 1976; Djibouti 1977; Zimbabwe 1980; Namibia 1990; discussed in J. Isawa Elaigwu and Ali A. Mazrui, 'Nation-Building and Changing Political Structures', in Ali A. Mazrui and C. Wondji (eds), *General History of Africa* VIII (Paris: UNESCO, 1993), pp. 456–61.

5   Locksley Edmondson, 'Africa and the Developing Regions', in Ali A. Mazrui and C. Wondji (eds), *General History of Africa* VIII (Paris: UNESCO, 1993), pp. 829–70.

6   Adekeye Adebajo, 'Towers of Babel? The African Union and the European Union', in Adekeye Adebajo (ed.), *The Curse of Berlin: Africa After the Cold War* (Scottsville: University of KwaZulu-Natal Press, 2010), p. 263.

7   Andrew Moravcsik, 'Negotiating the Single European Act: National Interests and Conventional Statecraft in the European Community', *International Organization*, vol. 45 (Winter 1991): 19–56.

8   Ravenhill, 'The Future of Regionalism in Africa', p. 206. See also Adekeye Adebajo, 'A Tale of Three Cassandras: Jean Monnet, RaÚl Prebisch, and Adebayo Adedeji', in Levine and Nagar (eds), *Region-Building in Africa*, pp. 53–69.

9   Gambari, *Political and Comparative Dimensions of Regional Integration*, pp. 2–3.

10 Pinder and Usherwood, *The European Union*, pp. 82–3.

11 Robert D. A. Henderson, 'The Southern African Customs Union: Politics of Dependence', in Onwuka, and Sesay (eds), *The Future of Regionalism in Africa*, pp. 225–53. See also Richard Gibb, 'Southern Africa in Transition: Prospects and Problems Facing Regional Integration', *Journal of Modern African Studies*, vol. 36, no. 2 (1998): 287–306; Asante, *Regionalisation and Africa's Development*.

12 Joseph S. Nye, 'East African Economic Integration', *Journal of Modern African Studies*, vol. 1, no. 4 (1966): 475–502.

13 See the Southern African Customs Union (SACU) and the establishment of SACU, which was initially formed in 1889 between the British Colony of Cape of Good Hope and the Orange Free State Boer Republic. www.sacu.int/show.php?id=394.

14 A. Adedeji, 'Comparative Strategies of Economic Decolonization in Africa', in Mazrui and Wondji (eds), *General History of Africa, VIII*, pp. 407–17.

15 Samuel K. B. Asante, 'The Years of Preparation: Adedeji and the ECA', in Samuel K. B. Asante (ed.), *African Development: Adebayo Adedeji's Alternative Strategies* (Ibadan, Nigeria: Spectrum Books, 1999), pp. 18–21.

16 Asante, 'The Years of Preparation: Adedeji and the ECA', p. 21.

17 Asante, 'The Years of Preparation: Adedeji and the ECA', pp. 22–4.

18 Adedeji, 'Comparative Strategies of Economic Decolonization in Africa', p. 413.

19 Rok Ajulu, 'Introduction: The New EAC: Linking Subregional and Continental Integration Initiatives', in Rok Ajulu (ed.), *The Making of a Region* (Johannesburg: Institute for Global Dialogue, 2005), p. 17.

20 See also Adekeye Adebajo, 'The Peacekeeping Travails of the OAU and the Regional Economic Communities', in John Akokpari, Angela Ndinga-Muvumba and Tim Murithi (eds), *The African Union and Its Institutions* (Johannesburg: Jacana, 2008), pp. 148–9.

21 Colin Legum, *Pan-Africanism: Short Political Guide*, rev. edn (London: Pall Mall, 1965), pp. 146–7.

22 Assis Malaquias, 'Dysfunctional Foreign Policy: Angola's Unsuccessful Quest for Security Since Independence', in Korwa Gombe Adar and Rok Ajulu (eds),

Globalization and Emerging Trends in African States' Foreign Policy-Making Process: A Comparative Perspective of Southern Africa (Aldershot: Ashgate, 2002), p. 118.
23 Khabele Matlosa and Kebapetse Lotshwao, *Political Integration and Democratisation in Southern Africa: Progress, Problems, and Prospects* (Gaborone: University of Botswana Press, December 2009). See also Gabriël H. Oosthuizen, *The Southern African Development Community: The Organisation, Its Policies, and Prospects* (Midrand: Institute for Global Dialogue, 2006).
24 Jonathan C. Momba and Fay Gadsden, 'Zambia: Nonviolent Strategies against Colonialism, 1900s–1960s', in Maciej J. Bartkowski (ed.), *Recovering Non-Violent History: Civil Resistance in Liberation Struggles* (Boulder, CO: Lynne Rienner, 2013), pp. 71–88.
25 Oosthuizen, *The Southern African Development Community*, pp. 55–6.
26 Zacarias, 'SADC: From a System to Community of Security?', p. 1.
27 Hedley Bull, *An Anarchical Society: A Study of Order in World Politics* (London: Macmillan, 1977), p. 10.
28 Bull, *An Anarchical Society*, p. 13. See also review by Geoffrey Goodwin, in *Royal Institute of International Affairs*, vol. 54, no. 1 (January 1978): 92–4.
29 Khadiagala, *Allies in Adversity*, p. 3.
30 Abillah H. Omari and Paulino Macaringue, 'Southern African Security in Historical Perspective', in Gavin Cawthra, Andre du Pisani and Abillah Omari (eds), *Security and Democracy in Southern Africa* (Johannesburg: Wits University Press, 2007), pp. 50–1. See also Malaquias, 'Dysfunctional Foreign Policy', p. 20.
31 Omari and Macaringue, 'Southern African Security in Historical Perspective', pp. 50–1. See also William A. Lindeke, 'From Confrontation to Pragmatic Cooperation: United States of America-Namibia Relations', in Anton Bösl, André du Pisani and Dennis U Zaire (eds), *Namibia's Foreign Relations: Historic contexts, Current Dimensions, and Perspectives for the 21st Century* (Windhoek: Macmillan Education Namibia, 2014), pp. 181–210.
32 Khadiagala, *Allies in Adversity*, p. 23.
33 Angola Briefings, *Review of African Political Economy*, no. 5 (October 1981): 85.
34 Chris Saunders, 'Namibian Diplomacy before Independence', in Anton Bösl, André du Pisani and Dennis U. Zaire (eds), *Namibia's Foreign Relations: Historic Contexts, Current Dimensions, and Perspectives for the 21st Century* (Windhoek: Macmillan Education Namibia, 2014), pp. 27–36.
35 Khadiagala, *Allies in Adversity*.
36 Gerhard Erasmus, 'Namibia and the Southern African Development Community', in AntonBösl, André du Pisani and Dennis U. Zaire (eds), *Namibia's Foreign Relations: Historic contexts, Current Dimensions, and Perspectives for the 21st Century* (Windhoek: Macmillan Education Namibia, 2014), pp. 211–30.
37 Khadiagala, *Allies in Adversity*, p. 227.
38 United Nations (UN) Yearbook of International Trade Statistics 1974, vol. III, cited in Manfield Bienefield and Duncan Innes, 'Capital Accumulation and South Africa', *Review of African Political Economy*, no. 7 (1976), pp. 48–9.
39 UN Yearbook of International Trade Statistics, 1974, pp. 48–9.
40 Mel Gurtov, 'Realism and Corporate Globalism in Theory and Practice', in Mel Gurtov (ed.), *Global Politics in the Human Interest*, 5th edn (Boulder, CO: Lynne Rienner, 2007), pp. 33–4.
41 Khadiagala, *Allies in Adversity*, p. 23.
42 Khadiagala, *Allies in Adversity*, p. 23.

43. Khadiagala, *Allies in Adversity*, p. 27.
44. Khadiagala, *Allies in Adversity*, p. 27.
45. Angola Briefings, 1981.
46. Lionel Cliffe and Peter Lawrence, 'The Struggle for the State in Southern Africa', *Review of African Political Economy*, vol. 3, no. 5 (October 1981): 10–11.
47. Joseph Hanlon, *Beggar Your Neighbours: Apartheid Power in South Africa* (London: Currey, 1986), pp. 235–8.
48. Anglin, 'Economic Liberation and Regional Cooperation in Southern Africa: SADCC and PTA', pp. 681–711.
49. Jonathan Mayuyuka Kaunda, 'Continuity and Change in Malawi's Foreign Policy-Making', in Korwa Gombe Adar and Rok Ajulu (eds), *Globalisation and Emerging Trends in African States' Foreign Policy-Making Process* (Aldershot: Ashgate, 2002), p. 79. See also Hanlon, *Beggar Your Neighbours*, pp. 238–40.
50. Khadiagala, *Allies in Adversity*, p. 228.
51. Khadiagala, *Allies in Adversity*, p. 177.
52. Khadiagala, *Allies in Adversity*, pp. 150–1.
53. Lindeke, 'From Confrontation to Pragmatic Cooperation: United States of America-Namibia Relations', p. 185.
54. Lindeke, 'From Confrontation to Pragmatic Cooperation: United States of America-Namibia Relations', p. 185.
55. Gurtov, 'Realism and Corporate Globalism in Theory and Practice', p. 26.
56. Gurtov, 'Realism and Corporate Globalism in Theory and Practice', p. 21.
57. Victor A. Olorunsola, and Dan Muhwezi, 'State Responses to Disintegration and Withdrawal: Adjustments in the Political Economy', in Keller and Donald Rothchild (eds), *Africa in the New International Order*, pp. 189–207.
58. Stephan, Power, Hervey and Fonseca, *The Scramble for Africa in the 21st Century: A View from the South*', pp. 320–1.
59. Ruth First, *Power in Africa* (New York: Pantheon, 1970), p. 110. Cited in Stephan, Power, Hervey and Fonseca, *The Scramble for Africa in the 21st Century*, pp. 320–1.
60. Khadiagala, *Allies in Adversity*, p. 9.
61. Khadiagala, *Allies in Adversity*.
62. Khadiagala, *Allies in Adversity*.
63. Hanlon, *Beggar Your Neighbours*, p. 246.
64. Hanlon, *Beggar Your Neighbours*, p. 246. See also Centre for Conflict Resolution Report, *South Africa in Southern Africa* (November 2012), http://www.ccr.org.za.
65. Colin Stoneman, 'Foreign Capital and Reconstruction of Zimbabwe', *Review of African Political Economy*, no. 11 (January–April 1978): pp. 70–1.
66. Bienefield and Innes, 'Capital Accumulation and South Africa', pp. 40–6.
67. Lindeke, 'From Confrontation to Pragmatic Cooperation: United States of America-Namibia Relations', p. 185.
68. Lindeke, 'From Confrontation to Pragmatic Cooperation: United States of America-Namibia Relations', p. 191.
69. Bienefield and Innes, 'Capital Accumulation and South Africa', p. 44.
70. Hanlon, *Beggar Your Neighbours*, p. 169.
71. Hanlon, *Beggar Your Neighbours*, p. 170.
72. Hanlon, *Beggar Your Neighbours*, p. 78. Mine workers in South Africa for the years 1974, 1980 and 1984, respectively, were from neighbouring countries to South Africa and totalled as follows: Angola – 108; 291; and 48; Botswana – 333,57; 23,200; and 26,433; Lesotho – 134,667; 140,746; and 138,443; Malawi – 137,676; 32,319; and

29,268; Mozambique – 139,993; 56,424; and 60,407; Swaziland – 9,984; 19,853; and 16,823; Zambia – 703; 918; and 1,274; and Zimbabwe – 5,691; 10,377, and 7,492. Remittances paid by South Africa to Southern African member states for the periods 1980; and 1983: Angola – Zero remittances paid; Botswana – R32 million; and R47.6 million; Lesotho – R153.3 million and R280.6 million; Malawi – R30.7 million and R51.3 million; Mozambique – R66.6 million and R116.8 million; Swaziland – R13.2 million and R32.1 million; Zambia – R600,000 and R1 million; and Zimbabwe – R15.4 million and R8.7 million.

73 Hanlon, *Beggar Your Neighbours*, p. 281.
74 Khadiagala, *Allies in Adversity*.
75 Hanlon, *Beggar Your Neighbours*, p. 238.
76 Keohane and Nye, *Power and Interdependence*, pp. 19–31. See also James Zaffiro, 'Exceptionality in External Affairs: Botswana in the African and Global Arenas', in Stephen Wright (ed.), *African Foreign Policies* (Boulder, CO: Westview Press, 1999).
77 Personal interview with Adebayo Adedeji, Ijebu-Ode, Ogun State, Nigeria (19 December 2010); and Somerset West, South Africa (13–15 December 2011).
78 Zacarias, 'SADC: From a System to Community of Security?', pp. 44–61.
79 Zacarias, 'SADC: From a System to Community of Security?', pp. 44–61.
80 European Union and Southern African Development Community seminar on 'The Regional Integration Process' (in collaboration with the Centre d'Etude d'Afrique Noire, Institut d' Eudes Politiques of Bordeaux), Brussels and Paris (12–15 June 1995), p. 11.
81 Oosthuizen, *The Southern African Development Community*, pp. 53–4.
82 Jan Isaksen, *Restructuring SADC – Progress and Problems* (Bergen, Norway: Chr. Michelsen Institute, 2002), pp. 1–102.
83 SADC Summit Communiqué, Salisbury, Zimbabwe, 20 July 1981.
84 Matlosa and Lotshwao, *Political Integration and Democratisation in Southern Africa* (Gaborone: University of Botswana Press, 2009).
85 Garth le Pere and Elling N. Tjønneland, 'Which Way SADC? Advancing Cooperation and Integration in Southern Africa', *Institute for Global Dialogue Occasional Paper*, no. 50 (2005). See also Oosthuizen, *The Southern African Development Community*, pp. 61–3.
86 Overseas Development Institute (ODI) Briefing Paper, 'Sanctions and South Africa's Neighbours' (May 1987).
87 Anglin, 'Economic Liberation and Regional Cooperation in Southern Africa: SADCC and PTA'.
88 le Pere and Tjønneland, 'Which Way SADC? Advancing Cooperation and Integration in Southern Africa'.
89 le Pere and Tjønneland, 'Which Way SADC? Advancing Cooperation and Integration in Southern Africa'.
90 Kaire Mbuende, 'Namibia and the Southern African Development Community', in Anton Bösl, André du Pisani and Dennis U Zaire (eds), *Namibia's Foreign Relations: Historic contexts, Current Dimensions, and Perspectives for the 21st Century* (Windhoek: Macmillan Education Namibia, 2014), pp. 231–52.
91 Chinyamata Chipeta and Robert Davies, *Regional Relations and Cooperation Post-Apartheid* (Gaborone: SADC, 1993), pp. 129–30.
92 SADCC's sectoral activities and responsibilities as overseen by its member states comprised the following: Angola – energy; Botswana – agriculture research, livestock production, and animal disease control; Lesotho – environment and

land management, and water; Malawi – inland fisheries, forestry, and wildlife; Mauritius – tourism; Mozambique – culture, information, and sports, and transport and communications; Namibia – marine fisheries and resources, and legal sector; Swaziland – human resources development; Tanzania – industry and trade; Zambia – employment and labour, and mining; Zimbabwe – crop sector, and food, agriculture, and natural resources; and later, South Africa (which joined SADC in 1994) – finance and investment, and health. See also the typology provided in, Lee, *The Political Economy of Regionalism in Southern Africa*, p. 51.

93 Oosthuizen, *The Southern African Development Community*, p. 64.
94 Oosthuizen, *The Southern African Development Community*. See also Matlosa, and Lotshwao, 'Political Integration and Democratisation in Southern Africa'.
95 le Pere and Tjønneland, 'Which Way SADC? Advancing Cooperation and Integration in Southern Africa'; see also Isaksen, *Restructuring SADC – Progress and Problems*.
96 Nagar, 'Towards a Pax Africana: Southern African Development Community's Architecture and Evolving Peacekeeping Efforts, 1996-2009'.
97 Chris Alden and Garth le Pere, 'South Africa's Post-Apartheid Foreign Policy – from Reconciliation to Revival?', *Adelphi Paper*, no. 362 (2003): 58–9.
98 Alden and le Pere, 'South Africa's Post-Apartheid Foreign Policy'.
99 Omari and Macaringue, 'Southern African Security in Historical Perspective', pp. 51–9. See also Nagar, 'Towards a Pax Africana'.
100 Naison Ngoma, *Prospects for a Security Community in Southern Africa: An Analysis of Regional Security in the Southern African Development Community* (Tshwane, Pretoria: Institute for Security Studies (ISS) 2005).
101 Naison Ngoma, 'The Organ on Politics, Defence and Security: The Rise and Fall of a Security Model?', *Prospects for a Security Community in Southern Africa: An Analysis of Regional Security in the Southern African Development Community* (Tshwane (Pretoria): Institute for Security Studies (ISS), 2005), pp. 141–73. See also Nagar, 'Towards a Pax Africana'.
102 Ngoma, 'The Organ on Politics, Defence and Security: The Rise and Fall of a Security Model?'.
103 Nagar, 'Towards a Pax Africana'.
104 SADC Extraordinary Summits and Communiqués, Namibia, Windhoek, 9 March, 2001; and Gaborone, Botswana, 17–18 August 2005.
105 Adekeye Adebajo, 'Security, Governance, and Economic Issues in the SADC Region', Presentation made to the Swiss Agency for Development and Cooperation (SIDA), Tshwane (25 June 2014).
106 See the discussion on SADCC's Sectoral Activities in Lee, *The Political Economy of Regionalism in Southern Africa*, p. 50. See also Oosthuizen, *The Southern African Development Community*, pp. 61–3.
107 Adekeye Adebajo, 'The Peacekeeping Travails of the AU and the Regional Economic Communities', in John Akokpari, Angela Ndinga-Muvumba and Tim Murithi (eds), *The African Union and Its Institutions* (Auckland Park, South Africa: Jacana Media, 2008), pp. 131–61.
108 Paul-Henri Bischoff, 'How Far, Where To? Regionalism, the Southern African Development Community and Decision-Making into the Millenium', in Adar and Ajulu (eds), *Globalisation and Emerging Trends in African States' Foreign Policy-Making Process*, pp. 288–333. See also Elling N. Tjønneland, 'SADC Restructuring, Pioritisation and Donors, 2006-2008', in Jonathan Mayuyuka Kaunda and Farai Zizhou (eds), *Furthering Southern African Integration: Proceedings of the 2008*

FOPRISA Annual Conference (Botswana: Lightbooks, 2009). See also Nagar,'Towards a Pax Africana'.
109 Adebajo, 'Southern Africa's Fledgling Security Architecture'. See also SADC website, http://www.sadc.int/opds. See also Bischoff, 'How Far, Where To? Regionalism, the Southern African Development Community and Decision-Making into the Millennium', pp. 295–9.
110 'SADC's Main Institutions and Office-Bearers', in Oosthuizen, *The Southern African Development Community*, pp. 217–25.
111 Omari and Macaringue, 'Southern African Security in Historical Perspective', p. 54. See also Nagar, 'Towards a Pax Africana'.
112 Adebajo, 'Southern Africa's Fledgling Security Architecture'.
113 Adebajo, 'Southern Africa's Fledgling Security Architecture'.
114 Ngoma, *Prospects for a Security Community in Southern Africa*, pp. 147–50.
115 SADC, Strategic Indicative Plan for the Organ on Politics, Defence and Security Cooperation (OPDSC), http://www.sadc.int/.
116 Elling N Tjønneland, Jan Isaksen and Garth le Pere, 'SADC's Restructuring and Emerging Policies: Options for Norwegian Support', *Report of the Norwegian Embassy*, 2005, p. 21.
117 Personal Interviews. Conducted at SADC Secretariat, 2009, 2011 and 2013.
118 Matlosa, and Lotshwao, *Political Integration and Democratisation in Southern Africa*, p. 13.
119 Tjønneland, Isaksen and le Pere, 'SADC's Restructuring and Emerging Policies: Options for Norwegian Support'.
120 Tjønneland, Isaksen and le Pere, 'SADC's Restructuring and Emerging Policies: Options for Norwegian Support'.
121 SADC Summit of the Troika of the Organ on Politics, Defence and Security Cooperation of the Southern African Development Community, Maseru, Kingdom of Lesotho (21–22 February 2010), http://www.sadc.int/.
122 Nagar, 'Towards a Pax Africana'. See also CCR, 'Governance and Security Challenges in Post-Apartheid Southern Africa', *CCR Report* (2012).
123 Personal Meeting, held on the poor performance of SADC SNCs and attempts to remedy the structures, meeting held with GIZ, Germany, 20 February 2015, Cape Town, South Africa.
124 See Nagar and Mutasa, 'The Implementation Gap of the Regional Integration Agenda', *CCR Seminar Report*, Cape Town, July 2017. See also Matlosa and Lotshwao, '*Political Integration and Democratisation in Southern Africa*', p. 14. See also Tjønneland, 'SADC Restructuring, Prioritisation and Donors, 2006–2008'.
125 Personal Interview, Confidential, 2013 and 2014.
126 Tjønneland, 'SADC Restructuring, Prioritisation and Donors, 2006–2008', p. 19.
127 Tjønneland, 'SADC Restructuring, Prioritisation and Donors, 2006–2008', p. 19.
128 Tjønneland, 'SADC Restructuring, Prioritisation and Donors, 2006–2008', pp. 22–3.
129 Tjønneland, 'SADC Restructuring, Prioritisation and Donors, 2006–2008', pp. 21–32. See also CCR, 'Governance and Security Challenges in Post-Apartheid Southern Africa', *CCR Report* (2012).
130 The SADC Capacity Development Framework lists ten intervention areas. These are: leadership skills development and review of management processes; policy and strategy development; programme management; implementation of Secretariat performance management and appraisal system; internalisation of the Secretariat vision, mission and values; human resource development; development of

administrative management competencies; financial management development; accounting and procurement of services; and implementation of the SADC/ICP partnership framework.

131 Elaine Friedland, 'The Southern African Development Coordination Conference and the West: Cooperation or Conflict?', *Journal of Modern African Studies*, vol. 23, no. 2 (June 1985): 287–314.

132 Roger Leys and Arne Tostensen, 'Regional Cooperation in Southern Africa: The Southern African Development Co-ordination Conference', *Scandinavian Perspectives on Africa, Review of African Political Economy*, vol. 23 (January–April 1982): 55–71.

133 Tom Øostergaard, 'Aiming beyond Conventional Development Assistance: An Analysis of Nordic Aid to the SADCC Region', in Bertil Odén and Haroub Othman, *Regional Cooperation in Southern Africa: A Post-Apartheid Perspective* (Uppsala: Scandinavian Institute of African Studies, 1989), pp. 127–80. See also Moeletsi Mbeki, *Profile of Political Conflicts in Southern Africa* (Harare: Nehanda, 1987), p. 87.

134 Anglin, 'Economic Liberation and Regional Cooperation in Southern Africa: SADCC and PTA'.

135 Leys and Tostensen, 'Regional Cooperation in Southern Africa: The Southern African Development Co-ordination Conference'.

136 Peter J. Schraeder, 'Continuity and Change in the United States' Foreign Policy towards Southern Africa', in Korwa Gombe Adar and Rok Ajulu (eds), *Globalization and Emerging Trends in African States' Foreign Policy-Making Process: A Comparative Perspective of Southern Africa* (Aldershot: Ashgate, 2002), pp. 332–3.

137 Schraeder, 'Continuity and Change in the United States' Foreign Policy towards Southern Africa', pp. 332–3.

138 Khadiagala, *Allies in Adversity*, p. 237.

139 See also SADC Summit Communiques, http://www.sadc.int/files/3913/5292/8384/SADC_SUMMIT_COMMUNIQUES_1980-2006.pdf.

140 Øostergaard, 'Aiming beyond Conventional Development Assistance'; Friedland, 'The Southern African Development Coordination Conference and the West'; Anglin, 'Economic Liberation and Regional Cooperation in Southern Africa'; and Peter Meyns, 'Present Structures and Future Challenges of Regional Cooperation and Integration in Southern Africa', *Africana Studia, Edição da Fundação Eng. Antônio de Almeida*, no. 1 (1999), pp. 85–107.

141 Anglin, 'Economic Liberation and Regional Cooperation in Southern Africa: SADCC and PTA'; and Meyns, 'Present Structures and Future Challenges of Regional Cooperation and Integration in Southern Africa'. See also SADC Summit Communiques, http://www.sadc.int/files/3913/5292/8384/SADC_SUMMIT_COMMUNIQUES_1980-2006.pdf.

142 SADCC Communiqué, Arusha, Tanzania, 9 August 1985, http://www.sadc.int.

143 The Joint Declaration on Expanded Economic and Cultural Cooperation between the Nordic Countries and the SADCC member states were signed in January 1986, in Luanda, see SADCC/SADC Heads of State and Government Summit Communiqués 1980–2000; and SADCC Summit Communiqué, Luanda, Angola, 22 August 1986, http://www.sadc.int. See also SADC Summit Communiques, http://www.sadc.int/files/3913/5292/8384/SADC_SUMMIT_COMMUNIQUES_1980-2006.pdf.

144 Øostergaard, 'Aiming beyond Conventional Development Assistance', pp. 137 and 149. See also Rasul Ahmed Minja, 'Security Architecture in Sub–Saharan Africa and

Collective Security Challenges: The EAC and SADC in Comparative Perspective', *DuEpublico, University of Duisburg-Essen* (December 2012), http://duepublico.uni-duisburg-essen.de/servlets/DerivateServlet/Derivate-32068/Minja_Diss.pdf.
145 SADCC Summit Communiqué, Luanda, Angola, 22 August 1986, http://www.sadc.int.
146 SADCC Summit Communiqué, Luanda, Angola, 22 August 1986, http://www.sadc.int.
147 Øostergaard, 'Aiming beyond Conventional Development Assistance'.
148 Øostergaard, 'Aiming beyond Conventional Development Assistance'.
149 Bremmer, 'State Capitalism Comes of Age: The End of the Free Market?', pp. 40–55.
150 Kwame A. Ninsin, 'Three Levels of State Reordering: The Structural Aspects', in Donald Rothchild and Naomi Chazan (eds), *The Precarious Balance: State and Society in Africa* (Boulder, CO: Westview Press, 1988), pp. 265–81.
151 Rothchild and Chazan, *The Precarious Balance*, pp. 265–81.
152 Crawford Young, 'The African Colonial State and Its Political Legacy', in Rothchild and Chazan, *The Precarious Balance*, pp. 25–66.
153 Øostergaard, 'Aiming beyond Conventional Development Assistance', p. 153.
154 Øostergaard, 'Aiming beyond Conventional Development Assistance', p. 153.
155 Friedland, 'The Southern African Development Coordination Conference and the West: Cooperation or Conflict?', pp. 287–314.
156 African Development Bank (AfDB), *Economic Integration in Southern Africa*, vol. 2 (Tunisia: AfDB, 1993), p. 271.
157 SADCC Summit Communiqué, 26 August 1990, Gaborone, Botswana; and SADCC Summit Communiqué, 26 August 1991, Arusha, Tanzania.
158 Khadiagala, *Allies in Adversity*.
159 Khadiagala, *Allies in Adversity*, p. 243.
160 Baldwin, 'Openness and Growth: What's the Empirical Relationship?', pp. 499–525.
161 SADCC Summit Communiqué, Luanda, Angola, 22 August 1986.
162 Khadiagala, *Allies in Adversity*, p. 262.
163 Bischoff, 'How Far, Where To?', p. 288. See also Schraeder, 'Continuity and Change in the United States' Foreign Policy towards Southern Africa', pp. 332–3.
164 Nagar, 'Towards a Pax Africana'.
165 OECD/DAC Meeting on Development Challenges and the Role of Aid in Southern Africa, Windhoek, Namibia, 7–8 September 1993 (SG/NR (93) 33, http://www.oecd.org.
166 Personal interview, confidential, 2013.
167 Personal interview, confidential, 2013.
168 Anglin, 'Economic Liberation and Regional Cooperation in Southern Africa', p. 684.
169 Anglin, 'Economic Liberation and Regional Cooperation in Southern Africa', pp. 681–711.
170 UNECA 'Annual Report 29 May 1984–29 April 1985', Economic and Social Council Official Records, 1985, Supplement no.15, E/1985/36, E/ECA/CM.11/81, p. 28.
171 Edmond J. Keller, 'Understanding Conflicts in the Horn of Africa', in Chandra Lekha Sriram and Zoe Nielsen (eds), *Exploring Subregional Conflict Opportunities for Conflict Prevention* (Boulder, CO: Lynne Rienner, 2004), p. 44.
172 The results for the average annual growth rate of GDP percentage for the period 1980–7 were obtained from the World Development Report, *World Bank* (1989), pp. 164–9; and pp. 174–5.
173 UNECA Annual Report 29 May 1984–29 April 1985, p. 70.

174 Sanmi Ajiki, *Adebayo Adedeji: A Rainbow in the Sky of Time (His Vision; His Mission; His Life and Times)* (Nigeria: Newswatch Books, 2000), p. 279.
175 Asante, 'The Years of Preparation: Adedeji and the ECA', p. 151.
176 Bax Nomvete, 'The PTA, a Historical Perspective and Objectives (PTA/PUB/11/4, 4 March 1987)', cited in GIGA, 'The Preferential Trade Area (PTA) for Eastern and Southern Africa: Achievements, Problems and Prospects' *Spectrum*, vol. 24, no. 2 (1989): 157–71. See also Lee, *The Political Economy of Regionalism in Southern Africa*, p. 86; and Kwaku, 'The African Economic Community: Problems and Prospects: The Politics of Economic Integration in Africa'.
177 GIGA, 'The PTA for Eastern and Southern Africa'.
178 Anglin, 'Economic Liberation and Regional Cooperation in Southern Africa', p. 688.
179 Anglin, 'Economic Liberation and Regional Cooperation in Southern Africa', p. 688.
180 Nomvete, 'The PTA, a Historical Perspective and Objectives', pp. 9–10.
181 Nomvete, 'The PTA, a Historical Perspective and Objectives', pp. 9–10.
182 Kenneth Kaoma Mwenda, *The Dynamics of Market Integration: African Stock Exchanges in the New Millennium* (Florida: Brown Walker Press, 2000).
183 Susan Hall, 'The Preferential Trade Area (PTA) for Eastern and Southern African States: Strategy, Progress, and Problems', Working Paper, Institute for Development Studies (1987).
184 Anglin, 'Economic Liberation and Regional Cooperation in Southern Africa'. See also GIGA, 'The Preferential Trade Area (PTA) for Eastern and Southern Africa', p. 168, http://www.herald.co.zw/wp-content/uploads/2015/04/sadc.jpg.
185 AfDB, 'Economic Integration in Southern Africa', p. 19. See also Tichaona Zindoga, 'SADC and the Politics of Regional Integration', *The Herald* (28 April 2015), http://www.herald.co.zw/sadc-and-the-politics-of-regional-integration/.
186 International Monetary Fund (IMF): Direction of Trade Statistics: Year-book 1988, pp. 248–429, cited in GIGA, 'The PTA for Eastern and Southern Africa', p. 165.
187 Anglin, 'Economic Liberation and Regional Cooperation in Southern Africa: SADCC and PTA'.
188 Jacob Viner, *The Customs Union Issue* (New York: Carnegie Endowment for International Peace; and London: Stevens and Sons, 1950). See also AfDB, 'Southern Africa Regional Integration Strategy Paper 2011-15', www.afdb.org.
189 Peter Anyang' Nyong'o (ed.), *Regional Integration in Africa Unfinished Agenda* (Nairobi: African Academy of Sciences, 1990), p. 151.
190 Nyong'o, *Regional Integration in Africa Unfinished Agenda*.
191 Yasmin Carrim, *The Preferential Trade Area for Eastern and Southern Africa and COMESA: Call for Suspension* (Cape Town: University of the Western Cape, 1994), p. 4.
192 Padamja Khandelwal, 'COMESA, EAC and SADC: Prospects and Challenges for Regional Trade Integration', *International Monetary Fund*, Working Paper no. WP/04/227 (2004), p. 5.
193 UNECA, 'Assessing Regional Integration in Africa, IV', p. 231.
194 Khandelwal, 'COMESA, EAC and SADC: Prospects and Challenges for Regional Trade Integration', p. 5.
195 Meyns, 'Present Structures and Future Challenges of Regional Cooperation and Integration in Southern Africa', pp. 85–107.
196 Personal interview, conducted with Simba Makoni, Kariba Lake, June 2011.
197 Romer, 'Increasing Returns and Long-Run Growth', pp. 1002–37.

198 AfDB, *Economic Integration in Southern Africa*, p. 249. See also James J. Hentz, 'The Southern African Security Order: Regional Economic Integration and Security among Developing States', *Review of International Studies*, vol. 35, no. 51 (2009): 189–213; and Theo Neethling, 'Pursuing a Functional Security Community in Southern Africa: Is It Possible After All?', *Strategic Review for Southern Africa*, vol. 25, no. 1 (May 2003), <ttps://www.questia.com/library/journal/1G1-109504763/pursuing-a-functional-security-community-in-southern.
199 AfDB, *Economic Integration in Southern Africa*, pp. 250–5.
200 World Bank, 'Mozambique Industrial Sector Study: the development of industrial policy and reform of the business environment', *Industry and Energy Operations Division, Southern African Department*, 1999; cited in AfDB, *Economic Integration in Southern Africa*, p. 249.
201 Zaffiro, 'Exceptionality in External Affairs', p. 72. See also 'SA Attempting to Squeeze Hyundai Botswana-Built Cars out of the Market', *Daily News*, 5 May 1994, p. 2.
202 AfDB, *Economic Integration in Southern Africa*, p. 171.
203 AfDB, *Economic Integration in Southern Africa*, p. 171.
204 Dollar, 'Outward-Oriented Developing Economies Really Do Grow More Rapidly: Evidence from 95 LDCs, 1976–85', 1992.
205 See also Victor Azarya, 'Reordering State–Society Relations: Incorporation and Disengagement', pp. 3–24, and Young, 'The African Colonial State and Its Political Legacy', pp. 25–66, both in Rothchild and Chazan (eds), *The Precarious Balance*, 1988.
206 Ninsin, 'Three Levels of State Reordering: The Structural Aspects', pp. 265–81.
207 Khadiagala, *Allies in Adversity*, p. 231.
208 AfDB, *Economic Integration in Southern Africa*, p. 26.
209 Chipeta and Davies, *Regional Relations and Cooperation Post-Apartheid*.
210 SADC Summit Communiqué 1991, Arusha, Tanzania, 26 August 1991. See also SADC Summit Communiques, http://www.sadc.int/files/3913/5292/8384/SADC_SUMMIT_COMMUNIQUES_1980–2006.pdf.
211 Simba Makoni, 'Foreword', in Chipeta and Davies, *Regional Relations and Cooperation Post-Apartheid* (Gaborone: SADC, 1993), pp. iii–iv.
212 Personal interview, Simba Makoni, Kariba Lake, 10 June 2011.
213 Makoni, 'Foreword', pp. iii–iv.
214 Personal interview, Simba Makoni, Kariba Lake, 10 June 2011.
215 Chipeta and Davies, *Regional Relations and Cooperation Post-Apartheid*, pp. 1–142. See also *The Courier*, 'A Fresh Look at Africa', no. 134 (July/August 1992), http://aei.pitt.edu/39179/1/Courier.134.pdf.
216 Fabrizio Carmignami, 'A Note on Income Converge Effects in Regional Integration Agreements', *Economic Analysis Division, United Nations Economic Commission for Europe (UNECE)* (2007).
217 Chipeta and Davies, *Regional Relations and Cooperation Post-Apartheid*, pp. 1–142.
218 Bax D. Nomvete, 'Regional Integration in Africa, a Path Strewn with Obstacles', *The Courier (EC Courier)*, no. 142 (November–December 1993).
219 Nomvete, 'Regional Integration in Africa, a Path Strewn with Obstacles'.
220 European Union and Southern African Development Community seminar on 'The Regional Integration Process', 1995, pp. 3–215. Opening addresses by Peter Pooley, deputy director general for Development – EC; Alain Azouaou, deputy head of Southern Africa and Indian Ocean Department, MAE, France; Kaire Mbuende,

executive secretary, SADC; M. C. Lekaukau, chairman, SADC Standing Committee of Officials; and Jacques Delors, former president of the European Commission.
221 Meyns, 'Present Structures and Future Challenges of Regional Cooperation and Integration in Southern Africa'.
222 See also Agreed Minutes of the Meeting between the SADCC Secretariat and the PTA Secretariat, Gaborone (mimeo), 9 March 1991. Cited in Meyns (1999). See also SADC Summit Communiques, http://www.sadc.int/files/3913/5292/8384/SADC_SUMMIT_COMMUNIQUES_1980-2006.pdf.
223 Meyns, 'Present Structures and Future Challenges of Regional Cooperation and Integration in Southern Africa'.
224 Personal interview, Simba Makoni, Kariba Lake, 10 June 2011.
225 SADCC Summit Communiqué, Windhoek, Namibia, 17 August 1992. See also SADC Summit Communiques, http://www.sadc.int/files/3913/5292/8384/SADC_SUMMIT_COMMUNIQUES_1980-2006.pdf.
226 SADCC Summit Communiqué, Windhoek, Namibia, 17 August 1992.
227 SADCC Summit Communiqué, Windhoek, Namibia, 17 August 1992.
228 SADCC Summit Communiqué, Windhoek, Namibia, 17 August 1992. See also SADC Summit Communiques, http://www.sadc.int/files/3913/5292/8384/SADC_SUMMIT_COMMUNIQUES_1980-2006.pdf.
229 SADCC Summit Communiqué, Windhoek, Namibia, 17 August 1992.
230 SADCC Summit Communiqué, Windhoek, Namibia, 17 August 1992.
231 SADCC Summit Communiqué, Windhoek, Namibia, 17 August 1992.
232 SADC Summit Communiqué, Swaziland, 1993.
233 Makoni, 'Foreword'.
234 SADC Summit Communiqué, Swaziland, 1993.
235 Personal Interview, Simba Makoni, Kariba Lake, 10 June 2011.
236 Fadzai Gwaradzimba, 'SADCC and the Future of Southern African Regionalism', *African Studies Association: A Journal of Opinion*, vol. 21, no. 1/2 (1993): 51–9.
237 SADC Summit Communiqué, Swaziland, 1993.
238 Personal interview, Simba Makoni, Kariba Lake, 10 June 2011.
239 Chipeta and Davies, *Regional Relations and Cooperation Post-Apartheid*, p. 89.
240 Chipeta and Davies, *Regional Relations and Cooperation Post-Apartheid*, p. 89.
241 SADC Summit Communiqué, Gaborone, 29 August 1994.
242 Personal interview, Ambassador Welile Nhlapo, Cape Town, South Africa, July 2013.
243 See also Adebayo Adedeji, *South Africa and Africa: Within or Apart* (London: Zed Books, 1996), p. 81.
244 Ben Turok, 'Building a progressive consensus', in Ben Turok (ed.), *The Controversy about Economic Growth* (Johannesburg: Jacana, 2011), p. 184.
245 *See* Congress of South African Trade Unions (COSATU), http://www.cosatu.org.za/.
246 Gavin Maasdorp, 'A Vision for Economic Integration and Cooperation in Southern Africa', report of the meeting of 21 January 1994 with South African departments: Finance and Foreign Affairs; Trade and Industry; Central Economic Advisory Centre; the Development Bank of Southern Africa (DBSA); the Industrial Development Corporation (IDC); and Chamber of Commerce (SACOB) (partially attended), in James J. Hentz, 'South Africa and the Political Economy of Regional Cooperation in Southern Africa', *Journal of Modern African Studies*, vol. 43, no. 1 (March, 2005): 21–51. See also Gavin A. Maasdorp, *Rethinking Economic Cooperation in Southern Africa: Trade and Investment* (Johannesburg: Konrad-Adenauer Stiftung, 1993).

247 Hentz, 'South Africa and the Political Economy of Regional Cooperation in Southern Africa', pp. 21–51.
248 Landsberg, *The Quiet Diplomacy of Liberation*, pp. 196–8.
249 Hentz, 'South Africa and the Political Economy of Regional Cooperation in Southern Africa', p. 31.
250 Hentz, 'South Africa and the Political Economy of Regional Cooperation in Southern Africa', p. 29.
251 Hentz, 'South Africa and the Political Economy of Regional Cooperation in Southern Africa', p. 34. Personal interview, conducted with AU ACP/EU Official (Brussels), Cape Town, 2014. See also Vickers, 'South Africa's Economic Diplomacy in a Changing Global Order', pp. 112–34. See also David Monyae, 'The Evolving "Doctrine" of Multilateralism in South Africa's Africa Policy', in Chris Landsberg and Jo-Ansie van Wyk (eds), *South African Foreign Policy Review* (Johannesburg: IGD, 2012), pp. 139–51.
252 Personal interviews conducted at DIRCO, Pretoria, 2014; and with a DTI official in Pretoria, 2014.
253 Personal interview, confidential, 2014.
254 SADC Summit Communiqué, Botswana, 29 August 1994. See also SADC Summit Communiques, http://www.sadc.int/files/3913/5292/8384/SADC_SUMMIT_COMMUNIQUES_1980-2006.pdf.
255 SADC Summit Communiqué, Botswana, 29 August 1994. See also SADC Summit Communiques, http://www.sadc.int/files/3913/5292/8384/SADC_SUMMIT_COMMUNIQUES_1980-2006.pdf.
256 SADC Summit Communiqué, Johannesburg, 28 August 1995.
257 SADC Summit Communiqué, Johannesburg, 28 August 1995.
258 SADC Summit Communiqué, Johannesburg, 28 August 1995. See also SADC Summit Communiques, http://www.sadc.int/files/3913/5292/8384/SADC_SUMMIT_COMMUNIQUES_1980-2006.pdf.
259 SADC Summit Communiqué, Johannesburg, 28 August 1995.
260 SADC Summit Communiqué, Maseru, 24 August 1996.
261 Maria Ramos, discussion on SADC's regional macroeconomic convergence in the *European Union and Southern African Development Community Seminar on 'The Regional Integration Process'*, 1995.
262 Ramos, discussion on SADC's regional macroeconomic convergence, p. 17.
263 SADC Summit Communiqué, Blantyre, Malawi, 8 August 1997. See also SADC Summit Communiques, http://www.sadc.int/files/3913/5292/8384/SADC_SUMMIT_COMMUNIQUES_1980-2006.pdf.
264 SADC Summit Communiqué, Blantyre, Malawi, 8 August 1997.
265 Gilbert M. Khadiagala, 'The SADCC and Its Approaches to African Regionalism', in Chris Saunders, Gwinyayi Dzinesa and Dawn Nagar (eds), *Region-Building in Southern Africa: Progress, Problems and Prospects* (London: Zed Books, 2012), p. 25.
266 Khadiagala, 'The SADCC and Its Approaches to African Regionalism', p. 25.
267 SADC Summit Communiqué, Botswana, 29 August 1994.
268 SADC Summit Meeting, Maseru, 24 August 1996. See also Martha Belete Hailu, 'Regional Economic Integration in Africa: Challenges and Prospects', *Mizan Law Review*, vol. 8, no. 2 (2014), http://www.ajol.info/index.php/mlr/article/view/117543/107100.

4 The era of convergence: COMESA, EAC and SADC

1. The Common Market for Eastern and Southern Africa, *Final Communiqué of the COMESA-EAC-SADC Tripartite Summit of Heads of State and Government*, 'Vision: Towards a Single Market', 'Theme: Deepening COMESA-EAC-SADC Integration', 22 October 2008, Kampala, Uganda.
2. Formal conversations with former South African foreign affairs minister Aziz Pahad, Lagos, Nigeria, 9 June 2012; and at a Centre for Conflict Resolution (CCR) Public Dialogue, 'The Diplomacy of Transformation: South African Foreign Policy and Statecraft', Cape Town, South Africa (3 May 2011), http://www.ccr.org.za/index.php/events/public-dialogues/item/652-no-154.
3. Christopher Clapham, 'The Changing World of Regional Integration in Africa', in Christopher Clapham, Gregg Mills, Anna Morner and Elizabeth Sidiropoulos (eds), *Regional Integration in Southern Africa* (Cape Town: South African Institute for International Affairs (SAIIA), 2001), p. 62.
4. See World Bank's Indicators reported on South Africa's total GDP for the period 2000-10, http://data.worldbank.org/indicator/NY.GDP.MKTP.CD?page=2.
5. Adedeji, *South Africa and Africa: Within or Apart*, p. 81.
6. Judi Hudson, 'Economic Expansion into Africa', in Adekeye Adebajo, Adebayo Adedeji and Chris Landsberg (eds), *South Africa in Africa: The Post-Apartheid Era* (Scottsville: University of KwaZulu-Natal Press, 2007).
7. COMESA's nineteen member states include Burundi, Comoros, the DRC, Djibouti, Egypt, Eritrea, Ethiopia, Kenya, Libya, Madagascar, Malawi, Mauritius, Rwanda, Seychelles, Sudan, Swaziland, Uganda, Zambia and Zimbabwe.
8. Edmond J. Keller, 'Understanding Conflicts in the Horn of Africa', in Chandra Lekha Sriram and Zoe Nielsen (eds), *Exploring Subregional Conflict Opportunities for Conflict Prevention* (Boulder, CO: Lynne Rienner, 2004), p. 44.
9. Keller, 'Understanding Conflicts in the Horn of Africa', p. 39.
10. SADC Communiqué, Pretoria, 23 August 1998.
11. SADC Strategic Indicative Plan for the Organ on Politics, Defence and Security Cooperation, http://www.sadc.int/.
12. See 'The Organ on Politics, Defence and Security: The Rise and Fall of a Security Model?', in Ngoma, *Prospects for a Security Community in Southern Africa*.
13. Vale, *Security and Politics in South Africa*, p. 175.
14. Landsberg, *The Quiet Diplomacy of Liberation*, pp. 173-4.
15. Matlosa and Lotshwao, *Political Integration and Democratisation in Southern Africa*.
16. Ngoma, 'The Organ on Politics, Defence and Security'.
17. Landsberg, *The Quiet Diplomacy of Liberation*, pp. 164-6. See also Clapham, 'The Changing World of Regional Integration in Africa', pp. 59-70.
18. Landsberg, *The Quiet Diplomacy of Liberation*.
19. Matlosa and Lotshwao, *Political Integration and Democratisation in Southern Africa*, p. 14. See also Tjønneland, 'SADC Restructuring, Prioritisation and Donors, 2006-2008'.
20. Matlosa and Lotshwao, *Political Integration and Democratisation in Southern Africa*.
21. Landsberg, *The Quiet Diplomacy of Liberation*, p. 173.
22. Landsberg, *The Quiet Diplomacy of Liberation*, p. 173.
23. Landsberg, *The Quiet Diplomacy of Liberation*.
24. Pierre De Vos, 'UCT Law Faculty statement on suspension of SADC Tribunal' (19 September 2012), http://constitutionallyspeaking.co.za/

uct-law-faculty-statement-on-suspension-of-sadc-tribunal/. See also CCR, 'Governance and Security Challenges in Post-Apartheid Southern Africa', *CCR Report* (2012).
25 Laurie Nathan, 'Solidarity Trumps Rule of Law', *Mail and Guardian* (30 November 2012), p. 21. See also Laurie Nathan, *The Disbanding of the SADC Tribunal: A Cautionary Tale* (Pretoria: Centre for Mediation in Africa, University of Pretoria, 2009).
26 Landsberg, *The Quiet Diplomacy of Liberation*, p. 174.
27 Gilbert M. Khadiagala, 'Forging Regional Foreign Policies in SADC: A Framework for Analysis', in Charles Harvey (ed.), *Proceedings of the 2009 FOPRISA Annual Conference* (Botswana: Lightbooks, 2010), p. 82. See also CCR, 'Governance and Security Challenges in Post-Apartheid Southern Africa', *CCR Report* (2012).
28 Landsberg, *The Quiet Diplomacy of Liberation*.
29 Landsberg, *The Quiet Diplomacy of* Liberation, p. 174.
30 See Vale, 'Ordering Southern Africa', in *Security and Politics in South Africa*.
31 Khabele Matlosa, 'Regional Security in Southern Africa'; and Devon Curtis, 'South Africa: "Exporting Peace" to the Great Lakes Region?', both in Adebajo, Adedeji and Landsberg (eds), *South Africa in Africa*. See also Vale, 'Ordering Southern Africa'. See also Soko, 'The Political Economy of Regional Integration in Southern Africa', 2007.
32 Brittany Kesselman, 'African Peace and Security Agenda', *Pax-Africana*, vol. 5, no. 1 (March 2009). See also CCR, 'Governance and Security Challenges in Post-Apartheid Southern Africa'.
33 SADC, 'Agreement Amending the Treaty of the Southern African Development Community', Blantyre, Malawi, 2001.
34 See CCR, 'Governance and Security Challenges in Post-Apartheid Southern Africa'. Zimbabwe's Ministry of Finance, the International Monetary Fund and the Economist Intelligence Unit had forecast growth rates of 8, 6 and 2.2 per cent, respectively, for 2013. See Economist Intelligence Unit, 'Country Report: Zimbabwe', 30 November 2012, p. 21.
35 Peter Batchelor and Paul Dunne, 'The Restructuring of South Africa's Defence Industry', *African Security Review*, vol. 7, no. 6 (1998): 27-43.
36 Adebayo Adedeji, architect of regional integration in Africa since the early 1970s, established ECOWAS between 1971 and 1975, was the minister of economic reconstruction and development in Nigeria, was executive secretary of the UN Economic Commission for Africa from 1975 to 1991 and developed the Preferential Trade Area (PTA), which later became COMESA.
37 See Adebayo Adedeji, 'Within or Apart', in Adebayo Adedeji (ed.), *South Africa in Africa: Within or Apart?* (London: Zed Books, 1996).
38 See Adedeji, *South Africa in Africa: Within or Apart?*
39 See Adedeji, *South Africa in Africa: Within or Apart?*
40 Adebayo Adedeji, 'Political Economy: Looking Inside from the Outside', in Adebajo, Adedeji and Landsberg (eds), *South Africa in Africa*.
41 Adedeji, 'Political Economy: Looking Inside from the Outside'.
42 Sam Moyo and Ruth Hall, 'Conflict and Land Reform in Southern Africa', in Adebajo, Adedeji and Landsberg (eds), *South Africa in Africa*.
43 *The Economist*, 'A Sad and Sorry Decline', Middle East and Africa (29 June 2013).
44 Chris Alden and Mills Soko, 'South Africa's Economic Relations with Africa: Hegemony and Its Discontents', *Journal of Modern African Studies*, vol. 43,

no. 3 (2005): 367–92; and Vickers, 'South Africa's Economic Policy in a Changing Global Order'.
45 SADC's four SDIs are energy, oil and gas extraction, electrical power generation, and water and transport; cited in Saunders, Dzinesa and Nagar (eds), *Region-Building in Southern Africa*, p. 132.
46 Tore Horvei, 'Powering the Region: South Africa in the Southern Africa Power Pool', in David Simon (ed.), *South Africa in Southern Africa: Reconfiguring the Region* (Oxford: James Currey, 1998). See also Stephan, Power, Hervey and Fonseca, *The Scramble for Africa in the 21st Century*.
47 King-Akerele and Asiedu, *Accelerating Africa's Integration Through Micro-Regionalism*.
48 Ravenhill, 'The "New East Asian Regionalism": A Political Domino Effect'.
49 SADC, 'Structure and Patterns of Trade' report (the statistics are adopted from the World Bank database).
50 Horvei, 'Powering the Region: South Africa in the Southern Africa Power Pool'. See also Dawn Nagar, 'Economic Integration', in Saunders, Dzinesa and Nagar (eds), *Region-Building in Southern Africa*, p. 132; and SADC *Today*, vol. 10, no. 2 (August 2007).
51 Horvei, 'Powering the Region: South Africa in the Southern Africa Power Pool'. See also Nagar, 'Economic Integration', p. 132.
52 SAPP, *Annual Report*, 2014, https:www.sapp.co.zw. See also Alison Chikova, 'Energy Trading in the Southern African Power Pool', *SAPP* (March 2009).
53 Agathe Maupin, 'Building a Regional Electricity Market: SAPP Challenges', South African Institute of International Affairs, Case Study 4 (2013).
54 Saunders, Dzinesa and Nagar, *Region-Building in Southern Africa*, p. 133.
55 SADC *Today*, vol. 10, no. 2 (August 2007).
56 SADC *Today*, vol. 10, no. 2 (August 2007).
57 Saunders, Dzinesa and Nagar, *Region-Building in Southern Africa*, p. 133. See also Horvei, 'Powering the Region: South Africa in the Southern Africa Power Pool'.
58 Monyae, 'The Evolving "Doctrine" of Multilateralism in South Africa's Africa Policy', p. 149. See also Vickers, 'South Africa's Economic Policy in a Changing Global Order', pp. 112–34.
59 Judi Hudson, 'Economic Expansion into Africa', in Adebajo, Adedeji and Landsberg (eds), *South Africa in Africa*, pp. 128–49.
60 Jenkins and Thomas, "The Macro-economic Frameworks', p. 55.
61 SADC Mozambique report, http://www.sadc.int/; http://www.sadctrade.org/files/Intra–SADC–trade–performance–review–2006–4–mozambique.pdf, pp. 86–7.
62 SADC *Today*, vol. 10, no. 2 (August 2007).
63 Hazelwood, 'The End of the East African Community', pp. 172–87.
64 Jacob Viner, *The Customs Union Issue* (New York: Carnegie Endowment for International Peace; and London: Stevens and Sons, 1950).
65 Gambari, *Political and Comparative Dimensions of Regional Integration*.
66 Nomvete, 'Regional Integration in Africa, a Path Strewn with Obstacles'.
67 See the discussion on new modern world systems in Gilpin, *The Political Economy of International Relations*, pp. 67–9.
68 Soko, 'The Political Economy of Regional Integration in Southern Africa'.
69 Lee, *The Political Economy of Regionalism in Southern Africa*; Alden and Soko, 'South Africa's Economic Relations with Africa: Hegemony and Its Discontents'.
70 ODI Briefing Paper, 'Sanctions and South Africa's Neighbours', May 1987.
71 Pinder and Usherwood, *The European Union*, pp. 82–3.

72 Charles Mutasa, 'A Critique of the EU's Common Agricultural Policy', in Adekeye Adebajo and Kaye Whiteman (eds), *The EU and Africa from Eurafrique to Afro-Europa* (Johannesburg: Wits University Press, 2013), p. 249.
73 Mutasa, 'A Critique of the EU's Common Agricultural Policy', pp. 237–56.
74 Lee, *Political Economy of Regionalism in Southern Africa*, p. 218.
75 Lee, *Political Economy of Regionalism in Southern Africa*, p. 90.
76 Soko, 'The Political Economy of Regional Integration in Southern Africa'.
77 'Impact of Regional Trade Deals on Clothing and Textile Sector – a Global Assessment: Management Briefing: South Africa', *Just Style* (22 April 2008).
78 James Hentz, 'South Africa and the Political Economy of Regional Cooperation in Southern Africa', *Journal of Modern African Studies*, vol. 43, no. 1 (March 2005), pp. 21–51.
79 Alden and Soko, 'South Africa's Economic Relations with Africa'.
80 'Impact of Regional Trade Deals on Clothing and Textile Sector'.
81 Vickers, 'South Africa's Economic Policy in a Changing Global Order', pp. 112–34.
82 See also Daniel H. Levine and Dawn Nagar, 'Security and Governance in the Great Lakes Region', *Centre for Conflict Resolution Seminar Report*, vol. 51 (August 2015).
83 Soko, 'The Political Economy of Regional Integration in Southern Africa', p. 2.
84 UNCTAD, 'Trade and Development Report' (2012), pp. 1–34, http://unctad.org/en/PublicationsLibrary/tdr2012overview_en.pdf.
85 EU GFA Consulting and GTZ, SADC 2008, 'Free Trade Area, Growth, Development and Wealth Creation'. See also AfDB, *Southern Africa Regional Integration Strategy Paper, 2011–2015*, http://www.afdb.org/en/news-and-events/article/afdb-approves-regional-integration-strategy-for-Southern-africa-7883/.
86 Lee, *Political Economy of Regionalism in Southern Africa*, pp. 122–6. See also AfDB, 'Economic Integration in Southern Africa', p. 38.
87 Lee, *Political Economy of Regionalism in Southern Africa*, pp. 198–9.
88 Liam Halligan, 'Global Africa: The Last Investment Frontier?', in Adebajo and Whiteman (eds), *The EU and Africa*, p. 183.
89 African Union, Yamoussoukro Declaration 1999, http://au.int/ar/sites/default/files/Yamoussoukro%20Decision%20-%20Regulatory%20Framework-EN.pdf.
90 Personal interview, September 2014. COMESA document: Amos Marawa, Infrastructure Development, *Infrastructure Development Directorate* (2010, 2014). See also InterVISTAS Consulting, 'Transforming Intra-African Air Connectivity: The Economic Benefits of Implementing the Yamoussoukro Decision' (July 2014).
91 Abuja Treaty, 1991, http://www.au.int/en/sites/default/files/TREATY_ESTABLISHING_THE_AFRICAN_ECONOMIC_COMMUNITY.pdf.
92 COMESA, *Treaty Establishing the Common Market for Eastern and Southern Africa*, adopted 5 November 1993, entered into force 8 December 1994, http://www.comesa.int/attachments/article/28/COMESA_Treaty.pdf, Article 87.
93 SADC, *Protocol on Transport, Communications and Meteorology in the Southern African Development Community (SADC) Region*, adopted 24 August 1996, entered into force 1 July 1998, http://www.sadc.int/files/7613/5292/8370/Protocol_on_Transport_Communications_and_Meteorology_1996.pdf, Article 9.
94 EAC, *Treaty for the Establishment of the East African Community*, adopted 30 November 1999, entered into force 7 July 2000, http://www.eac.int/legal/index.php?option=com_docman&task=doc_details&gid=166&Itemid=28, Article 92.
95 COMESA document: Marawa, 'Infrastructure Development'.

96 COMESA Secretariat, September 2014. See also: The US Trade and Development Agency (USTDA) Supports COMESA Regional Airspace Management Project. The $443,300 were conferred during a signing ceremony at the COMESA Forum that took place in Nairobi. US ambassador to Zambia, Carmen Martinez, and COMESA and former assistant secretary general, Sindiso N. Ngwenya (currently COMESA secretary general), signed the agreement on behalf of the US government and COMESA, 22 May 2007. See also the 2007 Comprehensive Report on U.S. Trade and Investment Policy Toward Sub-Saharan Africa and Implementation of the African Growth and Opportunity Act, https://agoa.info/images/documents/2990/2007_AGOA_Report.pdf, p. 55.
97 UNECA, 'Movement of Goods and Services in Africa' (2011). See also AfDB, 'Statistics on Africa Report, 2013' (2013).
98 UNECA, 'Assessing Regional Integration in Africa, V: Harmonizing Policies to Transform the Trading Environment' (2012), p. 11.
99 COMESA documents: Marawa, 'Infrastructure Development'; and COMESA-EAC-SADC Tripartite Framework: State of Play, Report of the Chair of the Tripartite Task Force, February 2011.
100 COMESA documents: Marawa, 'Infrastructure Development'; and COMESA-EAC-SADC Tripartite Framework: State of Play, February 2011.
101 COMESA document: COMESA-EAC-SADC Tripartite Framework: State of Play, February 2011.
102 COMESA document: COMESA-EAC-SADC Tripartite Framework: State of Play, February 2011.
103 COMESA document: Marawa, 'Infrastructure Development'.
104 COMESA document: Marawa, 'Infrastructure Development'.
105 Memorandum of Understanding on Inter Regional Cooperation and Integration Amongst COMESA, EAC and SADC, p. 3. Document obtained from COMESA Secretariat, August 2014. See also Tralac website: http://www.tralac.org/wp-content/blogs.dir/12/files/2011/uploads/FinalCommuniqueKampala_20081022.pdf.
106 UNECA, 'Assessing Regional Integration in Africa, V: Harmonizing Policies to Transform the Trading Environment'.
107 COMESA-EAC-SADC Second Tripartite Summit Communiqué, 12 June 2011, Sandton, Johannesburg, document obtained from COMESA Secretariat, August 2014, p. 4.
108 The International Bank for Reconstruction and Development/the World Bank, 'South Africa Economic Update Focus on Export Competitiveness' (2014), p. 36.
109 Sourced from InterVISTAS Consulting, 'Transforming Intra-African Air Connectivity', 2014, p. 27.
110 COMESA-EAC-SADC Second Tripartite Summit Communiqué, 12 June 2011. Upper Airspace is a controlled airspace that is below the division level and outside the terminal or airport airspace. It includes airways linking the airport with the upper airspace. Usually, air traffic is channelled along specified air routes and each air route is part of a network of generally fixed air routes within a flight information region (FIR). In terms of airspace control, (a) control zone (CTR) has a local air traffic control (ATC) and usually a circular area around the airport; (b) terminal control area (TMA) is your local ATC area reporting on incoming and outgoing flights between CTR and the Control Area (CTA); (c) the CTA is the general ATC within FIR below certain flight levels (lower airspace); and (d) the upper airspace control area is general ATC across FIRs. Upper airspace

heights differ according to countries. See International Civil Aviation Organization (ICAO), www.icao.int/.
111 See COMESA document, *Annual Report*, http://www.comesa.int/attachments/article/21/comesa_annualReport%202011_12_final.pdf.
112 'Open Skies: Transforming Intra-African Air Connectivity: The Economic Benefits of Implementing the Yamoussoukro Decision, IATA in partnership with AFCAC and AFRAA', InterVISTAS Consulting (July 2014), p. 110. See also Chris Giles, 'Sky's the Limit as Africa Makes Major Move towards Aviation Single Market', 31 January 2018, https://edition.cnn.com/2018/01/31/africa/african-union-single-air-airline/index.html.
113 See Kieron Monks, 'United States of Africa? African Union Launches All-Africa Passport', 19 July 2016, https://edition.cnn.com/2016/07/05/africa/african-union-passport/index.html.
114 See also Tralac website: http://www.tralac.org/wp-content/blogs.dir/12/files/2011/uploads/FinalCommuniqueKampala_20081022.pdf.
115 COMESA-EAC-SADC Tripartite Framework: State of Play, 2011.
116 COMESA-EAC-SADC Tripartite Framework: State of Play, 2011.
117 See also Tralac website: http://www.tralac.org/wp-content/blogs.dir/12/files/2011/uploads/FinalCommuniqueKampala_20081022.pdf.
118 Trade Law Centre for Southern Africa, 'Monitoring Regional Integration in Southern Africa'. See also Draft TFTA; and Ambassador A. J. V. Mwapachu, 'Report by the Chair of the Tripartite Task Force, Secretary-General of the EAC' (2011), http://www.eac.int/Tripartite-summit.html?showall=1.
119 COMESA Monetary Union, www.comesa.int.
120 European Central Bank, Eurosystem, 'Study of the Establishment of a Monetary Union among the Partner States of the East African Community' (2010). See also Janusz Rosiek and Robert W. Wlodarczyk, 'Comparative Analysis of the EU–27 Countries Labour Markets' Convergence', *Economics and Management*, Cracow University of Economics, Poland, vol. 17, no. 1 (2012), http://www.ecoman.ktu.lt/index.php/Ekv/article/view/2270/1752.
121 SADC Macroeconomic Policies and Convergence, TIFI Directorate (February 2012).
122 Jenkins and Thomas, 'The Macro-economic Frameworks', p. 7.
123 Fingleton, Garretsen and Martin, 'Shocking Aspects of Monetary Union: The Vulnerability of Regions in Euroland', p. 5: 'The symmetry condition means that economies should be roughly similar and synchronised so that shocks are symmetrical where all countries are roughly affected the same.'
124 COMESA Secretariat, 'Regional Integration', vol. 2 (2013). See also Munetsi Madakufamba, 'Region Takes Giant Step toward African Economic Community', *Southern African News Features* (SANF) vol. 9, no. 1 (January 2009), http://www.sardc.net/en/southern-african-news-features/region-takes-giant-step-toward-african-economic-community/.
125 Previous meetings of the TTCM were held in November 2014 and January 2015.
126 COMESA document: Tripartite Update, Trade and Customs Committee Meeting (9 February 2015).
127 COMESA-EAC-SADC Tripartite Summit, 'Communique of the Third Tripartite Summit, Vision: Towards a Single Market, Theme: Deepening COMESA-EAC-SADC Integration', Sharm El Sheikh, Arab Republic of Egypt, 10 June 2015, http://www.tralac.org/images/Resources/Tripartite_FTA/Third_Tripartite_Summit_Communique_10062015.pdf.

128 COMESA document: Tripartite Update, 2015. See also Edward Kafeero, 'Customs Law of the East African Community in Light of WTO Law and the Revised Kyoto Convention', *Westfälische, Wilhelms University*, Münster (2009), http://www.wwu-customs.de/research-activities/completed-projects/customs-law-of-the-east-african-community-in-light-of-wto-law-and-the-revised-kyoto-convention/.
129 Personal interviews, August and September 2014.
130 COMESA-EAC-SADC February 2011 Summit Report of the Chair of the TTF. See also SADC *Today*, May 2012.
131 Carlos Lopes, 'Mega Trade Agreement a Step Forward for the Continent', *UNECA* (12 June 2015), http://www.uneca.org/stories/mega-trade-agreement-step-forward-continent-%E2%80%93-carlos-lopes.
132 Personal interview, Lusaka, August 2014.
133 COMESA document: Tripartite Update, 2015.
134 COMESA document: Tripartite Update, 2015.
135 COMESA, 'COMESA Maintains High Confidence from Development Partners as It Turn 25 This Year [2019]", *COMESA E-Letter*, 5 April 2019, https://www.comesa.int/wp-content/uploads/2019/04/e-comesa-newsletter_579.pdf.
136 See South Africa's Department of International Relations and Cooperation (DIRCO), 'Remarks by President Jacob Zuma, during the South Africa/Zimbabwe Business Forum Meeting on the Occasion of President Mugabe's State Visit to South Africa, Pretoria', 9 April 2015, http://www.dirco.gov.za/docs/speeches/2015/jzum0409.htm.
137 UNECA, 'Status of Integration in Africa (SIA IV)', p. 10.
138 AU Programme for Infrastructure Development in Africa (PIDA), 'Interconnecting, Integrating, and Transforming a Continent: The Regional Infrastructure that Africa Needs to Integrate and Grow through 2020' (SOFRECO-Led Consortium [SOFRECO, MWH, Nathan, SOFRECOM, SYSTRA, ASCON and CABIRA]), p. 18.
139 UNECA, 'Movement of Goods and Services in Africa', p. 95.
140 AU, *Programme for Infrastructure Development in Africa: Addressing the Infrastructure Gap in Africa, to Speed Up Regional Integration*, Seventh Conference of African Ministers in Charge of Integration (4–18 July 2014), http://www.au-pida.org/.
141 UNECA, 'Assessing Regional Integration in Africa, IV', p. 105.
142 UNECA, 'Assessing Regional Integration in Africa, IV', p. 105.
143 An executive summary of the Regional Infrastructure Development Master Plan, as well as sectoral documents, can be found at SADC, 'Infrastructure', http://www.sadc.int/themes/infrastructure/.
144 See article by Deloitte and Touche, 'Partnering for Future Prosperity Delivering Successful Globally Competitive South African Cities' (2012), http://deloitteblog.co.za.www102.cpt1.host-h.net/wp-content/uploads/2012/08/How-do-SA-cities-increase-global-competitiveness-by-improving-their-physical-infrastructure.pdf.
145 Deloitte and Touche, 'Partnering for Future Prosperity Delivering Successful Globally Competitive South African Cities'.
146 Budget speech of South African finance minister Pravin Gordhan (27 February 2013), http://www.info.gov.za/speeches/docs/2013/budget2013.pdf, p. 16.
147 See Tamsin Oxford, 'Signs of New Era for SA Rail', *Mail and Guardian* (17 July 2015), http://mg.co.za/article/2015-07-17-signs-of-new-era-for-sa-rail.
148 See discussion by Transport World Africa, 'Smooth Flow of Cargo' (25 September 2014), http://www.transportworldafrica.co.za/2014/09/25/smooth-flow-of-cargo/.
149 AfDB, *Southern Africa Regional Integration Strategy Paper, 2011–15*.

150 See Deloitte and Touche, 'Partnering for Future Prosperity Delivering Successful Globally Competitive South African Cities', p. 8. See also Terence Creamer, 'SA Moves to Procure 7761 MW of Baseload IPP Power by 2025' (29 October 2012), http://www.polity.org.za.
151 Creamer, 'SA Moves to Procure 7761 MW of Baseload IPP Power by 2025', 2012.
152 See IATA, https://www.iata.org/policy/promoting-aviation/Pages/saatm.aspx. Accessed August 2019.
153 Africa/World News, 'COMESA at Twenty: Of the Successes, Challenges and Promises', *Addis Standard* (7 April 2015), http://addisstandard.com/comesa-at-twenty-of-the-successes-challenges-and-promises/.

5 Convergence and consolidation of multiple memberships: An attempted convergence

1 See also SADC Summit Communiques, http://www.sadc.int/files/3913/5292/8384/SADC_SUMMIT_COMMUNIQUES_1980-2006.pdf.
2 COMESA, EAC and SADC, *Final Communiqué*, p. 3. See also James Gathii, 'African Regional Trade Agreements as Flexible Legal Regimes', *North Carolina Journal of International Law and Commercial Regulation*, vol. 35, no. 3 (2010): 573.
3 COMESA, EAC and SADC, *Memorandum of Understanding on Inter-Regional Cooperation and Integration amongst COMESA, EAC and SADC*, unpublished official document, COMESA Secretariat August 2014, p. 3.
4 See Nagar, doctoral thesis, Wits University.
5 Nagar, 'Strengthening Policy Development on Inter-Regional Cooperation between the ACP and the AU'.
6 Raimo Väyrynen, 'Regionalism: Old and New', *International Studies Review*, vol. 5, no. 1 (March 2003): 25–51.
7 Trade has been fully liberalised in the EAC; however, the community is still faced with extensive non-tariff barriers. See EAC, *Status of Elimination of Non-Tariff Barriers in the East African Community*, vol. 8 (December 2014), https://www.eatradehub.org/status_of_elimination_of_non_tariff_bareers_in_the_east_african_community_volume_8_december_2014; European Commission, 'The Eastern African Community (EAC)', Fact Sheet on the Economic Partnership Agreements (October 2014), http://trade.ec.europa.eu/doclib/docs/2009/january/tradoc_142194.pdf.
8 See Trade Law Centre for Southern Africa (Tralac), *Cape to Cairo: Making the Tripartite Free Trade Area Work* (Tralac: Stellenbosch, 2011), p. 5: 'Swaziland has continuously benefited from a derogation to participate in COMESA as a non–reciprocal member of the FTA. … [Its] exporters enjoy non–reciprocal favourable access in COMESA markets while COMESA exporters face trade barriers in Swaziland.'
9 Väyrynen, 'Regionalism: Old and New', pp. 25–51.
10 Neamin Ashenafi, 'Ethiopia Admonishes Eritrea over South Sudan', *The Reporter*, vol. XVIII, no. 916 (29 March 2014), http://thereporterethiopia.com/issues/Reporter-Issue-916.pdf.
11 Ashenafi, 'Ethiopia Admonishes Eritrea over South Sudan'. See also Khalil Charles, 'Sudan Is Preparing Its Strategy for a Conflict with Its Neighbours', *Middle East Monitor* (8 January 2018), https://www.middleeastmonitor.com/20180108-sudan-is-preparing-its-strategy-for-a-conflict-with-its-neighbours/.

12 Kris Berwouts, 'DRC: President Tshisekedi's Leash Just Got a Little Tighter', *African Arguments*, 2 April 2019, https://africanarguments.org/2019/04/02/drc-president-tshisekedi-leash-tighter/.
13 See discussion by Tewodros Makonnen and Halellujah Lulie, 'Ethiopia, Regional Integration and the COMESA Free Trade Area', *South African International Affairs*, Occasional Paper 198 (August 2014): 1–28.
14 See International Coalition for the Responsibility to Protect (ICRtoP), http://icrtopblog.org/2015/01/16/an-indispensable-protection-tool-assessing-the-force-intervention-brigade-in-the-drc/.
15 Lopes, 'Mega Trade Agreement a Step Forward for the Continent'.
16 Lopes, 'Mega Trade Agreement a Step Forward for the Continent'. See also Gerhard Erasmus, 'The Tripartite FTA: Technical Features, Potential and Implementation', *Tralac* (18 June 2015), https://www.tralac.org/news/article/7574-tralac-s-daily-news-selection-19-june-2015.html.
17 Personal interview, Windhoek, August 2014.
18 Mirjam van Riesen, 'The Old Man and the Seas: The Future of the ACP/EU Relationship', *The Broker* (June 23, 2011). See also ODI Briefing Paper, 'Sanctions and South Africa's Neighbours' (1987), https://www.odi.org/sites/odi.org.uk/files/odi-assets/publications-opinion-files/6724.pdf.
19 Personal Interview, confidential, 22 August 2014.
20 Erasmus, 'The Tripartite FTA: Technical Features, Potential and Implementation'.
21 Makonnen and Lulie, 'Ethiopia, Regional Integration and the COMESA Free Trade Area', pp. 1–28.
22 See discussion by Makonnen and Lulie, 'Ethiopia, Regional Integration and the COMESA Free Trade Area', pp. 1–28.
23 Makonnen and Lulie, 'Ethiopia, Regional Integration and the COMESA Free Trade Area', p. 13.
24 See SAIIA, 'SACU Report', January 2007.
25 COMESA-EAC-SADC Tripartite Summit of Heads of State and Government, Final Communiqué, Kampala, Uganda, 22 October 2008, p. 3; see also Article 1 of the Memorandum of Understanding on Inter-Regional Cooperation and Integration amongst COMESA, EAC and SADC. Document obtained from COMESA Secretariat, August 2014, p. 3.
26 COMESA-EAC-SADC Second Tripartite Summit Communiqué, 12 June 2011, p. 4.
27 COMESA-EAC-SADC Tripartite Summit, 'Communique of the Third Tripartite Summit', 2015.
28 Final Communiqué of the COMESA-EAC-SADC Tripartite Summit of Heads State and Government, 'Vision: Towards a Single Market, Theme: Deepening COMESA-EAC-SADC Integration', Kampala, Uganda (22 October 2008), p. 3. Document obtained from COMESA Secretariat, August 2014: 'Variable geometry is a principle that allows for member states of a regional grouping to cooperate separately from other members as well as flexibility for progression in cooperation in a variety of areas and at different speeds.' See also Gathii, 'Neo-Liberal Turn in Regional Trade Agreements', pp. 647–8.
29 COMESA-EAC-SADC Tripartite Summit of Heads of State and Government, Final Communiqué, 2008.
30 Krugman, 'What's New about the "New Economic Geography"?', pp. 7–17. See also Martin, 'EMU versus the Regions?', pp. 23–4.

31 Marshall, *Principles of Economics*, cited in Nattrass, Wakeford and Muradzikwa, *Macro Economics Theory and Policy in South Africa*, p. 15:

> Marshallian-type economies refer to many of the assumptions that are similar to the foundational models for macro–economic and neoclassical models. These are: price adjustment in individual markets to ensure that no surpluses or gluts prevail; wage adjustment to ensure full employment; and the interest rate fluctuates to bring savings into line with investment. Typically it is assumed that under conditions of perfect competition, the operation of market forces will ensure that all resources are optimally allocated. Markets are assumed to be perfectly competitive and characterised by many buyers and sellers, homogeneous products, perfect knowledge and perfect factor mobility. The value of the economy is therefore measured by nominal and real values (the equilibrium values of real [real values are obtained by deflating nominal values by a price index] variables (employment, output) are determined in the labour and goods markets, whereas nominal [nominal values are, e.g., wages and output] variables (current prices) are determined in the money market). Given that real variables are not affected by changes in the money supply in such a model, money is then neutral. Hence this generates two parts of the theory: (i) a theory of how equilibrium output and employment are determined, and, (ii) a theory of how the aggregate price level is determined.

32 Gathii, 'African Regional Trade Agreements as Flexible Legal Regimes', pp. 666–7. See also Jagdish Bhagwati, *The World Trading System at Risk* (Princeton, NJ: Princeton University Press, 1991).
33 Krugman, 'What's New about the "New Economic Geography"?', pp. 7–17. See also Martin, 'EMU versus the Regions?', pp. 23–4.
34 Krugman, 'What's New about the "New Economic Geography"?', pp. 7–17. See also Martin, 'EMU versus the Regions?', pp. 23–4.
35 Gathii, 'African Regional Trade Agreements as Flexible Legal Regimes', p. 653.
36 Gathii, 'African Regional Trade Agreements as Flexible Legal Regimes', p. 653.
37 Gathii, 'African Regional Trade Agreements as Flexible Legal Regimes', p. 653.
38 Gathii, 'Neo-Liberal Turn in Regional Trade Agreements', 2011, p. 36. See also Panagariya, 'The Regionalism Debate', p. 36.
39 Erasmus, 'The Tripartite FTA'.
40 Peter Nyong'o, *Regional Integration in Africa*, pp. 280–1.
41 Peter Nyong'o. *Regional Integration in Africa*, pp. 280–1.
42 WTO report on Sri Lanka's tea trade, https://www.wto.org/english/tratop_e/tpr_e/g128_e.doc, p. 26.
43 Gathii, *African Regional Trade Agreements as Legal Regimes*, p. 677. See also Gathii, 'Neo-Liberal Turn in Regional Trade Agreements', pp. 1–50.
44 Panagariya, 'The Regionalism Debate', pp. 36.
45 Panagariya, 'The Regionalism Debate', p. 647. See also Bhagwati, *The World Trading System at Risk*.
46 Jenkins, Leape and Thomas (eds), *Gaining from Trade in Southern Africa*, pp. 2–3.
47 European Union, 'Southern African Region and the EU Complete Negotiations for an Economic Partnership Agreement', 22 July 2014, http://trade.ec.europa.eu/doclib/docs/2015/october/tradoc_153915.pdf.

48 See European Economic Commission, 'Overview of Economic Partnership Agreements', http://ec.europa.eu/trade/policy/countries-and-regions/development/economic-partnerships.
49 European Union, 'Southern African region and the EU complete negotiations for an Economic Partnership Agreement'.
50 Sindiso Ngwenya, 'Great Strides in Africa's Unity', *The Habari Network: Proposals for a More Effective African Growth and Opportunity Act* (Zambia: Common Market for Eastern and Southern African States (COMESA), February 2015), p. 21.
51 Gathii, 'African Regional Trade Agreements as Flexible Legal Regimes', p. 658. See also Panagariya, 'The Regionalism Debate'.
52 Friedrich Ebert Stiftung (FES), 'Deepening Integration in SADC', *Regional Integration in Southern Africa*, vol. 6 (December 2006).
53 FES, 'Deepening Integration in SADC'.
54 Erasmus, 'The Tripartite FTA'. See also COMESA-EAC-SADC Tripartite Trade and Customs Committee Meeting, 9 February 2015.
55 Brendan Vickers, 'SADC's International Trade Relations', in Charles Harvey (ed.), *Proceedings of the 2009 the Formative Process Research on Integration in Southern Africa (FOPRISA) Annual Conference*, 2010, pp. 129–49.
56 Paul Brenton, Frank Flatters and Paul Kalenga, 'Rules of Origin and SADC: The Case for Change in the Mid Term Review of the Trade Protocol', *Africa Region Working Paper Series* no. 83 (June 2005), p. iv. See also Gathii, 'Neo-Liberal Turn in Regional Trade Agreements'; and Gathii, *African Regional Trade Agreements as Legal Regimes*.
57 US AGOA trade with COMESA, https://ustr.gov/countries-regions/africa/regional-economic-communities-rec/common-market-eastern-and-Southern-africa-comesa.
58 Brenton, Flatters and Kalenga, 'Rules of Origin and SADC', pp. 1–44.
59 US AGOA trade with COMESA. See also Nomfundo Xenia Ngwenya, 'The United States', in Saunders, Dzinesa and Nagar (eds), *Region-Building in Southern Africa* (London: Zed Books, 2012), pp. 264–81.
60 Prince Heto, 'An AGOA with Even More Teeth', *Habari Network* (2015), p. 8. http://www.thehabarinetwork.com/.
61 AGOA trade with Southern Africa, http://www.ustr.gov/countries-regions/africa/Southern-africa/south-africa.
62 Stephen Lande, 'The Lande Opus on a Transformational AGOA'; and 'Great Strides in Africa's Unity', *Habari Network* (2015), pp. 4–6.
63 US trade with EAC, http://www.ustr.gov/countries-regions/africa/regional-economic-communities-rec; https://ustr.gov/countries-regions/africa/regional-economic-communities-rec/east-african-community.
64 Panagariya, 'The Regionalism Debate', p. 36.
65 Panagariya, 'The Regionalism Debate', p. 36.
66 This section of the chapter on South Africa in SACU was authored as a previous version in Dawn Nagar, 'The Era of Convergence: COMESA and SADC', in Daniel H. Levine and Dawn Nagar, *Region-Building in Africa*, pp. 191–212.
67 Brendan Vickers, 'South Africa's Trade Strategy and the BRICS', 2011. http://www.thedti.gov.za/sme_development/sumit/The%20BRICS%20Formation%20Benefits%20for%20the%20SMME%20sector%20Dr%20Brendan%20Vic.pdf. See also South African Government News Agency, 'SADC Ministers Discuss Integration, Industrialisation', *SA News Agency*, 28 April 2015, http://www.sanews.gov.za/africa/sadc-ministers-discuss-integration-industrialisation.

68 World Bank, 'South Africa Economic Update: Focus on Export Competitiveness', 2014, p. 31.
69 Personal interview conducted in Zambia, August 2014, with key COMESA officials who attended this summit. See important press release: Everson Mushava and Owen Gagare, 'Red Faces as SA, Namibia, Refuse to Sign SADC Trade Protocol', *News Day* (19 August 2014), https://www.newsday.co.zw/2014/08/19/red-faces-sa-namibia-refuse-sign-sadc-trade-protocol/.
70 Personal interview conducted at COMESA Secretariat, 22 August 2014. See also Mushava and Gagare, 'Red faces as South Africa, Namibia Refuse to Sign SADC Trade Protocol'.
71 See 'Zimbabwe, Russia Sign $3bn Platinum Deal', http://www.fin24.com/Economy/Zimbabwe-Russia-sign-3bn-platinum-deal-20140916. Personal interview, Confidential, 2014. See also 'Zimbabwe Commissions Chinese-Built Power Plant', *Xinhaunet* (26 July 2019), http://www.xinhuanet.com/english/2018-03/28/c_137072390.htm.
72 Personal interview conducted at SACU Secretariat, August 2014.
73 See description of 'swing countries' by Peter Draper, Durrel Halleson and Philip Alves,'SACU Regional Integration and the Overlap Issue in Southern Africa: From Spaghetti to Cannelloni?', *South African Institute of International Affairs*, Trade Policy Report no. 15 (January 2007), p. 21. A swing country is defined in the region by SACU as a country whose decisions will have significant bearing on SACU's trade significantly with South Africa. Such countries are Zimbabwe, Zambia, Malawi, Angola, the DRC and Kenya because of their population size, GDP and access to natural resources.
74 The range 2005–13 has been chosen as the assessment period because it is the period for which the most accurate relevant data are available from the World Bank Economic Indicators.
75 Barro and Sala-i-Martin, 'Convergence across States and Regions', pp. 112–13.
76 'COMESA-EAC-SADC Tripartite Trade and Customs Committee Meeting', Update, 9 February 2015.
77 Personal interview, Windhoek, August 2014.
78 Hudson,' Economic Expansion into Africa', pp. 128–49.
79 World Bank, 'South Africa Economic Update: Focus on Export Competitiveness', pp. 24–9.
80 World Bank, 'South Africa Economic Update: Focus on Export Competitiveness', p. 24.
81 World Bank, 'South Africa Economic Update: Focus on Export Competitiveness', p. 29.
82 Vickers, 'South Africa's Economic Diplomacy in a Changing Global Order', pp. 112–38.
83 Vickers, 'South Africa's Economic Diplomacy', pp. 129–30. See also Richard Gibb, 'Southern Africa in Transition: Prospects and Problems Facing Regional Integration', *Journal of Modern African Studies*, vol. 36, no. 2 (1998): 287–306.
84 Venables, 'Regional Integration Agreements: A Force for Convergence or Divergence?', pp. 1–17.
85 World Bank, 'GDP (Current US$)', http://data.worldbank.org/indicator/NY.GDP.MKTP.CD.
86 'Fears of More Violence in Lesotho after Killing of Ex-Army Boss', News24 (29 June 2015), http://www.news24.com/Africa/News/Fears-of-more-violence-in-Lesotho-after-killing-of-ex-army-boss-20150629.

87 'Platinum Miners in South Africa Go on Strike', *The Guardian* (London) (23 January 2014).
88 See article by Rene Vollgraaff, 'Eskom Has Slashed R400bn off SA's Economy in Last Seven Years', *Bloomberg* (8 April 2015), http://www.biznews.com/undictated/2015/04/08/eskom-slashed-10-off-the-size-of-sas-economy-in-seven-years/.
89 Office of the United States Trade Representative (USTR), '[Former] President Obama Removes Swaziland, Reinstates Madagascar for AGOA Benefits' (June 2014), https://ustr.gov/about-us/policy-offices/press-office/press-releases/2014/June/President-Obama-removes-Swaziland-reinstates-Madagascar-for-AGOA-Benefits.
90 USTR, 'Eswatini', https://ustr.gov/countries-regions/africa/southern-africa/eswatini.
91 Walter Mattli, *The Logic of Regional Integration*, p. 41.
92 Jorge Iván Canales–Kriljenko, Farayi Gwenhamo and Saji Thomas, 'Inward and Outward Spillovers in the SACU Area', *International Monetary Fund* Working Paper no. WP/13/31 (January 2013), https://www.imf.org/external/pubs/ft/wp/2013/wp1331.pdf. Data available from the South Africa Department of Trade and Industry (DTI): http://tradestats.thedti.gov.za/ReportFolders/reportFolders.aspx?sCS_referer=&sCS_ChosenLang=en.
93 Gathii, 'African Regional Trade Agreements', pp. 648–53; Panagariya, 'The Regionalism Debate', p. 36.
94 South African Foreign Policy Initiative (SAFPI), 'Namibia Sticks to Its EPA Guns' (18 December 2012), https://www.namibian.com.na/103603/archive-read/Namibia-sticks-to-its-EPA-guns. See also Vickers, 'SADC's International Trade Relations', pp. 129–49.
95 Putnam, 'Diplomacy and Domestic Politics: The Logic of Two-Level Games', p. 434. See also Stephan, Power, Hervey and Fonseca, *The Scramble for Africa in the 21st Century*, p. 224.
96 Putnam, 'Diplomacy and Domestic Politics: The Logic of Two-Level Games', p. 434. See also James Hentz, 'South Africa and the "Three-Level Game": Regionalism, Globalization and Domestic Politics', *Journal of Commonwealth and Comparative Politics*, vol. 46, no. 4 (2008): 490–515.
97 World Bank, 'South Africa Economic Update: Focus on Export Competitiveness', p. 35.
98 World Bank, 'South Africa Economic Update: Focus on Export Competitiveness', p. 35.
99 Dowrick and Nguyen, 'OECD Comparative Economic Growth 1950–85', p. 1010.
100 Jenkins and Thomas, 'The Macro-economic Frameworks', pp. 24–57; Lee, *The Political Economy of Regionalism in Southern Africa*, p. 217.
101 Barro and Sala-i-Martin, *Economic Growth*, pp. 16–21.
102 UN, *World Economic Situation 2015*, p. 112.
103 COMESA, EAC and SADC, *Final Communiqué*, p. 3. See also Gathii, 'African Regional Trade Agreements', p. 573.
104 COMESA, EAC and SADC, *Memorandum of Understanding on Inter-Regional Cooperation and Integration amongst COMESA, EAC and SADC*, p. 3.
105 Krugman, 'The Myth of Asia's Miracle', p. 67.
106 Brenton, Flatters and Kalenga, 'Rules of Origin and SADC', p. iv.
107 Dowrick and Nguyen, 'OECD Comparative Economic Growth 1950–85', p. 1010.
108 Jagdish N. Bhagwati, *The World Trading System at Risk* (Princeton, NJ: Princeton University Press, 2014), cited in Gathii, 'African Regional Trade Agreements', p. 657; Gathii, 'Neo-Liberal Turn in Regional Trade Agreements', pp. 1–50.

109 Gathii, *African Regional Trade Agreements as Legal Regimes*, p. xxix.
110 Mthuli Ncube, 'China the Biggest External Risk to Africa's Growth Outlook', *Terence CreamerMedia*, 3 September 2015.
111 Mike Haworth, 'How the US-China Trade War Is Likely to Affect SA', *Moneyweb* (3 July 2019), https://www.moneyweb.co.za/moneyweb-opinion/soapbox/how-the-us-china-trade-war-is-likely-to-affect-sa/.
112 Mthuli Ncube, 'China the Biggest External Risk to Africa's Growth Outlook'.
113 See World Bank Indicators reported on South Africa's total GDP for the period 2000–10, http://data.worldbank.org/indicator/NY.GDP.MKTP.CD?page=2.
114 UN, *World Economic Situation 2015*, p. 112.
115 UN, *World Economic Situation 2015*, p. 112.
116 See BusinessTech, 'South Africa's GDP Growth for 2018 Crawls to 0.8%' (5 March 2019), https://businesstech.co.za/news/finance/303364/south-africas-gdp-growth-for-2018-crawls-to-0-8/.
117 UN, *World Economic Situation 2015*, p. 112.
118 Personal interview, Windhoek, August 2014.

6 Pan-African economic integration

1 African Development Bank, 'Economic Outlook 2019', https://www.afdb.org/en/knowledge/publications/african-economic-outlook/.
2 See AU on the CFTA process, https://au.int/en/pressreleases/20180321/list-african-countries-signed-establishment-african-continental-free-trade. See also UNECA, https://www.uneca.org/publications/african-continental-free-trade-area-questions-answers.
3 Sindiso Ngwenya, 'Great Strides in Africa's Unity', p. 21.
4 See discussions by the African Development Bank (ADB), 'African Economic Outlook 2019: Integrating for Africa's Economic Prosperity', 2019, https://www.afdb.org/fileadmin/uploads/afdb/Documents/Publications/African_Economic_Outlook_2018_-_EN.pdf.
5 See, e.g., Jamie de Melo, 'The African Continental Free Trade Area: An Integration Trilemma', *Economic Research Forum*, 28 January 2019, https://theforum.erf.org.eg/2019/01/28/african-continental-free-trade-area-integration-trilemma/.
6 See discussion on Nigeria in the *Vanguard*, 'CFTA: I won't allow Nigeria to be dumping ground —Buhari', 22 March 2018, https://www.vanguardngr.com/2018/03/cfta-wont-allow-nigeria-dumping-ground-buhari/.
7 See discussion on Nigeria in 'Nigeria Signs African Free Trade Area', British Broadcasting Corporation (BBC) News (7 July 2019), https://www.bbc.com/news/world-africa-48899701.
8 COMESA document: Tripartite Update, 2017.
9 Paul R. Krugman, 'Growing World Trade: Causes and Consequences', *Brookings Papers on Economic Activity*, vol. 1 (1995): 327–77. Margaret MacMillan and Dani Rodrik, 'Globalization, Structural Change and Productivity Growth', in Marc Bacchetta and Marion Jansen (eds), *Making Globalisation Socially Sustainable* (Geneva: World Trade Organization (WTO) and International Labour Organization (ILO), 2011), pp. 49–80.

10 This section of the chapter on agro-processing of leather products is based on my personal conceptualisation of this project and research that I conducted, outlined in a concept note for a policy seminar concluded for Friedrich-Ebert-Stiftung, Johannesburg, South Africa, in October 2017. See also Nicholas Norbrook, 'South Africa's Industrial Policy Is Bearing Fruit', 14 June 2017, http://www.theafricareport.com/Interview/south-africa-industrial-policy-is-bearing-fruit.html (accessed 10 August 2017). See also Nagar, 'The Politics and Economics of Regional Integration', pp. 204 and 266.
11 See South African Revenue Services (SARS), 'South Africa's Exports and Imports 2016 with Major Trading Partners', http://www.sars.gov.za/ClientSegments/Customs-Excise/Trade-Statistics/Pages/Merchandise-Trade-Statistics.aspx (accessed 24 March 2017).
12 For the most robust study on the leather sector in Africa, see the Addis Ababa-based Common Market for Eastern and Southern Africa's Leather and Leather Products Institute (LLPI), https://www.allpi.int/.
13 See South African Skin, Hide and Leather Council, https://leatherpanel.org/content/south-african-skin-hide-and-leather-council.
14 See South African Skin, Hide and Leather Council.
15 DTI, 2015–16 annual report.
16 See New Economic Partnership for Africa's Development (NEPAD), meeting of the Southern African Business Forum, May 2016, Johannesburg.
17 This vision of economic growth is based on Jackson Ombui, a Kenyan professor at the Department of Public Health, Pharmacology and Toxicology at the Faculty of Veterinary Medicine, heading the Leather Science and Technology Training Programmes at the University of Nairobi, Kenya.
18 EU Leather producers, *see* EU Commission, 18 August 2017 <https://ec.europa.eu/growth/sectors/fashion/leather/eu-industry_en>.
19 World Bank, 'South Africa Economic Update: Promoting Domestic Competition Between Firms Could Help Spur Growth, Reduce Poverty', February 2016 <http://www.worldbank.org/en/country/southafrica/publication/south-africa-economic-update-promoting-faster-growth-poverty-alleviation-through-competition>.
20 World Bank, 'South Africa Economic Update'.
21 UNECA, 'Urbanization and Industrialization for Africa's Transformation', 2017 <https://www.uneca.org/sites/default/files/PublicationFiles/web_en_era-2017_01.pdf>.
22 The Kenyan Government included leather development in its Vision 2030 policy document. This vision spurs economic growth, and in 2012 the Kenyan government deployed Jackson Ombui, a Kenyan Professor at the Department of Public Health, Pharmacology and Toxicology at the Faculty of Veterinary Medicine, heading the Leather Science and Technology Training Programmes at the University of Nairobi, Kenya.
23 Nicholas Norbrook, 'Interview: Rob Davies, Minister of Trade and Industry, South Africa', 13 June 2016, in discussion with Rob Davies in the Africa Report, https://www.theafricareport.com/618/interview-rob-davies-minister-of-trade-and-industry-south-africa/.
24 Jan Tinbergen (ed.), *Shaping the World Economy: An Analysis of World Trade Flows in Shaping the World Economy* (New York: Twentieth Century Fund, 1962).
25 See World Bank Economic Data on the European Union, https://data.worldbank.org/indicator/NY.GDP.MKTP.CD?locations=EU-US-CN. Accessed August 2019.

26 Nagar, 'COMESA and SADC: The Era of Convergence? Economic Growth', in Daniel Levine and Dawn Nagar (eds), *Region-Building In Africa: Political and Economic Challenges* (New York: Palgrave, 2016), pp. 191–212.
27 See African, Caribbean and Pacific (ACP) Ambassadorial Working Group (AWG), *Transforming the ACP Group into an Effective Global Player*, on Final Report of the AWG on the Future Perspectives of the African Caribbean and Pacific Group (Brussels, 2 December 2014), pp. 38–42, http://www.acp.int/content/transforming-acp-group-effective-global-player-transformer-le-groupe-acp-en-un-acteur-mondia.
28 See European Centre for Development Policy Management (ECDPM) Report, 'Challenges for Africa-EU Relations in 2017', *Challenges Paper* no. 8 (January 2017), https://www.consilium.europa.eu/en/policies/eu-budgetary-system/multiannual-financial-framework/mff-negotiations/.
29 Joseph Hanlon, *Beggar Your Neighbours: Apartheid Power in South Africa* (London: Currey, 1986), pp. 169–70, 326.
30 See Andrew Sherriff, Niels Keijzer, Geert Laporte and Marc de Tollenaere, 'Negotiating a New Agreement with the ACP Post-2020: What Is at Stake in the Coming Months', *European Centre for Development Policy Management: (ECDPM)*, 15 January 2018, http://ecdpm.org/talking-points/negotiating-new-agreement-acp-post-2020-coming-months/.
31 See EU Commission, 'EU Trade with the Caribbean', http://ec.europa.eu/trade/policy/countries-and-regions/regions/caribbean.
32 Liam Halligan, 'Global Africa: The Last Investment Frontier?', in Adebajo and Whiteman, *The EU and Africa*, p. 183.
33 United Nations University Institute for Environment and Human Security, *World Risk Report 2016*.
34 Halligan, 'Global Africa', p. 184.
35 See Pacific Islands Forum Fisheries Agency (FFA) report, 'Blue Economy in the Pacific Region; Case Study: The Sustainable Management of Tuna Resources', July 2017, http://www.europarl.europa.eu/intcoop/acp/2017_vanuatu/pdf/blue-economy.pdf. See also the UN's seventeen SDGs of Agenda 2030, http://www.un.org/sustainabledevelopment/blog/2015/12/sustainable-development-goals-kick-off-with-start-of-new-year.
36 See Patrick Gomes, 'Unlocking the Potential of the Blue Economy', *In Depth News*, 8 June 2017, https://archive-2016-2017-indepthnews.net/index.php/sustainability/oceans-seas-and-marine-resources/1193-unlocking-the-potential-of-the-blue-economy.
37 See reports on the SDGs by the UNECA and ECLAC, https://www.uneca.org/stories/integrated-approach-sdgs-and-agenda-2063; and http://www.cepal.org/en/news/eclac-presents-model-institutional-framework-sustainable-development-goals-implementation.
38 See Francois Vreÿ, 'Tapping into Africa's Trillion-Dollar Blue Economy', *Cable News Network (CNN)*, 30 May 2017, http://edition.cnn.com/2017/05/30/africa/africa-blue-economy/index.html. See also the AU's 2050 Strategy, 'Africa's Integrated Maritime (AIM) Strategy', 2015, http://cggrps.org/wp-content/uploads/2050-AIM-Strategy_EN.pdf.
39 European Union, Aviation Africa, 'Second International Conference on Global Navigation Satellite Systems (GNSS/EGNOS) Technologies and Applications for the Development of Africa', 17–18 May 2017, http://www.aviation-africa.eu/news/second-international-conference-gnss-systems-gnssegnos-technologies-and-applications.

40 Upper airspace is a controlled airspace that is below the division level and outside the terminal or airport airspace. It includes airways linking the airport with the upper airspace. Usually, air traffic is channelled along specified air routes and each air route is part of a network of generally fixed air routes within a flight information region (FIR). In terms of airspace control, (a) control zone (CTR) has a local air traffic control (ATC) and usually a circular area around the airport; (b) terminal control area (TMA) is the local ATC area reporting on incoming and outgoing flights between CTR and the control area (CTA); (c) the CTA is the general ATC within an FIR below certain flight levels (lower airspace); and (d) the upper airspace control area has general ATC across FIRs. Upper airspace heights differ according to countries. See International Civil Aviation Organization (ICAO), www.icao.int (accessed 10 January 2015), cited in Nagar, 'The Politics and Economics of Regional Integration', pp. 175–6.
41 See World Bank Economic Indicators, 'Pacific Region', http://www.worldbank.org/en/country/pacificislands/overview.
42 See Weather Observer report, 6 September 2017, https://antiguaobserver.com/one-dead-after-hurricane-irma-destroyed-barbuda.
43 United Nations University Institute for Environment and Human Security, *World Risk Report 2016*, https://collections.unu.edu/eserv/UNU:5763/WorldRiskReport2016_small_meta.pdf.
44 United Nations University Institute for Environment and Human Security, *World Risk Report 2016*, pp. 48–9.
45 See Peter C. Gutkind and Immanuel Wallerstein (eds), *The Political Economy of Contemporary Africa* (California: Sage, 1976), pp. 30–57, cited in Kaye Whiteman and Dawn Nagar, 'From Eurafrique to Afro-Europa: Africa and Europe in a New Century', *CCR Report* (11–13 September 2008).

7 Pan-African security convergence: The evolution of collective security

1 Nagar, 'Pillars of Africa's Peace and Security Architecture: The African Standby Force', in Karbo and Virk (eds), *Towards a New Pax-Africana*, pp. 65–79.
2 Buzan and Wæver, *Regions and Powers*, p. 52.
3 Buzan and Wæver, *Regions and Powers*, p. 46.
4 General Carl von Clausewitz, *On War* (Chapel Hill, NC: Project Gutenberg, 1874, 1909, 2006), pp. 1–141.
5 Landsberg, *The Quiet Diplomacy of Liberation*, pp. 159–71. See also Adekeye Adebajo, *UN Peacekeeping in Africa: From the Suez Crisis to the Sudan Conflicts* (Boulder, CO: Lynne Rienner, 2011), p. 80. See also Annemarie Peen Rodt, 'Taking Stock of EU Military Conflict Management', *Journal of Contemporary European Research*, vol. 7, no. 1 (2011): 41–60, http://www.jcer.net/index.php/jcer/article/view/184/262.
6 This section is based on Nagar, 'Pillars of Africa's Peace and Security Architecture'.
7 Adebayo Adedeji, 'Comparative Strategies of Economic Decolonization in Africa', in Ali A. Mazrui and C. Wondji (eds), *General History of Africa, Vol. 8: Africa since 1935* (Oxford: Currey, 1999), pp. 407–17.
8 Arthur Boutellis and Paul D. Williams, *Peace Operations, the African Union, and the United Nations: Toward More Effective Partnerships* (New York: International Peace Institute (IPI), April 2013). See also Dawn Nagar, 'Defence Review: Who Will Keep the Peace?', *Sunday Independent*, 12 April 2015.

9 Franke Benedikt, *Security Cooperation in Africa: A Reappraisal* (Boulder, CO: Rienner, 2009), pp. 166–76; Eastern Africa Standby Force (EASF), 'History and Background', http://www.easfcom.org/index.php/en/about-easf/history-and-background.
10 EASF, 'History and Background'; and EASF, 'EASF Structures', http://www.easfcom.org/index.php/en/about-easf/easf-structures.
11 'Egypt, Ethiopia, and Sudan to Start Negotiations on Nile Water Dispute', Ahram Online, 18 June 2013, http://english.ahram.org.eg/NewsContent/1/64/74322/Egypt/Politics-/Egypt,-Sudan-and-Ethiopia-to-startnegotiations-on.aspx.
12 See Rex Chikoko, 'Chissano, Mbeki to Visit Malawi over Lake Border Row', Africa Review, 11 July 2013, http://www.africareview.com/news/Chissano--Mbeki-to-visit-Malawi-over-lake-border-row/979180-1911710sqgxovz/index.html.
13 Protocol Relating to the Establishment of the Peace and Security Council of the African Union, adopted at the First Ordinary Session of the African Union, Durban, 9 July 2002. See also Jakkie Cilliers, 'The African Standby Force: An Update on Progress', Paper no. 160 (Tshwane: ISS, 2008).
14 On the African Standby Force, see http://www.peaceau.org/en/page/82-african-standby-force-asf-amani-africa-1.
15 See a discussion on fighting terrorism in the Horn of Africa: https://www.globalcenter.org/events/engaging-civil-society-actors-in-the-rehabilitation-and-reintegration-of-individuals-associated-with-and-affected-by-terrorism/.
16 Buzan and Wæver, *Regions and Powers*, pp. 47–8.
17 Paul Taylor and A. J. R. Groom, *International Institutions at Work* (London: Pinter, 2006).
18 See discussion on totalitarian regimes in Juan Linz, *Totalitarian and Authoritarian Regimes* (Boulder, CO: Lynne Rienner, 2000).
19 See also SADC Summit of the Double Troika Plus Troop Contributing Countries, DRC and Madagascar (29 January 2015), www.sadc.int.
20 Institute for Security Studies, 'New "Super" Combat Brigade: Creation of an African Elite?', June 2013, https://issafrica.org/amp/iss-today/new-super-combat-brigade-creation-of-an-african-elite.
21 Boutellis and Williams, *Peace Operations, the African Union and the United Nations*, p. 6.
22 United Nations document: '"Intervention Brigade" Authorized as Security Council Grants Mandate Renewal for United Nations Mission in Democratic Republic of Congo', 28 March 2013, http://www.un.org/press/en/2013/sc10964.doc.htm.
23 Conflict in the DRC, focused on by the International Crisis Group, https://www.crisisgroup.org/africa/central-africa/democratic-republic-congo. In Africa, on the whole, there is an alarming number of a hundred thousand children being forced into rebel movements and militia groups to form part of rebel movements and their gendarmerie. See statistics provided by Child Soldiers Organisation, https://www.childsoldiers.org/.
24 Paul Mulindwa, 'Uganda', 'Security and Governance in the Great Lakes Region', paper presented at *CCR Seminar* (9–10 May 2015); see CCR, seminar report, no. 51, 2015.
25 Mulindwa, 'Uganda'.
26 Henry Wasswa, 'Will Uganda Pay Up for Congo Occupation?', *Global Policy Forum* (26 July 2007), https://www.globalpolicy.org/component/content/article/163/28685.html.
27 See CCR, seminar report, no. 51, 2015.
28 Mulindwa, 'Uganda'.

29 United Nations High Commissioner for Refugees (UNHCR), 'Thousands of Refugees Continue to Flee Burundi', 30 June 2015, with UN refugee estimates at 66,612 from Burundi in Tanzania; 56,508 in Rwanda; 11,500 in the Congo; 9,038 in Uganda; and 400 in Zambia. http://www.unhcr.org/55929f206.html.
30 AfDB Strategy Paper, 'Burundi 2012–16' (October 2011). See also Economy Watch, http://www.economywatch.com/economic-statistics/country/Burundi/.
31 BBC, 'Burundi President Pierre Nkurunziza Sworn In for Third Term', 2015.
32 World Bank, 'The World Bank's Rwanda Economic Update: Seizing the Opportunities for Growth with a Special Focus on Harnessing the Demographic Dividend' (29 January 2014), https://www.worldbank.org/en/news/press-release/2014/01/29/the-world-banks-rwanda-economic-update-seizing-the-opportunities-for-growth-with-a-special-focus-on-harnessing-the-demographic-dividend.
33 World Bank statistics on Rwanda's donor funding, http://search.worldbank.org/all?qterm=Rwanda%27s+donor+funds+recieved+at+2013&title=&filetype=.
34 See CCR seminar report, no. 51, 2015.
35 United Nations Environment Programme (UNEP) and the Mission des Nations Unies en République Démocratique du Congo (MONSUCO), 'Experts' Background Report on Illegal Exploitation and Trade in Natural Resources Benefitting Organized Criminal Groups and Recommendations on MONSUCO's Role in Fostering Stability and Peace in Eastern DR Congo', 15 April 2015, http://wedocs.unep.org/handle/20.500.11822/22074?show=full. See also ECDPM Report, 'Artisanal Mining in the Democratic Republic of Congo: Time to Get Down to Earth' (March 2018), https://ecdpm.org/wp-content/uploads/DP-223-Artisanal-gold-mining-in-DRC.pdf.
36 UNEP and MONSUCO, 'Experts' Background Report'.
37 See discussion, 'South Sudanese Vice President Ready to Offer Positions to Rebel Leader', *Sudan Tribune* (17 June 2015), http://www.sudantribune.com/spip.php?article55367.
38 UNEP and MONSUCO, 'Experts' Background Report'.
39 UNEP and MONSUCO, 'Experts' Background Report'.
40 UNEP and MONSUCO, 'Experts' Background Report'.
41 UNEP and MONSUCO, 'Experts' Background Report'.
42 UNEP and MONSUCO, 'Experts' Background Report'.
43 COMESA Thirty-Second Meeting of the Council of Ministers, Kinshasa, DRC, 22–24 February 2014, CS/CM/XXX11/2.
44 COMESA defines a new strategy for its peace and security framework, https://www.comesa.int/services/governance-peace-and-security-unit/.
45 Balaam and Veseth, *Introduction to Political Economy*, pp. 110–27.
46 The African Renaissance and International Co-operation Fund Act, Act No. 51 of 2000, https://www.gov.za/documents/african-renaissance-and-international-co-operation-fund-act.
47 Nagar, 'Defence Review: Who Will Keep the Peace?', *Sunday Independent* (12 April 2015), p. 16.
48 Tom Head, 'Revealed: What Load Shedding Has Cost the SA Economy in 2019', *The South African*, 18 March 2019, https://www.thesouthafrican.com/news/eskom-load-shedding-latest-cost-in-2019/.
49 The World Fact Book, Central Intelligence Agency, United States, 2015, https://www.cia.gov/library/publications/the-world-factbook/geos/print_sf.html.
50 Nagar, 'Regional Economic Integration', in Saunders, Dzinesa and Nagar (eds), *Region-Building in Southern Africa*, pp. 131–47.

51 World Bank, 'Proposed Grant of $73.1 million for the DRC', http://www-wds.worldbank.org/external/default/WDSContentServer/WDSP/IB/2014/03/05/000456286_20140305164405/Rendered/INDEX/774200REPLACEM0140Box382121B00OUO90.txt.
52 NCACC, *Third Quarterly Report*, 2014.
53 See discussion in Landsberg and van Wyk (eds), *South African Foreign Policy Review*, pp. 90–1.
54 SADC Extraordinary Summit of the Double Troika Communique, 3 July 2015, http://www.sadc.int/files/8114/3598/7203/Draft_Communique_on_3_July__2135hrs_corrected.pdf.
55 Anthoni van Nieuwkerk, 'A Review of South Africa's Peace Diplomacy since 1994', in Landsberg and van Wyk (eds), *South African Foreign Policy Review*, pp. 84–107.
56 Francis Deng and J. Stephen Morrison, *US Policy to End Sudan's War: Report of the CSIS Task Force on U.S.–Sudan Policy* (Washington, DC: Center for Strategic and International Studies, 2001), p. 3.
57 See African Union, 'African Charter on Human and People's Rights', http://www.achpr.org/instruments/achpr/.
58 See COMESA profile, https://www.comesa.int/comesa-institutions/.
59 Reuters, 'Zambia Seeks to Block Arms for Zimbabwe', *New York Times* (22 April 2008).
60 Henning Melber, 'Global Trade Regimes and Multi-Polarity: The US and Chinese Scramble for African Resources and Markets', in Roger Southall and Henning Melber (eds), *A New Scramble for Africa: Imperialism, Investment and Development* (Scottsville: University of KwaZulu-Natal Press, 2009), p. 74. See also Reuters, 'Zambia Seeks to Block Arms for Zimbabwe'.
61 Reuters, 'Zambia Seeks to Block Arms for Zimbabwe'.
62 COMESA Observer Mission in Zimbabwe in July 2013, https://www.eisa.org.za/pdf/zim2013comesa.pdf.
63 COMESA Observer Mission in Malawi's May 2014 elections, https://www.comesa.int/wp-content/uploads/2019/02/2015-Comesa-Annual-Report.pdf.
64 Seifulaziz Milas, 'Egypt/Ethiopia: There Will Be No Water War in the Nile Basin Because No One Can Afford It', *African Arguments* (10 June 2013), http://allafrica.com/stories/201306110820.html.
65 See Milas, 'Africa' https://allafrica.com/stories/201306110820.html. See also 'Egypt: Ethiopian Envoy Lauds Sudan's Stance on Nile Dam, Criticizes Egypt', *Sudan Tribune* (11 June 2013), https://sudantribune.com/spip.php?article46915. Zeryhun Kassa, 'Ethiopia: Hailemariam – Egypt Goes to War over Nile Only If Leaders Go Mad', *All Africa* (12 June 2013).
66 See Milas, 'Africa'. See also Kassa, 'Ethiopia'.
67 See Marthe van der Wolf, 'Egypt: Ethiopia, Egypt Meet to Ease Nile Dam Tensions', *All Africa* (18 June 2013).
68 Personal interview, August 2014.
69 UN document, S/2014/740, report of the secretary general on the situation with respect to piracy and armed robbery at sea off the coast of Somalia (16 October 2014), http://www.un.org/en/ga/search/view_doc.asp?symbol=S/2014/740.
70 COMESA document: 'COMESDA–EU Launch a Programme to Fight Piracy' (12 September 2014).
Personal interview, August 2014.
71 SADC–EU Ministerial Political Dialogue Communique (Maputo, Mozambique) (20 March 2013).

72 Jens Vestergaard Madsen, Conor Seyle, Kellie Brandt, Ben Purser, Heather Randall, and Kellie Roy, *The State of Maritime Piracy*, Oceans beyond Piracy Project: One Earth Future Foundation (2013), http://oceansbeyondpiracy.org/sites/default/files/attachments/SoP2013-Digital.pdf.
73 UN document, S/2014/740, report of the secretary general on the situation with respect to piracy and armed robbery at sea off the coast of Somalia (16 October 2014), p. 2.
74 COMESA document: 'COMESDA–EU Launch a Programme to Fight Piracy'.

8 Analysis and normative proposals: Pan-African convergence theories

1 Nagar, 'Strengthening Policy Development on Inter-Regional Cooperation between the ACP and the AU', *Concept Note*.
2 Erasmus, 'The Tripartite FTA'.
3 Gathii, 'Neo-Liberal Turn in Regional Trade Agreements', pp. 1–50; Panagariya, 'The Regionalism Debate', pp. 1–60; and Bhagwati, *The World Trading System at Risk*.
4 Panagariya, 'The Regionalism Debate', p. 36.
5 World Bank, 'South Africa Economic Update: Focus on Export Competitiveness', p. 31.
6 Krugman, 'The Myth of Asia's Miracle'. See also Dowrick and Nguyen, 'OECD Comparative Economic Growth 1950–85', p. 1010.
7 World Bank, 'South Africa Economic Update: Focus on Export Competitiveness', p. 35.
8 World Bank, 'South Africa Economic Update: Focus on Export Competitiveness', p. 35. See also Galor, 'Convergence? Inferences from Theoretical Models'; Durlauf and Johnson, 'Multiple Regimes and Cross Country Growth Behaviour', pp. 365–84; Quah, 'Convergence Empirics across Economics with (Some) Capital Mobility'.
9 European Union, 'Southern African Region and the EU Complete Negotiations for an Economic Partnership Agreement'.
10 O Nying'uro, 'The EAC's Prospects on the Global Stage', pp. 31–44.
11 See critical scholars provide insight on these debates in Nagar and Mutasa (eds), *Africa and the World*.
12 Personal interview, Lusaka, August 2014.
13 Barro and Sala-i-Martin, 'Convergence across States', pp. 112–13.
14 See CCR, *South Africa in Southern Africa* (November 2012).
15 World Bank, 'South Africa Economic Update: Focus on Export Competitiveness', p. 34.
16 Panagariya, 'The Regionalism Debate', pp. 1–60.
17 See also Africa/World News, 'COMESA at Twenty: Of the Successes, Challenges and Promises'.
18 Gathii, 'Neo-Liberal Turn in Regional Trade Agreements'.
19 Paul Kalenga, 'COMESA-EAC-SADC Tripartite Mechanism on Non-Tariff Barriers to Trade', *World Trade Report* (2012), p. 117.
20 Nagar, 'Pillars of Africa's Peace and Security Architecture: The African Standby Force', Karbo and Virk (eds), *Towards a New Pax-Africana*, pp. 65–79.

9 Conclusion

1. Lamy, 'Regional Integration in Africa: Ambitions and Vicissitudes'.
2. See also Gathii, 'Neo-Liberal Turn in Regional Trade Agreements', pp. 1–50; and Gathii, *African Regional Trade Agreements as Legal Regimes*, pp. 572–667.
3. Personal interview with SADC Secretariat, Gaborone, Botswana, July 2013.
4. See AU, '689th PSC Meeting on the AU Peace Fund and the AU-UN Partnership for Predictable Financing of AU Peace and Security Activities', 2017, www.peaceau.org/en/article/689th-psc-meeting-on-the-au-peace-fund-and-the-au-un-partnership-for-predictable-financing-of-au-peace-and-security-activities.

Bibliography

Acharya, Amitav. 'Regional Security Complexes in the Third World: Stability and Collaboration'. Unpublished Essay. 1992.

Adebajo, Adekeye. 'Security, Governance, and Economic Issues in the SADC Region'. *Presentation Made to the Swiss Agency for Development and Cooperation (SIDA)*. Tshwane (25 June 2014).

Adebajo, Adekeye. 'Southern Africa's Fledgling Security Architecture'. In *The African Union and Its Institutions*, edited by John Akokpari, Angela Ndinga-Muvumba and Tim Murithi. Auckland Park, South Africa: Jacana Media, 2008.

Adebajo, Adekeye. 'The Peacekeeping Travails of the AU and the Regional Economic Communities'. In *The African Union and Its Institutions*, edited by John Akokpari, Angela Ndinga-Muvumba and Tim Murithi. Auckland Park, South Africa: Jacana Media, 2008.

Adebajo, Adekeye. 'Towers of Babel? The African Union and the European Union'. In *The Curse of Berlin: Africa after the Cold War*, edited by Adekeye Adebajo. Scottsville: University of KwaZulu-Natal Press, 2010.

Adebajo, Adekeye. *UN Peacekeeping in Africa: From the Suez Crisis to the Sudan Conflicts*. Boulder, CO: Lynne Rienner, 2011.

Adedeji, Adebayo. 'Political Economy: Looking Inside from the Outside'. In *South Africa in Africa: The Post-Apartheid Era*, edited by Adekeye Adebajo, Adebayo Adedeji and Chris Landsberg. Scottsville: University of KwaZulu-Natal Press, 2007.

Adedeji, Adebayo. *South Africa and Africa: Within or Apart*. London: Zed Books, 1996.

Aghrout, Ahmed. 'Africa's Experiences with Regional Cooperation and Integration: Assessing Some Groupings'. *Istituto Italiano per l'Africa el'Oriente (IsIAO)* (1992).

Ajiki, Sanmi. 'The Challenger – AAF-SAP'. In *Adebayo Adedeji: A Rainbow in the Sky of Time His Vision; His Mission; His Life and Times*. Lagos, Nigeria: Newswatch Books, 2000.

Ajulu, Rok. 'African Security: Can Regional Organisations Play a Role?'. In *Peace in Africa: Towards a Collaborative Security Regime*, edited by Shannon Field. Johannesburg: Institute for Global Dialogue, 2004.

Akokpari, John. 'Dilemmas of Regional Integration and Development in Africa'. In *The African Union and Its Institutions*, edited by John Akokpari, Angela Ndinga-Muvumba and Timothy Murithi. Auckland Park, South Africa: Jacana Media, 2008.

Alden, Chris, and Garth le Pere. 'South Africa's Post-Apartheid Foreign Policy – from Reconciliation to Revival?' *Adelphi Paper*, 43, no. 362 (2003): 71–76.

Alden, Chris, and Maxi Schoeman, 'South Africa's Symbolic Hegemony in Africa', *London School of Economics, London; and University of Pretoria, South Africa*, 52 no. 2 (2015): 239–254.

Alden, Chris, and Mills Soko. 'South Africa's Economic Relations with Africa: Hegemony and Its Discontents'. *Journal of Modern African Studies* 43, no. 3 (2005): 367–92.

Ali, Ali Abdel Gadir. 'The Rediscovery of the African Alternative Framework to Structural Adjustment Programmes'. In *African Development in the 21st Century: Adebayo Adedeji's Theories and Contributions*, edited by Amos Sawyer, Afeikhena Jerome and Ejeviome Eloho Otobo. Johannesburg: Wits University Press, 2015.

Anglin, Douglas. 'Economic Liberation and Regional Cooperation in Southern Africa'. *International Organisation* 37, no. 4 (1983): 681–711.

Angola Briefings. *Review of African Political Economy*, no. 5 (October 1981).

Asante, Samuel K. B. *Regionalisation and Africa's Development: Expectations, Reality and Challenges*. London: Palgrave Macmillan, 1997.

Asante, Samuel K. B. 'The Years of Preparation: Adedeji and the ECA'. In *African Development: Adebayo Adedeji's Alternative Strategies*. Asante. Lagos: Spectrum, 1991.

Asante, Samuel K. B., and David Chanaiwa. 'Pan-Africanism and Regional Integration'. In *General History of Africa, VIII: Africa Since 1935*, edited by Ali A. Mazrui and C. Wondji. Paris: UNESCO, 1993.

Ashenafi, Neamin. 'Ethiopia Admonishes Eritrea over South Sudan'. *The Reporter* XVIII, no. 916 (2014). https://allafrica.com/stories/201403311126.html. Accessed July 2019.

Azarya, Victor. 'Reordering State-Society Relations: Incorporation and Disengagement'. In *The Precarious Balance: State and Society in Africa*, edited by Donald Rothchild and Naomi Chazan. Boulder: Westview Press, 1988.

Balaam, David, and Michael Veseth. *Introduction to Political Economy*. Upper Saddle River: Pearson Prentice Hall, 2001.

Balassa, Bela. *The Theory of Economic Integration*. Homewood: Richard D. Irwin, 1961.

Baldwin, Robert E. 'Openness and Growth: What's the Empirical Relationship?'. In *Challenges to Globalization: Analyzing the Economics*, edited by Robert E. Baldwin and L. Alan Winters. Chicago: Chicago University Press, 2004.

Barro, Robert J. 'Economic Growth in a Cross Section of Countries'. *Quarterly Journal of Economics* 106 no. 2 (1991): 407–43.

Barro, Robert J., and Xavier Sala-i-Martin. 'Convergence Across States and Regions'. *Brookings Papers on Economic Activity* 1 (1991).

Barro, Robert J., and Xavier Sala-i-Martin. *Economic Growth*. 2nd ed. Cambridge: MIT Press, 2004.

Batchelor, Peter, and Paul Dunne. 'The Restructuring of South Africa's Defence Industry'. *African Security Review* 7, no. 6 (1998): 27–43.

Baumol, William J. 'Productivity Growth, Convergence, and Welfare: What the Long-Run Data Show'. *American Economic Review* 76, no. 5 (December 1986): 1072–85.

Ben-David, Dan. 'Trade and Convergence among Countries'. *Journal of International Economics* 40 no. 3–4 (May 1996): 279–98.

Berlin, Isaiah. *Auguste Comte Memorial Lectures 1953–1962*. London: Athlone Press, 1964.

Besada, Hany, Ariane Goetz and Karolina Werner. 'African Solutions for African Problems and Shared R2P'. In *Crafting an African Security Architecture*, edited by Hany Besada. Burlington: Ashgate, 2010.

Bhagwati, Jagdish. *The World Trading System at Risk*. Princeton: Princeton University Press, 1991.

Bienefield, Manfield, and Duncan Innes. 'Capital Accumulation and South Africa'. *Review of African Political Economy*, no. 7 (1976): 31–55.

Bischoff, Paul-Henri. 'How Far, Where To? Regionalism, the Southern African Development Community and Decision-Making into the Millenium'. In *Globalisation and Emerging Trends in African States' Foreign Policy-Making Process*, edited by Korwa Gombe Adar and Rok Ajulu. Aldershot: Ashgate, 2002.

Boutellis, Arthur, and Williams Paul. *Peace Operations, the African Union and the United Nations: Toward More Effective Partnerships*. New York: International Peace Institute (IPI), April 2013.

Bremmer, Ian. 'State Capitalism Comes of Age: The End of the Free Market?'. *Foreign Affairs* 88, no. 3 (May/June 2009).

Brenton, Paul, Frank Flatters and Paul Kalenga. 'Rules of Origin and SADC: The Case for Change in the Mid Term Review of the Trade Protocol'. *Africa Region Working Paper Series No. 83* (June 2005).

Bull, Hedley. *An Anarchical Society: A Study of Order in World Politics*. London: Macmillan, 1977.

Buzan, Barry, and Ole Wæver. *Regions and Powers: The Structure of International Security*. London: Cambridge University Press, 2003.

Callaghy, Thomas M. 'The State and the Development of Capitalism in Africa: Theoretical, Historical, and Comparative Reflections'. In *The Precarious Balance: State and Society in Africa*, edited by Donald Rothchild and Naomi Chazan. 1988.

Canales-Kriljenko, Jorge Iván, Farayi Gwenhamo and Saji Thomas. 'Inward and Outward Spillovers in the SACU Area'. *International Monetary Fund*. Working Paper no. WP/13/31. (January 2013).

Carmignami, Fabrizio. 'A Note on Income Converge Effects in Regional Integration Agreements'. *Economic Analysis Division, United Nations Economic Commission for Europe (UNECE)* (2007).

Carrim, Yasmin. *The Preferential Trade Area for Eastern and Southern Africa and COMESA: Call for Suspension*. Cape Town: University of the Western Cape, 1994.

Cass, David. 'Optimum Growth in an Aggregate Model of Capital Accumulation'. *Review of Economic Studies* 32, no. 3 (1965): 233–40.

Chikova, Alison. 'Energy Trading in the Southern African Power Pool'. *SAPP*. (March 2009). https:www.sapp.co.zw. Accessed October 2010.

Chipeta, Chinyamata, and Robert Davies. *Regional Relations and Cooperation Post-Apartheid*. Gaborone: SADC, 1993.

Clapham, Christopher. 'The Changing World of Regional Integration in Africa'. In *Regional Integration in Southern Africa: Comparative International Perspective*, edited by Christopher Clapham, Gregg Mills, Anna Morner and Elizabeth Sidiropoulos. Cape Town: South African Institute for International Affairs (SAIIA), 2001.

Cliffe, Lionel, and Peter Lawrence. 'The Struggle for the State in Southern Africa'. *Review of African Political Economy* 3, no. 5 (October 1981): 4–11.

Creamer, Terence. 'SA Moves to Procure 7761 MW of Baseload IPP Power by 2025'. 29 October 2012, http://www.polity.org.za. Accessed December 2012.

Curtis, Devon. 'South Africa: "Exporting Peace" to the Great Lakes Region?' In *South Africa in Africa: The Post-Apartheid Era*, edited by Adekeye Adebajo, Adebayo Adedeji and Chris Landsberg. Scottsville: University of KwaZulu-Natal Press, 2007.

Davies, Rob. 'South Africa in Southern Africa'. Seminar Report. *Centre for Conflict Resolution* (November 2012).

Deloitte and Touche. 'Partnering for Future Prosperity Delivering Successful Globally Competitive South African Cities'. (2012). http://deloitteblog.co.za.www102.cpt1.host-h.net/wp-content/uploads/2012/08/How-do-SA-cities-increase-global-competitiveness-by-improving-their-physical-infrastructure.pdf. Accessed December 2012.

Dersso, Solomon A. 'The Role and Place of the African Standby Force within the African Peace and Security Architecture'. *Institute for Security Studies, Paper 209*, January 2009.

Deutsch, Karl W., et al. *Political Community and the North Atlantic Area: International Organisation in light of Historical Experience*. Princeton, NJ: Princeton University Press, 1957.

De Vos, Pierre. 'UCT Law Faculty Statement on Suspension of SADC Tribunal'. 19 September 2012. http://constitutionallyspeaking.co.za/uct-law-faculty-statement-on-suspension-of-sadc-tribunal/. Accessed December 2013.

Dollar, David. 'Outward-Oriented Developing Economies Really Do Grow More Rapidly: Evidence from 95 LDCs, 1976–1985'. *World Bank Economic Development and Cultural Change* 40, no. 3 (April 1992): 523–44.

Dowrick, Steve, and Duc-Tho Nguyen. 'OECD Comparative Economic Growth 1950–85: Catch-Up and Convergence'. *The American Economic Review* 79, no. 5 (December 1989):1010–30.

Draper, Peter. 'Implementing Development Corridors: Lessons from the Maputo Corridor'. *SAIIA Policy Briefing* 54 (2012).

Draper, Peter, Durrel Halleson and Philip Alves. 'SACU Regional Integration and the Overlap Issue in Southern Africa: From Spaghetti to Cannelloni?'. *South African Institute of International Affairs*, Trade Policy Report no. 15 (January 2007).

Durlauf, Steven N., and Paul A. Johnson, 'Multiple Regimes and Cross Country Growth Behaviour'. *Journal of Applied Econometrics* 10, no. 4. (October–December 1995): 365–84.

ECDPM Report. 'Artisanal Mining in the Democratic Republic of Congo: Time to Get Down to Earth' (March 2018). https://ecdpm.org/wp-content/uploads/DP-223-Artisanal-gold-mining-in-DRC.pdf. Accessed July 2019.

Edmondson, Locksley. 'Africa and the Developing Regions'. In *General History of Africa, VIII: Africa since 1935*, edited by Ali A. Mazrui and C. Wondji. Paris: UNESCO, 1993.

Edwin, Walter, and Orondo Orchoro. 'Trade and Industrial Development in the EAC'. In *The Making of A Region*, edited by Rok Ajulu, 127–134. Johannesburg: Institute for Global Dialogue, 2005.

Elaigwu, J. Isawa, and Ali A. Mazrui. 'Nation-Building and Changing Political Structures'. In *General History of Africa, VIII: Africa since 1935*, edited by Ali A. Mazrui and C. Wondji. Paris: UNESCO, 1993.

Erasmus, Gerhard. 'Namibia and the Southern African Development Community'. In *Namibia's Foreign Relations: Historic Contexts, Current Dimensions, and Perspectives for the 21st Century*, edited by Anton Bösl, André du Pisani and Dennis U Zaire. Windhoek: Macmillan Education Namibia, 2014.

Erasmus, Gerhard. 'The Tripartite FTA: Technical Features, Potential and Implementation'. *Tralac*. 18 June 2015. http://www.tralac.org/discussions/article/7568-the-Tripartite-fta-technical-features-potential-and-implementation.html. Accessed February 2016.

Evans, Osabuohien, and Efobi Uchenna. 'Trade Outcomes in Africa's Regional Economic Communities and Institutional Quality: Some Policy Prescriptions', *Petroleum – Gas University of Ploiesti Bulletin, Technical Series*, 64, no. 4 (October 2012).

Fingleton, Bernard, Harry Garretsen and Ron Martin. 'Shocking Aspects of Monetary Union: The Vulnerability of Regions in Euroland'. *Special Issue of Journal of Economic Geography on the Future of Europe* (2 April 2014).

First, Ruth. *Power in Africa*. New York: Pantheon, 1970.

Flatters, Frank. Eemeritus Professor at Queens University Canada on SADC Rules of Origin, See discussion in Southern African International SAIIA SADC Barometer 1 (March 2003).

Friedland, Elaine. 'The Southern African Development Coordination Conference and the West: Cooperation or Conflict?' *Journal of Modern African Studies* 23, no. 2 (June 1985): 287–314.

Friedmann, John. 'A General Theory of Polarized Development'. In *The Political Economy of International Relations*, edited by Robert Gilpin. Princeton: Yale University Press, 1987.

Galor, Oded. 'Convergence? Inferences from Theoretical Models'. *The Economic Journal* 106, no. 437 (July 1996):1056–69.

Gambari, I. A. *Political and Comparative Dimensions of Regional Integration: the Case of ECOWAS*. Atlantic Highlands: Humanities Press International, 1991.

Gathii, James Thuo, 'Neo-Liberal Turn in Regional Trade Agreements'. *Albany Law School Legal Studies, Research Paper Series*, no. 40 (2010–2011).

Gathii, James Thuo. 'African Regional Trade Agreements as Flexible Legal Regimes'. *North Carolina Journal of International Law and Commercial Regulation* 35, no. 3 (2010): 571–668.

Gathii, James Thuo. *African Regional Trade Agreements As Legal Regimes*. London: Cambridge University Press, 2011.

Gerschenkron, Alexander. 'Economic Backwardness in Historical Perspective'. In *The Progress of Under-developed Areas*, edited by Bert F. Hoselitz. Chicago: University of Chicago Press, 1952.

Gibb, Richard. *Rationalisation or Redundancy? Making Eastern and Southern Africa's Regional Trade Units Relevant*. The Brenthurst Foundation (2006).

Gibb, Richard. 'Southern Africa in Transition: Prospects and Problems Facing Regional Integration'. *Journal of Modern African Studies* 36, no. 2 (1998): 287–306.

GIGA. 'The Preferential Trade Area PTA for Eastern and Southern Africa: Achievements, Problems and Prospects'. *Spectrum* 24, no. 2 (1989): 157–71.

Gillson, Ian. 'Deepening Regional Integration to Eliminate the Fragmented Goods Market in Southern Africa'. *World Bank*. 2012.

Gilpin, Robert. *The Political Economy of International Relations*. Princeton: Yale University Press, 1987.

Gordhan, Pravin. Budget Speech of South African Finance Minister. 27 February 2013. https://www.gov.za/minister-finance-pravin-gordhan-presents-2013-budget-speech. Accessed July 2019.

Gould, Jonathan, and John O'Donnell. 'ECB Launches 1 Trillion Euro Rescue Plan to Revive Euro Economy'. *Reuters*. 22 January 2015.

Griffith, Richard. 'The Dynamics and States of European Construction, 1945–1995, SADC-EU'. *Seminar on the Regional Integration Process*, 1995.

Grossman, Gene M., and Elhanan Helpman. 'Endogenous Innovation in the Theory of Growth'. *Journal of Economic Perspectives* 8, no. 1 (Winter 1994): 23–44.

Gurtov, Mel. 'Realism and Corporate Globalism in Theory and Practice'. In *Global Politics in the Human Interest*, 5th edn, edited by Mel Gurtov. Boulder, Colorado: Lynne Rienner, 2007.

Gwaradzimba, Fadzai. 'SADCC and the Future of Southern African Regionalism'. *African Studies Association: A Journal of Opinion* 21, no. 1/2 (1993): 51–9.

Haarløv, Jens. *Regional Cooperation in Southern Africa: Central Elements of the SADCC Venture*. University of Bonn, Centre for Development Research (CDR), 1988.

Haas, Ernest. *The Uniting of Europe*. Stanford: Stanford University Press, 1958.

Haberler, Gottfried. 'Some Problems in the Pure Theory of International Trade'. *The Economic Journal* 50, no. 238 (June 1950): 223–40.

Hailu, Martha Belete. 'Regional Economic Integration in Africa: Challenges and Prospects'. *Mizan Law Review*, 8, no. 2 (2014): 299–332.
Hall, Susan. 'The Preferential Trade Area (PTA) for Eastern and Southern African States: Strategy, Progress, and Problems'. *Working paper Institute for Development Studies* (1987).
Halligan, Liam. 'Global Africa: The Last Investment Frontier?' In *The EU and Africa*, edited by Adekeye Adebajo and Kaye Whiteman. London: Hurst; New York: Columbia University Press; and Johnnesburg: Wits University Press, 2013.
Hanlon, Joseph. *Beggar Your Neighbours: Apartheid Power in South Africa*. London: Currey, 1986.
Hansen, Garry D. 'Indivisible Labor and the Business Cycle'. *Journal of Monetary Economics* 16 (1985): 309–27.
Hazelwood, Arthur, 'The End of the East African Community: What are the Lessons for Regional Integration Schemes?' In *The Future of Regionalism in Africa*, edited by Ralph I. Onwuka and Amadu Sesay. London: Macmillan, 1985.
Henderson, Robert D. A. 'The Southern African Customs Union: Politics of Dependence'. In *The Future of Regionalism in Africa*, edited by Ralph I. Onwuka and Amadu Sesay, Basingstoke: Macmillan Press, 1985.
Hennink, Monique, Inge Hutter and Ajay Bailey. *Qualitative Research Methods*, London: Sage, 2011.
Hentz, James J. 'South Africa and the Political Economy of Regional Cooperation in Southern Africa'. *Journal of Modern African Studies* 43, no. 1 (March 2005): 21–51.
Hentz, James J. 'South Africa and the "Three-Level Game": Regionalism, Globalization and Domestic Politics', *Journal of Commonwealth and Comparative Politics* 46, no. 4 (2008): 490–515.
Hentz, James J. 'The Southern African Security Order: Regional Economic Integration and Security among Developing States', *Review of International Studies*, 35, no. 51 (2009): 189–213.
Heto, Prince. 'An AGOA with Even More Teeth'. *Habari Network*, 2015. http://www.thehabarinetwork.com/an-agoa-with-even-more-teeth. Accessed July 2019.
Hettne, Björn, and Fredrik Söderbaum. 'The New Regionalism Approach'. *Politeia* 17, no. 3 (1998): 6–21.
Hettne, Björn, and Fredrik Söderbaum. 'Theorising the Rise of Regionness'. *New Political Economy* 5, no. 3 (December 1999): 457–72.
Hettne, Björn, András Inotai and Osvaldo Sunkel. *Globalism and the New Regionalism, Volume I*. London: Palgrave Macmillan, 1999.
Horvei, Tore. 'Powering the Region: South Africa in the Southern Africa Power Pool'. In *South Africa in Southern Africa: Reconfiguring the Region*, edited by David Simon. Oxford: James Currey, 1998.
Hudson, Judi. 'Economic Expansion into Africa'. In *South Africa in Africa: The Post-Apartheid Era*, edited by Adekeye Adebajo, Adebayo Adedeji and Chris Landsberg. Scottsville: University of KwaZulu-Natal Press, 2007.
Isaksen, Jan. *Restructuring SADC – Progress and Problems*. Bergen, Norway: Chr. Michelsen Institute, 2002.
Jefferis, Keith R. 'The Process of Monetary Integration in the SADC Region'. *Journal of Southern African Studies* 33, no. 1 (March 2007): 83–106.
Jenkins, Carolyn, and Lynne Thomas. 'The Macro-Economic Frameworks'. In *Gaining from Trade in Southern Africa: Complementary Policies to Underpin the SADC*

Free Trade Area, edited by Carolyn Jenkins, Jonathan Leape and Lynne Thomas. London: Palgrave Macmillian, 2000.
Jenkins, Carolyn, Jonathan Leape and Lynne Thomas. *Gaining from Trade in Southern Africa: Complementary Policies to Underpin the SADC Free Trade Area*. London: Palgrave Macmillian, 2000.
Kafeero, Edward. 'Customs Law of the East African Community in Light of WTO Law and the Revised Kyoto Convention', *Westfälische, Wilhelms University*, Münster (2009).
Kalenga, Paul. 'COMESA-EAC-SADC Tripartite Mechanism on Non-Tariff Barriers to Trade'. *World Trade Report*. 2012.
Kant, I. 'Empirical and a Priori Knowledge'. In *The structure of Scientific Thought*, edited by Edward H. Madden. Cambridge, Massachusetts: Riverside Press, 1960.
Kassa, Zeryhun. 'Ethiopia: Hailemariam – Egypt Goes to War over Nile Only If Leaders Go Mad'. *All Africa* (12 June 2013).
Kaunda, Jonathan Mayuyuka. 'Continuity and Change in Malawi's Foreign Policy-Making'. In *Globalization and Emerging Trends in African States' Foreign Policy-Making Process: A Comparative Perspective of Southern Africa*, edited by Korwa Gombe Adar and Rok Ajulu. Aldershot: Ashgate, 2002.
Kaunda, Mayuyuka Jonathan, and Farai Zizhou. eds. *Furthering Southern African Integration: Proceedings of the 2008 FOPRISA Annual Conference*, Botswana: Lightbooks, 2009.
Keller, Edmond J. 'Understanding Conflicts in the Horn of Africa'. In *Exploring Subregional Conflict Opportunities for Conflict Prevention*, edited by Chandra Lekha Sriram and Zoe Nielsen. Boulder: Lynne Rienner, 2004.
Keohane, Robert O. 'International Institutions: Two Approaches'. *International Studies Quarterly* 32, no. 4 (December 1988): 379–96.
Keohane, Robert O., and Joseph S. Nye. *Power and Interdependence*. 3rd ed. New York: Longman, 2001.
Kesselman, Brittany. 'African Peace and Security Agenda'. *Pax-Africana* 5, no. 1 (March 2009).
Khadiagala, Gilbert M. *Allies in Adversity: The Frontline States in Southern Africa Security 1975–1993*. Athens: Ohio University Press, 1994.
Khadiagala, Gilbert M. 'Forging Regional Foreign Policies in SADC: A Framework for Analysis'. In *Proceedings of the 2009 FOPRISA Annual Conference*, edited by Charles Harvey. Botswana: Lightbooks Lentswe La Lesedi, 2010.
Khadiagala, Gilbert M. 'The SADCC and Its Approaches to African Regionalism'. In *Region-Building in Southern Africa: Progress, Problems and Prospects*, edited by Chris Saunders, Gwinyayi Dzinesa and Dawn Nagar. London: Zed Books, 2012.
Khandelwal, Padamja. 'COMESA, EAC and SADC: Prospects and Challenges for Regional Trade Integration'. *International Monetary Fund, Working Paper no. WP/04/22*, 2004.
King-Akerele, Olubanke, and Kojo Boafo Asiedu. *Accelerating Africa's Integration Through Micro-Regionalism: The case of Zambia-Malawi-Mozambique Growth Triangle and Its Impact*. Tema: Digibooks, 2013.
Krugman, Paul. 'The Myth of Asia's Miracle'. *Foreign Affairs* 73, no. 6 (November/December 1994): 62–78.
Krugman, Paul. 'What's New about the "New Economic Geography"?' *Oxford Review of Economic Policy* 14, no. 2 (1998): 7–17.
Krugman, Paul R. 'Growing World Trade: Causes and Consequences'. *Brookings Papers on Economic Activity* 1 (1995): 327–77.

Kuhn, Thomas S. *The Structure of Scientific Revolutions*. Chicago: University of Chicago Press, 1970.

Kuwali, Dan, and Dawn Nagar. 'Towards a New Pax-Africana: Making, Keeping and Building Peace in Post-Cold War Africa', *CCR*, 28–30 August 2013.

Kwaku, Danso. 'The African Economic Community: Problems and Prospects: The Politics of Economic Integration in Africa'. *Africa Today*, Fall 1995.

Lamy, Pascal. 'Regional Integration in Africa: Ambitions and Vicissitudes'. *Policy Paper 43, Jacques Delors Institute*. Last modified 2010.

Lande, Stephen. 'The Lande Opus on a Transformational AGOA'. *The Habari Network: Proposals for a More Effective African Growth and Opportunity Act*. Zambia: The Common Market for Eastern and Southern African States COMESA, 2015.

Landsberg, Chris. *The Quiet Diplomacy of Liberation: International Politics and South Africa's Transition*. Johannesburg: Jacana Media, 2004.

Landsberg, Chris, and Jo-Ansie van Wyk. *South African Foreign Policy Review*. Johannesburg: IGD. 2012.

le Pere, Garth, and Elling N. Tjønneland. 'Which Way SADC?: Advancing Cooperation and Integration in Southern Africa'. *Institute for Global Dialogue Occasional Paper*, no. 50 (2005).

Lee, Margaret C. *The Political Economy of Regionalism in Southern Africa*. Cape Town: University of Cape Town (UCT) Press, 2003.

Legum, Colin. *Pan-Africanism: Short Political Guide*. Rev. ed. London: Pall Mall, 1965.

Legum, Margaret. 'Nyerere's Challenge'. In *A Dialogue of the Deaf: Essays on Africa and the United Nations*, edited by Adekeye Adebajo and Helen Scanlon. Johannesburg: Jacana, 2006.

Levine, Daniel H., and Dawn Nagar. 'Security and Governance in the Great Lakes Region'. *Centre for Conflict Resolution Seminar Report* 51 (August 2015).

Leys, Roger, and Arne Tostensen. 'Regional Cooperation in Southern Africa: The Southern African Development Co-ordination Conference'. *Scandinavian Perspectives on Africa, Review of African Political Economy* 23 (January–April 1982).

Limão, Nuno, and Anthony J. Venables. *Infrastructure, Geographical Disadvantage, Transport Costs and Trade*. London: London School of Economics, 20 December 2000.

Lindberg, Leon N. *The Political Dynamics of European Integration*. Stanford: Stanford University Press, 1963.

Lindeke, William A. 'From Confrontation to Pragmatic Cooperation: United States of America-Namibia Relations'. In *Namibia's Foreign Relations: Historic contexts, Current Dimensions, and Perspectives for the 21st Century*, edited by Anton Bösl, André du Pisani and Dennis U. Zaire. Windhoek: Macmillan Education Namibia, 2014.

Linz, Juan. *Totalitarian and Authoritarian Regimes*. Boulder: Lynne Rienner, 2000.

Lopes, Carlos. 'Mega Trade Agreement a Step Forward for the Continent'. *UNECA*, 12 June 2015. http://www.uneca.org/stories/mega-trade-agreement-step-forward-continent-%E2%80%93-carlos-lopes.

Lucas, Robert 'On the Mechanics of Economic Development'. *Journal of Monetary Economics* 22, no. 1 (1988): 3–42.

Maasdorp, Gavin. 'A Vision for Economic Integration and Cooperation in Southern Africa'. Cited in James J. Hentz, 'South Africa and the Political Economy of Regional Cooperation in Southern Africa', *Journal of Modern African Studies* 43, no. 1 (March, 2005): 21–51.

Maasdorp, Gavin A. *Rethinking Economic Cooperation in Southern Africa: Trade and Investment*. Johannesburg: Konrad-Adenauer Stiftung, 1993.
MacMillan, Margaret, and Dani Rodrik. 'Globalization, Structural Change and Productivity Growth'. In *Making Globalisation Socially Sustainable*, edited by Marc Bacchetta and Marion Jansen. Geneva: World Trade Organization [WTO] and International Labour Organization [ILO], 2011.
Madakufamba, Munetsi. 'Region Takes Giant Step toward African Economic Community', *Southern African News Features*, SANF 09, no. 01 (January 2009).
Makoni, Simba. 'Foreword'. In *Regional Relations and Cooperation Post-Apartheid*, Chinyamata Chipeta and Robert Davies. Gaborone: SADC, 1993.
Makonnen, Tewodros, and Halellujah Lulie. 'Ethiopia, Regional Integration and the COMESA Free Trade Area'. *South African International Affairs*, Occasional Paper 198 (August 2014).
Malan, Mark. 'The Crisis in External Response'. In *Peace, Profit or Plunder? The Privatisation of Security in War-Torn African Societies*, edited by Pretoria: Institute for Security Studies, 1999.
Malaquias, Assis. 'Dysfunctional Foreign Policy: Angola's Unsuccessful Quest for Security Since Independence'. In *Globalization and Emerging Trends in African States' Foreign Policy-Making Process: A Comparative Perspective of Southern Africa*, edited by Korwa Gombe Adar and Rok Ajulu. Aldershot: Ashgate, 2002.
Malewezi, Justin. 'Regional Integration: The Path to Prosperity?' In *Regional Integration in Southern Africa: Comparative International Perspective*, edited by Christopher Clapham, Greg Mills, Anna Morner and Elizabeth Sidiropoulos. Cape Town: South African Institute for International Affairs [SAIIA], 2001.
Mankiw, Gregory N., David Romer and David N. Weil. 'A Contribution to the Empirics of Economic Growth'. *Quarterly Journal of Economics* 107, no. 2 (1992): 407–37.
Mansfield, Edward. 'Effects of International Politics on Regionalism in International Trade'. In *Regional Integration and the Global Trading System*, edited by Kym Anderson and Richard Blackhurst. New York: Harvester Wheatsheaf, 1993.
Mansfield, Edward, and Helen V. Milner. 'The Domestic Politics of Preferential Trade Agreements in Hard Times'. *Department of Political Science*. 2014.
Marawa, Amos. Infrastructure Development, COMESA Document. *Infrastructure Development Directorate*. 2010, 2014.
Marchand, Marianne H., Morten Bøås and Timothy M. Shaw. 'The Political Economy of New Regionalisms'. *Third World Quarterly* 20, no. 5 (1999): 897–910.
Marshall, Alfred. *Principles of Economics*. London: Macmillan, 1920. Cited in, Nattrass, Wakeford and Muradzikwa. *Macro Economics Theory and Policy in South Africa*, 3rd edn. London: Macmillan, 2003.
Martin, Guy. *African World Politics: A Pan-African Perspective*. Trenton: Africa World Press, 2002.
Martin, Lisa. 'Interests, Power and Multilateralism'. *International Organization* 46, no. 4 (Autumn 1992): 765–92.
Martin, Ron. 'EMU Versus the Regions? Regional Convergence and Divergence in Euroland'. *ESRC Centre for Business Research*, Working Paper no. 179. September 2000.
Matlosa, Khabele. 'Regional Security in Southern Africa'. In *South Africa in Africa: The Post-Apartheid Era*, edited by Adekeye Adebajo, Adebayo Adedeji and Chris Landsberg. Scottsville: University of KwaZulu-Natal Press, 2007.

Matlosa, Khabele, and Kebapetse Lotshwao. *Political Integration and Democratisation in Southern Africa: Progress, Problems, and Prospects*. Gaborone: University of Botswana Press, December 2009.

Mattli, Walter. *The Logic of Regional Integration: Europe and Beyond*. Cambridge: Cambridge University Press, 1999.

Maupin, Agathe. 'Building a Regional Electricity Market: SAPP Challenges'. *South African Institute of International Affairs*. Case Study 4 (2013).

Mbeki, Moeletsi. *Profile of Political Conflicts in Southern Africa*. Harare: Nehanda Publishers, 1987.

Mbuende, Kaire. 'Namibia and the Southern African Development Community'. In *Namibia's Foreign Relations*, edited by du Pisani Bösl and U Zaire. Namibia: Macmillan Education, 2014.

Meier, Gerald M. 'The Old Generation of Development Economists and the New'. In *Frontiers of Development Economics: The Future in Perspective*, edited by Gerald M. Meier and J. Stiglitz. Oxford: Oxford University Press, 2001.

Melber, Henning. 'Global Trade Regimes and Multi-Polarity: The US and Chinese Scramble for African Resources and Markets'. In *A New Scramble for Africa: Imperialism, Investment and Development*, edited by Roger Southall and Henning Melber. Scottsville: University of KwaZulu-Natal Press, 2009.

Meyns, Peter. 'Present Structures and Future Challenges of Regional Cooperation and Integration in Southern Africa'. *Africana Studia, Edição da Fundação Eng. Antônio de Almeida*, no. 1 (1999).

Milas, Seifulaziz. *Africa: There Will Be No Water War in the Nile Basin Because No One Can Afford It*. 10 June 2013.

Mills, Gregg. *Why Africa Is Poor and What Africans Can Do about It*. Johannesburg: Penguin Books, 2011.

Minja, Rasul Ahmed. *Security Architecture in Sub-Saharan Africa and Collective Security Challenges: The EAC and SADC in Comparative Perspective*. DuEpublico: University of Duisburg-Essen, December, 2012.

Mitrany, David. 'A Functional Approach to World Organization'. *Royal Institute of International Affairs* 24, no. 3 (1948): 350–63.

Mitrany, David. *A Working Peace System*. Chicago: Quadrangle Books, 1966.

Mittelman, James H. 'Rethinking the "New Regionalism" in the Context of Globalization'. *Global Governance* 2, no. 2 (May–August 1996): 189–213.

Momba, Jonathan C., and Fay Gadsden. 'Zambia: Nonviolent Strategies against Colonialism, 1900s–1960s'. In *Recovering Non-Violent History: Civil Resistance in Liberation Struggles*, edited by Maciej J. Bartkowski. Boulder: Lynne Rienner, 2013.

Monyae, David. 'The Evolving "Doctrine" of Multilateralism in South Africa's Africa Policy'. In *South African Foreign Policy Review*, edited by Chris Landsberg and Jo-Ansie van Wyk. Pretoria: Africa Institute of South Africa, 2012, pp. 139–51.

Moravcsik, Andrew. 'Negotiating the Single European Act: National Interests and Conventional Statecraft in the European Community'. *International Organization*, vol. 45 (Winter 1991): 19–56.

Motumi, Tsepe. 'Logistical and Capacity Considerations Surrounding a Standby Force'. In *Peace in Africa: Towards a Collaborative Security Regime*, edited by Shannon Field. Johannesburg: Institute for Global Dialogue, 2004.

Mouton, Johann. *Basic Concepts in the Methodology of the Social Sciences*. Pretoria: Human Sciences Research Council [HSRC], 1988.

Moyo, Sam, and Ruth Hall. 'Conflict and Land Reform in Southern Africa'. In *South Africa in Africa*, edited by Adekeye Adebajo, Adebayo Adedeji and Chris Landsberg. 2007.

Mukisa, S., and Bankole Thompson. 'Prerequisites for Economic Integration in Africa: An Analysis of the Abuja Treaty', *Africa Today*, 4th Quarter, 42, no. 4 (1995).

Mulindwa, Paul. 'Uganda'. 'Security and Governance in the Great Lakes Region'. Paper presented at *CCR Seminar*, 9–10 May 2015.

Mushava, Everson, and Owen Gagare. 'Red Faces as SA, Namibia, Refuse to Sign SADC Trade Protocol'. *News Day*. 19 August 2014.

Mutasa, Charles. 'A Critique of the EU's Common Agricultural Policy'. In *The EU and Africa From Eurafrique to Afro-Europa*. Johannesburg: Wits University Press, 2013.

Mwenda, Kenneth Kaoma. *The Dynamics of Market Integration: African Stock Exchanges In the New Millennium*. Florida: Brown Walker Press, 2000.

Mytelka, Lynn. 'Building Partnerships For Innovation: A New Role for South-South Cooperation'. In *Regional Integration and Cooperation in West Africa*, edited by Réal Lavergne. Trenton, NJ: Africa World Press, 1997.

Mytelka, Lynn. *Regional Development in a Global Economy: The Multinational Corporation, Technology and Andean Integration*. New Haven: Yale University Press, 1979.

Nagar (Alley), Dawn. 'Research Methodology'. In *An Examination of the South African Correctional Services' Policy with Respect to Children Living with their Mothers in Prison*. Master's book, University of Port Elizabeth (UPE), 2007.

Nagar, Dawn. 'Defence Review: Who Will Keep the Peace?' *The Sunday Independent*. 12 April 2015.

Nagar, Dawn. 'Economic Integration'. In *Region-Building in Southern Africa: Progress, Problems, and Prospects*, edited by Chris Saunders, Gwinyayi Dzinesa and Dawn Nagar. London: Zed Books, 2012.

Nagar, Dawn. 'Towards a New Pax Africana: The Politics of Peacekeeping in Africa'. *CCR Seminar Paper*. August 2013.

Nagar, Dawn. 'Towards a Pax Africana: Southern African Development Community's Architecture and Evolving Peacekeeping Efforts, 1996–2009'. Master's thesis, University of Cape Town, 2010.

Nathan, Laurie. 'Solidarity Trumps Rule of Law'. *Mail and Guardian*. 30 November 2012.

Nathan, Laurie. *The Disbanding of the SADC Tribunal: A Cautionary Tale*. Pretoria: Centre for Mediation in Africa, University of Pretoria, 2009.

Nattrass, Nicoli, Jeremy Wakeford and Samson Muradzikwa. *Macro Economics Theory and Policy in South Africa*, 3rd edn. Cape Town: David Philip Publishers, 2003.

Ncube, Mthuli. 'China the Biggest External Risk to Africa's Growth Outlook'. *Terence Creamer Media*. 3 September 2015.

Neethling, Theo. 'Pursuing a Functional Security Community in Southern Africa: Is It Possible After All?'. *Strategic Review for Southern Africa*, 25, no. 1 (May 2003).

Ngoma, Naison. 'Prospects for a Security Community in Southern Africa'. In *Prospects for a Security Community in Southern Africa: An Analysis of Regional Security in the Southern African Development Community*, edited by Naison Ngoma. Pretoria: Institute for Security Studies, 2005.

Ngoma, Naison. *Prospects for a Security Community in Southern Africa: An Analysis of Regional Security in the Southern African Development Community*. Tshwane (Pretoria): Institute for Security Studies (ISS), 2005.

Ngwenya, Nomfundo Xenia. 'The United States'. In *Region-Building in Southern Africa*, edited by Chris Saunders, Gwinyayi Dzinesa and Dawn Nagar. London: Zed Books, 2012.

Ngwenya, Sindiso. 'Great Strides in Africa's Unity'. *The Habari Network: Proposals for a More Effective African Growth and Opportunity Act*. Zambia: Common Market for Eastern and Southern African States (COMESA), 2015.

Ninsin, Kwame A. 'Three Levels of State Reordering: The Structural Aspects'. In *The Precarious Balance: State and Society in Africa*, edited by Donald Rothchild and Naomi Chazan. Boulder: Westview Press, 1988.

Nomvete, Bax. 'The PTA, a Historical Perspective and Objectives (PTA/PUB/11/4, 4 March 1987)'. Cited in GIGA, 'The Preferential Trade Area (PTA) for Eastern and Southern Africa: Achievements, Problems and Prospects'. *Spectrum* 24, no. 2 (1989): 157–71.

Nomvete, Bax D. 'Regional Integration in Africa, a Path Strewn with Obstacles'. *The Courier (EC Courier)*, no. 142 (November–December 1993).

Nye, Joseph. *Pan-Africanism and East African Integration*. Princeton: Harvard University Press, 1965.

Nye, Joseph S., and Robert O. Keohane. 'Transnational Relations and World Politics'. *International Organization* 25, no. 3 (Summer 1971): 329–49.

Nyong'o, Peter Anyang' (ed.). *Regional Integration in Africa: Unfinished Agenda*. Nairobi: African Academy of Sciences, 1990.

Nzewi, Ogochukwu. 'The Challenges of Post-1990 Regional Integration in Africa: Pan-African Parliament'. *Centre for Policy Studies Policy Brief 57*. Johannesburg, South Africa: Centre for Policy Studies [CPS], April 2009.

O Nying'uro, Phillip. 'The EAC's Prospects on the Global Stage'. In *The Making of A Region*, edited by Rok Ajulu. Johannesburg: Institute for Global Dialogue, 2005.

Ocampo, José Antonio, and Joseph E. Stiglitz. *Capital Market Liberalization and Development*. New York: Oxford University Press, 2010.

Olorunsola, Victor A., and Dan Muhwezi. 'State Responses to Disintegration and Withdrawal: Adjustments in the Political Economy'. In *Africa in the New International Order: Rethinking State Sovereignty and Regional Security*, edited by Edmond J. Keller and Donald Rothchild. London: Lynne Rienner Pub, 1996.

Omari, Abillah H., and Paulino Macaringue. 'Southern African Security in Historical Perspective'. In *Security and Democracy in Southern Africa*, edited by Gavin Cawthra, Andre du Pisani and Abillah Omari. Johannesburg: Wits University Press, 2007.

Øostergaard, Tom. 'Aiming Beyond Conventional Development Assistance: An Analysis of Nordic Aid to the SADCC Region'. In *Regional Cooperation in Southern Africa: A Post-Apartheid Perspective*, edited by Bertil Odén and Haroub Othman. Uppsala: The Scandinavian Institute of African Studies, 1989.

Oosthuizen, Gabriël H. 'SADC's Main Institutions and Office-Bearers'. In *The Southern African Development Community: The Organisation, Its Policies, and Prospects*, edited by Gabriël H. Oosthuizen. Midrand: Institute for Global Dialogue, 2006.

Orchoro, Walter. 'Trade and Industrial Development in the EAC'. In *The Making of A Region*, edited by Rok Ajulu, 127–134. Johannesburg: Institute for Global Dialogue, 2005.

Oxford, Tamsin. 'Signs of New Era for SA Rail'. *Mail and Guardian*. 17 July 2015, http://mg.co.za/article/2015-07-17-signs-of-new-era-for-sa-rail. Accessed July 2016.

Panagariya, Arvind. 'The Regionalism Debate: An Overview', *World Economy* 22, no. 4 (1999): 477–512.

Papadimitriou, Dimitri B. *Contributions to Economic Theory, Policy, Development and Finance: Essays in Honor of Jan A. Kregel*. London: Palgrave Macmillan, 2014.

Peet, Richard. *Unholy Trinity: The IMF, World Bank, and WTO*. 2nd ed. London: Zed Books, 2009.

Pinder, John, and Simon Usherwood. *The European Union: A Very Short Introduction*. Oxford: Oxford University Press, 2007.

Polanyi, Michael. *Science, Faith, and Society: A Searching Examination of the Meaning and Nature of Scientific Inquiry*. US: University of Chicago Press, 1964.

Prescott, Edward C. 'Robert M. Solow's Neoclassical Growth Model: An Influential Contribution to Economics'. *The Scandinavian Journal of Economics* 90, no. 1 (March 1988): 7–12.

Punch, Keith F. *Introduction to Social Research: Quantitative and Qualitative Approaches*. London: Sage, 2005.

Putnam, Robert D. 'Diplomacy and Domestic Politics: The Logic of Two-Level Games'. *International Organizations*, 42, no. 3 (1988): 427–60.

Quah, Danny. 'Convergence Empirics Across Countries with (Some) Capital Mobility'. Centre for Economic Performance Discussion Paper No. 257. (August 1995).

Quah, Danny. 'Convergence Empirics Across Countries with (Some) Capital Mobility'. *Journal of Economics Growth* 1 (1996).

Ramos, Maria. 'Discussion on SADC's Regional Macroeconomic Convergence'. In *The European Union and Southern African Development Community Seminar Entitled* 'The Regional Integration Process'. 1995.

Ravenhill, John. 'The Future of Regionalism in Africa'. In *The Future of Regionalism in Africa*, edited by Ralph I. Onwuka and Amadu Sesay. Macmillan Education, 1985.

Ravenhill, John. 'Regional Integration in Africa: Theory and Practice'. *Paper Presented on Region-Building and Regional Integration in Africa*. Cape Town, South Africa: Centre for Conflict Resolution, April 2014.

Ravenhill, John. 'The "New East Asian Regionalism": A Political Domino Effect'. *Review of International Political Economy* 17, no. 2 (2010): 178–208.

Robson, Peter. *Economic Integration in Africa*. Evanston: Northwestern University Press, 1968.

Rodrik, Dani. 'An African Growth Miracle?' *The National Bureau of Economic Research*, Working Paper, no. 20188, June 2014.

Rodriquez, Francisco, and Dani Rodrik. 'Trade Policy and Economic Growth: A Skeptic's Guide to the Cross-National Evidence'. *National Bureau of Economic Research (NBER) Macroeconomics Annual 2000* 15 January 2001.

Rodt, Annemarie Peen. 'Taking Stock of EU Military Conflict Management', *Journal of Contemporary European Research*, 7, no. 1 (2011): 41–60.

Romer, Paul M. 'Increasing Returns and Long Run Growth'. *Journal of Political Economy* 94, no. 5 (1986): 1002–37.

Rosberg, Jr., Carl G. 'The Federation of Rhodesia and Nyasaland: Problems of Democratic Government'. *Annals of the American Academy of Political and Social Science* 306 (July 1956).

Rose, Gideon. 'Neoclassical Realism and Theories of Foreign Policy'. *World Politics* 51, no. 1 (October 1998): 144–72.

Rosiek, Janusz, and Robert W. Wlodarczyk. 'Comparative Analysis of the EU-27 Countries Labour Markets' Convergence', *Economics and Management, Cracow University of Economics*, Poland, 17, no. 1 (2012): 216–22.

Roux, Andre. 'South Africa and the UN Intervention Brigade in the DRC'. *ISS Today*. 24 (2013).

Ryan, Ciaran. 'China Sneezes – How Sick Will SA Get?' *Finweek*. 13 August 2015. http://finweek.com/2015/09/03/cover-the-global-economic-super-cycle-is-over/.

Saunders, Chris. 'Namibian Diplomacy before Independence'. In *Namibia's Foreign Relations*: Historic contexts, current dimensions, and perspectives for the 21st Century, edited by du Pisani Bösl and U. Zaire. Namibia: Macmillan Education, 2014.

Saunders, Chris, Gwinyayi Dzinesa and Dawn Nagar. *Region-Building in Southern Africa: Progress, Problems, and Prospects*. London: Zed Books, 2012.

Schraeder, Peter J. 'Continuity and Change in the United States' Foreign Policy Towards Southern Africa'. In *Globalization and Emerging Trends in African States' Foreign Policy-Making Process*, edited by Korwa Gombe Adar and Rok Ajulu. Aldershot: Ashgate: 2002.

Schultz, Theodore W. *Transforming Traditional Agriculture*. New Haven, CT: Yale University Press, 1964. Cited in Gilpin, *The Political Economy of International Relations*, Princeton, NJ: Yale University Press, 1987.

Seim, Line Tøndel. 'Export Performance and Trade Facilitation in SADC'. In *Towards Political and Economic Integration in Africa*, edited by Gavin Cawthra and Jonathan Mayuyuka Kaunda. Botswana: Light Books, 2008.

Shipman, M. D. *The Limitations of Social Research*, 4th edn. New York: Routledge, 2014.

Siebert, John. 'R2P and the IGAD Sub-Region: IGAD's Contribution to Africa's Emerging R2P-Oriented Security Culture'. In *Crafting an African Security Architecture*, edited by Hany Besada, 89–108. Burlington: Ashgate, 2010.

Slaughter, Matthew J. 'Trade Liberalization and Per Capita Income Convergence: A Difference-In-Differences Analysis'. *Journal of International Economics* 55 (2001): 203–28.

Slocum-Bradley, Nikki. 'The Zambia-Malawi-Mozambique Growth Triangle (ZMM-GT): Discursive Region-Building in Africa and Consequences for Development'. In *Afro-Regions: The Dynamics of Cross-Border Micro-Regionalism in Africa*, edited by Fredrik Söderbaum and Ian Taylor. Stockholm: Elanders Sverige, 2008.

Snyder, Jack. *Myths of Empire: Domestic Politics and International Ambition*. Ithaca: Cornell University Press, 1991.

Söderbaum, Fredrik, and Ian Taylor. *Afro-Regions: The Dynamics of Cross-Border Micro-Regionalism in Africa*. Stockholm: Elanders Sverige, 2008.

Soko, Mills. 'The Political Economy of Regional Integration in Southern Africa', *Notre Europe*, 2007.

Solow, Robert. 'A Contribution to the Theory of Economic Growth'. *The Quarterly Journal of Economics* 70, no. 1 (February 1956): 65–94.

Stephan, Harry, Michael Power, Angus Fane Hervey and Raymond Steenkamp Fonseca. *The Scramble for Africa in the 21st Century: A View from the South*. Cape Town: Renaissance Press, 2006.

Stoneman, Colin. 'Foreign Capital and Zimbabwe'. *Review of African Political Economy*, no. 11 (January–April 1978): 62–83.

Strassler, Robert B. *The Landmark Thucydides: A Comprehensive Guide to the Polepennesian War*. New York: Free Press, 1996.

Sy, Amadou. 'Convergence or Divergence: Discussing Structural Transformation in Africa during the G20'. *Brookings Institution*. 2014. http://www.brookings.edu/blogs/africa-in-focus/

posts/2014/11/14-convergence-divergence-structural-transformation-africa-g20-sy. Accessed July 2015.

Taylor, Ian. 'African Unity at 50: From Non-Interference to Non-Indifference'. *E-International Relations*. 25 June 2013.

Taylor, Ian. 'Globalization and Regionalization in Africa: Reactions to Attempts at Neo-Liberal Regionalism'. *Review of International Political Economy* 10, no. 2 (May 2003): 310–330.

Taylor, Paul, and A. J. R. Groom. *International Institutions at Work*. London: Pinter, 2006.

Thelen, Kathleen, and Sven Steinmo. 'Historical Institutionalism in Comparative Politics'. In *Structuring Politics: Historical Institutionalism in Comparative Analysis*, edited by Sven Steinmo, Kathleen Thelen and Frank Longstreth. Cambridge: Cambridge University Press, 1992.

Tjønneland, Elling. 'SADC Restructuring, Prioritisation and Donors, 2006–2008', 2009. In *Jonathan Mayuyuka Kaunda and Farai Zizhou: Furthering Southern African integration. Proceedings of the 2008 FOPRISA Annual Conference. (FOPRISA report no.7)*, edited by Jonathan Mayuyuka Kaunda and Farai Zizhou. Gaborone: Lightbooks.

Tjønneland, Elling N., Jan Isaksen and Garth le Pere. 'SADC's Restructuring and Emerging Policies: Options for Norwegian Support'. *Report of the Norwegian Embassy*, 2005.

Turner, Daniel. 'Qualitative Interview Design: A Practical Guide for Novice Investigators', *The Qualitative Report*, 15, 3 (May 2010): 754–60.

Turok, Ben. 'Building a Progressive Consensus'. In *The Controversy about Economic Growth*, edited by Ben Turok. Johannesburg: Jacana, 2011.

Vale, Peter. *Security and Politics in South Africa: The Regional Dimension*. Cape Town: Cape Town University Press, 2003.

Van Der Wolf, Roger Southall and Henning Melber. 'Egypt: Ethiopia, Egypt Meet to Ease Nile Dam Tensions'. *All Africa*. 18 June 2013.

Van Nieuwkerk, Anthoni. 'A Review of South Africa's Peace Diplomacy since 1994'. In *South African Foreign Policy Review*, edited by Chris Landsberg and Jo-Ansie van Wyk. Pretoria: Africa Institute of South Africa, 2012.

Väyrynen, Raimo. 'Regionalism: Old and New'. *International Studies Review* 5, no. 1 (2003): 25–51.

Venables, Anthony J. 'Regional Integration Agreements: A Force for Convergence or Divergence?' *Policy Research Working Paper*, no. 2260 (December 1999).

Vestergaard, Madsen, Jens, Conor Seyle, Kellie Brandt, Ben Purser, Heather Randall and Kellie Roy. 'The State of Maritime Piracy', *Oceans beyond Piracy Project: One Earth Future Foundation*. 2013.

Vickers, Brendan. *Industrial Policy In the Southern African Customs Union: Past Experiences, Future Plans*. Johannesburg: Institute for Global Dialogue, 2008.

Vickers, Brendan. 'SADC's International Trade Relations'. In *Proceedings of the 2009 the Formative Process Research on Integration in Southern Africa (FOPRISA) Annual Conference*, edited by Charles Harvey. 2010.

Vickers, Brendan. 'South Africa's Economic Diplomacy in a Changing Global Order'. In *South African Foreign Policy Review*, edited by Chris Landsberg and Jo-Ansie van Wyk. Pretoria: Africa Institute of South Africa and Institute for Global Dialogue, 2012.

Viner, Jacob. *The Customs Union Issue*. New York: Carnegie Endowment for International Peace, 1950.

Vollgraaff, Rene. 'Eskom Has Slashed R400bn off SA's Economy in Last Seven Years'. *Bloomberg*. 8 April 2015. http://www.biznews.com/undictated/2015/04/08/eskom-slashed-10-off-the-size-of-sas-economy-in-seven-years/. Accessed July 2015.

Von Clausewitz, General Carl. *On War*. Chapel Hill: Project Gutenberg, 1874, 1909, 2006.

Wallerstein, Immanuel. 'Regional Unity and African Unity'. In *Africa: The Politics of Independence and Unity*, edited by Immanuel Wallerstein. Lincoln: University of Nebraska Press, 2005.

Warleigh-Lack, Alex. 'Towards a Conceptual Framework for Regionalisation: Bridging "New Regionalism" and "Integration Theory"', *Review of International Political Economy* 13, no. 5 (December 2006): 750–71.

Wasswa, Henry. 'Will Uganda Pay Up for Congo Occupation?', *Global Policy Forum* (26 July 2007), https://www.globalpolicy.org/component/content/article/163/28685.html. Accessed July 2015.

Willetts, Peter. 'Transnational actors and International Organizations in Global Politics'. In *The Globalization of World Politics*, 2nd ed., edited by John Baylis and Steve Smith. Oxford: Oxford University Press, 2001.

Young, Crawford. 'The African Colonial State and Its Political Legacy'. In *The Precarious Balance: State and Society in Africa*, edited by Donald Rothchild and Naomi Chazan. Boulder: Westview Press, 1988.

Zacarias, Agostinho. 'SADC: From a System to Community of Security?' *African Security Review* 7, no. 6 (1998): 44–61.

Zaffiro, James. 'Exceptionality in External Affairs: Botswana in the African and Global Arenas'. In *African Foreign Policies*, edited by Stephen Wright. Boulder: Westview, 1999.

Zartman, I. William. 'African Regional Security and Changing Patterns of Relations'. In *Africa in the New International Order: Rethinking State Sovereignty and Regional Security*, edited by Edmond J. Keller and Donald Rothchild. London: Lynne Rienner, 1996.

Zindoga, Tichaona. 'Sadc and the Politics of Regional Integration', *The Herald*. 28 April 2015.

Zizhou, F.B. 'Modalities and Scenarios For Establishing a Tripartite Free Trade Area'. In *From Cape To Cairo: Exploring The COMESA-EAC-SADC Tripartite FTA Report*, Friedrich Ebert Stiftung. Proceedings of the Sixth Southern African Forum on Trade (SAFT) held in Pretoria, South Africa, 3–4 August 2009. Johannesburg: Institute for Global Dialogue, 2009.

Organisational reports, websites and articles

Africa/World News. 'COMESA at Twenty: Of the Successes, Challenges and Promises', *Addis Standard*, 7 April 2015. http://addisstandard.com/comesa-at-twenty-of-the-successes-challenges-and-promises/. Accessed July 2015.

African Development Bank. 'Burundi 2012–2016 Strategy Paper'. October 2011. https://www.afdb.org/en/documents/document/2012-2016-burundi-country-strategy-paper-25829. Accessed July 2019.

African Development Bank. 'Eastern Africa Regional Integration Strategy Paper 2011–2015'. Revised Draft for Regional Team Meeting. October 2010: 8, table 1. http://www.afdb.org/fileadmin/uploads/afdb/Documents/Project-and-Operations/RISP-East%20

Africa%20-%20Shortened%20Draft%20-%20Pre%20OpsCom%20Version%20-%20 Revision%2028%2010%202010%20RR%20Clean.pdf. Accessed July 2016.

African Development Bank (AfDB). *Economic Integration in Southern Africa 2*, Tunisia, 1993.

African Development Bank. 'Statistics on Africa Report, 2013'. https://unctad.org/en/PublicationsLibrary/aldcafrica2013_en.pdf. Accessed July 2019.

African Development Bank. *Southern Africa Regional Integration Strategy Paper, 2011–2015*. https://www.afdb.org/en/documents/document/2011-2015-southern-africa-regional-integration-strategy-paper-22186. Accessed July 2019.

African Union (AU), 'African Charter on Human and People's Rights', http://www.achpr.org/instruments/achpr/. Accessed July 2016.

African Union. 'Peace and Security, Post-Conflict Reconstruction and Development Programme'. http://www.peaceau.org/en/page/70-post-conflict-reconstruction-and-development-pcrd. Accessed July 2016.

African Union. *Programme for Infrastructure Development in Africa: Addressing the Infrastructure Gap in Africa, to Speed Up Regional Integration*. Seventh Conference of African Ministers in Charge of Integration1 (4–18 July 2014).

African Union. Yamoussoukro Declaration 1999. http://au.int/ar/sites/default/files/Yamoussoukro%20Decision%20-%20Regulatory%20Framework-EN.pdf. Accessed July 2016.

African Union Programme for Infrastructure Development in Africa (PIDA). 'Interconnecting, Integrating, and Transforming a Continent: The Regional Infrastructure that Africa Needs to Integrate and Grow through 2020'. SOFRECO-Led Consortium [SOFRECO, MWH, Nathan, SOFRECOM, SYSTRA, ASCON, and CABIRA].

African Union Strategy for Regional Integration. 'Towards a Common Market for Agricultural Products'. Charter of the organization of African Unity and the AEC Treaty, Article 3(c) and (d). 1999. https://au.int/en/ea/ric. Accessed July 2019.

British Broadcasting Corporation (BBC). 'Burundi President Pierre Nkurunziza Sworn in for Third Term'. 2015.

Centre for Conflict Resolution (CCR), 'Peacebuilding in Post-Cold War Africa: Progress, Problems and Prospects', *CCR Report*. 25–28 August 2009.

Centre for Conflict Resolution. 'Security and Governance in the Great Lakes Region'. *CCR Seminar Report*. August 2015. www.ccr.org.za. Accessed July 2016.

Centre for Conflict Resolution. *South Africa in Southern Africa*. Report. November 2012. http://www.ccr.org.za/index.php/media-release/reports/seminar-reports?start=10. Accessed July 2016.

Centre for Conflict Resolution Public Dialogue. 'The Diplomacy of Transformation: South African Foreign Policy and Statecraft'. Cape Town. 3 May 2011. http://www.ccr.org.za/index.php/events/public-dialogues/item/652-no-154. Accessed July 2016.

CEWARN. http://cewarn.org/index.php?option=com_content&view=article&id=51&Itemid=53. Accessed July 2016.

Child Soldiers Organisation. https://www.childsoldiers.org/. Accessed July 2019.

COMESA. Common Market for Eastern and Southern Africa (COMESA). *Treaty Establishing the Common Market for Eastern and Southern Africa*, adopted 5 November 1993, entered into force 8 December 1994. https://www.comesa.int/comesa-institutions/. Accessed July 2019.

COMESA. Common Market for Eastern and Southern Africa Monetary Union, www.comesa.int. Accessed July 2016.

COMESA. Marawa, Infrastructure Development, *Infrastructure Development Directorate*, 2010, 2014. Document obtained from COMESA Secretariat August 2014.

COMESA. Memorandum of Understanding on Inter Regional Cooperation and Integration amongst COMESA, EAC and SADC. Document obtained from COMESA Secretariat. August 2014.

COMESA. Observer Mission in Malawi's May 2014 Elections. https://www.comesa.int/wp-content/uploads/2019/02/2015-Comesa-Annual-Report.pdf. Accessed July 2019.

COMESA. Observer Mission in Zimbabwe in July 2013. https://eisa.org.za/pdf/zim2013au2.pdf. Accessed July 2015.

COMESA. Secretariat, 'Regional Integration' 2, 2013. https://www.comesa.int/wp-content/uploads/2019/03/key-issues-on-intergration-ii_final_final_cutout_print.pdf. Accessed July 2014.

COMESA. Thirty-Second Meeting of the Council of Ministers, Kinshasa, DRC, 22–24 February 2014, CS/CM/XXX11/2. https://www.comesa.int/wp-content/uploads/2019/02/comesa-gazette-2014_october.pdf. Accessed July 2019.

COMESA Document. 'COMESA-EU Launch a Programme to Fight Piracy'. 12 September 2014. https://www.tralac.org/news/article/6301-comesa-eu-team-up-against-piracy.html. Accessed July 2019.

COMESA Secretariat. Article 1 of the Memorandum of Understanding on Inter-Regional Cooperation and Integration amongst COMESA, EAC, and SADC. Document obtained from COMESA Secretariat August 2014.

COMESA, EAC and SADC. Memorandum of Understanding on Inter-Regional Cooperation and Integration amongst COMESA, EAC and SADC, unpublished official document, COMESA Secretariat August 2014.

COMESA-EAC-SADC. February 2011 Summit Report of the Chair of the TTF. Document obtained from COMESA Secretariat. August 2014.

COMESA-EAC-SADC. Second Tripartite Summit Communique, 12 June 2011. Sandton, Johannesburg. Document obtained from COMESA Secretariat. August 2014.

COMESA-EAC-SADC. Tripartite Summit. 'Communique of the third Tripartite Summit. Vision: Towards A Single Market. Theme: Deepening COMESA-EAC-SADC Integration', Sharm El Sheikh, Arab Republic of Egypt, 10 June 2015.

COMESA-EAC-SADC. Tripartite Summit of Heads of State and Government. Final Communiqué. 2008. Document obtained from COMESA Secretariat. August 2014.

COMESA-EAC-SADC. Tripartite Trade and Customs Committee Meeting (TTCC). Update, 9 February 2015. Document obtained from COMESA Secretariat.

Daily News. 'SA Attempting to Squeeze Hyundai Botswana-Built Cars Out of the Market'. *Daily News*. 5 May 1994.

Department of International Relations and Cooperation (DIRCO). 'Remarks by President Jacob Zuma, during the South Africa/Zimbabwe Business Forum Meeting on the occasion of Former President Mugabe's State Visit to South Africa', Pretoria, 9 April 2015.

East African Community. Ambassador A. J. V. Mwapachu. 'Report by the Chair of the Tripartite Task Force, Secretary-General of the EAC.' (2011).

East African Community. *Status of Elimination of Non-Tariff Barriers in the East African Community* 8. December 2014.

East African Community (EAC). *Treaty for the Establishment of the East African Community*, adopted 30 November 1999, entered into force 7 July 2000, Art. 92.

Economist. 'A Flawed Plan for Africa', *Financial Times*, 13 July 1989.

Economist. 'A Sad and Sorry Decline'. Middle East and Africa. 29 June 2013.

Economist Intelligence Unit. 'Country Report: Zimbabwe'. 30 November 2012.
Economy Watch. http://www.economywatch.com/economic-statistics/country/Burundi/. Accessed July 2014.
European Union. European Commission's Economic Partnership Agreements. http://ec.europa.eu/trade/policy/countries-and-regions/development/economic-partnerships/. Accessed July 2019.
European Union (EU). GFA consulting and GTZ, SADC 2008. 'Free Trade Area, Growth, Development and Wealth Creation'.
European Union. 'Regional Integration in Africa'. 2011. http://www.delorsinstitute.eu/011-2423-Regional-Integrations-in-Africa-ambitions-and-vicissitudes.html. Accessed September 2012.
European Union. 'Southern African Region and the EU Complete Negotiations for an Economic Partnership Agreement'. 22 July 2014. http://trade.ec.europa.eu/doclib/press/index.cfm?id=940.
European Union and Southern African Development Community. Seminar on, 'The Regional Integration Process'. In collaboration with the Centre d'Etude d'Afrique Noire, Institut d' Eudes Politiques of Bordeaux. Brussels and Paris, 12–15 June 1995: 11.
European Union. European Central Bank, Eurosystem. 'Study of the Establishment of a Monetary Union among the Partner States of the East African Community'. 2010.
European Union. European Commission. 'The Eastern African Community (EAC)'. Fact Sheet on the Economic Partnership Agreements. October 2014. http://trade.ec.europa.eu/doclib/docs/2009/january/tradoc_142194.pdf. Accessed November 2015.
Fin24. 'Zim Starts $533 Million Power Project with China'. 16 September 2014. https://www.fin24.com/Economy/Zim-starts-533m-power-project-with-China-20140905. Accessed July 2019.
Friedrich Ebert Stiftung (FES), 'Deepening Integration in SADC'. *Regional Integration in Southern Africa* 6 (December 2006).
Institute for Security Studies. 'Is the Force Intervention Brigade Neutral?' 27 November 2014. https://issafrica.org/iss-today/is-the-force-intervention-brigade-neutral. Accessed July 2019.
International Civil Aviation Organization (ICAO). www.icao.int. Accessed July 2016.
International Coalition for the Responsibility to Protect (ICRtoP). http://icrtopblog.org/2015/01/16/an-indispensable-protection-tool-assessing-the-force-intervention-brigade-in-the-drc/. Accessed July 2016.
International Crisis Group. Conflict in the Democratic Republic of Congo. https://www.crisisgroup.org/africa/central-africa/democratic-republic-congo. Accessed July 2019.
International Monetary Fund (IMF). Direction of Trade Statistics: Year-Book 1988. Cited in, GIGA, 'The Preferential Trade Area for Eastern and Southern Africa: Achievements, Problems and Prospects'. 1989.
InterVistas Consulting. 'Transforming Intra-African Air Connectivity: The Economic Benefits of Implementing the Yamoussoukro Decision'. July 2014.
Just Style. 'Impact of Regional Trade Deals on Clothing and Textile Sector: A Global Assessment: Management Briefing: South Africa', *Just Style* (ProQuest Information and Learning Company) (Journal-Code: JSYL). 22 April 2008.
Maputo Corridor Logistics Initiative. 2013. http://www.mcli.co.za/mcli-web/mdc/mdc-timeline.htm. Accessed September 2014.
News24. 'Fears of More Violence in Lesotho After Killing of Ex-Army Boss'. *News24*. 29 June 2015. http://www.news24.com/Africa/News/Fears-of-more-violence-in-Lesotho-after-killing-of-ex-army-boss-20150629. Accessed September 2016.

Nordiska Afrikainstitutet. *Regionalism and Regional Integration in Africa: A Debate of Current Aspects and Issues, Discussion Paper 11*, Uppsala, Sweden, 2001.

Office of the United States Trade Representative (USTR). 'President Obama Removes Swaziland, Reinstates Madagascar for AGOA Benefits'. June 2014. https://ustr.gov/about-us/policy-offices/press-office/press-releases/2014/June/President-Obama-removes-Swaziland-reinstates-Madagascar-for-AGOA-Benefits. Accessed September 2016.

Organisation for Economic Co-Operation and Development (OECD)/DAC. Meeting on Development Challenges and the Role of Aid in Southern Africa, Windhoek, Namibia, 7–8 September 1993 (SG/NR (93) 33), http://www.oecd.org/officialdocuments/publicdisplaydocumentpdf/?cote=SG/NR(93)33&docLanguage=En. Accessed July 2016.

Organization of the Petroleum Exporting Countries (OPEC). Brief History and its establishment in 1960. http://www.opec.org/opec_web/en/about_us/24.htm. Accessed July 2016.

Overseas Development Institute (ODI). 'Sanctions and South Africa's Neighbours'. Briefing Paper. May 1987.

Reuters. 'Zambia Seeks to Block Arms for Zimbabwe', *New York Times*. 22 April 2008.

SADC. 'Agreement Amending the Treaty of the Southern African Development Community'. Blantyre: Malawi, 2001. https://www.sadc.int/about-sadc/overview/history-and-treaty/. Accessed July 2019.

SADC. Communiqué. Pretoria. 23 August 1998. www.sadc.int. Accessed July 2016.

SADC. 'The DRC Declarations on M23'. 18 December 2013. https://www.sadc.int/files/7013/8718/4213/M23_DECLARATION_ENGLSH0001.pdf. Accessed July 2019.

SADC. Extraordinary Summits and Communiqués. Namibia, Windhoek, 9 March 2001; and Gaborone, Botswana, 17–18 August 2005. https://www.sadc.int/files/3913/5292/8384/SADC_SUMMIT_COMMUNIQUES_1980-2006.pdf. Accessed July 2019.

SADC. Extraordinary Summit of the Double Troika Communique. 3 July 2015. http://www.sadc.int/files/8114/3598/7203/Draft_Communique_on_3_July__2135hrs_corrected.pdf. Accessed July 2019.

SADC. The Joint Declaration on Expanded Economic and Cultural Cooperation between the Nordic Countries and the SADCC member states were signed in January 1986. In Luanda, *see the*, SADCC/SADC Heads of State and Government Summit Communiqués 1980–2000. https://www.sadc.int/files/3913/5292/8384/SADC_SUMMIT_COMMUNIQUES_1980-2006.pdf. Accessed July 2019.

SADC. Mozambique Report. https://www.sadc.int/information-services/sadc-statistics/sadc-statiyearbook/. 2006. Accessed August 2019.

SADC. *Protocol on Transport, Communications and Meteorology in the Southern African Development Community (SADC) Region*, adopted 24 August 1996, entered into force 1 July 1998. http://www.sadc.int/files/7613/5292/8370/Protocol_on_Transport_Communications_and_Meteorology_1996.pdf, Art. 9. Accessed July 2016.

SADC. Regional Infrastructure Development Master Plan: Infrastructure'. http://www.sadc.int/themes/infrastructure/. Accessed July 2016.

SADC. Strategic Indicative Plan for the Organ on Politics, Defence and Security Cooperation (OPDSC). http://www.sadc.int/fi les/9113/6492/3812/sipo_en_3.pdf. Accessed July 2016.

SADC. Summit Communiqué. Blantyre, Malawi. 8 August 1997. www.sadc.int. Accessed July 2016.

SADC. Summit Communiqué. Botswana. 29 August 1994. www.sadc.int. Accessed July 2016.
SADC. Summit Communiqué. Johannesburg. 28 August 1995. www.sadc.int. Accessed July 2016.
SADC. Summit Communiqué. Maseru. 24 August 1996. www.sadc.int. Accessed July 2016.
SADC. Summit Communiqué. Swaziland. 1993. www.sadc.int. Accessed July 2016.
SADC. Summit of the Double Troika Plus Troop Contributing Countries, DRC and Madagascar. 29 January 2015. https://www.sadc.int/news-events/news/summit-double-troika-plus-troop-contributing-countries-democ/. Accessed July 2019.
SADC. Summit of the Troika of the Organ on Politics, Defence and Security Cooperation of the Southern African Development Community, Maseru, Kingdom of Lesotho (21–22 February 2010). https://www.sadc.int/about-sadc/sadc-institutions/org/. Accessed July 2016.
SADC. *Today* (May 2012). www.sadc.int. Accessed July 2016.
SADC. *Today* 10, no. 2 (August 2007). www.sadc.int. Accessed July 2016.
SADCC. Communiqué, Arusha, Tanzania, 9 August 1985. www.sadc.int. Accessed July 2016.
SADCC. Summit Communiqué, 26 August 1990, Gaborone, Botswana. www.sadc.int. Accessed July 2016.
SADCC. Summit Communiqué, Arusha, Tanzania, 26 August 1991. www.sadc.int. Accessed July 2016.
SADCC. Summit Communiqué, Luanda, Angola, 22 August 1986. www.sadc.int. Accessed July 2016.
SADCC. Summit Communiqué. Salisbury, Zimbabwe, 20 July 1981. www.sadc.int. Accessed July 2016.
SADCC. Summit Communiqué. Windhoek, Namibia. 17 August 1992. www.sadc.int. Accessed July 2016.
SADC-EU. Ministerial Political Dialogue Communique. Maputo, Mozambique. 20 March 2013. http://www.sadc.int . Accessed July 2016.
SAPP. *Annual Report*. 2014. https:www.sapp.co.zw. Accessed July 2016.
Security Council Report. 'Democratic Republic of the Congo, Expected Council Action'. http://www.securitycouncilreport.org/monthly-forecast/2015-03/democratic_republic_of_the_congo_7.php. Accessed July 2016.
South Africa Department of Trade and Industry (DTI). http://tradestats.thedti.gov.za/ReportFolders/reportFolders.aspx?sCS_referer=&sCS_ChosenLang=en. Accessed July 2016.
South African Foreign Policy Initiative (SAFPI). 'Namibia Sticks to Its EPA Guns'. 18 December 2012. https://www.namibian.com.na/103603/archive-read/Namibia-sticks-to-its-EPA-guns. Accessed July 2019.
South African Government. The African Renaissance and International Co-operation Fund Act, Act No. 51 of 2000. http://www.dfa.gov.za/chiefstatelawadvicer/documents/acts/africanrenaissanceandinternationalcooperationact.pdf. Accessed July 2016.
South African Government News Agency. 'SADC Ministers Discuss Integration, Industrialisation', *SA News Agency*, 28 April 2015.
South African Institute of International Affairs (SAIIA). 'SACU Report'. January 2007.
South African Institute of International Affairs. 'SADC Barometer'. Issue 8. March 2005: 6.
South African National Conventional Arms Control Committee (NCACC). *Third Quarterly Report*. July–September 2014.

Southern African Customs Union (SACU) and US trade in 2013. https://ustr.gov/countries-regions/africa/regional-economic-communities-rec/Southern-african-customs-union-sacu. Accessed July 2016.

Sudan Tribune. 'Egypt: Ethiopian Envoy Lauds Sudan's Stance on Nile Dam, Criticizes Egypt'. *Sudan Tribune*. 11 June 2013.

Sudan Tribune. 'South Sudanese Vice President Ready to Offer Positions to Rebel Leader'. *Sudan Tribune*. 17 June 2015.

The Courier. 'A Fresh Look at Africa', no. 134, July/August 1992.

The Guardian. 'Platinum Miners in South Africa Go On Strike'. *The Guardian*. London, 23 January 2014.

Trade Law Centre for Southern Africa. 'Monitoring Regional Integration in Southern Africa'.

Trade Law Centre for Southern Africa (Tralac). *From Cape To Cairo: Making the Tripartite Free Trade Area Work*. Stellenbosch, South Africa: Tralac, 2011.

Transport World Africa. 'Smooth Flow of Cargo'. 25 September 2014. http://www.transportworldafrica.co.za/2014/09/25/smooth-flow-of-cargo/. Accessed July 2016.

UNECA. Abuja Treaty 1991. http://repository.uneca.org/handle/10855/21721. Accessed July 2016.

UNECA. 'Annual Report 29 May 1984–29 April 1985'. Economic and Social Council Official Records, Supplement no.15, E/1985/36, E/ECA/CM.11/81, 1985: 28. http://repository.uneca.org/handle/10855/3534. Accessed July 2019.

UNECA. Annual Report 29 May 1984–29 April 1985: Economic Commission for Africa, 1985.

UNECA. 'Assessing Regional Integration in Africa'. 2008. https://www.uneca.org/sites/default/files/PublicationFiles/aria4full.pdf. Accessed July 2019.

UNECA. 'Assessing Regional Integration in Africa, IV'. 2011. http://siteresources.worldbank.org/INTAFRREGINICOO/Resources/1587517-1271810608103/UNECA-4th-Africa-RI-Assessment-May2010.pdf. Accessed July 2019.

UNECA. 'Assessing Regional Integration in Africa V: Harmonizing Policies to Transform'. Last modified 2012. http://new.uneca.org/aria/aria5.aspx. Accessed July 2019.

UNECA. 'Assessing Regional Integration in Africa V: Towards a Continental Free Trade Area'. 2012. https://repository.uneca.org/handle/10855/22110. Accessed July 2019.

UNECA. Empirical Evidence on Macroeconomic Convergence in African RECs. United Nations Economic Commission for Africa, 'Macroeconomic Convergence in African RECs 'Assessing Regional Integration in Africa', 2008: 137. https://www.uneca.org/publications/assessing-regional-integration-africa-iii. Accessed July 2019.

UNECA. Lagos Plan of Action and Final Act of Lagos. UNECA http://repository.uneca.org/handle/10855/14129. Accessed July 2016.

UNECA. 'Macroeconomic Policy and Institutional Convergence of Member States in the Southern African Development Community'. https://www.uneca.org/sites/default/files/PublicationFiles/aria5_print_uneca_fin_20_july_1.pdf. Accessed July 2016.

UNECA. 'Movement of Goods and Services in Africa V'. 2012. https://unctad.org/en/PublicationsLibrary/presspb2018d4_en.pdf. Accessed August 2019.

UNECA. '*The Mutual Review of Development Effectiveness in Africa: Promise and Performance*'. Report. Addis Ababa: United Nations Economic Commission for Africa, 2013.

UNECA. 'Status of Integration in Africa (SIA IV)'. 2012. https://au.int/sites/default/files/newsevents/workingdocuments/26630-wd-highlights_rev1_en.pdf. Accessed July 2019.

United Nations. Security Council Report, 'Democratic Republic of the Congo'. http://www.un.org/press/en/2014/sc11268.doc.htm. Accessed July 2016.

United Nations. *World Economic Situation* 2015.

United Nations Conference on Trade and Development (UNCTAD). 'Trade and Development Report'. 2012: http://unctad.org/en/PublicationsLibrary/tdr2012overview_en.pdf. Accessed July 2016.

United Nations Conference on Trade and Development (UNCTAD) Trade and Development Report. *Policies for Inclusive Development and Balanced Growth*. 2012: 103–4. http://unctad.org/en/publicationslibrary/tdr2012_en.pdf. Accessed July 2016.

United Nations (UN) document. ' "Intervention Brigade" Authorized as Security Council Grants Mandate Renewal for United Nations Mission in Democratic Republic of Congo'. 28 March 2013. http://www.un.org/press/en/2013/sc10964.doc.htm. Accessed July 2016.

United Nations document. http://www.un.org/press/en/2014/sc11268.doc.htm. Accessed July 2016.

United Nations document S/2014/740. Report of the Secretary-General on the situation with respect to piracy and armed robbery at sea off the coast of Somalia. 16 October 2014. http://www.un.org/en/ga/search/view_doc.asp?symbol=S/2014/740. Accessed July 2016.

United Nations Environment Programme (UNEP) and the Mission des Nations Unies en République Démocratique du Congo (MONSUCO). 'Experts' background report on illegal exploitation and trade in natural resources benefitting organized criminal groups and recommendations on MONUSCO's role in fostering stability and peace in eastern DR Congo'. 15 April 2015.

United Nations Security Council (UNSC) SC/11172. 'Security Council Extends Mandate of AU mission in Somalia, Requests Increase in Troop Strength'. 12 November 2013, http://www.un.org/press/en/2013/sc11172.doc.htm. Accessed July 2016.

United Nations Yearbook of International Trade Statistics 1974. vol. III, cited in, Manfield Bienefield and Duncan Innes, 'Capital Accumulation and South Africa'. *Review of African Political Economy*, no. 7 (1976).

United States AGOA Trade with COMESA. https://ustr.gov/countries-regions/africa/regional-economic-communities-rec/common-market-eastern-and-Southern-africa-comesa. Accessed July 2016.

United States Trade Representative (USTR). AGOA trade with Southern Africa. http://www.ustr.gov/countries-regions/africa/Southern-africa/south-africa. Accessed July 2016.

United States Trade with EAC. http://www.ustr.gov/countries-regions/africa/regional-economic-communities-rec OR https://ustr.gov/countries-regions/africa/regional-economic-communities-rec/east-african-community. Accessed July 2016.

United States (USTR). 'Eswatini'. https://ustr.gov/countries-regions/africa/Southern-africa/eswatini. Accessed July 2016.

World Bank. 'De-Fragmenting Africa: Deepening Regional Trade Integration in Goods and Services'. 2012. https://openknowledge.worldbank.org/bitstream/handle/10986/12385/684900ESW0Whit00Box367921B00PUBLIC0.pdf?sequence=1. Accessed July 2016.

World Bank. 'GDP (current US$)'. http://data.worldbank.org/indicator/NY.GDP.MKTP.CD. Accessed July 2016.

World Bank. 'Mozambique Industrial Sector Study: the Development of Industrial Policy and Reform of the Business Environment'. *Industry and Energy Operations Division, Southern African Department*, 1999.

World Bank. 'Proposed Grant of $73.1 million for the DRC'. http://www-wds.worldbank.org/external/default/WDSContentServer/WDSP/IB/2014/03/05/000456286_20140305164405/Rendered/INDEX/774200REPLACEM0140Box382121B00OUO90.txt. Accessed July 2016.

World Bank. 'South Africa Economic Update: Focus on Export Competitiveness'. 2014.

World Bank. 'The World Bank's Rwanda Economic Update: Seizing the Opportunities for Growth with a Special focus on Harnessing the Demographic Dividend'. 29 January 2014. http://www.worldbank.org/en/news/press-release/2014/01/29/the-world-banks-rwanda-economic-update-seizing-the-opportunities-for-growth-with-a-special-focus-on-harnessing-the-demographic-dividend. Accessed July 2016.

World Bank Indicators. South Africa's total GDP for the periods 2000–2010. https://data.worldbank.org/indicator/NY.GDP.MKTP.KD.ZG?locations=ZA. Accessed July 2019.

World Bank Statistics on Rwanda's Donor Funding. https://www.worldbank.org/en/country/rwanda/overview. Accessed July 2019.

World Development Report. *World Bank* (1989). www.worldbank.org. Accessed July 2014.

World Fact Book. Central Intelligence Agency. United States. 2015. https://www.cia.gov/library/publications/the-world-factbook/fields/print_2116.html. Accessed July 2016.

Index

absolute convergence (catch-up process) 28, 29, 133
Abuja Treaty (1991) 21, 43, 86, 104, 106, 142, 180
ACFTA *see* Continental Free Trade Agreement (CFTA)
Acharya, Amitav 8, 13
ACIRC *see* African Capacity for Immediate Response to Crises (ACIRC)
ACP *see* Africa, Caribbean and Pacific (ACP) group of states
ACRT *see* African Regional Centre for Technology Design and Manufacturing (ACRT)
Addis Ababa 121, 124, 170
Adedeji, Adebayo 45, 53, 68, 95
ADF *see* Allied Democratic Forces (ADF)
ADF-NALU *see* Allied Democratic Forces–National Army for the Liberation of Uganda (ADF-NALU)
AEC *see* African Economic Community (AEC)
AfDB *see* African Development Bank (AfDB)
Africa, Caribbean and Pacific (ACP) group of states 2, 149, 150
   Africa–Europe trade relations 14, 31–2
   blue economy 163–6
   Cotonou Agreement with Europe 7, 12, 120, 159, 185, 188, 190
   EU's relationship with 159–62
   post-Cotonou agenda 160, 162, 163, 164, 165, 194
   Programming of Regional Cooperation Funds 64
African Capacity for Immediate Response to Crises (ACIRC) 13, 171–2
African Common Market 5, 45, 46
African Continental Free Trade Agreement (ACFTA) *see* Continental Free Trade Agreement (CFTA)
African Development Bank (AfDB) 9, 104, 115
African Economic Community (AEC) 21, 80, 82, 86, 87
African Growth and Opportunity Act (AGOA) 6, 12, 119, 120, 123
   rules of origin and 125, 127–31, 142, 186
   trade agreements with the United States 101, 134, 138, 186
   trade with COMESA and South Africa 128–30
African National Congress (ANC) 31, 47, 55, 66, 78, 84
African Peace and Security Architecture (APSA) 3, 8, 167, 169, 170
African Peer Review Mechanism (APRM) 31
African Regional Centre for Engineering Design and Manufacturing (ARCEDEM) 68
African Regional Centre for Technology Design and Manufacturing (ACRT) 68
African Regional Transport Infrastructure Network (ARTIN) 114
African Renaissance and International Cooperation Fund (ARF) 177, 178
African Standby Force (ASF) 2, 3, 167, 169–70, 177, 192
African Union (AU) 3, 9, 16, 23, 31, 192, 194–5
   Abuja Treaty of 1991 21, 142
   Agenda 2063 12, 150
   CFTA establishment 147, 148
   Constitutive Act of 2000 21
   intra-African trade boost by 5
   military intervention tool set up 171–2
   non-support by the United Nations 172
   Peace and Security Council (PSC) 169, 194
   regional integration, agenda on 22

Roadmap and Planning Element (PLANELM) 169–70
2050 Africa's Integrated Maritime (AIM) strategy 164
Africa's Priority Programme for Economic Recovery (APPER) 68
Afrikaanse Handelsinstituut (AHI) 84
AGOA *see* African Growth and Opportunity Act (AGOA)
agro-processing 115, 123, 149, 153–5, 157–8
AHI *see* Afrikaanse Handelsinstituut (AHI)
airspace market 104–5, 107–8, 114, 116, 164
Ajulu, Rok 41
Akokpari, John 19
alliance theory 14, 42
Allied Democratic Forces (ADF) 172
Allied Democratic Forces–National Army for the Liberation of Uganda (ADF-NALU) 173
Amin, Idi 17
ANC *see* African National Congress (ANC)
Anglin, Douglas 50, 54, 63, 67, 69
Angola 2, 53, 63, 83, 95, 144 *see also* National Union for the Total Independence of Angola (*União Nacional para a Independência Total de Angola*) (UNITA)
  colonialism and independence 47
  COMESA member 88
  economy 15, 17
  exports from SADCC to 57, 64, 76
  FLS member 47
  MULPOC funding 68
  Mutual Defence Pact 57–8, 59, 94
  oil production and trading 52
  participation in FLS involvement 19
  PTA member 4, 69
  skills shortage in 76
APDP *see* Automotive Production and Development Programme (APDP)
APPER *see* Africa's Priority Programme for Economic Recovery (APPER)
APRM *see* African Peer Review Mechanism (APRM)
APSA *see* African Peace and Security Architecture (APSA)

ARCEDEM *see* African Regional Centre for Engineering Design and Manufacturing (ARCEDEM)
ARF *see* African Renaissance and International Cooperation Fund (ARF)
Armed Forces of the Democratic Republic of the Congo (*Forces Armées de la République Démocratique du Congo*) (FARDC) 176, 178
ARTIN *see* African Regional Transport Infrastructure Network (ARTIN)
Asante, Samuel K. B. 18, 44
ASEAN *see* Association of Southeast Asian Nations (ASEAN)
ASF *see* African Standby Force (ASF)
'Asian Miracle' 32
Asiedu, Kojo 21–2, 96
Association of Southeast Asian Nations (ASEAN) 16, 22, 96
ASYCUDA *see* Automated System for Customs Data (ASYCUDA)
AU *see* African Union (AU)
Australia 144, 152, 162
Austria 52
Automated System for Customs Data (ASYCUDA) 73
automotive industry 152, 155, 189
Automotive Production and Development Programme (APDP) 152

β *see* beta-convergence (β)
Balassa, Bela 22
Baldwin, Robert 38, 66
Baltic states 34, 110
Banda 49, 50, 52, 53
Bandung Afro-Asian Conference (1955) 44
Barro, Robert 28–9, 133, 189
Baumol, William 37
Beijing 12, 154, 159, 185
Belgium 47, 52, 160, 165
Ben-David, Dan 30
Besada, Hany 41
beta-convergence (β) 28, 133, 134
Bhagwati, Jagdish 126, 143, 186
BLNE *see* Botswana, Lesotho, Namibia and Eswatini (BLNE)
Bøås, Morten 19

Botswana 5, 17, 48, 53, 76, 115 *see also* Botswana, Lesotho, Namibia and Eswatini (BLNE)
   border dispute with Namibia 93
   COMESA, EAC and SADC member 8, 60
   exports from SADCC to 57, 64
   FLS member 47
   JPC member 78
   metal producer 52
   MULPOC funding 68
   PTA member 4, 69
   skills shortage in 76
   trade growth convergence of 134, 136
Botswana, Lesotho, Namibia and Eswatini (BLNE) 7, 19–20, 31, 45, 83, 126, 131, 134, 138–9, 140, 144, 188
BP *see* British Petroleum (BP)
Brazil 38, 76, 144, 152 *see also* Brazil-Russia-India-China-South Africa (BRICS)
Brazil-Russia-India-China-South Africa (BRICS) 6, 13, 31, 119, 127, 133, 140–2, 143, 188
Bremmer, Ian 24, 65
Brenton, Paul 128
BRICS *see* Brazil-Russia-India-China-South Africa (BRICS)
Brink, Brian 101
Britain 14, 30, 34, 45, 52, 63, 109, 165
British Petroleum (BP) 52, 160
Brussels 12, 34, 44, 63, 112, 159, 160, 185, 188, 190
Buhari, Muhammadu 148
Bull, Headley 47
Burundi 71, 112 *see also* Democratic Republic of the Congo (DRC)
   agricultural country 173–4
   CEPGL member 46
   COMESA, EAC and SADC member 8, 72
   conflicts in 83, 93, 173
   PTA member 4, 69
Buzan, Barry 8, 13, 42, 168, 171, 172

Callaghy, Thomas 39
Canada 63, 144
Canadian International Development Assistance (CIDA) 65
CAP *see* Common Agriculture Policy (CAP)
capitalism 24, 30, 65
Carmignami, Fabrizio 80
Cass, David 26
Castro, Fidel 50
CEAO *see* West African Economic Community (*Communauté économique de l' Afrique de l'oust*) (CEAO)
CEN–SAD *see* Community of Sahel-Saharan States (CEN–SAD)
Central Intelligence Agency (CIA) (US) 177
CEOs *see* chief executive officers (CEOs)
CEPGL *see* Economic Community of the Great Lakes Countries (*Communauté économique des pays des Grands Lacs*) (CEPGL)
CFTA *see* Continental Free Trade Area (CFTA)
chief executive officers (CEOs) 105
China 2, 7, 132, 133, 148, 179 *see also* Brazil-Russia-India-China-South Africa (BRICS)
   Doha Round process 24
   economic slowdown 143–4
   G-5 Sahel initiative 13
   G20 Summit meeting 37
   leather trade 151, 152, 154
CIA *see* Central Intelligence Agency (CIA) (US)
CIDA *see* Canadian International Development Assistance (CIDA)
Clapham, Christopher 92
CMA *see* Common Monetary Area (CMA)
Cold War 46
colonialism 4, 23, 44, 45, 47, 54, 57
COMESA-EAC-SADC
   air markets for 107–8
   airspace liberalisation, harmonised policies for 103–5 (*see also* Yamoussoukro Declaration (YD))
   diplomacy during 1998–2008 103–5
   endowment factors, lack of 23
   free trade in 28, 72, 73, 91, 92, 100, 147
   infrastructure gaps as trade barriers 191
   JCA for liberalised airspace 105, 107, 108

multiple memberships in 104–5, 119, 123, 132 (*see also* multiple memberships)
regional integration processes 100–1
regional security management by 21, 38, 40, 41, 168, 171, 173, 177–83, 191–2
rules of origin for 113–14, 127–8, 186
sugar production in 102–3
trade divergence in 101
trade partnership in 2008 2, 5, 23
Tripartite Agreement 105, 106–14, 117, 148 (*see also* Tripartite Free Trade Agreement (TFTA))
Tripartite Task Force 105, 107, 109
variable geometry and 124–7
COMESA *see* Common Market for Eastern and Southern Africa (COMESA)
Common Agriculture Policy (CAP) 101
Common Market for Eastern and Southern Africa (COMESA)
and AGOA markets 128–30
convergence with EAC and SADC 12, 105 (*see also* COMESA-EAC-SADC)
establishment and evolution 4, 9, 46, 72–4, 88
institutional architecture of 72–4
macroeconomic convergence, addressing of 110
member states 72, 88–9
merging of PTA and SADC into 82, 84, 85–6, 88
non-tariff barriers, removal of 72, 73, 110, 111
post rationalisation process 5
principles of member states 180–1
profile of 180–1
trade 28, 72–3, 128–30
treaty 69, 71
variable geometry approach to liberalise trade 6, 23
Common Monetary Area (CMA) 6, 35, 86–7
Community of Sahel-Saharan States (CEN-SAD) 122
Comprehensive Peace Accord (CPA) 179
Congress of South African Trade Unions (COSATU) 84
Continental Free Trade Area (CFTA) 23, 43, 91, 182, 185, 186, 187, 189–90, 193
establishment and evolution 2–6, 11, 13, 147, 159
open markets and free trade 3, 12
phases and protocols 148
ratification 147, 148, 167
convergence *see also* divergence and convergence
absolute 28, 29, 133
beta- 28, 133, 134
club 28, 29
conditional 29
economic *see* economic convergence
economic growth 28, 33, 133, 149
historical evolution of 4
increase through productivity 37
macroeconomic 34, 35, 86, 87, 109, 110
regional 12, 13, 32, 33, 35, 72–4, 97, 123
security *see* Pan-African security convergence; regional security convergence
sigma- 28, 133
trade growth 134–8
COSATU *see* Congress of South African Trade Unions (COSATU)
Cotonou Agreement 7, 12, 120, 159, 185, 188, 190
CPA *see* Comprehensive Peace Accord (CPA)
Cuba 48
customs unions 3, 6, 27, 106, 112, 113, 121, 139 *see also* Southern African Customs Union (SACU)
EAC 2, 5, 121, 122, 147
interlinking of 46, 169
Kenya-Uganda 44
multiple memberships, accommodation of 105, 126
purpose of 30, 80–1, 105, 109, 187
for tariff elimination 81, 109

DAC *see* Development Assistance Committee (DAC)
DAM *see* day-ahead market (DAM)
Davies, Rob 28, 84, 155, 157
day-ahead market (DAM) 97

DBSA *see* Development Bank of Southern Africa (DBSA)
Democratic Forces for the Liberation of Rwanda (*Forces démocratiques de libération du Rwanda*) (FDLR) 172, 174
Democratic Republic of the Congo (DRC) 13, 46, 57, 72, 95, 115, 147, 181, 182
  conflicts in 83, 93–4, 121, 123, 171, 172–3, 192
  independence of 54
  Inga project 101–2, 177–8
  Kinshasa 174, 176
  power generation projects in 116, 177–8
  smuggling of resources in 174–6
Denmark 64
Department for International Development (DFID) 109
Department of International Relations and Cooperation (DIRCO) 31, 85
Department of Peacekeeping Operations (DPKO) 172
Department of Trade and Industry (DTI) 85, 152, 157
Deutsch, Karl 14–15, 41
Development Assistance Committee (DAC) 66
Development Bank of Southern Africa (DBSA) 9, 62, 84, 85, 89
developmental integration 20, 22, 36, 65, 96–103
DFID *see* Department for International Development (DFID)
diamonds
  exports 48, 52, 127, 144
  extraction/production 52
  smuggling 51, 171, 173, 174, 176
Diop, Cheikh Anta 44
DIRCO *see* Department of International Relations and Cooperation (DIRCO)
divergence *see also* divergence and convergence
  core versus peripheral economies 22–3, 100 (*see also* peripheral economies)
  economic inequality and, 2–3
  of economic integration 109
  historical evolution of 4
  regional trade policies, cause for 3, 12

divergence and convergence 1–4, 9, 10, 11
  in free trade agreements 30–3, 100
  Galor's theory on 29
  of macroeconomic policies within regions 33–5
  and multiple memberships 36–8
  in neoclassical economics 24–7
  of Pan-Africanism within regional integration 14–20
  of regional integration 1, 2, 24
Djibouti 4, 69, 70, 71, 123, 124, 128, 147, 170
Doha Round process 24, 112
Dollar, David 33, 76
'domino theory' (proliferation of membership) 36–7
Dowrick, Steve 7, 28, 140, 143, 187
DPKO *see* Department of Peacekeeping Operations (DPKO)
DRC *see* Democratic Republic of the Congo (DRC)
DTI *see* Department of Trade and Industry (DTI)
Dubois, William E.B. 30
Durlauf, Steven 29

EAC *see* East African Community (EAC)
EACB *see* East African Central Bank (EACB)
EAMU *see* East African Monetary Union (EAMU)
EAPP *see* East African Power Pool (EAPP)
EASBRIG *see* Eastern African Standby Brigade (EASBRIG)
EASF *see* Eastern Africa Standby Force (EASF)
EASFCOM *see* East African Standby Force Coordination Mechanism (EASFCOM)
East African Central Bank (EACB) 110
East African Community (EAC)
  convergence with COMESA and SADC 12, 105 (*see also* COMESA-EAC-SADC)
  customs union 2, 5, 121, 122, 147
  economic partnership agreement with the EU, 161–2
  establishment and evolution 4, 9, 16, 19, 46, 67

failure of 16–17
free trade in 28, 72, 73, 100
infrastructure development 115
Kenya-Uganda Customs Union 44
relations with PTA 5, 67–72
trade with the US 130
Treaty 104, 110
variable geometry approach to liberalise trade 6, 23
East African Monetary Union (EAMU) 110
East African Power Pool (EAPP) 116
East African Standby Force Coordination Mechanism (EASFCOM) 170
Eastern Africa 1, 4, 16, 17, 21, 35, 41, 46, 67, 69, 169, 170 *see also individual organisations*
Eastern Africa Standby Force (EASF) 169–70
Eastern African Standby Brigade (EASBRIG) 169–70
Eastern and Southern African Management Institute (ESAMI) 68
ECA *see* United Nations Economic Commission for Africa (UNECA)
ECB *see* European Central Bank (ECB)
ECCAS *see* Economic Community for Central African States (ECCAS)
ECLA *see* Economic Commission for Latin America (ECLA)
ECLAC *see* Economic Commission for Latin America and the Caribbean (ECLAC)
Economic and Social Council (ECOSOC) 45
Economic Coal and Steel Community (ECSC) 15, 16
Economic Commission for Latin America (ECLA) 26, 44
Economic Commission for Latin America and the Caribbean (ECLAC) 44, 164
Economic Community for Central African States (ECCAS) 122, 169, 195
Economic Community of the Great Lakes Countries (*Communauté économique des pays des Grands Lacs*) (CEPGL) 46, 122
Economic Community of West African States (ECOWAS) 16, 41, 46, 169, 181

economic convergence 2, 4, 11, 53, 76, 87, 106–9, 119, 120, 125, 131, 133, 139, 147, 148, 162–3, 167
economic growth
classical model of 25–6
convergence 28, 33, 133, 149
divergence and/or convergence 24–7
factors that inhibit 2–3, 15–16, 17
federalist views on 15
growth triangles for 21–2, 96
open markets and open trade 12, 22–4
socio- 1, 10, 96, 119, 153, 180
by trade liberalisation 27–30, 32, 35, 149
economic inequality 2–3, 149
economic integration 16, 22, 23, 35, 37 *see also* Pan-African economic integration; regional economic integration
Africa's journey through 81–9
classical economic growth model of 25
divergence of 109
intraregional trade for 8, 35, 149–58
Krugman's hypothesis 32
neoclassical theory 6–7, 12
political integration as foundation for 43–4
regional integration within 18
regional wars targeting 17, 21, 67
Solow theory 25–6
Economic Partnership Agreements (EPAs) 6, 12–13, 22, 93, 112, 119, 144
between EAC and EU 161–2, 186
members 126–7
rules of origin and 127–31
SADC agreement 126–7, 188
ECOSOC *see* Economic and Social Council (ECOSOC)
ECOWAS *see* Economic Community of West African States (ECOWAS)
ECSC *see* Economic Coal and Steel Community (ECSC)
EEC *see* European Economic Commission (EEC)
EFTA *see* European Free Trade Association (EFTA)
Egypt 72, 142
core economy in Africa 15, 150
disputes with Ethiopia 121, 182
TFTA ratification 114, 121

trade 2, 8, 12, 31
Tripartite Summit (2015) 111, 113, 114
EMU *see* European Monetary
    Union (EMU)
endogenous growth 16, 25, 27, 32, 33,
    37–8, 74, 92, 99, 117, 140, 143, 186,
    187, 189
EPAs *see* Economic Partnership
    Agreements (EPAs)
Erasmus, Gerhard 125–6
Eritrea 68, 72, 93, 114, 121, 123, 170, 181
Erwin, Alec 85
ESAMI *see* Eastern and Southern African
    Management Institute (ESAMI)
Eskom 96–8, 101, 116, 117, 144, 177
Eswatini 5, 7, 47, 53, 83, 121 *see also*
    Botswana, Lesotho, Namibia and
    Eswatini (BLNE)
  COMESA, EAC and SADC member 8
  exports from SADCC to 57, 64
  Maputo Corridor Joint Operating
    Centre 115–16
  PTA member 4, 69
  skills shortage in 76
  TFTA signatory 133
  trade growth convergence of 134, 138
  trilateral monetary agreement 35
  Tripartite Common Monetary Area 86–7
Ethiopia
  COMESA, EAC and SADC member 8
  disputes with Egypt 121, 182
  leather markets 152, 153, 154, 155, 189
  Ogaden War 68, 93
  PAFMECA grouping 46
  power generation projects in 116, 181–2
  PTA member 4, 68, 69
EU *see* European Union (EU)
EU-SA TDCA *see* Trade Development and
    Cooperation agreement (TDCA)
Europe 2, 8, 37 *see also* European
    organisations
  ACP–EU Cotonou Agreement 7, 12 (*see
    also* Cotonou Agreement)
  Bretton Woods system, collapse of 30
  club convergence in 28
  economic policy, convergence of 18
  industrialisation in 25
  restructuring of SADC Secretariat 57, 60
  supranationalism and sovereignty 14–15

trade with Africa 14, 31, 44
European Central Bank (ECB) 34
European Commission 34, 53, 160
European Economic Commission (EEC)
    29, 30, 54, 65, 101, 159
European Free Trade Association
    (EFTA) 29
European Monetary Union (EMU) 34
European Union (EU) 6, 9, 22, 80, 85, 110
  Britain's exit from the 14, 34
  economic partnership agreement with
    EAC, 161–2, 186
  exports to Southern Africa 127
  funding and assessment for SADC
    60, 62, 93
  Cotonou Agreement with ACP 7, 12,
    120, 159, 185, 188, 190
  Germany's investments in 37
  Multiannual Financial Framework
    (MFF) 160
  relationship with ACP bloc 159–62
  segregation of South Africa to the ACP
    bloc 32
  a supranational entity 15
  trade agreement with South Africa
    see Trade Development and
    Cooperation agreement (TDCA)

FARDC *see* Armed Forces of the
    Democratic Republic of the Congo
    (*Forces Armées de la République
    Démocratique du Congo*) (FARDC)
FDI *see* foreign direct investment (FDI)
FDLR *see* Democratic Forces for the
    Liberation of Rwanda (*Forces
    démocratiques de libération du
    Rwanda*) (FDLR)
federalism 14, 15
FIB *see* Force Intervention Brigade (FIB)
Fingleton, Bernard 34, 110
First, Ruth 51
Flatters, Frank 33, 128
FLS *see* Frontline States (FLS)
Fonseca, Raymond Steenkamp 23, 96
Force Intervention Brigade (FIB) 123
foreign direct investment (FDI) 38
Fourth Industrial Revolution (4IR) 7, 149
4IR *see* Fourth Industrial Revolution (4IR)
France 45, 70, 160, 165, 170, 188

Cross-Border Joint Force
    operationalisation 13
  a eurozone member state 34
  funding for SADCC 63
  interference in Pan-African unity 30
  investments in Rhodesia 52
  support to Zaire 47
Frank, Andre Gunder 100
free trade 11, 23
  areas/agreements *see* free trade areas/
    free trade agreements (FTAs)
  divergence and convergence in 3, 12,
    30–3, 100
free trade areas/free trade agreements
    (FTAs) 24, 30–3, 36, 68, 72, 74, 85,
    119, 120, 133
  CFTA *see* Continental Free Trade
    Area (CFTA)
  in COMESA-EAC-SADC 28, 72, 73, 91,
    92, 100, 147
  crisscrossing 37, 126, 191
  spaghetti-bowl concept in 126,
    130–1, 191
  TFTA *see* Tripartite Free Trade
    Area (TFTA)
FRELIMO *see* Mozambique Liberation
    Front (FRELIMO)
Friedland, Elaine 63, 65
Friedmann, John 22, 190
Froman, Michael 134, 138
Frontline States (FLS) 4, 14, 58, 63, 74,
    83, 87, 88
  alliance formation 46–9, 51
  defence and security function 57
  détente, use of 49–50
  and external actors 51–3
  formation 19, 46–7
  goals of 46–7
  security objectives of 42
FTAs *see* free trade areas/free trade
    agreements (FTAs)
functionalism 14, 15

Galor, Oded 29
Gambari, Ibrahim 7, 17, 18, 27, 32, 100
Gambia 2, 147
Garretsen, Harry 34, 110
Gathii, James 36, 125, 126, 139, 143,
    186, 191

GATT *see* General Agreement on Tariffs
    and Trade (GATT)
GDP *see* gross domestic product (GDP)
General Agreement on Tariffs and Trade
    (GATT) 3, 24, 29, 31, 80, 126,
    127, 129 *see also* World Trade
    Organization (WTO)
GERD *see* Grand Ethiopian Renaissance
    Dam (GERD)
Germany 26, 34, 37, 52, 61, 63, 160, 165
Gerschenkron, Alexander 26
Ghana 30, 44, 45, 147, 169
Gibb, Richard 35, 44
Gilpin, Robert 26, 36
GNP *see* gross national product (GNP)
Goetz, Ariane 41
Grand Ethiopian Renaissance Dam
    (GERD) 121
gravity theory of trade 7, 159
Great Lakes conflicts 94, 123, 171, 174, 177,
    179, 183
Greece 34, 110
Griffith, Richard 30
gross domestic product (GDP) 21,
    33, 54, 68
gross national product (GNP) 64, 68, 69, 80
Grossman, Gene 37
Group of Twenty (G-20) 20
growth accounting tautology 32–3
G20 Africa-Conference (2017) 37
G-20 *see* Group of Twenty (G-20)
G20 Summit 37
Gurtov, Mel 49
Gwaradzimba, Fadzai 83

Haarløv, Jens 36
Haas, Ernest 15, 18
Hansen, Gary 27
HAT *see* High Transitional Authority
    (*Haute Autorité de la
    Transition*) (HAT)
Hazelwood, Arthur 100
HCTs *see* High Commission
    Territories (HCTs)
HDI *see* Human Development Index (HDI)
Helpman, Elhanan 37
Henderson, Robert 44
Hervey, Angus Fane 23, 96
Hettne, Björn 19, 20, 21

High Commission Territories (HCTs) 45
High Transitional Authority (*Haute Autorité de la Transition*) (HAT) 95
Horve, Tore 96
Human Development Index (HDI) 95

ICGLR *see* International Conference on the Great Lakes Region (ICGLR)
ICJ *see* International Court of Justice (ICJ)
ICM *see* Integrated Committee of Ministers (ICM)
IDT *see* Independent Development Trust (IDT)
IGAD *see* Intergovernmental Authority for Development (IGAD)
IGADD *see* Intergovernmental Authority for Drought and Development (IGADD)
IMF *see* International Monetary Fund (IMF)
IMO *see* International Maritime Organization (IMO)
import substitution 26, 27, 32, 190
Independent Development Trust (IDT) 84
India 24, 44, 148, 151, 152 *see also* Brazil-Russia-India-China-South Africa (BRICS)
industrialisation 5, 25, 28, 31, 37, 44, 74, 106, 155
  agro- 7, 149, 193
  funding for projects 65
  value-addition/value-driven 7, 16, 33, 125, 140, 143, 150, 153, 159, 185, 187
Inotai, András 20
Integrated Committee of Ministers (ICM) 59–60
Integrated Resource Plan (IRP) 116
Intergovernmental Authority for Development (IGAD) 41, 114, 169, 181, 195
Intergovernmental Authority for Drought and Development (IGADD) 68
International Conference on the Great Lakes Region (ICGLR) 195
International Court of Justice (ICJ) 93
International Maritime Organization (IMO) 182
International Monetary Fund (IMF) 50, 66

International Standard Industrial Classification (ISIC) 74–6
Inter-State Defence and Security Committee (ISDSC) 57, 58, 60
Inter-State Politics and Diplomacy Committee (ISPDC) 58, 60
intraregional trade 30, 72, 114, 143, 165, 189
  for economic integration 8, 35, 149–58
  impediments to 56, 63, 123
  increase of 24, 69, 139, 144 (*see also* 'two-level game' theory)
  unequal nature of 3
  value-added production through 16, 92
Ireland 34, 110
IRP *see* Integrated Resource Plan (IRP)
Isaksen, Jan 59
ISDSC *see* Inter-State Defence and Security Committee (ISDSC)
ISIC *see* International Standard Industrial Classification (ISIC)
Ismail, Faizel 85
ISPDC *see* Inter-State Politics and Diplomacy Committee (ISPDC)
Italy 34, 52, 95, 152, 160, 165

Japan 26, 30, 52, 63, 104, 152
JCA *see* Joint Competition Authority (JCA)
Jenkins, Carolyn 33, 35, 98, 110, 126, 140
Jefferis, Keith 35
JOC *see* Maputo Corridor Joint Operating Centre (JOC)
Johnson, Paul 29
Johor–Singapore–Riau Growth Triangle 22, 96
Joint Competition Authority (JCA) 105, 107, 108
Joint Planning Committee (JPC) 78, 79–80, 82, 83, 84
JPC *see* Joint Planning Committee (JPC)

Kagame, Paul 148, 174
Kalenga, Paul 128, 191
Kaunda, Kenneth 46, 48–50
Khadiagala, Gilbert 14, 42, 47, 49, 50, 51, 66, 77, 87
Khama, Seretse 46
Kéïta, Modibo 44
Kenya 141, 142, 144

cooperatives, formation of 158
core economy in Africa 15, 16–17, 71, 150
EAC member 16, 46
leather markets 152, 153–4, 155, 158, 189
Leather Science and Technology Training Programme 158
power generation projects in 116
PTA member 4, 68, 69
TFTA ratification 114, 121, 124
trade 2, 8, 12, 31
Keohane, Robert 18, 38, 53
Kibaki, Mwai 124
King-Akerele, Olubanke 21–2, 96
Kiplagat, Bethuel 181
Klerk, F. W. de 31
Krugman, Paul 32–3, 125, 142–3, 149, 186–7

labour
low-cost 22, 87, 96
migration 20, 23, 50, 52–3, 109, 191
productivity 26, 28
restrictions on 100
semi-skilled 22, 92, 96, 117, 140, 189
skilled 22, 32, 96
specialised 32, 125, 154
unskilled 92, 117
Lagos Plan of Action (LPA) 19, 30, 81
Lamu Port for Southern Sudan–Ethiopia Transport corridor (LAPSSET) 124
Lamy, Pascal 16, 17, 193
Lande, Stephen 129
Landsberg, Chris 94
LAPSSET see Lamu Port for Southern Sudan–Ethiopia Transport corridor (LAPSSET)
LDC see least developed country (LDC)
LDF see Lesotho Defence Force (LDF)
Leape, Jonathan 126
least developed country (LDC) 12, 18, 26, 28, 29, 32, 44, 96, 100, 124, 148, 163, 185
leather industry 55, 75, 127, 128, 149–59, 189
Lee, Margaret 18
Lesotho 5, 7, 47, 53, 83, 177 see also Botswana, Lesotho, Namibia and Eswatini (BLNE)

COMESA, EAC and SADC member 8, 88
exports from SADCC to 57, 64
income convergence study on 80
military coup by South Africa 93, 179
PTA member 4, 69
skills shortage in 76
trade growth convergence of 134, 137
trilateral monetary agreement 35
Tripartite Common Monetary Area 86–7
Lesotho Defence Force (LDF) 93
Leys, Roger 63
Libya 45, 72, 114, 128, 169
Lindberg, Leon 15
Lindeke, William 50–1
Lomé Convention (1975) 64, 72, 101, 159, 160
Lord's Resistance Army/Movement (LRA) 173
Love, Alexander R. 66
LPA see Lagos Plan of Action (LPA)
LRA see Lord's Resistance Army/Movement (LRA)
Lucas, Robert 27, 29
Lusaka 19, 48, 50, 54, 65, 67, 81, 104, 105, 111, 114, 176

Maasdorp, Gavin 84, 85
Machar, Riek 174
MacMillan, Margaret 149
Macro-Economic Research Group (MERG) 84
Madagascar 4, 54, 70, 72, 95, 124, 169, 173, 179, 182
Makoni, Simba 79, 80, 81
Malawi 21, 46, 47, 53, 63, 83, 115, 123 see also Nyasaland; Zambia–Malawi–Mozambique Growth Triangle (ZMM-GT)
access to railways 17, 50
COMESA, EAC and SADC member 8, 88, 181
exports from SADCC to 64, 76
income convergence study on 80
independence of 54
PTA member 4, 69
regional détente policy 50
skills shortage in 76

technology transfer in fishing
industry 65
trade with Mozambique 50, 52
Malewezi, Justin 7, 23
Mandela, Nelson 31, 57, 94, 95
Mankiw, Gregory 29
Mansfield, Edward 40
MANU *see* Mozambican African National Union (MANU)
Manuel, Trevor 84
manufacturing value added (MVA) 75-6
Maputo 6, 17, 58, 63, 98, 116
Maputo Corridor and Logistics Initiative (MCLI) 100, 116
Maputo Corridor Joint Operating Centre (JOC) 115-16
Maputo Development Corridor (MDC) 20, 22, 96, 98, 99, 100, 115-16, 189
March 23 rebel group movement (M23) 123, 172, 174, 176
Marchand, Marianne 19
Martin, Ron 32, 34, 110, 125
Mattli, Walter 7, 139
Mauritius 4, 61, 69, 71-2, 86, 88, 164, 165, 181, 182
Mayardit, Salva Kiir 174
Mazrui, Ali 7
Mbeki, Thabo 31, 94-5
Mbuende, Kaire 54, 55, 58, 66
MC *see* ministerial committee (MC)
MCLI *see* Maputo Corridor and Logistics Initiative (MCLI)
MDC *see* Maputo Development Corridor (MDC)
MDGs *see* Millennium Development Goals (MDGs)
Meier, Gerald 17, 25
memorandum of understanding (MOU)
SADCC 54, 64
Tripartite Agreement 5, 106, 109, 112, 124
Mercado Común del Sur (MERCOSUR) 16
mercantilist policies 39, 51, 88
MERCOSUR *see* Mercado Com ún del Sur (MERCOSUR)
MERG *see* Macro-Economic Research Group (MERG)
Merkel, Angela 37
Meyns, Peter 63, 81

MFN *see* most-favoured nation (MFN)
migration of labour 20, 23, 50, 52-3, 109, 191
Millennium Development Goals (MDGs) 67
Mills, Gregg 20
Minh, Ho Chi 44
mining industries/mining sector 20, 51, 52-3, 63, 76, 114, 115, 144, 161, 163, 165, 174, 176
ministerial committee (MC) 58-9
Mitrany, David 15, 18
Mittleman, James 19, 20
MNCs *see* multinational corporations (MNCs)
MONUSCO *see* United Nations Organisation Stabilisation Mission in the Democratic Republic of the Congo (*Mission de l'Organisation des Nations Unies pour la Stabilisation en République Démocratique du Congo*) (MONUSCO)
Moravcsik, Andrew 18
Morocco 45, 47, 169
Morsi, Mohamed 181
Moscow 132
most-favoured nation (MFN) 37, 73, 80, 111, 126, 128, 186, 191
MOU *see* memorandum of understanding (MOU)
Mozambican African National Union (MANU) 46
Mozambican National Resistance (*Resistência Nacional Moçambicana*) (RENAMO) 50
Mozambique 6, 17, 46, 53, 63, 83, 112, 115, 144 *see also* associated organisations
bilateral trade with South Africa 96, 98-100 (*see also* Maputo Development Corridor (MDC))
colonialism and independence 47
COMESA member 88
exports from SADCC to 57, 64
FLS member 47
income convergence study on 80
JPC member 78
macro-regions in 21

Maputo Corridor Joint Operating
  Centre 115–16
Nacala in 50, 63
participation in FLS involvement 19
Portuguese coup 47
SADCC member 4
skills shortage in 76
trade with Malawi 50, 52
Mozambique Liberation Front (FRELIMO)
  19, 46, 47, 48
MPLA *see* Popular Movement for the
  Liberation of Angola (MPLA)
M23 *see* March 23 rebel group
  movement (M23)
Mugabe, Robert 49, 57, 93, 94, 132, 181
Muhwezi, Dan 51
MULPOCs *see* multi-national
  programming and operational
  centres (MULPOCs)
multinational corporations (MNCs) 20,
  71, 102
multi-national programming
  and operational centres
  (MULPOCs) 67–8
multiple memberships 12, 23, 36, 89, 119–
  45, 186, 188, 190–1
  accommodation by customs union
    105, 126
  case of South Africa in SACU 138–42
  challenges in COMESA-EAC-SADC
    104–5, 119, 120, 123, 125–6, 132
  management of 121–4, 138–42
  regional arrangements in 131–8
  in TFTA 5, 6, 123, 138
Muscat, Jason 143, 144
MVA *see* manufacturing value
  added (MVA)
Mwanawasa, Levy 181
Mwinyihija, Mwinyikione 152
Mytelka, Lynn 7, 17, 27, 32

Namibia 5, 7, 19, 45 *see also* Botswana,
  Lesotho, Namibia and
  Eswatini (BLNE)
border dispute with Botswana 93
diamond exports 52, 144
independence of 79
Mutual Defence Pact 57–8, 59, 94
PTA member 4, 69

TFTA signatory 123, 133
trade growth convergence of 134, 137
Tripartite Common Monetary Area
  86–7
Walvis Bay retrieval 79
Nathan, Laurie 94
National African Union of Independent
  Mozambique (UNAMI) 46
National Bargaining Council for the
  Leather Industry (NCBLI) 155
National Conventional Arms Control
  Committee (NCACC) 178
National Democratic Union of
  Mozambique (UDENAMO) 46
National Development Plan (NDP) 96, 154
National Industrial Policy Framework
  (NIPF) 96
National Party (NP) 31
National Resistance Army (NRA) 173
National Skills Development Strategy
  (NSDS) 155
National Union for the Total Independence
  of Angola (*União Nacional para
  a Independência Total de Angola*)
  (UNITA) 47, 50–1
NCACC *see* National Conventional Arms
  Control Committee (NCACC)
NCBLI *see* National Bargaining Council for
  the Leather Industry (NCBLI)
Ncube, Mthuli 143, 144
NDP *see* National Development
  Plan (NDP)
Nehru, Jawaharlal 44
neoclassical economic integration theory
  6–7, 11–12
neoclassical economics 3, 9, 11–12, 24–7,
  28, 30, 38, 91–2, 99–100
neoclassical growth model 26, 27, 28, 29,
  30, 35, 141
neoclassical realism 11, 24, 36, 38–42
neo-functionalism 14, 15, 18
neorealist security convergence 3, 9, 13
NEPAD *see* New Partnership for Africa's
  Development (NEPAD)
New Growth Path (NGP) 96
New International Economic Order
  (NIEO) 64
New Partnership for Africa's Development
  (NEPAD) 9, 31, 114–15, 152

New Regionalism Approach/Theory
 (NRA/T) 20–1
New York 13, 170
Ngavirue, Z. 66
Ngoma, Naison 41
NGP see New Growth Path (NGP)
Nguyen, Duc-Tho 7, 28, 140, 143, 187
Ngwenya, Sindiso 111, 147
NIEO see New International Economic
 Order (NIEO)
Nigeria 15, 68, 144, 148, 169
NIPF see National Industrial Policy
 Framework (NIPF)
Nkrumah, Kwame 30, 31, 44, 45, 168–9
Nkurunziza, Pierre 174
Nomvete, Bax 70, 80
non-tariff barriers 35, 72, 73, 81, 109,
 111, 126
non-trade barriers (NTBs) 4, 5, 73
NP see National Party (NP)
NRA see National Resistance Army
 (NRA)
NRA/T see New Regionalism Approach/
 Theory (NRA/T)
NSDS see National Skills Development
 Strategy (NSDS)
NTBs see non-trade barriers (NTBs)
Nyasaland 17, 21, 46, 51 see also Malawi
Nye, Joseph 18, 38, 53
Nyerere, Julius 46
Nyong'o, Peter Anyang' 126
Nzewi, Ogochukwu 33

O Nying'uro, Phillip 7, 37, 188
OAU see Organization of African
 Unity (OAU)
Obama, Barack 129
OCAs see optimum currency areas (OCAs)
Ochoro, Walter 27, 33
OECD see Organisation for
 Economic Co-operation and
 Development (OECD)
Ogaden Wars 68, 93
Olorunsola, Victor 51
Øostergaard, Tom 63
OPDS see Organ on Politics, Defence and
 Security (OPDS)
OPDSC see Organ on Politics, Defence and
 Security Cooperation (OPDSC)

OPEC see Organization of Petroleum
 Exporting Countries (OPEC)
open markets 6, 37, 70, 88, 99–100, 117,
 120, 124, 132, 142, 185 see also
 open trade
 and divergence 3, 12
 and regional integration 14, 22–4
open trade 14, 22, 29, 87, 100, 101, 120,
 133, 142 see also open markets
optimum currency areas (OCAs) 34,
 35, 110
Orchoro, Walter 7
Organ on Politics, Defence and Security
 (OPDS) 57, 58, 59
Organ on Politics, Defence and Security
 Cooperation (OPDSC) 58–9, 60,
 93, 179
Organisation for Economic Co-operation
 and Development (OECD) 28, 63,
 66, 95, 101, 190
Organization of African Unity (OAU) 16,
 21, 46, 49, 80–1, 87, 103, 169
Organization of Petroleum Exporting
 Countries (OPEC) 17, 26, 30
σ see sigma-convergence (σ)

PAC see Pan-African Congress (PAC)
PAFMECA see Pan-African Movement
 for East and Central Africa
 (PAFMECA)
Pakistan 151
Pan-African Congress (PAC) 44, 55, 78
Pan-African economic integration 1–3, 9,
 31, 121, 147–66, 185
 divergence in achievement of 3, 12
 evolution of 5
 factors that determine 8
 five-pronged approach for promotion
  of 188–90
 poor infrastructure as barrier to 8,
  12–13, 17, 21
 theory 7, 148–9
Pan-African Movement for East and
 Central Africa (PAFMECA) 46
Pan-African Parliament (PAP) 5, 31, 114
Pan-African security convergence 1, 2, 3,
 167–83, 191–2
 collective security, achievement
  of 168–70

against piracy 182, 191
regional security management *see*
    regional security; regional security
    complex (RSC)
against smuggling 174–6
South Africa's role in 168, 171, 172,
    176, 177–83
state interventions in conflict
    areas 178–9
theory 8–9, 167–8
Pan-Africanism 1, 2, 6, 10, 168
    birth and death of 43–5
    evolution 11
    free trade agreements and 30–3
    towards modernity 20–2
    modernity to dependency 22–4
    within regional integration 14–20, 87
    reincarnate 45–9
Panagariya, Arvind 36, 126, 130, 139,
    186, 191
PAP *see* Pan-African Parliament (PAP)
PCRD *see* Post-Conflict Reconstruction
    and Development
    Programme (PCRD)
Peace and Security Council (PSC), 169, 194
Pere, Garth le 56, 59
peripheral economies 15, 22–3, 24, 34, 36,
    100, 159
PIDA *see* Programme for Infrastructure
    Development in Africa (PIDA)
PLANELM *see* Roadmap and Planning
    Element (PLANELM) 169–70
policy of détente 5, 49–51
Popular Movement for the Liberation of
    Angola (MPLA) 47, 48, 50
Post-Conflict Reconstruction and
    Development Programme
    (PCRD) 178
Power, Michael 23, 96
power sector 97–8, 102, 114, 116,
    177, 181–2
Prebisch, Raúl 26, 44
Preferential Trade Area (PTA)
    derogations to member states' budget
        contribution 71
    for eastern and Southern Africa 16, 69
    economic indicators 68, 69
    formation 4, 16, 19, 46, 67–72
    historical challenges 4

industrial development in Africa 69
key goals 17
legal instruments, establishment of 70–1
members 4, 68, 69, 83–4
merging into COMESA 82, 84, 85–6
merging with SADCC 81, 82, 83
North and South 85, 119–20
objectives of 70
obstacles faced by 70
rationalisation period of 74, 80–8
regional conflicts in member states
    68, 83, 93
relations with EAC 5, 67–72
and SADCC 19, 40
successor to *see* Common Market for
    Eastern and Southern Africa
    (COMESA)
trade 70, 71–2
treaty 4, 70, 72
Prescott, Edward 27
Pretoria 4, 31, 48, 49, 83, 93
Programme for Infrastructure
    Development in Africa
    (PIDA) 114–15
protectionism 24, 26, 32, 189
PSC *see* Peace and Security Council (PSC)
PTA *see* Preferential Trade Area (PTA)
Putnam, Robert 23–4, 139, 190

Qaddafi, Muammar 31
Quah, Danny 29
quantitative easing programme 34
Quebec 22, 96

racism/racial discrimination 4, 19,
    30, 45, 57
Rajoelina, Andry 95
Ramaphosa, Cyril 179
Ramos, Maria 87
Ramsamy, Prega 58
rationalisation 4, 5, 40, 43, 55, 92, 119
    of PTA 74, 80–8
    of SADCC 74–89
Ravalomanana, Marc 95
Ravenhill, John 20, 21, 22, 36
realism 3, 8, 38, 159, 167, 192
    classical 39
    defensive 39
    neo- 3, 9, 13, 38, 39, 177

neoclassical 11, 24, 36, 38–42
offensive 39
RECs *see* regional economic communities (RECs)
regional cooperation 16, 19, 21, 55, 86
inter- 112, 164
sub- 4, 69
regional economic communities (RECs) 2, 5, 9, 11, 16 *see also* Common Market for Eastern and Southern Africa (COMESA); East African Community (EAC); Southern African Development Community (SADC)
in Africa 21, 67
free trade areas, creation by 28, 72, 73, 91, 92 (*see also* Tripartite Free Trade Agreement (TFTA))
multiple memberships in 36–8
regional integration through 24, 67, 100–1
regional security management 21, 38, 40, 41, 168, 171, 173, 177–83, 191–2
regional trade boost by 35
trade liberalisation 6, 100, 110
regional economic integration 1, 8, 11, 14–15, 28, 44, 60, 120, 181
Regional Indicative Strategic Development Plan (RISDP) 61
regional integration 1, 2, 3, 5–7
agreements 80
within economic integration 18
exploitation of functional spillover effects 36
globalisation as a constraint in 17, 23–4, 30
lack of policies for economic growth 15–16
negotiation, power of 18
neoclassical economic 6–7, 11–12, 120, 142
in the 1970s 18
obstacles of 28
oil crisis as a hurdle to 17, 24, 30
open markets and open trade 14, 22–4
Pan-Africanism within 14–20, 87
phases of 54
processes 6, 14–16, 23, 40, 82, 87, 100–1, 142, 193
through RECs 24, 67, 100–1

South Africa's role in 20–2
state capitalism, impact on 24, 65
supranationalism and sovereignty 14–15, 18
theories 6–7, 9, 11–14 (*see also* Pan-African economic integration; Pan-African security convergence)
UNECA's efforts towards 16–17, 67
regional integration agreement (RIA) 80
Regional Payment and Settlement System (REPSS) 74, 189
Regional Peacekeeping Training Centre (RPTC) 61
regional security 1, 2, 57, 58, 67, 92 *see also* regional security complex (RSC)
convergence 3, 13–14
management by RECs 21, 38, 40, 41, 168, 171, 173, 177–83, 191–2
neglect of 93
neoclassical realist approach to 38–42
within regionalism 8–9, 13, 21
regional security complex (RSC) 8–9, 13, 171–6
framework 8, 13, 168, 171
qualification for 171
regional trade agreements 16, 100, 126, 127, 128, 131, 132–3, 142, 143, 152, 191
regionalisation 5, 18, 19, 20
regionalism 46, 66
apartheid 4, 19
by cooperation between eastern and Southern states 67–8
functional 45, 169
macro- 20, 21
micro- 20, 21, 22, 96–7, 99–100, 116, 117
new 18, 20–2
old 18–19
open 36, 80
regional security within 8–9, 13, 21
sub- 20
views on 18–19
Reilly, Gavin 84
REIPPP *see* Renewable Energy Independent Power Producer Programme (REIPPP)
RENAMO *see* Mozambican National Resistance (*Resistência Nacional Moçambicana*) (RENAMO)

Renewable Energy Independent
    Power Producer Programme
    (REIPPP) 116
REPSS *see* Regional Payment and
    Settlement System (REPSS)
Responsibility to Protect (R2P) 41
Rhodesia 4, 17, 21, 45, 46, 48–9, 50, 51–2
    see also Zambia
Rhodesian Iron and Steel Corporation
    (RISCO) 52
RIA *see* regional integration
    agreement (RIA)
RISCO *see* Rhodesian Iron and Steel
    Corporation (RISCO)
RISDP *see* Regional Indicative Strategic
    Development Plan (RISDP)
Rodrik, Dani 31, 36, 149
Rodriquez, Francisco 31, 36
Romer, David 29
Romer, Paul 27, 29
ROOs *see* rules of origin (ROOs)
Rose, Gideon 39, 40
RPTC *see* Regional Peacekeeping Training
    Centre (RPTC)
RSC *see* regional security complex
    (RSC)
R2P *see* Responsibility to Protect
    (R2P)
rules of origin (ROOs) 5, 7, 71, 109, 112,
    120, 123, 126, 140, 148, 189, 191
    in AGOA trade agreements 125, 127–31,
      142, 186
    for COMESA-EAC-SADC bloc 113–14,
      127–8, 186
    divergence of trade policies 33
    EU–SA FTA 101
    and external trade agreements 125,
      127–31, 142
    on leather products 152–3
    restrictive 101, 128, 143
Russia 132, 144 *see also* Brazil-Russia-
    India-China-South Africa (BRICS)
Rwanda *see also* Democratic Republic of
    the Congo (DRC)
    CEPGL member 46
    CFTA agreement at 148
    COMESA, EAC and SADC member 8
    conflicts in 123, 171, 173
    genocide in 68, 83, 93, 174

a hegemonic state 13
PTA member 4, 69
Rylander, Sten 66

SAATM *see* Single African Air Transport
    Market (SAATM)
SACCAR *see* Southern African Centre
    for Cooperation in Agricultural
    Research (SACCAR)
SACTWU *see* South African Clothing and
    Textile Workers Union (SACTWU)
SACU *see* Southern African Customs
    Union (SACU)
SADC National Committees (SNCs) 60, 94
SADC Programme of Action (SPA) 55, 83
SADC *see* Southern African Development
    Community (SADC)
SADCC *see* Southern African
    Development Coordination
    Conference (SADCC)
SAFTO *see* South African Foreign Trade
    Organisation (SAFTO)
Sala-i-Martin, Xavier 28–9, 133, 189
Samuelson, Paul 25
SANDF *see* South African National
    Defence Force (SANDF)
SAP *see* structural adjustment
    programme (SAP)
SAPP *see* Southern African Power
    Pool (SAPP)
SASSA *see* South African Social Security
    Agency (SASSA)
SATCC *see* Standing Committee of
    Officials (SATCC)
SATUCC *see* Southern African Trade
    Union Coordination Council
    (SATUCC)
Saudi Arabia 38
Savimbi, Jonas 50
Schäuble, Wolfgang 37
Schultz, Theodore W. 26
SDGs *see* sustainable development
    goals (SDGs)
SDI *see* Spatial Development
    Initiative (SDI)
Second World War 15, 25, 26, 44, 45
security sector reform (SSR) 178
Seko, Mobutu Sese 47, 51
Senghor, Lamine 44

SETA *see* Skills Education Training
    Authority (SETA)
SHALC *see* South African Skin, Hide and
    Leather Council (SHALC)
Shaw, Timothy 19
SIDS *see* small island developing
    states (SIDS)
Siebert, John 41
sigma-convergence (σ) 28, 133
Single African Air Transport Market
    (SAATM) 108
SIPO *see* Strategic Indicative Plan of the
    Organ (SIPO)
SITC *see* Standard International Trade
    Classification (SITC)
Skills Education Training Authority
    (SETA) 155
Slaughter, Matthew 29
Slocum-Bradley, Nikki 21
small island developing states (SIDS)
    163, 164
small, micro, and medium enterprises
    (SMMEs) 15–16, 158
Smith, Ian 48, 50
SMMEs *see* small, micro, and medium
    enterprises (SMMEs)
SNCs *see* SADC National
    Committees (SNCs)
Society for Worldwide Interbank Financial
    Telecommunication (SWIFT) 74
Söderbaum, Fredrik 21–2
Soko, Mills 102
Solow, Robert 25–7
Somalia 4, 46, 68, 69, 70, 93, 169, 170, 182
South Africa 4, 5, 6–8, 115 *see also* South
    African organisations
  ACP–EU Cotonou Agreement 7, 12 (*see
    also* Cotonou Agreement)
  and AGOA markets 128–9
  agricultural exports from SADCC
    to 76–7
  Anglo-American Corporation 52
  attachment to SACU 2, 7, 19–20,
    132, 133
  bilateral trade with Mozambique 96, 98–
    100 (*see also* Maputo Development
    Corridor (MDC))
  bilateral trade with Zimbabwe 77, 78
  core economy in Africa 15, 100, 150

economic growth policies 96
Eskom's financial difficulties, solving
    of 96–7
export trade 76–8, 92, 101, 151
functionalist approach to
    integration 31–2
hegemony of 6–7, 12, 13, 20, 102,
    138, 177
import trade 150, 152
influence on SADCC 17
infrastructure development 141
    (*see also* Spatial Development
    Initiative (SDI))
leather processing chain 155–7 (*see also*
    leather industry)
manufacturing sector of 74–6
Maputo Corridor Joint Operating
    Centre 115–16
micro-regional developmental
    integration approach 20–2,
    96–7, 99–100
military coup in Lesotho 93, 179
mining sector 52, 144
in Pan-African security convergence,
    role of 168, 171, 172, 176, 177–83
power sector 97–8, 102 (*see also* Eskom)
open trade with SADC 101–2
regional détente with Zambia 49–50
regional development in 19, 20, 22, 54,
    84–5, 96, 115, 132
regional trade in 77–8, 92
and SACU relations for economic
    integration 138–42
TFTA ratification 114, 121
trade agreement with EU *see* Trade
    Development and Cooperation
    agreement (TDCA)
trade growth convergence of 134, 136–8
trade relations with ACP bloc 31–2
trade with BRICS 141
trilateral monetary agreement 35
Tripartite Common Monetary Area 86–7
United States, relations with 52
South African Clothing and Textile
    Workers Union (SACTWU) 155
South African Foreign Trade Organisation
    (SAFTO) 77
South African National Defence Force
    (SANDF) 84, 93, 177

South African Skin, Hide and Leather Council (SHALC) 152, 156
South African Social Security Agency (SASSA) 96
South Korea 76, 152
South West Africa People's Organization (SWAPO) 47, 48
Southern African Centre for Cooperation in Agricultural Research (SACCAR) 54
Southern African Customs Union (SACU) 5, 9, 70, 74, 76, 80, 83, 85, 88, 112, 119
  agreement on trade 19, 48–9
  Article 31 121
  attachment of South Africa to 2, 7, 19–20, 132, 133
  convergence 31, 131
  establishment 19–20, 44–5
  multiple memberships 12, 87
  regional economic integration 6–7, 11–12, 16
  South Africa's approach for economic integration 138–42
  trade in member states 24, 48–9, 134–6
Southern African Development Community (SADC) 1, 2, 3, 35, 41 *see also* Southern African Development Coordination Conference (SADCC)
  Capacity Development Framework 61
  Committee of Ambassadors 60
  convergence with COMESA and EAC 12, 105 (*see also* COMESA-EAC-SADC)
  Council of Ministers 59–60, 61, 63, 82
  EPA agreement 126–7, 188
  establishment and evolution 4, 9, 57–62
  free trade area 28, 74, 85, 117
  funding for 59, 60, 62–7
  governance issues in member states 94
  institutional architecture of 57–62
  merging into COMESA 82, 84, 85–6, 88
  Mutual Defence Pact 57–8, 59, 94
  OPDS establishment and operationalisation 58–9
  open trade with South Africa 101–2
  post rationalisation process 5
  Regional Infrastructure Master Plan 115
  Resident Mission 83
  restructuring of Secretariat 57, 60, 61–2, 93
  Secretariat 57–62, 67
  security policies 57–9
  staffing for Secretariat 57, 59, 61
  trade liberalisation in 124
  trade protocol 93, 124, 132
  transformation of SADCC to 81–2
  treaty/Treaty 61, 82, 95
  tribunal 94
  Troika system 58, 59–60, 179
  variable geometry approach to liberalise trade 6, 23
  Windhoek Summit 61, 66, 82
Southern African Development Coordination Conference (SADCC) 9, 17, 19 *see also* Southern African Development Community (SADC)
  action programme 55, 83
  agricultural exports to South Africa 76–7
  annual consultative conference 55, 56, 58, 61
  challenges faced by 4, 55–6, 58
  cross-border investment projects, review by 76–7
  food shortages faced by 65–6, 79, 83, 95
  formation 46, 53–7
  functions 54
  funding for 55, 62–7
  Joint Declaration on Expanded Economic and Cultural Cooperation 64
  JPC, establishment of (*see* Joint Planning Committee (JPC))
  Macro-Framework Study 80, 83
  manufacturing value-added (MVA) of 76
  member states 4, 53, 55–6
  merging with PTA 81, 82, 83
  Nordic countries, dependence on 63–5, 88
  Programming of Regional Cooperation Funds 64
  and PTA 19, 40
  rationalisation period of 74–89
  trade 4, 56–7, 63, 64, 76–9
  transformation to SADC 81–2

Southern African Power Pool (SAPP) 22, 96–8, 116, 117
Southern African Trade Union Coordination Council (SATUCC) 154
sovereignty 14–15, 18, 39, 41, 79, 94, 112, 125, 143, 169
Soviet Union 25, 48
SPA *see* SADC Programme of Action (SPA)
Spain 34, 52, 76, 95, 110, 160
'spatial agglomeration' 28, 189
Spatial Development Initiative (SDI) 20, 96, 99, 141
spillover 40, 65, 133, 142
 of economic to political cooperation 18
 functional 15, 28, 36, 44
 knowledge 23, 38
 production 23, 37
 regional 98
 technology/technological 23, 25, 32, 37, 100, 125, 154
SPLA *see* Sudan People's Liberation Army (SPLA)
SPLM/A *see* Sudan People's Liberation Movement/Army (SPLM/A)
SPLM-IO *see* Sudan People's Liberation Movement in Opposition (SPLM-IO)
Sri Lanka 126
SSR *see* security sector reform (SSR)
Standard International Trade Classification (SITC) 48, 57
Standing Committee of Officials (SATCC) 54, 63
Stephan, Harry 23, 96
Strategic Indicative Plan of the Organ (SIPO) 59, 61, 62
structural adjustment programme (SAP) 77
Sudan 41, 104, 124, 169, 182
 livestock holder 153
 military coup in 68
 power generation projects in 116
 South 121, 123, 171, 179–80, 181
Sudan People's Liberation Army (SPLA) 173
Sudan People's Liberation Movement/Army (SPLM/A) 179–80
Sudan People's Liberation Movement in Opposition (SPLM-IO) 174
sugar industry 53, 56, 57, 85, 99, 101, 102–3, 117, 127, 128, 149, 150, 163
Sundry, Ron 101
Sunkel, Osvaldo 20
supranationalism 14–15
sustainable development goals (SDGs) 160, 163, 164
Sylvester-Williams, Henry 30
SWAPO *see* South West Africa People's Organization (SWAPO)
Swaziland *see* Eswatini
SWIFT *see* Society for Worldwide Interbank Financial Telecommunication (SWIFT)
Switzerland 52

Tanzania 53, 63, 65, 83, 115, 123
 COMESA member 88
 EAC member 16, 46
 economy of 17
 exports from SADCC to 57, 64
 FLS member 47, 48
 income convergence study on 80
 independence of 54
 MULPOC funding 68
 participation in FLS involvement 19
 power generation projects in 116
 PTA member 4, 69
 unaccounted funds in 51
Taylor, Ian 20, 21
TBTs *see* technical barriers to trade (TBTs)
TCSO *see* Tripartite Committee of Senior Officials (TCSO)
TDCA *see* Trade, Development and Cooperation Agreement (TDCA)
technical barriers to trade (TBTs) 33, 111, 162, 191
technology and skills, transference of 16, 65, 97, 109, 125, 151, 154–5, 186
terms of reference (TOR) 59, 105
textile industry 55, 56, 57, 64, 75–6, 85, 101, 127, 129, 149, 150, 155, 160
TFP *see* total factor productivity (TFP)
TFTA *see* Tripartite Free Trade Agreement (TFTA)
Thailand 151
Thomas, Lynne 33, 35, 99, 110, 126, 140

Tinbergen, Jan 7, 159
Tjønneland, Elling 56, 59
TOR *see* terms of reference (TOR)
Tostensen, Arne 63
total factor productivity (TFP) 7, 28–9, 140, 143, 186–7
Touré, Sékou 44
TPSF *see* Trade Policy and Strategy Framework (TPSF)
trade *see also* Continental Free Trade Area (CFTA); free trade; Tripartite Free Trade Agreement (TFTA)
  divergence based on world systems theory 22–3, 100 (*see also* peripheral economies)
  intercontinental 12–13, 30, 31, 104
  interregional 5, 16, 68, 125, 140, 143, 163, 187, 189
  intracontinental 2, 107, 148, 167, 185
  intraregional *see* intraregional trade
  liberalisation *see* trade liberalisation
  open 14, 22, 29, 87, 100, 101, 120, 133, 142
  poor infrastructure as barrier to 8, 12–13, 17, 21, 56, 104, 191
  protectionism 26, 189
Trade, Development and Cooperation Agreement (TDCA) 22, 32, 85, 100–1, 126, 127, 160
trade liberalisation 5, 17, 24, 37, 65, 70, 91–2
  for economic growth 27–30, 32, 35, 74, 100, 149
  income convergence, effects on 29, 30, 80, 133
  open markets and 120, 124
  RECs and 6, 100, 110
  regional 81, 110
  in SADC 124
Trade Policy and Strategy Framework (TPSF) 96
Tripartite Committee of Senior Officials (TCSO) 111
Tripartite Free Trade Agreement (TFTA) 1, 11, 121–4, 128, 131, 133, 143, 147, 148
  establishment and evolution 5, 9, 91, 106–9

memorandum of understanding (MOU) 5, 106, 109, 112, 124
multiple memberships 5, 6, 123, 138 (*see also* multiple memberships)
1998–2008 92–6
principle of acquis 147–8, 187
progress towards convergence 109–16
regional infrastructure, progress in 114–16
roadmap for Tripartite merger implementation 109–11
Tripartite free trade area, establishment of 109, 111–14
Tripartite imports 112–13
Tripartite Summit
  2008 105, 106–7, 109, 112, 114, 124, 193
  2011 106, 108, 111, 114
  2015 111, 113, 121, 138
  2017 113–14
variable geometry and 124–7
Tripartite Task Force (TTF) 105, 107, 109
Tripartite Technical Committee on Industrial Development (TTCID) 111
Tripartite Technical Working Groups (TTWGs) 111
Tripartite Trade and Customs Committee (TTCM) 111, 112, 113
Tripartite Trade and Customs Committee Meeting (TTCC) 113
Tripartite Trade Negotiating Forum (TTNF) 111, 112, 113
Troika system/Double Troika 58, 59–60, 179
Tshisekedi, Félix 121
Tshwane 31, 32, 96, 120, 154, 155, 160, 177, 179, 185
TTCC *see* Tripartite Trade and Customs Committee Meeting (TTCC)
TTCID *see* Tripartite Technical Committee on Industrial Development (TTCID)
TTCM *see* Tripartite Trade and Customs Committee (TTCM)
TTF *see* Tripartite Task Force (TTF)
TTNF *see* Tripartite Trade Negotiating Forum (TTNF)

TTWGs *see* Tripartite Technical Working Groups (TTWGs)
Tunisia 45
Turok, Ben 84
'two-level game' theory 23–4, 139, 190

UAPTA *see* Unit of Account of the Preferential Trade Area (UAPTA)
UDENAMO *see* National Democratic Union of Mozambique (UDENAMO)
UFIR *see* Upper Flight Information Region (UFIR)
Uganda 121, 141, 144 *see also* Democratic Republic of the Congo (DRC)
  COMESA, EAC and SADC member 8, 16, 46
  conflicts in 123, 171, 173
  a hegemonic state 13
  power generation projects in 116
  PTA member 4, 69
  TFTA ratification 114, 121
UNAMI *see* National African Union of Independent Mozambique (UNAMI)
UNCTAD *see* United Nations Conference on Trade and Development (UNCTAD)
UNDP *see* United Nations Development Programme (UNDP)
UNECA *see* United Nations Economic Commission for Africa (UNECA)
UNEP *see* United Nations Environment Programme (UNEP)
UNIDAT *see* United Nations Multinational Interdisciplinary Development Advisory Teams (UNIDAT)
Unit of Account of the Preferential Trade Area (UAPTA) 70–1
UNITA *see* National Union for the Total Independence of Angola (*União Nacional para a Independência Total de Angola*) (UNITA)
United Nations Conference on Trade and Development (UNCTAD) 26, 37, 102, 135, 136, 137, 138, 140
United Nations Development Programme (UNDP) 95

United Nations Economic Commission for Africa (UNECA) 9, 69, 139, 164
  EAC creation assistance 16, 67
  efforts towards regional integration 16–17, 67
  establishment and role 45–6, 80
  macroeconomic policies, tests by 33–4
  MULPOCs, setting up of 67
United Nations Environment Programme (UNEP) 174, 175
United Nations Multinational Interdisciplinary Development Advisory Teams (UNIDAT) 67
United Nations Organisation Stabilisation Mission in the Democratic Republic of the Congo (*Mission de l'Organisation des Nations Unies pour la Stabilisation en République Démocratique du Congo*) (MONUSCO) 175
United Nations Programme for Action for African Economic Recovery and Development (UN-PAAERD) 68
United States 2, 7, 9, 31, 37 *see also* New York; Washington
  AGOA and trade agreements with the 101, 134, 138, 186
  club convergence in 28
  G-5 Sahel initiative 13
  funding for SADCC 55, 66
  industrialisation in 25
  interference in Pan-African unity 30
  investments in Rhodesia 52
  South Africa, relations with 52
  support to South Africa by proxy wars 50
  support to Zaire 47
  trade with EAC countries 130
UN-PAAERD *see* United Nations Programme for Action for African Economic Recovery and Development (UN-PAAERD)
Upper Flight Information Region (UFIR) 108
US Trade and Development Agency (USTDA) 104
USTDA *see* US Trade and Development Agency (USTDA)

Vale, Peter 41
variable geometry approach 6, 12, 23, 106, 111, 113, 120, 123, 124–7, 142, 147, 148, 185, 187
Venables, Anthony 7, 36, 132–3, 134
Vickers, Brendan 132
Vietnam 44, 151
Viner, Jacob 72, 100
Von Clausewitz, General Carl 168
Vorster 48–50

Wæver, Ole 8, 13, 42, 168, 171, 172
Wallerstein, Immanuel 165
Warleigh-Lack, Alex 18–19, 20
Washington 12, 13, 159, 180, 185
Weil, David 29
Werner, Karolina 41
West African Economic Community (*Communauté économique de l' Afrique de l'oust*) (CEAO) 46
Wetangula, Moses 172
Windhoek Declaration (1992) 61, 66, 82
World Bank 50, 51–2, 66, 76, 115, 133, 139, 154, 187, 190
world systems theory 22–3, 100, 190
World Trade Organization (WTO) 3, 20, 24, 37, 80, 112, 113, 126, 127, 133, 186
WTO *see* World Trade Organization (WTO)

Yamoussoukro Declaration (YD) 103–4, 105, 107, 108, 117
YD *see* Yamoussoukro Declaration (YD)
Young, Crawford 65

Zacarias, Agostinho 40, 47, 51, 53, 88
Zaire 46, 47, 51, 52, 173
Zambia 46, 63, 83, 115, 144 *see also* Rhodesia; Zambia–Malawi–Mozambique Growth Triangle (ZMM-GT)
  access to railways 17
  COMESA, EAC and SADC member 8, 88
  exports from SADCC to 57, 64
  FLS member 47, 48
  hide producer 154
  income convergence study on 80
  independence of 54
  JPC member 78
  manufacturing sector 74, 75
  mining industry 20
  PTA member 4, 69
  regional détente with South Africa 49–50
  skills shortage in 76
  trade importer 48–9
Zambia–Malawi–Mozambique Growth Triangle (ZMM-GT) 21–2
ZANU *see* Zimbabwe African National Union (ZANU)
ZAPU *see* Zimbabwe African People's Union (ZAPU)
Zartman, William 40
Zimbabwe 19, 47, 53, 85, 113, 115, 132
  access to railways 17
  alignment with COMESA 101
  bilateral trade with South Africa 77, 78
  COMESA, EAC and SADC member 8, 88, 181
  disputes in 94, 95
  exports from SADCC to 64
  food shortages in 95
  hegemonic role in SADC/SADCC functioning 57–9, 63
  JPC member 78
  manufacturing sector 75, 76
  MULPOC funding 68
  Mutual Defence Pact 57–8, 59, 94
  PTA member 4, 69
  racial discrimination in 45
  role in FLS and ISDSC 57
  sugar producer 102
Zimbabwe African National Union (ZANU) 47, 48, 49
Zimbabwe African People's Union (ZAPU) 47
ZMM-GT *see* Zambia–Malawi–Mozambique Growth Triangle (ZMM-GT)
Zuma, Jacob 31, 177, 179

www.ingramcontent.com/pod-product-compliance
Lightning Source LLC
Chambersburg PA
CBHW070017010526
44117CB00011B/1609